Old Southwest to Old South

Old Southwest to Old South

MISSISSIPPI, 1798–1840

MIKE BUNN
and
CLAY WILLIAMS

University Press of Mississippi for the
Mississippi Historical Society and the
Mississippi Department of Archives and History / Jackson

Publication of this book was made possible
by a grant from the Phil Hardin Foundation.

The University Press of Mississippi is the scholarly publishing agency of the Mississippi Institutions of Higher Learning: Alcorn State University, Delta State University, Jackson State University, Mississippi State University, Mississippi University for Women, Mississippi Valley State University, University of Mississippi, and University of Southern Mississippi.

www.upress.state.ms.us

The University Press of Mississippi is a member
of the Association of University Presses.

Cover image: John James Audubon (1785–1851). *View of Natchez*. 1823. Oil on canvas. 29–3/8 x 38–3/8 inches. Purchased by the Greenville County Museum of Art with funds from the 2010 Museum Antiques Show, sponsored by Carolina First Bank. Chairman's Circle: AVX Corporation; Cherry, Bekaert & Holland, LLP; Rosa M. Eisenstadt; Tom and Linda Govreau; The Graham Foundation; Hartness International Charitable Fund; Bunny and Bob Hughes; Mary and Jeff Lawson; Bill and Esta McCrary; Milberg Factors, Inc.; Martha and Tracy Pellett; Jane and Clifford Roy; Thomas W. Styron; Triangle Construction; Mr. and Mrs. James S. Whitten.

Manufactured in the United States of America

First printing 2023
∞

Library of Congress Cataloging-in-Publication Data

Names: Bunn, Mike, author. | Williams, Clay, 1970– author.
Title: Old Southwest to Old South : Mississippi, 1798–1840 / Mike Bunn and Clay Williams.
Other titles: Heritage of Mississippi series.
Description: Jackson : University Press of Mississippi for the Mississippi Historical Society and the Mississippi Department of Archives and History, [2023] | Series: Heritage of Mississippi series | Includes bibliographical references and index.
Identifiers: LCCN 2022042579 (print) | LCCN 2022042580 (ebook) | ISBN 9781496843807 (hardback) | ISBN 9781496843821 (epub) | ISBN 9781496843791 (epub) | ISBN 9781496843838 (pdf) | ISBN 9781496843845 (pdf)
Subjects: LCSH: Mississippi—History. | Mississippi—History—18th century. | Mississippi—History—19th century.
Classification: LCC F341 .B86 2023 (print) | LCC F341 (ebook) | DDC 976.2/04—dc23/eng/20221019
LC record available at https://lccn.loc.gov/2022042579
LC ebook record available at https://lccn.loc.gov/2022042580

British Library Cataloging-in-Publication Data available

For the pioneering historians who sparked our interest in this incredible story,
Thomas D. Clark, John D. W. Guice, and Robert V. Haynes;
and for our long-suffering wives, Tonya and Kym,
who indulged us in the pursuit of its telling

Contents

Acknowledgments

We are indebted to many people for their assistance in the creation of this book. Two groups of individuals deserve special recognition in the limited space available here. We owe the deepest debt of gratitude to the Board of Editors of the Mississippi Historical Society's Heritage of Mississippi Series, who entrusted us to tell the story of this pivotal era in the state's past as a part of this landmark effort. We especially want to thank Dr. John F. Marszalek and Elbert Hilliard for their guidance and patience throughout this long process. We appreciate their careful review and editing of our first draft. We also owe a debt of gratitude to Nan Prince and Anne Webster who helped secure images for the book. It is an honor to be a part of this series, and we hope our work helps not only provide a solid overview of the time period, but inspires further research.

We want to extend a heartfelt thanks to the many historians whose work on this pivotal era inspired us to learn about it long before we contemplated writing its story and whose work fundamentally informed our own. Space precludes a full listing of all those worthy of mention, but among them are: James F. Barnett Jr., John K. Bettersworth, Bradley Bond, J. F. H. Claiborne, Thomas D. Clark, Everett Dick, Jack D. Elliott Jr., Porter L. Fortune Jr., John D. W. Guice, Jack D. L. Holmes, Robert V. Haynes, D. Clayton James, Charles D. Lowery, Richard A. McLemore, Edwin A. Miles, Frank L. Owsley, Dawson A. Phelps, Dunbar Rowland, William K. Scarborough, John Ray Skates, and Charles S. Sydnor. Anyone seeking to learn about Mississippi's frontier era will soon become familiar with these names and more. We count ourselves fortunate to be in their company.

Preface

The two men stood quietly, pausing to catch their breath after climbing to the top of a heavily wooded bluff that offered a commanding view of the gently rolling plains stretching into the distance. As they gazed across the lush expanse and observed the winding river meandering through it, they took solace, knowing their long journey was at its end. They looked at one another and smiled. Having set out from a nearby Choctaw Agency where the treaty granting this land to the United States government had recently been signed, they had traveled seeking a location containing some specific qualities. They had been meticulous in fulfilling their assignment, trudging through what was still mostly raw frontier, through forests and swamps, fields and plains, and hills and valleys, to seek a place near the center of the rapidly growing young state of Mississippi. They had been looking for a spot that also lay near a navigable stream where there would be good water, elevated ground, healthy air, fertile soil, and good timber. They had explored several locations that failed to meet all of those necessary qualifications, but now, as they scrutinized their surroundings, they knew they had achieved their goal. Thomas Hinds and William Lattimore had succeeded; they had found the site for the future capital of Mississippi.[1]

Following the signing of the Treaty of Doak's Stand in the fall of 1820, in which Mississippi gained a huge tract of land in the central portion of the state from the Choctaw, the legislature sought to move the seat of government. It had been located in the Old Natchez District, where it had resided since the establishment of the Mississippi Territory at the close of the eighteenth century. They now sought to move it to a more central location in the state. The state had grown tremendously since being admitted to the union in 1817, witnessing a dramatic increase in population and a steady expansion of its physical limits via treaties such as the one that precipitated the need for the relocation of the capital. Everything pointed toward future growth. Hinds, Lattimore, and James Patton had been selected as commissioners to find a spot near the state's geographic center and choose the most appropriate site for the capital from which its seemingly bright future would be administered. Hinds, a Creek War and War of 1812 hero, had served with Andrew Jackson as a treaty negotiator at Doak's Stand. Lattimore had served four terms as the territory's delegate to Congress and helped the territory achieve statehood. James Patton was a skilled surveyor and lieutenant governor, but his appointment came too late for him to participate in the expedition, so Hinds and Lattimore set out without him in November 1821.[2]

Standing atop what came to be known as Le Fleur's Bluff overlooking the Pearl River, the two men's thoughts must have turned to the past as much as the future they were helping to build. As they walked along the site of the former trading post established by French trader Louis Le Fleur, they likely could not help but think about Mississippi becoming a part of the United States after so many years of European control. France, Great Britain, and Spain had all at one time or another claimed the land they now walked upon, and those nation's influences were still being felt. Of course, at this time, they could not know that Le Fleur's wife's son, Greenwood Leflore, would one day sign the final Choctaw cession treaty that removed one of the last remaining Native American nations from the homeland that they and their ancestors had lived upon for thousands of years.[3]

Hinds may have thought of his military career, as he had waged war against the Creek nation to the east. It had been a contest that would eventually lead to thousands of white settlers moving onto these lands in search of a new chance at life, many of them reliant on the forced labor of enslaved African Americans to make their economic dreams become reality. Lattimore surely dwelt upon his past civic service, having witnessed the very beginnings of Mississippi's government as leaders sought to establish order among chaos as these new lands were organized. For nearly twenty years, the area that was now a rising state had been a territory of the United States. Long-term residents with European backgrounds had interacted with a swarm of new settlers and their slaves while Native Americans remained on the periphery of the new state's centers of development, controlling most of the land within Mississippi's boundaries but surely wondering what all the activity meant for their way of life. Hinds and Lattimore had both personally participated in transforming this frontier full of uncertainty into a region of prosperity poised for continued expansion. It had been a long road to this point, and they could only wonder what the next twenty years would bring. They could be sure, however, that they were getting an opportunity to participate in one more event that would have great significance for Mississippi's future.

If it were possible to tell them, Hinds and Lattimore might be saddened to know that the history of Mississippi during the era with which they were so familiar has been relatively neglected and far too often ignored in contemporary times. From professional historians to the general public, more attention generally has been given to other eras in the state's rich past, leaving its foundational epoch either mostly unknown or poorly understood. High school and college textbooks race through these formative years, barely scratching the surface of the times between European colonialism and the antebellum period immediately prior to the Civil War. Far too often, if these decades are discussed at all, it is simply as the first several years of a decades-long antebellum story revolving around little more than slavery, secession, and Civil War.

Few book-length works exist that detail this time period. *Frontiers in Conflict: The Old Southwest 1795–1840*, by Thomas D. Clark and John D. W. Guice, originally published in 1989, provides an excellent narrative and is in our opinion the standard on coverage of the era by which all scholars wading into the time period must be measured. This masterpiece, however, does not focus specifically on Mississippi. More recently, Robert V. Haynes wrote *The Mississippi Territory and the Southwest Frontier, 1798–1817*. Haynes, who has researched the topic for over fifty years, provides a detailed analysis of the political and international issues of Mississippi's territorial period, but he does not go into much detail regarding social and cultural development and ends his analysis with statehood. Richard A. McLemore's edited two-volume study, *A History of Mississippi*, which appeared in 1973, contains excellent chapters focusing on this era that remain authoritative reference resources on their subjects, but that project is more comprehensive in scope and of course covers the entirety of Mississippi's story. In truth those looking for focused narratives on this pivotal founding era in the state's past will find few books that treat the years under study here as a distinct, important phase of Mississippi history. In fact, this time period was not even originally scheduled to be a part of the Heritage of Mississippi Series as established by the Mississippi Historical Society in 1992 to cover the entire history of Mississippi era by era.[4]

The lack of attention to this critical era remains puzzling to say the least. These forty years laid the foundation for the future of the state. Historian Porter L. Fortune Jr. called it the "Formative Period," and one would be hard pressed to find a better descriptive. Certain key themes that still resonate today can trace their beginnings from this time period; troubled race relations, heavy reliance on certain agricultural pursuits, chronic political and sectional factionalism, educational shortcomings, and persistent economic inequities and difficulties, to name a few.[5]

During the span of a mere four decades, the state underwent a series of dramatic upheavals that shaped its early years and set the stage for much of its later development. The period featured the controversial end of Spanish rule, the contested formation of a territorial government, a devastating war, a difficult road to statehood, the writing of two state constitutions, the rise of cotton production as the dominant economic activity in the state, and the emotional stories of American Indian removal and the hardships of slavery. On top of that, the era is full of many colorful and exciting characters, many of whom have sadly enough become forgotten by the general public. The list includes William Dunbar, a successful planter, scientist, astronomer, surveyor, and explorer, regarded by many as Mississippi's Thomas Jefferson. George Poindexter, an early political leader, helped draft the state's first constitution and codified many of the state's early laws. And then there is Mississippi's version of Davy Crockett, frontiersman Sam Dale. Finally, American icons such as Aaron Burr and Andrew Jackson played a part in early Mississippi's story and made a tremendous impact on the state's history.

As public historians who have studied, written about, and spoken about this critical era for almost the entirety of our careers, we have come to a special appreciation of its impact on the development of Mississippi. We have explored its intriguing stories countless times intellectually and even physically, and have long made relating their importance to the general public one of our professional goals. As a consequence, we are also perhaps more aware than most of how some of its most important stories are frequently overlooked and misunderstood by the public, and how easily are formed indistinct generalizations about life during this era that are more applicable to either earlier or later periods.

Old Southwest to Old South: Mississippi, 1798–1840 seeks to tell the story of the state's founding era in a sweeping, straightforward, subject-driven narrative that gives these crucial years the attention they so richly deserve. We have taken to heart the broad audience to which the Heritage of Mississippi Series seeks to reach in our approach, and accordingly have designed our book uncompromisingly as directed more toward general readers with only a cursory familiarity with the era than the scholar who has spent decades researching and teaching about its major events. Still, we believe both groups will find something of merit within these pages.

We have eschewed a traditional textbook-like approach of dividing up the years we chronicle into equal groupings and attempting a conventional blow-by-blow account, instead arranging our chapters as discussions of the major themes we view as essential to understanding this period. This is for two reasons. One, the era's landmark political, military, and technological events are not scattered evenly over the forty years we cover in these pages; most are heavily weighted in the first two decades of its existence. At the same time, a great deal of the guiding forces shaping its physical and cultural development manifested themselves most readily in the second half of the period. Two, we felt it our duty to help readers go beyond just the major headline events of the period which might be placed on simple timelines to provide some description of how the people who called Mississippi home during this era lived, worked, and played. What lured them to this land, and what was their experience in settling it? What forces animated their pursuits once they arrived, and what factors guided the development of the society they ended up creating? How did they go about physically transforming a far-flung rural region into one of the most prosperous and rapidly growing states in the Deep South, thoroughly integrated economically, politically, and socially with its surrounding region, within the span of a mere four decades? We believe that understanding these stories not as separate events but as concurrent experiences offers a comprehensive and compelling way to explore Mississippi's coming of age in its foundational years. We also believe this approach will best complement the existing literature on the colonial, territorial, and early antebellum eras and help form a more distinct identity for the era under discussion.

Readers will notice that there is a good bit of discussion of the area that eventually became the state of Alabama in portions of this book. The reason is simple. Up until the time of Mississippi's statehood in 1817, or nearly half of the years we chronicle here, what we now know as Alabama was the eastern section of the Mississippi Territory. As such, it stood as fully a part of that political entity as any other section and figured significantly in its development. Mississippi and Alabama therefore share a common heritage in their territorial eras, and to attempt to understand Mississippi's developmental period as somehow separate would be to leave out essential parts of an inextricably linked origin story.

The twelve chapters of this book are accordingly arranged into what might be described as two broad groups highlighting the major themes we seek to address in their pages. Part one, including chapters 1 through 6, essentially seeks to chronicle the story of Mississippi's American settlement and governmental administration. One of the most complicated and consequential stories from the state's rich past, the results of these efforts influenced when, where, and how it came into American control. Chapters 1 and 2 detail the tumultuous process of establishing its contested borders and the sometimes chaotic attempt at the forming of adequate governmental institutions. Chapters 3 and 4 introduce readers to some of the most essential features in much of our story—how early settlers went about claiming their share of the land that drew them here, and their triumphs and travails in making their way here from diverse locations and circumstances near and far. Chapters 5 and 6 relate the pivotal stories of war, international intrigue, and political maneuvering that ultimately led to the setting of the state's borders as we now know them.

The second set of chapters is devoted to detailing the ways most of Mississippi's territorial and early statehood period residents actually lived their lives and how their efforts at community building laid the foundations for the development of state far into the future. Chapters 7 and 8 discuss the related stories of the dispossession of Native Americans of their ancestral lands and the rise of the slave-powered cotton agriculture enterprises that defined so much of the early state's economy and social structure. Chapters 9 and 10 give shape to some of the defining currents of daily life in territorial and early statehood era Mississippi, revealing how the fragility of life, a fiercely independent culture, an overwhelmingly rural landscape, and specific understandings of the role of education and religion in society worked together to shape its societal development. Finally, in chapters 11 and 12, we turn our attention to discussion of two broad topics that served as the literal and figurative building blocks for a great deal that would come after in

Mississippi—the unheralded but enormously consequential growth of trade and transportation networks and the creation of its first urban centers; and the full-throated endorsement of Jacksonian democracy and all it represented politically.

Our book is purposefully designed not to repeat work that has already been done. For instance, we saw no need to rehash in detail a blow-by-blow account of all the political fighting that took place during the territorial period, which scholars such as Dr. Haynes have already covered. Nor did we want to repeat too much information found in other volumes in the Heritage of Mississippi Series, such as James F. Barnett Jr.'s *Mississippi's American Indians* and Randy Sparks's *Religion in Mississippi* or in the forthcoming volume focusing on the institution of slavery in the state. We chose simply to summarize those authors' good work and point readers to their excellent scholarship to learn more for themselves. Our goal was to take advantage of all these significant studies and a host of others perhaps less well known to paint a broad picture of life in early Mississippi and to offer an introduction to the people, places, and events that guided its development.

Some topics are also admittedly more fully developed than others. Very few resources exist documenting the minutiae of daily life for women as compared to men, for example, and our narrative reflects this occasional disparity in scholarship and records. We believe readers will nonetheless find our treatment of the period to be as inclusive and balanced as can reasonably be expected given the realities of what is available to historians, and we provide a thorough introduction to the era. At the conclusion of our narrative, we hope to have proven that the four decades we chronicle witnessed Mississippi's transformation from a Native American–dominated region on America's periphery to an influential part of the American South at the height of an era of relative prosperity and ascendance that writer Joseph Glover Baldwin lastingly termed the "Flush Times." This incredible story has been mostly untold. Until now.[6]

Old Southwest to Old South

Introduction

The region that became the Mississippi Territory spanned an enormous swath of early America's southwestern frontier. It originally consisted of only a rectangular tract between the 31st parallel on the south and just above the 32nd on the north, bounded on the east by the state of Georgia and the west by the mighty Mississippi River. Large sections of territory were added above and below its original boundaries over the course of nearly two decades prior to statehood. Ultimately, before its division into the states of Mississippi and Alabama, the Territory stretched all the way from the Tennessee border southward to the Gulf of Mexico. The lure of this region, which many early settlers viewed as a veritable land of opportunity, is at the heart of the story of Mississippi's territorial and early statehood experience.

Dense primeval forests dominated most of this expansive landscape, their luxuriant growth awing those who encountered it. One traveler, passing through the southern portions of the state, raved at "immense forests whose depths the last rays of the sun could scarcely penetrate," while another rhapsodized about the "grandeur in the vast forests of the South, of which a northerner can form no adequate conception." It was a "canopy almost impervious to the sun, and beneath which wind arcades of the most magnificent dimensions." Trees of every description, from hardwoods to pine, evergreens to deciduous, could be found scattered around the area, offering the promise of ample building material at a time when wooden construction predominated.[1]

Because the land lay in a subtropical climate zone, thick vegetation of all sorts covered its surface. Canebrakes dotted the landscape, with stalks sometimes reaching as much as thirty feet high and so dense a man could not enter them. Flowers, shrubs, and vines of all types proliferated throughout the region. In the meadows that opened between patches of forest, tall grasses grew. A wide variety of indigenous wild fruits and berries—blueberries, strawberries, and blackberries among them—grew in portions of the state, as did a selection of edible vegetables and greens. Rich riverside bottomlands featured lush growth of innumerable species, while gently rolling hills and occasional prairies offered pristine vistas of a fertile land unlike anything most early settlers had seen.

The land abounded with game. Deer, rabbits, turkeys, and squirrels were plentiful, and huge flocks of birds could be seen, especially along the Mississippi and its tributaries. "Innumerable flocks of pigeons, which passed so near us that we were able to distinguish their eyes," greeted traveler Christian Schultz on a visit to the Natchez area. He bragged that with a pair of pistols loaded with birdshot he "killed 3 to 7 at every fire." Famed naturalist John James Audubon marveled at the spectacle of birds he encountered along the banks of the Mississippi River, and other travelers noted immense flocks of wild turkeys and innumerable varieties of fish swimming in the region's many streams. The country seemed positively exotic. Buffalo, having long disappeared in other parts of the South, had roamed in some areas of the territory within living memory of some of the area's inhabitants.[2]

The Mississippi Territory's wildness was only accentuated by the presence of several large predators, many now long vanished from the state. Travelers frequently mentioned the eerie glow of wolves' eyes twinkling in the firelight of their nighttime camps. Wolves became so common and such a nuisance to early herders that in 1837 the state legislature authorized bounties in several counties for wolf hides. Mountain lions (often called panthers at the time) and bears still roamed over the majority of the territory, and not infrequently attacks were made on the unwary hunter or trail walker. One visitor to territorial-period Natchez noticed several bizarre "leopard" skins hanging on the doors of some stores he passed. He naturally assumed these were imported, but they were in actuality probably the last of a population of large spotted cats whose habitat once extended into the area but are now long extinct.[3]

In contrast to the majesty of the area's many game animals and numerous other species of fauna that intrigued settlers and visitors, the land positively teemed with all manner of pest and vermin that could make life miserable for man and beast. Every conceivable variety of biting insect could be found in abundance, making travel and hunting in the thick forests and work in the cleared fields of the state frequently uncomfortable and at times unbearable. Judging from surviving correspondence, mosquitoes clearly ranked as public enemy number one. "One must always have a free hand to drive them [mosquitoes] away, and I assure you that in the woods I scarcely had time to draw a bead on game," disparaged one visitor who attempted to take in a little hunting. The torment did not end at bedtime, as he noted that "one can read, write, or sleep only under a kind of gauze tent, called a mosquito net." Another writer similarly observed that "the buzzing vampires" were "too blood-thirsty and numerous to mention, and to sleep without a 'bar' or netting was, to a thin-skinned Anglo-Saxon, utterly impossible." Perhaps summing up the situation with more clarity than any other, one particularly irritated traveler mentioned "mosquitoes" seventeen times in a letter to his wife, closing the missive with a note that "a damn, damn mosquito has won the day. Your harassed husband."[4]

The climate proved at once inviting and forbidding. As an emigrant's guide proclaimed, "The seasons are agreeable, the autumn and winter particularly . . . We know no place, where from September to April the weather is so uniformly pleasant." The rub came in those months not addressed, for as anyone remotely familiar with Mississippi then or now knows, the state features brutally hot summers and stifling humidity. Trying to do any sort of manual labor, much less live in homes prior to air conditioning, could be a tall order that required power of endurance as well as hardiness. While springs and autumns were pleasant, if brief, winters could be surprisingly frigid. This is true even today, as small annual snowfalls in the northern portions of the state are not unusual. Mississippi's early years, however, fell within a "little ice age" characterized by cooler than normal temperatures and some of the most severe winters on record in the region. World-renowned and well-traveled actor Tyrone Power arrived in Natchez in January 1816 during the midst of a harsh freeze. Temperatures below zero greeted him, causing him to later remark that "never did I feel cold so penetrating." Temperatures that year remained below normal in part owing to a volcanic eruption in the Dutch East Indies that put so much ash into the atmosphere that regular climatic patterns were temporarily interrupted. Farmers could usually count on adequate rainfall, but there were occasional droughts that devastated crops and ruined economies.[5]

As the weather could be almost simultaneously welcoming and adversarial, early Mississippians learned both to admire and fear the forces of nature they encountered and to have a healthy respect for things beyond their control. Noted British travel writer and scientist Charles Lyell reported of his conversation with a man who perhaps said it best when waxing philosophically about the mighty Mississippi. The man confided to Lyell that he "had lived on the great river long enough to admire it, for the ease with which it performs its mighty work; and to fear it, so often had he witnessed the wreck of vessels and the loss of lives." Nothing could cause quite as much immediate damage as the storms that periodically ravaged the landscape. In the southern reaches of the state, residents learned to watch for the signs of hurricanes approaching from the Gulf of Mexico, as these fearsome storms could wipe away years of construction in the course of a few hours and render a familiar landscape utterly unrecognizable.

Even more menacing in terms of their power, frequency, and random nature of destruction, however, were tornadoes. A particularly fierce one struck Natchez on May 7, 1840. Resident Horatio Eustis described the solemn aftermath to his father a few days later:

> It . . . demolished entirely the lower town leaving but one house standing there. In the upper town which is built mostly of brick many of the larger edifices, such as the Hotels, the churches, and the railroad depot, were either leveled with the dust or so minced that the walls must come down. The force of the wind was incredible.

> Iron spikes were borne by the blast with such force and direction as to be driven up to their heads, into the walls of houses . . . The present estimate of lives lost, is about 300, principally at the landing on the river bank where nearly every flat boat and steamboat was sunk or destroyed.[6]

Despite such a panoply of potential environmental troubles, most early settlers nonetheless regarded Mississippi as a veritable paradise because of the promise its fertile lands held. Overt boosterism such as the observations of author A. B. Meek rang true for many who sought their fortunes in the new state:

> . . . it is upon our section of the Union that these blessings are most amply bestowed. Beginning upon the eastern border of our State, and proceeding west to the farthest line of Louisiana, we pass over perhaps the most beautiful and fertile region that the sun looks upon in his diurnal travel. Its territories are everywhere, and in every direction, irrigated and linked together by noble and navigable rivers, which serve not merely to fructify the soil but to convey its productions to safe and commodious harbors. . . . When we add to these things, the blessings of a climate which is always genial and agreeable, whether viewed in the regal splendor of its summer days, or the milder manifestations of its moonlight evenings . . . we have a correct idea of the physical characteristics of that section of the Union in which we reside.[7]

Long before statehood, colonial authorities had raved about the area's suitability for settlement. Montfort Browne, lieutenant governor of the British colony of West Florida, which included portions of what became Mississippi, praised the land around Natchez in his evaluation of the region in the 1760s. Like many, he claimed the spot held "the most charming prospects in the world, extensive plains intermixed with beautiful hills, and small rivers . . . fruit trees of most excellent kinds, and strawberries as good in their kind as any in the world and in as great abundance." Another British colonial traveler, Edward Mease, explored the same area shortly after Browne and came away convinced that "No lands in North America can possibly exceed the banks of this noble river in fertility . . . the situation is inconceivably beautiful . . ." Early arrivals similarly described the area in glowing terms. Settlers of the Mississippi Territory's Tennessee River Valley, in what is now Alabama, were known to refer to the area as "Happy Valley," and those who settled along the Alabama River basin raved about its productive soils as the "Acadia of Southern America."[8]

By almost any measure, the land that would become Mississippi stood rich with potential and lured settlers with dreams of opportunity. The story of the forty-plus years of organization and development detailed in the pages that follow is to a large degree a chronicle of these immigrants', and their slaves', interaction with this verdant landscape. Within it Mississippi's pioneer settlers established farms and plantations, built roads and cities, and labored to create the economic and social systems that would determine the course of its development for generations into the future. Before any of that could happen, however, political ownership of this bountiful territory had to be clearly established. Thus Mississippi's story began not against a backdrop of the arrival of settlers seeking to wrest a profitable living from all the natural amenities the land offered, but instead one of strained international rivalry, political intrigue, and competing visions for the future.

CHAPTER 1

Becoming American

Mississippi's beginnings, like most of its history, started with controversy. The land that would eventually become the Mississippi Territory lay on the southwestern periphery of the borders of the new United States at the end of the Revolutionary War. Whether it was part of the new nation or belonged to Spain proved to be a point of some contention. After winning its independence from Great Britain, the 1783 Treaty of Paris established boundaries for the fledgling United States. The new nation stretched from the Atlantic Ocean to the Mississippi River and then from British Canada all the way south to Spanish Florida. Officials from Spain and the United States had different opinions on the location of the northern boundary of Spanish Florida, leading to more than a decade of simmering dispute. Bringing this issue to a resolution would form the opening act of Mississippi's colorful territorial drama and set the stage for its tumultuous development afterward.

The problem originated with the end of the French and Indian War, which established the British Colony of West Florida. The 1763 treaty ending that war initially set the northern boundary of this British possession at the 31st parallel. A year later, Great Britain moved the boundary northward to 32° 28', the point where the Yazoo River runs into the Mississippi River. During the Revolutionary War, Spain fought against Great Britain in an effort to win back some of its former colonial holdings and succeeded when Spanish forces gained possession of Baton Rouge, Natchez, Mobile, and Pensacola. In the 1783 Treaty, Britain officially ceded its Florida possessions to Spain, but without any clear mention of the northern boundary. The United States felt the boundary should be placed at 31°, whereas Spain felt the line lay further north. Simply put, whereas the United States made its claim based on the 1783 Treaty of Paris, Spain exerted its by right of conquest.[1]

The major difference between these two boundaries as it concerned development of the region lay in who could claim ownership of the Natchez District, the rich agricultural region along the Mississippi River's lower reaches containing some of the few thriving European settlements in what is now known as the Old Southwest. This frontier region, literally south and west of the nation's more populous eastern seaboard, is roughly defined as all the territory stretching between the Ocmulgee River in Georgia and south of the Tennessee River. Containing approximately 2,000 residents, the Natchez District had become an important area to Spanish officials and was coveted by the United States.[2]

The state of Georgia added to the confusion in 1783 by establishing the Mississippi River as its own western boundary. Two years later, by legislative enactment, Georgia officially created Bourbon County to encompass this expansion. This disputed area had been under the authority of the Spanish, who tried to maintain control of their region against encroachment not only from the United States government but from the rogue state of Georgia as well.[3]

Spain began obtaining control over the Natchez District when it captured Baton Rouge from the British in 1779. In the surrender agreement, British officials signed over Natchez as well. Spanish forces followed up this success by winning victories at Mobile and Pensacola that strengthened their hold on the territory, leading Britain to officially cede its southern possessions to Spain in 1783. Spain would spend the next ten years consolidating its control over the area by a number of methods such as establishing strong relations with the region's Native Americans, constructing several strategically located forts, and most importantly, developing the town of Natchez into a more permanent settlement to serve as a population and governmental center. Spanish leaders established a liberal land grant policy and did not force Catholicism on the local citizens. Although confronted by an ever-expanding United States government eager to take control over the region that it thought it legally owned, Spanish leaders were pleased with their efforts at strengthening their hold on the region. They would soon be stunned to learn their efforts had been wasted.[4]

Spain's control of the Natchez District officially ended with the Treaty of San Lorenzo, signed on October 27, 1795, in a monastery outside Madrid. Also known as Pinckney's Treaty (after American negotiator Thomas Pinckney), this accord settled the long-standing controversy over the boundary issue when Spain accepted the 31st parallel as the boundary between Spanish West Florida and the United States. Even more importantly, the treaty also allowed free navigation of the Mississippi River and the right of deposit in New Orleans. Traders would no longer have to pay duties to store merchandise in New Orleans before shipping items elsewhere.[5]

With the signage of the treaty, Spain abandoned its longtime policy of frontier defense. For years, Spanish leadership treated this region as a buffer to its more lucrative possessions in Mexico. Spain now felt forced to sign the compact due to fears of a strengthening alliance between Britain and the United States that grew out of Jay's Treaty from 1795. Spanish Prime Minister Manuel de Godoy was fearful of a combined British and American attack on his nation's North American possessions.[6]

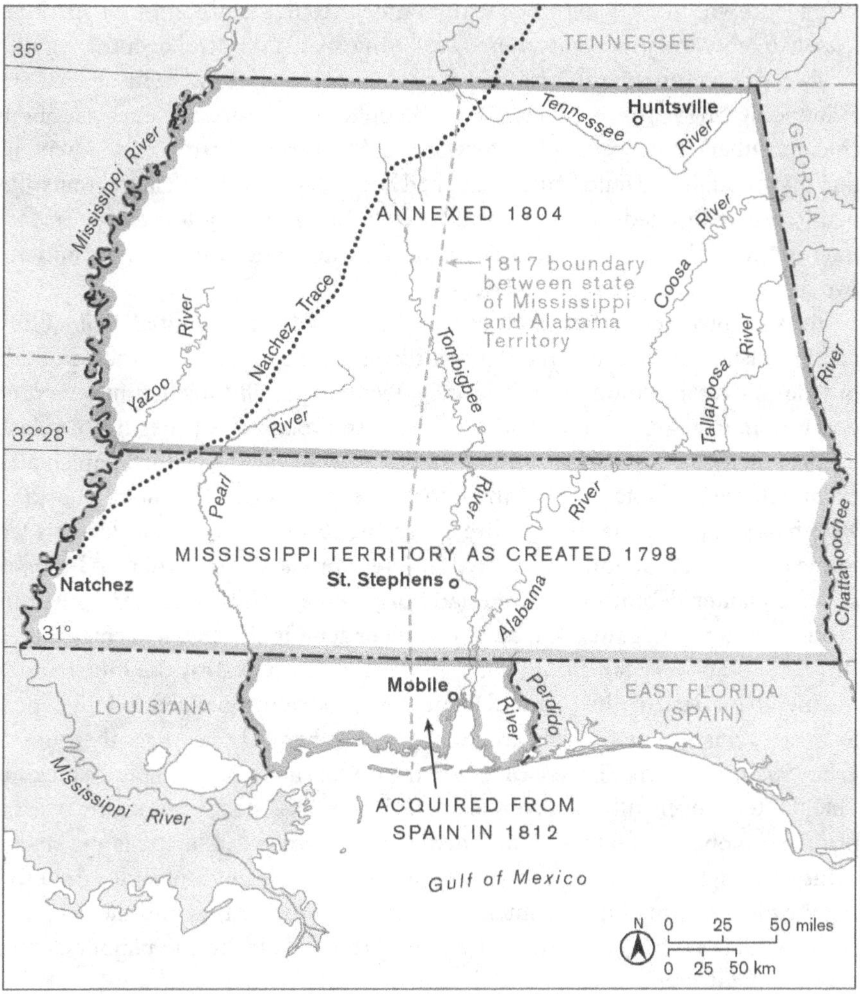

Figure 1.1. Growth of the Mississippi Territory. (University Press of Mississippi)

The ink on the treaty had not yet dried when Spanish leadership began having second thoughts on the accord. Francisco Luis Hector, Barón de Carondelet, governor of the Spanish colonies of Louisiana and West Florida, was upset from the start over the treaty. Along with others, he felt Spain had surrendered too much in the treaty when it allowed the United States free navigation of the Mississippi River with its right of deposit in New Orleans. He also felt that the treaty would turn the Native Americans against the Spanish, leading to the eventual fall of Louisiana and Florida. Carondelet had been trying for years to build upon the dissatisfaction of Tennesseans and Kentuckians who long had been upset with their country's inability to guarantee navigation of the Mississippi River. Carondelet sent agents with money to bribe the discontented citizens of Kentucky and Tennessee to rebel and join Spain, thereby securing Spanish control over the region.[7]

The region's inhabitants also had mixed feelings regarding their new rulers. Many settlers had prospered under Spanish policies and were apprehensive about change. Others, however, looked forward to American control and the benefits that they thought it would bring. Spain had been very liberal with land grants, but many settlers disliked monarchy and Catholicism. In reality, however, personal interests were the key factors in determining where one cast his favor, and the two biggest issues were land and debt.[8]

Tobacco production had exploded in the 1780s due to its initial profitability and Spanish subsidies. Production went from zero in 1779 to 589,000 pounds in 1786 to over a million pounds in 1789. Planters put all they had into its production, mortgaging homes and farms. These prosperous times did not last, unfortunately, as the markets in Spain were oversaturated and the Spanish also eventually found better quality tobacco at cheaper cost in Kentucky. Subsidies were halted, placing planters in dire economic straits. This economic crisis led to the creation of factions: the merchant/creditor class who were owed money and the planter/debtor group who had borrowed extensively to plant the crop. Planter Anthony Hutchins, who became a major actor in the drama to come, stated "the time is not very far distant when the planter must destroy the merchant or the merchant destroy the planter." Planters successfully managed to lobby local Spanish officials to obtain stay laws that granted them a break from their heavy debts. Spanish leadership were caught in the middle and unable to please anyone. The planters never fully forgave the Spanish, who had strongly encouraged the planting of tobacco and then abandoned them. Historian D. Clayton James stated, "This seemingly underlying controversy was the most important factor underlying the citizens' growing discontent with Spanish rule by 1795 and the origin of political factions in 1797, which bore strong resemblance to the planter-debtor and merchant-credit alignment."[9]

Spanish officials were totally uncommitted to following the terms of the treaty, and the population was confused and worried about the future. These circumstances called for levelheaded leadership to manage these affairs during this period of transition. The situation instead rested in the hands of Andrew Ellicott.

Born in 1754 in Pennsylvania to a Quaker family, Andrew Ellicott acquired vast experience in the surveying profession. His background included participating in the famous survey of the Mason-Dixon Line and helping establish boundaries between Georgia and North Carolina and Ohio and Pennsylvania. He helped lay out the national capital in Washington, DC; planned the city of Erie, Pennsylvania; and even became the first to measure Niagara Falls. Historian John C. Van Horne states that "A more highly qualified surveyor than Ellicott could hardly be found in the country." In contrast to his technical skills and experience, Ellicott lacked the necessary tact to handle the important job given to him by President George Washington, who commissioned him to be the nation's representative to survey and mark the boundary between Spanish possessions and the United States. He garnered advice from Secretary of State Timothy Pickering, who informed him of the importance of maintaining peace with the Spanish and the neighboring Indians. In meetings with President Washington, Ellicott had been warned to prevent Spain from delaying the implementation of the treaty and was advised to be wary of Americans working with the Spanish government in trying to detach Kentucky from the United States. It was surely clear to Ellicott that his mission was more complicated than simply surveying a boundary.[10]

Ellicott possessed no experience to handle this delicate diplomatic situation. Confusion existed as to who exactly was to establish control for the United States. Was this Ellicott's function or perhaps that of military commanders sent to take possession of Spanish forts in the region? It would become apparent that Ellicott was more than willing to take the responsibility himself.

Ellicott left Philadelphia on September 1, 1796, to begin his six-month journey to Natchez. He kept a journal that recorded his thoughts and actions during his trip until his return in 1800. His journal has proved invaluable in documenting the expedition and providing insight into his thoughts and motivations. After making his way down the Ohio River, Ellicott began his trip down the Mississippi and soon learned his mission would be even more difficult than he might have at first believed.[11]

His suspicions first arose when he arrived at the Spanish fort at New Madrid in what is now Missouri on February 2, 1797. The Spanish commandant tried to detain him, telling Ellicott of his orders not to allow any Americans to pass until the posts were evacuated. A few days later at Chickasaw Bluffs (present-day Memphis area), the commandant there appeared to be unaware of the treaty at all and had made no preparations to leave. On February 19 at Walnut Hills (present-day Vicksburg), officials asked Ellicott of his business. Ellicott saw impressive fortifications with no evidence that an evacuation would take place anytime soon. Ellicott surely must have been exasperated by what he had seen. The treaty specified that the garrisons should be withdrawn from the territory six months after the treaty had been ratified. Treaty ratifications were exchanged in April 1796, therefore meaning the Spanish should have withdrawn from the region by October 1796. Four months past that deadline and no progress had been made toward this effect.[12]

Ellicott's journey had not gone unnoticed, and he finally received word from Manuel Gayoso de Lemos, the Spanish governor of the district of Natchez. In the note, Gayoso asked Ellicott to leave his detachment of troops upriver to prevent any misunderstandings. Ellicott took the advice and finally arrived with only a handful of men to Natchez on February 24 to finally meet Gayoso and begin preparations for the task at hand.[13]

Tensions were high from the start between Ellicott and Gayoso. Ellicott had heard on his journey southward that the Spanish never intended to honor the terms of the treaty. Ellicott was anxious to begin marking the boundary and, perhaps even more importantly, assert American control. It was time to make a statement. At his encampment in Natchez, Ellicott defiantly and emphatically made the strongest declaration possible. On February 29, 1797, on a prominent hill in town, Ellicott's men hoisted the United States flag for all to see, boldly proclaiming American authority over the region. Spanish officials were aghast at this affront to their sovereignty and made pleas for the flag to be removed, but Ellicott would not be denied; he wrote in his journal that the "flag wore out upon the staff." Gayoso claimed he wanted the flag removed for fear that the Native Americans would become unruly, but considering the disregard he had seen on his journey southward about the treaty's enforcement, Ellicott must not have believed him. Ellicott began pestering Gayoso immediately to "name a day on which our operations should commence," meaning when the boundary could be properly marked so the Spanish could withdraw from United States territory.[14]

Gayoso gave various reasons for delaying the enforcement of the treaty. He feared a possible British attack from Canada, thereby putting all Spanish possessions in danger. Secondly, he wanted to make sure that land issues were settled so there would be no problems with people securing their claims. A third reason for delay lay in the desire for friendly relations to continue with the area's Native Americans. Gayoso claimed it would be "impossible for His Catholic Majesty to leave unprotected so many of his faithful subjects and expose other settlements to the revengeful disposition of discontented Indians." Another excuse involved the time needed to determine exactly what should be the condition of the forts at the time of the Spanish withdrawal: should they be dismantled or left intact?[15]

Ellicott was not to be denied and proved persistent in his desire for action, sometimes sending three notes a day to Gayoso. As time went by, Ellicott sensed Gayoso and the Spanish were not moving toward evacuation. At one point, he even witnessed cannon being removed from the fort at Natchez only to be returned days later. Gayoso felt that Ellicott was agitating settlers, while Ellicott claimed tensions were rising simply because of Spanish insincerity of executing the treaty by evacuating. The situation was turning critical and, like other tense historical events, all it needed was a spark to ignite a flame. That spark came in June from an unlikely source, an itinerant Baptist preacher.[16]

Barton Hannon, a shoemaker and lay Baptist preacher, started the controversy when he got permission in June 1797 to preach to Ellicott's men. As Ellicott stated in his journal, "The Minister being elated with the attention he had received on account of his sermon, and emboldened by having permission to speak publicly, he had with enthusiastic zeal, which was a little heightened by liquor, entered into a religious controversy in a disorderly part of town, generally inhabited at that time by Irish Roman Catholics, who took offense at the manner in which he treated the tenets of the church, and in revenge, gave him a beating." After the altercation, Hannon proceeded to meet with Gayoso and demanded justice. Gayoso eventually felt threatened by the preacher and proceeded to throw him in jail. On his way to incarceration, Hannon yelled "Help me, fellow Americans" as he passed by Ellicott's camp. The seed for rebellion had been sown.[17]

Events now proceeded rapidly. A few days later on June 12, over 300 men gathered at Belk's Tavern on the Natchez Trace to discuss freeing Hannon and organizing a revolt. Lt. Percy "Crazy" Pope, who led the army contingent with Ellicott, advocated immediate assault, but Ellicott discouraged it. Many believed the fort to be mined, but a few brave souls decided to approach the fort, only to be turned away when shots were fired. The danger alarmed Gayoso enough to move himself and his family inside the fort for safety. Before long, a committee of citizens formed and sent a letter to Gayoso with a list of demands in order to restore peace. This action began the process of ending Spanish control over the Natchez District.[18]

The June 22, 1797, letter requested four main concessions from Gayoso. The committee demanded that citizens no longer be prosecuted or injured due to their neutral position prior to American occupation and that citizens no longer be required to serve in the Spanish militia except in case of riot or Indian attack. The laws of Spain were to be executed only in mildness or moderation, and a committee would be formed to preserve peace and promote justice. Faced with no real alternative, Gayoso quickly agreed to the propositions, and Governor Carondelet lent his approval shortly afterward. Gayoso would keep his title, but the real power was to be held by this newly elected committee—the unceremonious beginnings of American control of the region. By July, a "permanent" committee of seven had been established. But as historian Franklin Riley has observed, it was a serious mistake to create a governing body without clearly defined responsibilities and duties. Some citizens took exception to this newly formed governing body.[19]

Leading the uproar was Anthony Hutchins. Described as a man of "unlimited ambition" and "of an active, restless, and discontented spirit," Hutchins declared war on this new committee. Hutchins complained that the committee had not been truly mandated and authorized, that it consisted mainly of the merchant/creditor class, and that it would only be the tool of Ellicott, whom Hutchins despised. Hutchins tried to dissolve the committee in quick fashion, declaring, "I am the Organ and Oracle of the People, you are no committee. I will issue circular letters, and have another elected which shall be the Committee of the People."[20]

Gaining permission from acting Spanish Governor Stephen Minor, Hutchins secured new elections for September that led to the formation of a Committee of Safety and Correspondence. Minor had succeeded Gayoso, who had thankfully left his post in late July to assume Carondelet's position in New Orleans. With Spanish control basically over, two distinct factions vied to discredit each other and rule the district. Ellicott and Hutchins would lead those groups in these endeavors. Ellicott's group (Permanent Committee) consisted mainly of newcomers, merchants, and former favorites of the Spanish regime, whereas Hutchins's faction (Committee of Safety) contained mostly long-term residents, indebted famers, and opponents of Ellicott. After both factions formed, episodes took place that would be comedic if not for their sadness and the damage done to the tranquility in the district. The best example of this chicanery was a memorial that Hutchins's Committee of Safety sent to Congress that requested the removal of Ellicott. The memorial never arrived, having been stolen by men reputedly working for Ellicott. Minor summed it up best when he wrote Gayoso: "Generally speaking the People are getting heartily tired of all party business and American politicks [*sic*] is now becoming an old thing."[21]

The arrival of Captain Isaac Guion in late 1797 began calming matters. Guion had been assigned to take possession of certain posts held by Spanish garrisons, but he was also made aware of the discord in the community. He was told that it was his duty ". . . to conciliate all parties to the government of our country by every means in your power, avoiding, at the same time, any just cause of offense with the Spanish authorities. . . . It will be your duty to abstract yourself from all personal feuds and animosities, but you are to give your unequivocal protection to the friends of our government." Upon arrival, it did not take Guion long to assess the situation and determine that neither committee was good for the region. He called a meeting with the factional leaders and became so agitated that he had to excuse himself. In another comedic instance, he came into a meeting of Ellicott and others and after inquiring by what authority were they meeting, declared "you may all kiss my Arse; I will be harder upon you than Hutchins ever was." In a letter to the secretary of state in February 1798, Guion stated, "the inhabitants of this Country are very anxious for the establishment of some government from the executive of the United States." Guion obviously thought the situation would not dramatically improve until a legitimate government could be established. That could not happen until the Spanish completely evacuated.[22]

Spanish leadership finally determined that their hopes of holding on to the Natchez district had ended and that the time had come to evacuate. Gayoso issued orders to his commandants in January 1798 to evacuate. On March 23, the Spanish evacuated Fort Nogales at present-day Vicksburg, and on March 30, Ellicott recorded in his journal: "I rose . . . at five o'clock and walked to the fort, and found the last party, or rear guard just leaving it. . . . I went in, and enjoyed from the parapet, the pleasing prospects of gallies [*sic*] and boats leaving the shore and getting underway. They were out of sight of the town before daylight."

Guion sent official word that same day: "I have the honor to announce to your Excellency the evacuation of the posts of Walnut Hills and Natchez by the troops of his Catholic Majesty. . . . I have put a small guard in this post & the flag of the U. States now is waving over the rampart." A century of rule by various European nations had finally ended.[23]

With Spanish evacuation over and Guion now in command and maintaining order, Ellicott was finally able to proceed with his original mission of surveying and marking the 31st parallel, the boundary between the United States and Spanish West Florida. Working with representatives of the Spanish government who included Minor and William Dunbar, Ellicott began the process of marking the 381 miles from the Mississippi to the Chattahoochee River. The job proved as difficult as it sounded as the surveyors faced not only hostile Indians but "mosquitoes, malaria, canebrakes, torrential rains, and incompetent helpers." All was not horrible, as Dunbar did record that "the first twenty miles of country . . . is as fertile as any in the United States." Ellicott did not mark the last spot until February 1800, meaning the process took over twenty months. Once completed, Ellicott finally retuned north to Philadelphia where he had his journal published in 1803, providing a fascinating account of this transitionary period. Ellicott would conduct other boundary work and later became a mathematics teacher at West Point. He died in 1820.[24]

Even before the Spanish evacuation, the US government made arrangements for establishing authority in the region. On June 12, 1797, President John Adams recommended that Congress "erect a government for the district of Natchez." After debate the following spring, Congress created the Mississippi Territory on April 7, 1798. The act established boundaries for the territory that consisted of lands north of the 31st parallel and south of the mouth of the Yazoo River and east of Mississippi River and west of the Chattahoochee River. The territory would be expanded twice over the next two decades. In 1804, the northern boundary was extended to the Tennessee state line and nearly ten years later, President James Madison annexed additional land along the Gulf Coast. By 1813, the Mississippi Territory encompassed the boundaries of present-day Alabama and Mississippi. The original act creating the territory established for it a government similar to that of the one established for the Northwest Territory, but unlike that act it did not forbid the institution of slavery, which already existed and whose illegality would have been challenged by the region's residents.[25]

The territory's governmental structure would play a huge role in the events to come. The president, with consent of Congress, would appoint a governor, secretary, and three judges who could adopt laws and appoint civil and militia officers. After the territory's population reached 5,000 free adult males, an assembly could be elected and a delegate sent to Congress. This legislation created a very nondemocratic form of government to control a district that had already

Figure 1.2. Winthrop Sargent, first governor of Mississippi Territory. (Collection of the Museum Division, Mississippi Department of Archives and History, 1978.32.1)

had its share of authority issues. Anyone with foresight could have predicted the results to come.[26]

The choice of the territory's first governor would only add fuel to the fire. After initially choosing former Georgia governor George Matthews to serve and then withdrawing the name after protests, President John Adams selected Winthrop Sargent for the post. Sargent had many suitable qualifications for the job. He had a strong military background with service during the Revolutionary War and against the Native Americans in the northwest, and had territorial administrative experience as secretary of the Northwest Territory for ten years. George Washington himself even wrote a testimonial stating that Sargent "displayed a zeal, integrity and intelligence which did honor him as an officer and a gentleman."[27]

Sargent had some attributes, however, that would not mesh with the residents of his new frontier environment. Sargent was a strict Puritan from Massachusetts who abhorred frontier standards of morality and the institution of slavery. His Federalist views of strong centralized government also conflicted with a democracy-loving society. Historian Arthur H. DeRosier Jr. stated, "A worse choice could have scarcely been made."[28]

Aside from personality differences, Sargent faced a monumental task. The first issue Sargent had to solve involved land issues. France, Britain, and Spain had all issued land grants in the region, and the new government had to sort out these disputes. Georgia also complicated matters, as that state had claimed much of that land going back to the 1780s. In 1789 and 1795 the Georgia legislature passed Yazoo Land Acts that granted millions acres of land in the region to land companies, which then sold the land to settlers and speculators. One such act has long since been referred to as the Yazoo Land Frauds. Due to corruption and bribery, this legislation was rescinded one year later. DeRosier stated, "Nowhere in America were land policy difficulties more complex and more unsolvable than in the old Southwest."[29]

Second, most of the territory was inhabited by various Native American nations who were apprehensive after their ally Spain abandoned them to the ever-expanding United States. Sargent's new government would have to maintain peace between these tribes and land-hungry immigrants. The Spanish had cemented their friendship with the giving of gifts, and the new government lacked the money to continue this process. Sargent had nothing to offer and complained that many residents "were literally eaten out of house and home." Sargent wrote that "At this place the chactaw [*sic*] Indians frequently visit they are sometimes troublesome to the inhabitants by killing their cattle. . . . perhaps it might endeavor to keep them in good humour, by a little Bread, Beef, and liquor, and some trifling presents . . ." His addition of liquor is interesting as a few months later, he issued a proclamation prohibiting the giving or selling to Indians ". . . any Whiskey, Rum, Brandy, or other Ardent Spirits."[30]

Adopting laws became another important issue. Sargent needed the help of judges, and as historian Robert Haynes has said, "territorial judges were slow to arrive, loath to remain on the job, and eager to leave." One judge resided in the area, but the second one did not arrive until January 1799, when Sargent felt that he could begin adopting laws. Sargent reported to Secretary of State Pickering that "The Judge's arrival gives us (authority) to Legislate—it was most essential and we will set about it without delay though with much regret on my part at the want of Laws of several States. . . ." The writing of these laws would cause tremendous divisiveness in the community.[31]

Finally, there was the need to maintain order. The area had long been a refuge for escaped prisoners, border ruffians, fugitive murderers, and heavily burdened debtors, and Sargent needed to appoint sheriffs and justices of the peace to deal with issues of disorder. He would write that "We have no Prisons, no sufficient places of Confinement, and the Vilest offenders therefore Calculate with some Certainty upon impunity." As an indicator of this problem, one of the first public buildings constructed was a jail in Natchez. On top of this, setting up a militia for the territory's defense was of utmost concern. A strong militia was important for providing safety from possible Indian attacks as well as meeting any potential threat from European nations.[32]

After a tumultuous period of transition, the United States had finally removed the Spanish from its newly acquired territory and had established an official government. Residents were anxious to put the problems of the past aside and move toward solving the issues at hand. It would soon be clear that the new American rule would not put an end to this divisive environment. In fact, it would only get much worse!

CHAPTER 2

Tumultuous Territorial Government

After finally ridding the last European empire of its claim to the region, residents cautiously looked to the future. Many hoped the last few months of upheaval and disagreement would fade as they eagerly awaited the arrival of their new governor, Winthrop Sargent. Expectations were high as they waited to meet and talk with him and learn about his plans. Unfortunately, Sargent was in no condition to converse; the long journey down the Ohio and Mississippi Rivers from the Northwest Territory, where he had served as secretary for a decade, depleted his health. His illness was so severe that upon arrival on August 6, 1798, he was immediately taken to Concord, the home of former Spanish governors, to recover. The long journey and almost unbearable climate proved to be simply too much. Many thought his life hung in the balance; he would recover, but his declining health served as an omen of future troubles. Sargent's tenure as governor of the Mississippi Territory, as well as that of his successors, would be defined by constant turmoil.[1]

After spending nearly two weeks recovering, Sargent gave his initial address to his constituents at a public gathering in Natchez. Referring to the Northwest Ordinance of 1787 as being his framework, Sargent stressed the need for "a concise and clear code of laws, intelligible to the most common capacity," which would be executed with uniformity and fairness. He also told the crowd that the right to own property in slaves would be continued, that appointments would be made, and that a militia would be established. He intended the speech to serve as an introduction to the principles by which he planned to govern the new Territory, but his talk of creating "good citizens void of Jealousy of each other and emulous of public good" would soon prove ironic.[2]

Figure 2.1. Seal of Mississippi Territory, 1798, cast in Philadelphia, Pennsylvania (notice Mississippi is misspelled). (Collection of the Museum Division, Mississippi Department of Archives and History, 1981.33.1)

Jealousies quickly arose as Sargent decided to visit with several local citizens to gain an understanding of the community and the political environment. He first met with Andrew Ellicott. Sargent sought his opinion on the leading men of the district so he could make proper appointments. Sargent could not have made a poorer decision in whom he should place his trust, as there was no more divisive personality than Ellicott.[3]

Sargent moved quickly to establish his government. With other officials slow to arrive, he was forced to operate by executive decree. He appointed minor officials such as sheriffs and created necessary offices such as a probate court to administer estates, and in doing so chose two of Ellicott's favorites as judges. Sargent also organized the militia and appointed officers. In this case, he made sure to select a wide variety of individuals, including many of Ellicott's enemies, but all this did was make others mad. Sargent's critics saw his rule as arbitrary, and one even commented that "Royalty could do no more."[4]

Matters got even more contentious when Sargent moved to create a set of laws. By January 1799, Judge Daniel Tilton had arrived and with Judge Peter Bruin, Sargent felt it was time to establish a legal code for the Territory. The governor proved hesitant, however, feeling that he himself and the other two judges lacked adequate knowledge to formulate the laws. The critical issue became whether Sargent and his officials were simply adopting laws or creating new ones. Sargent later wrote to Secretary of State Timothy Pickering: "I have already Authorized you of the arrival of Judge Tilton, and in Consequence we are at length Legislating but destitute of the Laws of the several states we necessarily make instead of Adopting them the right to do which has heretofore been a Question." Without any strong set of laws to use as a model, they "made" laws instead of utilizing existing state/territorial statutes. This decision would generate problems in the future.[5]

By the end of February 1799, forty-six new laws, which soon became known derisively as "Sargent's Codes," had been drafted. These laws established rules and regulations for militia, various court systems, defined crimes and their punishments, and regulated marriages and taverns. These laws made many of Sargent's executive decrees official and also were in accordance with his strong desire to install order in a district that had for too long been lacking in such regard. They also would send his rapidly growing list of opponents into a frenzy.[6]

Opposition to Sargent grew quickly. Longtime agitator Anthony Hutchins, who had finally grown too old and infirm to cause much of a ruckus, passed his mantle of leadership on to others in his camp, principally Thomas Marston Green and Cato West, who had married into the Green family. These opponents and their cohorts would become known as the Green-West Faction or the West Junto. Sargent, unfortunately, did little to foster support for himself as tensions rose. His strict Puritan ways and haughty attitude did not sit well with many of the region's inhabitants, and his desire to establish strict law and order was not embraced either. No "man so frigid and sour" could ever gain friends and allies with a "free people."[7]

Sargent's opponents had many reasons to be upset. Some of the biggest complaints dealt with appointments, taxes, the militia, and uncertainty concerning distribution of land. Hatred of the territorial governor's new laws, however, became the focal point. Besides being upset at the harsh punishments mandated for crimes, many citizens did not like the way the laws were enacted. Sargent's opponents asserted that laws were only supposed to be adopted from existing legislation, not created from scratch. They believed that the legislation establishing the Mississippi Territory only allowed for adoption of "laws made in the original States as may best suit the circumstances of the country." Those in opposition banded together and did more than simply voice their complaints aloud, they took their grievances to the national government.[8]

Opponents to Sargent drafted a petition to Congress to lay out their concerns. Carried by Narsworthy Hunter, the petition listed several problems with the current government in the Mississippi Territory. Besides discussing the right of citizens to have their own voice in government, the main focus of the petition centered on the arbitrary mingling of "executive, legislative, and Judicial authorities" in the hands of "three or four individuals." The solution proposed was simple—grant the territory the second stage of government that would provide a bicameral legislature.[9]

Hunter found two allies in Congress to support this petition. Thomas Davis of Kentucky and William C. C. Claiborne of Tennessee sponsored legislation that moved the territory into the second stage of government. Hunter lobbied hard as well by exaggerating population numbers, reiterating complaints about the making of laws rather than simply adopting them, and discussing how citizens were upset about Sargent's appointments. Perhaps his strongest statement in criticizing the current government of the territory came when he said, "Can it be possible that an administration which from its earliest operations, have proved so repugnant to the public will and so fatal to the happiness of society, can ever be able to restore harmony, attach public confidence, and promote the general good? The thing is impossible." Hunter emphasized that only a legislative assembly could right these wrongs and appease the minds of the territory's citizens.[10]

Sargent had no choice but to conduct elections for a house of representatives of nine members. (The upper house in this bicameral legislature was a five-member legislative council appointed by the president from ten nominees selected by the House.) Sargent was adamant that the region's inhabitants were "unfitted in every view of the matter for that second stage of Order," but the election took place. And to further cement his disappointment and anger, the electorate voted in eight of his harshest critics, including West, Green, and Anthony Hutchins himself. Pouring salt on the open wound, the representatives chose Hunter as the territory's delegate to Congress.[11]

Sargent did not have to deal with a confrontational legislature long, because his fate soon became sealed. Thomas Jefferson's election as president in 1800 soon ended his term. Sargent journeyed east to defend himself and fight for his job, but the Republican Jefferson felt the need to satisfy many of his supporters' wishes by removing Sargent and appointing W. C. C. Claiborne to replace him. Sargent's political career was over. He had made mistakes and did not possess the personality nor temperament to succeed, but one wonders if any governor at this point in time could have succeeded. He eventually settled down to life as a planter until dying in New Orleans in 1820.[12]

Whereas Sargent's background provided ample experience for assuming this position, the young Claiborne's résumé was not quite as impressive. A native of Virginia, the twenty-six-year-old had already served as a congressional clerk, as a member of Tennessee's first constitutional convention, and on the Tennessee Supreme Court. As a congressman from Tennessee, he supported Jefferson, who rewarded him with this position. Appointed in May 1801, Claiborne arrived in Natchez that November. If he had hopes that with Sargent's departure, the political climate would improve, he would soon be disappointed.[13]

Upon arrival, Claiborne delivered an address to the legislative body in December that summarized his priorities and his goals for the future. He expressed the need for improvements in the judicial department and a strong concern for the formation of a proper militia amidst constant fears of Native American attack, slave revolts, and meddling by the Spanish. These issues and the continual struggle to resolve land disputes would dominate much of his time. He "formed a firm

Resolution to exercise the authority vested in me" and discussed how "Party Spirit, that Bane to happiness," was not in the best interest of man and the community. He ended with a call to "let us all unite, and enrich Society with the charms of harmony and Concord."[14]

Disregarding Claiborne's call for harmony, the legislature quickly fanned the flames of discord. It voted to move the capital away from Federalist-dominated Natchez six miles northeast to the new town of Washington. The territorial assembly also changed the county name of Pickering (named after Timothy Pickering, another hated Federalist) to Jefferson, and they repealed nearly a half dozen laws created by the previous governor. The hated "Sargent's Codes" would be no more.[15]

Plenty of other examples of factionalism occurred during Claiborne's tenure. Rival literary and cultural societies were formed; Republicans led by the Green family established the Mississippi Republican Society while Federalists created the Mississippi Society for the Acquisition and Dissemination of Useful Knowledge. Partisan newspapers were also launched in this era. Federalists started the territory's first newspaper, the *Mississippi Herald*, while Claiborne sought out other printers to print laws, circulars, and handbills.[16]

Bickering also delayed the establishment of an important educational institution. Claiborne called for a "seminary of learning," and the legislature responded by establishing Jefferson College in May 1802. The legislation, however, provided no source of funding, and left it up to donations to get the school off the ground. This action in turn led to disagreement over where to place the school. The Greens wanted it located near their home in Greenville in Jefferson County and offered donations of land and money. Similar donations of money and land were also offered to place the institution in the capital of Washington, which the governor preferred. Not until 1811 did classes finally begin at Jefferson College, which had been located in Washington. This entire controversy revealed that there were two Republican factions (Claiborne's group and the Green/West junto) and shoved Claiborne further and further to joining with the old-line Federalists.[17]

Claiborne had his hands full regardless of the constant political squabbles. He received help on the ever-present land issue when the US government in 1802 finally convinced Georgia to relinquish its western land claims. The following year, Congress passed a monumental land act that validated land claims prior to the Treaty of San Lorenzo (Pinckney's Treaty) and established a system for the sale of other lands. The act established two land offices in the Mississippi Territory and authorized the appointment of necessary officials who could register claims and settle disputes. This longstanding issue finally showed signs of being addressed.[18]

Issues with the Spanish to the south also dominated Claiborne's time. Spanish officials closed the port of New Orleans in 1802, causing great concern. Word that Spain had secretly sold Louisiana to France made matters worse. Spanish possession of southern lands was one thing, but Napoleon controlling the area economically as well as politically was something else entirely. Fortunately, French reverses in Europe and on the island of St. Dominique led the French ruler to sell all of France's Louisiana possessions to the United States. President Jefferson sent Claiborne to officially accept the transfer of the colony in December 1803. He did not know it at the time, but Claiborne would not return to his post, eventually becoming Louisiana's governor. He would find new challenges there, but probably was happy to put the Mississippi Territory behind him.[19]

The constant factionalism was not only related to people and party but was sectional as well. Established in 1800, Washington County encompassed the area of the territory east of the Pearl River. Separated by three hundred miles from the territorial government in Natchez, residents felt isolated and neglected. Court proceedings seldom occurred, and the economy struggled. Residents exporting their products down the rivers to Mobile had to pay high duties to the Spanish. Failing to get their grievances heard, residents in November 1803 petitioned Congress for division of the territory. It was the first mention of the possibility of splitting the territory, but it would be far from the last and become an issue every future governor would be forced to deal with in one way or another.[20]

The legislative assembly had its issues as well. One of the matters that proved most detrimental to the territory involved the assembly's failure to choose a new delegate to Congress in December 1804. Various candidates were considered, but party politics and disagreeable personalities prevented consensus. After six failed ballots and being exasperated by unfocused and useless conversations and debate, Speaker of the House Philander Smith terminated the balloting, leaving Mississippi without any voice or representation with the federal government for some time.[21]

Upon Claiborne's departure, Territorial Secretary Cato West assumed executive duties. Ambitious to a fault and leader of the Green/West faction, West now assumed his dream position. With powerful friends and family, he assumed that he would be appointed to the position on a permanent basis. As historian Robert Haynes states, "Political alignments were more likely to be based on familiar relationships than political ideologies or economic interests."[22]

To his utter despair, West did not get his wish. Thomas Jefferson first appointed Judge Ephraim Kirby to be governor but upon Kirby's sudden death, Jefferson took the advice of Isaac Briggs, the territory's surveyor and no friend of West, and appointed Robert Williams as permanent governor. In perhaps the greatest example of poor sportsmanship, West promptly returned to his estate in Greenville in Jefferson County and took the official government records with him. It took threats from the territorial assembly to finally force West to relinquish the papers.[23]

Robert Williams, Mississippi's third territorial governor, was a North Carolina native and a former congressman. He was serving as land commissioner for the district west of the Pearl River at the time of his appointment. Upon accepting the job from President Thomas Jefferson, he sought authority to hold on to that lucrative position and also asked permission to return to his native state for personal business. These decisions soon caused friction with the citizens of the territory. And Williams needed no further strikes against him, because his temperament did him no favors. Historian Robert Haynes summed it up nicely by describing him thusly: "Irascible in personality and dictatorial in style, Williams was incapable of building a sustained friendship with anyone but Briggs or instilling loyalty among his supporters. Instead, he attracted enemies as fast as honey draws flies."[24]

Like his predecessor Claiborne, Williams erred in his assessment of the territory's political stability. Williams explained that "Colonel West has had his political frolic, and all things are quiet." In reality, political tensions would not ease, and upon Williams leaving for North Carolina, one of the territorial period's most intriguing and divisive events took place.[25]

Aaron Burr, along with several boats of "adventurers," arrived in the territory in January 1807. The former vice president's political career had disintegrated after he killed Alexander Hamilton in a duel in 1804. Since then, rumors had run rampant concerning an alleged scheme masterminded by Burr that involved the separation of a few states such as Tennessee and Kentucky from the rest of the Union, as well as the invasion and capture of Spanish lands to the west that would be ruled by Burr. General James Wilkinson, who offered his services to the Spanish crown as a paid spy, was also rumored to be involved. When Wilkinson heard his name also being mentioned prominently in this plot, he decided to turn on his co-conspirator. The climate in the territory was filled with uncertainty and unrest.[26]

During Williams's visit to North Carolina to tend to his personal affairs, Territory Secretary Cowles Mead served as acting governor. Another ambitious politician, Mead had become a member of the Green faction when he married into the family. Not trusting Wilkinson or Burr, he activated the militia, stirring up even more intrigue. When he learned of his impending arrest, Burr voluntarily surrendered to territorial authorities in exchange for a guarantee of a trial in the Mississippi Territory. Burr was released on bond and a court date was set for the following month.[27]

Burr's appearance in the territory served as another example of the factionalism of the times. Several balls were held in his honor as many residents, including Federalists, were in awe of the famous Burr and were in favor of taking land from the Spanish. Rumor had it that Burr even fell in love with a local widow's daughter. Others, however, including Judge Thomas Rodney, were anxious to put Burr on trial for treason. Williams eventually returned to assume his duties and his presence seemed to calm the community. Burr's arraignment before a grand jury overwhelmed the small town of Washington, which had never experienced an event of such magnitude. The grand jury absolved Burr and actually condemned

Mead's heavy-handed actions. Judge Rodney was upset and wanted Burr held under his recognizance. Burr, still fearful of getting captured by Wilkinson, fled, only to be later captured and arrested near Mobile. He eventually stood trial in Richmond, where he was acquitted in a landmark verdict that set the precedent for trials involving treason.[28]

Although Burr was out of the picture, political maneuverings continued. Cowles Mead, stinging from the results of the Burr trial, still hoped to claim the governorship for himself. He withdrew from Williams's administration and formed a new faction with George Poindexter, a recent arrival in the territory who rose rapidly in local politics, and Ferdinand Claiborne, militia leader and brother of the former governor. Poindexter got elected as delegate to Congress and quickly worked on petitions to remove Williams from office. In an example of the strong animosity involved, Poindexter challenged Williams to a duel because of remarks the governor made about the militia. Williams declined the duel, however, due to his official obligations. Meanwhile, Mead and Claiborne soon were elected to the legislature and caused problems for Williams on that front.[29]

Williams did not sit quietly while his foes maneuvered around him. He blamed Mead for resurrecting "that party spirit which [had] formerly interrupted the individual happiness of the people, the harmony of Society and the public tranquility of this country, thereby weakening their confidence in the government." Williams took the offensive by removing government officials and militia officers, angering everyone and also causing a rash of resignations in protest. Judge Thomas Rodney wrote Poindexter that "The Conduct of the Govr Indeed is like That of a Man whose mind is deranged." Williams's strongest attempt to secure his power was his dismissing the legislature three times in a span of four months. This display of power did him no good, because the election of the summer of 1808 saw candidates on the "country ticket," supporters for Mead/Poindexter, triumph over many of Williams's supporters, known as the "city ticket."[30]

Growing disheartened with the entire affair, Williams finally decided he would leave office when his sponsor President Thomas Jefferson also moved on. Jefferson quickly chose Virginian David Holmes to replace Williams but told him to keep his withdrawal confidential until he was actually ready to leave. Word of course leaked, and in an act typical of the era, several legislators in an act of defiance of the governor purposely arrived late to the General Assembly in February 1809, delaying the start of the session by three days. A month later, Williams left Mississippi, but not before dissolving the Assembly yet again. His enemies did not seem to care as legislators had quite a "frolic," celebrating by parading through the streets of Washington.[31]

David Holmes arrived on June 30, 1809, to begin his term as the Mississippi Territory's fourth governor. It had been a tumultuous decade dominated by constant political discord, but the area finally had a leader who would calm the

Figure 2.2. David Holmes, last governor of Mississippi Territory and first governor of the state of Mississippi. (Collection of the Museum Division, Mississippi Department of Archives and History, 1978.36.1)

stormy waters. Pennsylvanian by birth, he had served twelve years in Congress, which perhaps honed his compromise skills. Importantly, too, Holmes had a more pleasant and agreeable personality than his predecessors. He also had no desire to use the position for political gain. Robert Haynes compared Holmes adeptly by saying, "He lacked the aloofness of Sargent, the intense ambition and youthful vigor of Claiborne, the egotism of West, the flamboyance of Mead, and the arbitrariness of Williams." Holmes summed it up soon after his arrival in a letter he sent to the president stating that he hoped to "Cherish peace and good will among the people."[32]

Luckily for Holmes, several factors led to a decreased atmosphere of strained factionalism. Several long-term agitators, such as Anthony Hutchins and Thomas M. Green, had passed away. Many simply also faded away from public office or chose to no longer antagonize the governor. More importantly, people's attention turned to other important events and circumstances. The growing population of the eastern counties threatened the power base of the Natchez area. Fears of the eastern section separating to form its own state became more of a possible reality, and citizens wondered how these new population trends would affect the path to statehood for the territory. Finally, international affairs also took center stage. Wars in Europe with Napoleon had a harmful effect on the United States, especially on maritime trade and the economy. These important issues finally outweighed petty personal differences and individual pursuits of power.[33]

Politics assumed a more manageable and civilized level, but no discussion of political squabbling would be complete without mention of the feud between George Poindexter and Andrew Marschalk. Poindexter had served in a variety of capacities such as attorney general, legislator, and territorial delegate, which had led to his being involved in a number of political quarrels. One of these disputes involved a duel with Abijah Hunt in 1811 that ended in Hunt's death and the rumor that Poindexter fired prematurely.[34]

First arriving in the Territory as an army lieutenant, Andrew Marschalk became one of the Territory's more prominent printers (he printed the first laws of the territory) and editor of several newspapers. He eventually allied with Governor Williams and began aiming his editorial gun at Poindexter. Over the course of several years, he accused Poindexter of dishonesty and the mishandling of public funds and even retold the unfortunate Hunt duel story again. Marschalk apparently went too far when he printed a story concerning Poindexter's alleged cowardice during the famous 1815 Battle of New Orleans against the British. Poindexter had served as aide-de-camp and initially had his own version printed in the *Mississippi Republican*. Marschalk answered this account by publishing a letter of a supposed eyewitness who claimed Poindexter fled the field as soon as the first shots were fired. An enraged Poindexter eventually encountered Marschalk and chased him through the streets of Washington with a brick. This incident led to both men spending time in jail.[35]

One could easily summarize government in Mississippi's territorial period in three words—bitter political factionalism. Various historians have attempted to state the reasons for such tension, but historian William B. Hamilton described it best when he summarized the political environment of Mississippi's birth: "Desire for office and power, petty geographical jealousies and sectionalism, the colonial relation with the United States, and personal and family relationship were the driving forces. They were, so to speak, what the shouting was all about."[36]

CHAPTER 3

The Land of Promise

To its free early American settlers, the millions of acres of relatively cheap and extremely productive land that lay within the Mississippi Territory formed "the land of promise, flowing with milk and honey." Fertile, abundant, and beckoning to those eager to make their fortune, the land that became the twentieth state sounded a clarion call for thousands throughout the nation in an age when land represented one of the surest paths to security and wealth. As sure a form of currency as any coin, bill, or note, the land held tangible promise that could be unlocked by anyone with the willingness to toil or the financial resources to purchase slaves for that purpose. Its sylvan beauty, both aesthetic and practical, captured the attention of early settlers in a profound way. "This is a fine fresh country, well watered and healthy, and the land produces very well," observed one optimistic visitor to early Mississippi who expressed the thoughts of thousands of his peers. "It is the opinion of the citizens of this country that it will be the best place of trade that is in America. . . ." The process of settling this luxuriant land, however, would prove more complicated than many could have dreamed.[1]

Mississippi had been claimed alternately by France, Great Britain, Spain, and even the state of Georgia prior to statehood, and each had issued titles to portions of its lands over time. This conflicting, overlapping tangle of existing deeds yielded tremendous confusion over legal ownership of land in the state that would occupy both territorial and state courts. There were very few land grants issued by the French, their dominion over the then sparsely inhabited territory having ended in 1763. Those grants handed down by the British in the Natchez District were usually the oldest, but they frequently overlapped the same areas later deeded to individuals by Spain, which held the area from the time of the American Revolution until the creation of the Mississippi Territory. Added on top of these grants in some places were those issued by Georgia, which had attempted to organize portions of the future state as "Bourbon County."[2]

All this confusion impeded the growth of the Territory in its early years and frustrated government officials. The hundreds of conflicting grants and surveys waiting to be untangled by American officials when the short-staffed administration of Governor Winthrop Sargent arrived in 1798 caused considerable delays in settlement. Surveyors and registers simply could not keep up with the flood of paperwork required to issue clear title to settlers, tying the hands of employees in the land offices. At one point in the territorial period, assistants working under the western district Surveyor General Isaac Briggs summarily quit because they could not do their job until the registers sorted through a mountain of claims. Surveying claims regularly ground to a halt owing to the backlog, causing much unrest and adding fuel to the fire of already rampant speculation.[3]

Partial resolution came in 1803, when Congress issued an act confirming the titles for all heads of families who held British or Spanish grants to lands that had been under cultivation prior to October 1795, and gave settlers without claims preemption rights of up to 640 acres of land under cultivation by that time. Those that had settled between 1795 and the date of the act were to be extended preemption rights as well. While on its surface the act seemed to solve some of the most pressing problems associated with the distribution of land, it did cause anguish for many because it required court action and filing fees to validate deeds issued by colonial powers. The portion of the act that authorized the appointment of land commissioners for two districts became the most consequential part of the act in resolving the backlog of title applicants. One office was located east of the Pearl River in Washington County, and the other was west of that river in Adams County. Later an office opened in Nashville, Tennessee, and subsequently moved to Huntsville, to serve the territory's northern reaches. The administrative centers were to sell at auction in an orderly fashion all unclaimed lands to which Indian title had been extinguished. The offices did a booming business in executing their charge, handling the sale of hundreds of thousands of acres of the Mississippi Territory in a mounting torrent of activity over the decade and a half prior to statehood. In the process, they became a critical linchpin in orchestrating the growth of the region and in its headlong pursuit of statehood.[4]

The presence of hordes of squatters in the Territory, their claims now having legal standing, exacerbated an already difficult situation for territorial officials by encouraging even more such behavior. With so little government presence in most quarters of the new territory and those officers present consumed with other duties, squatters wandered into almost every corner of the province and established their homes undisturbed; most were unmolested for considerable lengths of time, making it all the more difficult to honor legitimate claims when eventually attempted. It has been reported that upon Mississippi's statehood, there were more intruders, or illegal settlers, than legal residents in some counties. At public land sales, it was not uncommon for illegal squatters to attend and intimidate or otherwise threaten those who might wish to legally purchase the land on which squatters resided. The practice became such a problem during the early territorial years that auctions were occasionally scheduled outside of the affected region.[5]

Few intruders who received official word that they were living on land claimed by someone else willingly acquiesced to eviction. Indeed, in the rare case that authorities attempted to force illegal settlers off lands claimed by others, local governments might openly aid the squatters. Judge Harry Toulmin, an official residing north of Mobile in the "Tombigbee" settlements, lamented about the situation by asking a rhetorical question: "How can a jury be found in Monroe County to convict a man of intrusion—where every man is an intruder?" Even when authorities brought to bear efforts to remove illegal occupants of lands, the intruders enjoyed some degree of legal recourse. A group from Tennessee, for example, who had settled on the Cahaba River in what is now central Alabama, was granted a stay of eviction by President James Madison until they could harvest the crops they had planted. Officials often favorably received such appeals to "stay on until the harvest" lest they appear to mistreat the American settlers they encouraged to inhabit the territory. Such leniency only encouraged the extraction of resources from the land before it could be legally settled. Activities such as illegal timber cutting, including the rare and valuable cedar in south Mississippi, became a widespread problem in the chaos of the early territorial years and threatened to make the area a free-for-all to be plundered at will.[6]

Added to the influx of new arrivals seeking to legally settle were a handful of older residents who likewise held no clear title to the land on which they lived. Some of these individuals operated trading establishments and had become fixtures in the areas they served. "Indian countrymen," as they were known, had settled among the native towns years before any vestige of American authority appeared in their vicinity and established themselves in the unique niche of economic intermediary that American expansion facilitated. Abram Mordecai, for example, lived among the Creeks in the eastern portion of the Mississippi Territory for nearly two decades prior to statehood, trading with them for roots, hickory nut oil, and pelts, which he sold in markets such as New Orleans, Mobile, and Pensacola. In return, he exchanged a variety of trade goods in Creek villages which he brought back via pack horses. President Madison ultimately ordered the removal of these trespassers in December 1815, an executive action that, while not immediately solving the problem, certainly paved the way for its resolution by lending federal authority and resources to the understaffed local government. While the intrusion issue defied resolution by any single order or action, officials managed to clear up the most troublesome cases by the first years of statehood. Well into the state's formative era, however, squatters made up a significant portion of settlers.[7]

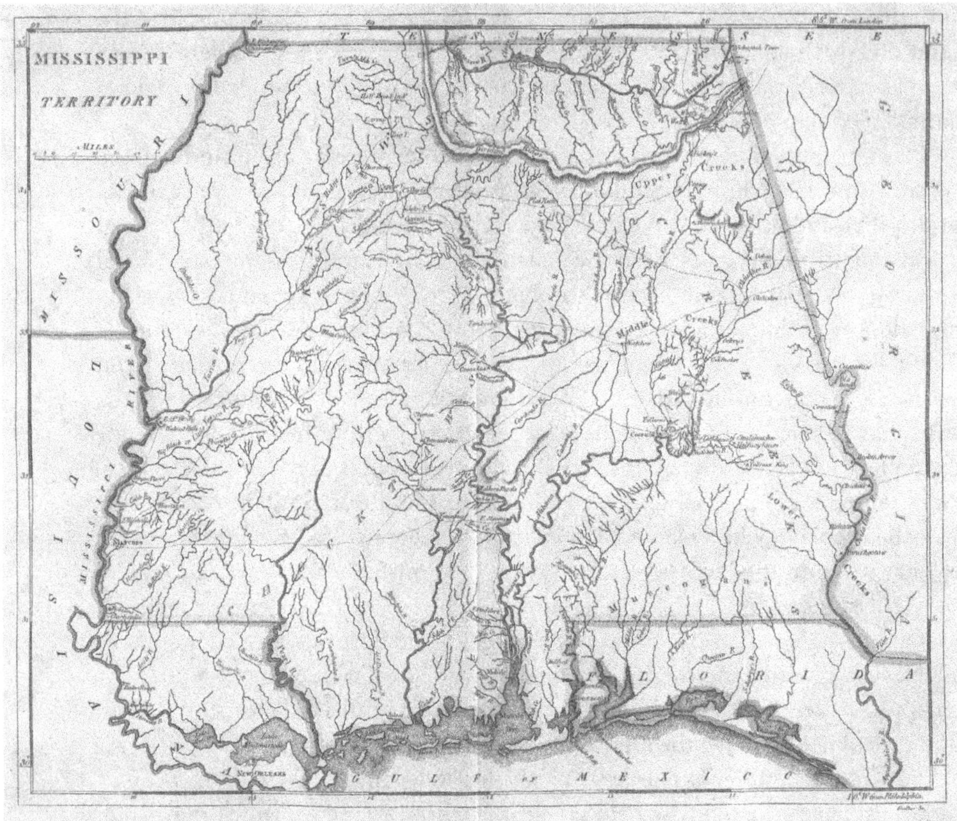

Figure 3.1. Map of Mississippi Territory, 1814. (Courtesy of the David Rumsey Map Collection)

In order for legal settlement to occur, Mississippi's lands had to be professionally surveyed into sections, ranges, and townships. These surveys proved to be no easy task in a sparsely settled frontier country that featured few decent roads and a significant Native American population. The surveyors who laid out the state into units of measurement that could be used to record land sales and deeds were true pioneers who, of necessity, literally were often the first Americans to ever walk on some of the grounds on which they worked. Almost year round, in all types of weather, they and their crews slogged through forests, meadows, and swamps dragging chains, blazing trees, placing stakes, and scribbling notes as they carved boundaries in the wilderness.

Levin Wailes's account of a 1809 survey of lands in southeast Mississippi along the Chickasawhay River provides a window into surveyors' experiences and vividly paints a portrait of a frontier that transitioned into statehood rather than one that neatly assumed a place as a sovereign government overnight. Wailes's daily notes are typical of those of countless surveyors. They contain entries detailing monotonous and laborious crossings of branches, clearing of paths, staking of corners, and notching of trees to mark the survey line. He and his crew subsisted for weeks at a time on the store of supplies they brought with them or what they could trade for with local Indians or area traders: food in the form of fish, beef, pork, butter, potatoes, corn, turkeys, ducks, apples, cheese, sweet potatoes, brandy, porter, and salt. Wailes's encounter with a group of Choctaws concerned about his presence and purpose is typical of the contacts that periodically took place along the borders of the territory and state until the long, sordid process of Indian Removal had been completed. On May 28, 1809, a Choctaw chief and his attendants stopped Wailes in his work to inform him (through a translator) that if he continued on his present line of survey, he would pass through the hunting lands of a village whose residents were "particularly averse to having their lands measured with a chain, and that it would be difficult to make such explanations as would enable them to discriminate between the guide lines and the proper Boundary between the United States and their nation. . . ." The next day a group of armed warriors appeared and threatened some Choctaws who were cooperating with Wailes, asserting that their people had not agreed to a boundary such as the one he was in the process of delineating. After much discussion, they allowed Wailes and his men to complete their survey to a certain point that represented a temporary compromise between the official orders of the American government and the concerns of apprehensive natives.[8]

Surveys, complete or not, became both the precursor to and the result of land sales. Early Mississippi positively buzzed with both. Word of mouth about the new lands would have been sufficient to generate a crowd of enthusiastic buyers, but public notices were sent out far and wide alerting the public of the coming sales. An advertisement that appeared in a New York paper typified their language, inviting "to this part of the country any number of the industrious part of those emigrants who, when arrived here, will be provided with lands, rent-free for three years, with cattle and corn at the usual prices of the country, until they can pay for them, and all other things wanting for immediate use." The notice even recommended the routes by which settlers might make their way south. In a flurry of activity, Mississippi Territory land offices sprang to life. For example, over 214,000 of 354,000 acres surveyed in Madison County, in the eastern section of the territory in the Great Bend of the Tennessee River, had been sold by June 1815. Sales in the entirety of the territory between October 1815 and September 1816 equaled nearly a third of the total acreage sold in the rest of the nation during that time.[9]

Land auctions were big events that frequently drew huge crowds. Temporary tent cities popped up in wilderness clearings as throngs of people ventured to the chosen spot from far and wide. After a few makeshift tables and chairs were set up, survey notes and maps spread out, and ledgers opened to record the transactions, officials had all the "office" they needed and opened for business. In a matter of several days, buyers bargained for the best lands at the best price on the best terms. The overwhelming majority made their purchases on credit under the terms of the liberal Land Law of 1800, which required a very small down payment and provided a generous number of years for repayment. With prime land selling for as little as two dollars an acre, it must have seemed like the chance of a lifetime. Of course, some of the choicest parcels had already been snatched up by wealthy insiders by the time the general public got a chance to bid, but there was so much acreage available that opportunities seemed plentiful enough.[10]

Inevitably, many individuals attempted to buy far more than they could actually afford and, through a combination of greed and unanticipated economic downturns, found themselves having difficulty paying the debt. As early as 1811, Mississippi Territory inhabitants sent a petition to Congress asking for modifications in contract terms and extensions on debts due, claiming that the decline in cotton prices made it impossible for them to make scheduled payments for land. What began as a trickle soon turned into a veritable flood of similar requests from all corners of the territory and became the source of much debate in the nation's capital. Secretary of the Treasury Albert Gallatin moved to stop the credit system at one point, but delegates, led by territorial representative William Lattimore, blocked him. However, the financial setbacks of the first major depression in United States history, known as the Panic of 1819, caused such widespread failure to pay debts on lands that Congress the following year instituted a system requiring cash purchases of land with a simultaneous lowering of the price and the amount eligible for purchase.

The root causes of the depression are tangled and complex, but at its heart lay a combination of overextension of credit in the heady years after the War of 1812, a rash of unregulated banking and questionable financial management of the Second Bank of the United States, lowered demand for cotton in Europe as overseas mills began to tap into markets in India, and declining prices for manufactured goods. The unpopular credit system did not stay in place long, as representatives from western states were able to push through the Relief Act of 1821 shortly afterward. By its terms, landowners unable to meet contracted payments could relinquish their lands and apply payments already made on the remainder, effectively allowing them to continue payments at reduced rate or spread installments out even longer. Western states and territories such as Mississippi actively encouraged settlement within their limits on such terms, as settlement and prosperity seemed interrelated, if not synonymous, and revenue from land taxes served as a key revenue source for local governments.[11]

With land a plentiful and desirable commodity that could be sold for large profits, naturally a certain amount of unscrupulous activities accompanied sales. Following the treaties of Doak's Stand (1820) and Dancing Rabbit Creek (1830), in which the Choctaws ceded enormous swaths of their homeland to the United States, Mississippi became a center of activity for land speculators. Groups of opportunistic investors had in various ways conspired to make a profit on the sale of public lands in Mississippi almost from the first public auction in the territorial days, usually attempting to work together to keep bids artificially low so that lands purchased could then be resold quickly at inflated prices. Sometimes, these groups worked together in "companies" to purchase huge tracts of acreage which they resold at higher prices later. At other times, speculators brazenly set up their own offices from which to sell lands with dubious titles. But the speculation that occurred in the 1830s in the state became notorious for its scale and complexity. In one speculator ring, an ad hoc land company persuaded participating members to invest sums ranging from $100 to $1,000, which was used as capital to make large purchases of land. Designated commissioners did the bidding on the company's behalf, working together to effectively purchase the entirety of the lands at auction at less than competitive prices, preventing private individuals from offering fair bids on smaller tracts. Company representatives even bribed some legitimate settlers to agree to withhold their planned bids. Their winnings were then quickly auctioned off to bidders at "normal" rates individuals expected to pay, and profits divided between company members according to their level of financial involvement in the scheme. With rates of return ranging between 40 and 50 percent of the initial investment, this type of speculation proved popular and attempts were made to duplicate it in other places. Various versions of this type of speculation took place, some in which minors were illegally conveyed ownership of tracts, or on occasion completely fictitious names assigned lands, all of which changed hands for higher prices at later resale. Even the most complex of these schemes should have been relatively easy to detect, but early Mississippi was still an emerging frontier state in the 1830s with vestiges of legal authority few and far between, "more wild west than Magnolia state" in the words of one historian.[12]

This wildness and the way the environment yielded itself to the making of fortunes became, in an abstract way, the very thing that made the land so appealing to settlers. The enhancement of one's fortunes and the promise of a better life animated emigration, but an additional, philosophical romance with the idea of an adventure into a new world held sway among early settlers. Their fascination only intensified with "the dark forest, the hooting of owls, the croaking of frogs, and the incessant chirping of crickets" that greeted them. For the thousands of pioneers who would lay the foundations for Mississippi society and culture, the state became the physical manifestation of their chance for a new start, having been "drawn to the new region by the promise of greater opportunities, by the promise of something, often intangible, better than what they left."[13]

So many settlers and slaves made their way to the Mississippi Territory between 1798 and Alabama's statehood in 1819 that its peopling is often referred to by

Figure 3.2. Drawing of a stagecoach, "luxurious" method of traveling for early settlers. (from *Forty Etchings, from Sketches Made with the Camera Lucida, in North America, in 1827 and 1828*, by Basil Hall)

historians of the era as the "Great Migration." On par for its time with any general movement of people in American history, this settling of what became Mississippi and Alabama is remembered as a milestone event in the region's development that contributed substantially to the trajectory of both its demographic and cultural development. This settlement was part of a larger western expansion of the United States. In 1800 there were only two states west of the Appalachians, containing a combined population of about 386,000. By 1820, eight new western states had been formed in the transmontane South that over two million people, a substantial portion of them enslaved, called home. When Mississippi assumed statehood in 1817, it did so as a center of growth in a dynamic new frontier of an expanding nation.[14]

The pace of the migration into the Mississippi Territory was startling, even for its time. In 1800 the vast Mississippi Territory had a mere three relatively sparsely populated counties, with only two, Adams and Pickering, located in what would become the state of Mississippi. These counties were located along the Mississippi River in the extreme southwestern section of the territory and contained a population of just a little over four thousand, including slaves. The lone county in the eastern section of the territory, Washington, north of Mobile along the Tombigbee River, claimed only 1,250 American inhabitants. Native Americans significantly outnumbered this small number of settlers in these early years of the Mississippi Territory's development, mainly the Choctaws and Chickasaws, who had dominated the landscape for hundreds of years. An avalanche of immigration would soon begin the process of a radical change in the region's population dynamics. By 1810, in the middle of an initial, and ultimately smaller, wave of migration that started with the formation of the territory in 1798 and ended with the outbreak of the War of 1812, the counties of the western portion of the territory (which became Mississippi) claimed 31,000 residents and the eastern section (which became Alabama) 9,000. At the conclusion of the brief but more dramatic second wave of migration, initiated at the conclusion of the war in 1815 and continuing until the economic uncertainty of the Panic of 1819, the state of Mississippi claimed 75,000 residents and the state of Alabama nearly 144,000. In the short span of a decade the population of Mississippi had more than doubled, while that of Alabama had multiplied an incredible sixteen times. While settlers set up homesteads throughout the territory, three areas received the bulk of the new arrivals; the Natchez area, the lower Tombigbee River valley region, and the Tennessee River Valley.[15]

Those who witnessed this movement of people through the wilderness of the Old Southwest were struck by the scale of what they saw. Their attempts to quantify the number of people and vehicles underscore their astonishment. Creek Indian Agent Benjamin Hawkins, whose agency lay along the Federal Road in central Georgia, scrupulously recorded details of what occurred in the region. He reported that in one five-month span in late 1811 and early 1812 he saw 120 wagons, eighty carts, three carriages, and exactly 3,726 people pass by as they followed the route westward. Another man, himself traveling against this tide of immigration as he ventured from the Mississippi Territory to eastern Georgia in 1816, reported that in the course of nine days he encountered 141 wagons, 102 carts, ten stages, fourteen gigs, two coaches, twenty-nine droves of cattle, twenty-seven droves of hogs, two droves of sheep, and an estimated 3,840 people. A visitor to the region who later recorded his experiences in book form noted that he "met an almost uninterrupted line of emigrants, with innumerable heavy and light wagons . . . there were also some lighter carriages. . . ." Even deep in the settled portions of the territory, the flow of emigrants startled established residents. A Natchez newspaper reported in 1818 that between ten and fifteen families passed by the city every day making their way to new homes in the territory, and that these numbers were steadily increasing.[16]

This "flood of humanity," in the words of historian Thomas P. Abernathy, came primarily from other Southern states and those along the eastern seaboard of the nation. It included notable numbers of natives of Pennsylvania, Connecticut, and New Jersey scattered throughout the territory, while the Tennessee River Valley overwhelmingly became a destination for people from the state of Tennessee. In virtually every other corner of the Mississippi Territory and the early state, Americans, slave and free, from Georgia, North Carolina, Virginia, and occasionally South Carolina provided the majority of new inhabitants.[17]

So massive and sudden did this westward migration occur in the eastern seaboard states of the South, especially Virginia and North Carolina, that many established residents feared the depopulation would wreck their economies, ruin their political standing, and permanently retard their development. A Richmond, Virginia, newspaper in 1816 disparaged that the western migration would inevitably lead to a dramatic population shift in which the "the pivot on which the union will balance will be the Allegheny Mountains, or west of them." It has been estimated that over 200,000 residents of North Carolina alone left that state for the Mississippi Valley between 1790 and 1815. Witnesses to this exodus often referred to those who ventured to the fertile lands of the Mississippi Territory as seized with "Alabama Fever" (in reference to the river that ran through some of the best lands in the eastern section of the province) and less often as "Mississippi Fever" because they were figuratively burning with a desire to have a piece of the rich new lands as soon as possible. A letter from North Carolina political leader James Graham to Tar Heel statesman Thomas Ruffin captured the simultaneous concern, wonder, and disdain with which some viewed the departure of so many of their neighbors:

> The *Alabama Feaver* [*sic*] rages here with great violence and has *carried off* vast numbers of our citizens. I am apprehensive, if it continues to spread as it has done, it will almost depopulate the country. There is no question that this feaver [*sic*] is contagious . . . , for as soon as one neighbor visits another who has just returned from the Alabama he immediately discovers the same symptoms which are exhibited by the person who has seen the allureing [*sic*] Alabama."[18]

While most of the new immigrants arrived from elsewhere in the United States, a substantial number hailed from Europe. These "old world" settlers, who came primarily from the British Isles with a smattering of French and Germans, often were fleeing the same sort of difficult economic conditions as their American-born neighbors and similarly hoping to find their fortune in the area's rich soil. Especially prominent among these groups were Scotch emigrants, who formed closely connected small settlements in several places such as the "Old Scotch Settlement" in Jefferson County. That community formed around 1805 by Scotch families who had first made their homes in North Carolina and Tennessee upon arrival in America. Learning of its presence via family and friends, others followed. While life in these settlement enclaves can be characterized as very similar to that of most others in the region, many residents spoke Gaelic as a first language for at least a generation and centered community life on the two Presbyterian churches they established. A sense of the close-knit nature of the settlement can be gleaned through a glance at an early register of Union Church, which contains the names of nearly two dozen congregants whose surname begins with "Mc." Elsewhere, in early Wayne County, a similar Scotch settlement existed and established a school around 1812 where Gaelic was spoken exclusively for a time.[19]

The Vine and Olive Colony, established in what is now western Alabama near the confluence of the Black Warrior and Tombigbee Rivers, is perhaps the most well-known ethnic community in the Mississippi Territory. Founded by a band of exiled veterans of Napoleon's defeated army and French refugees from a slave rebellion in Saint-Domingue (Haiti), the colony came about after an 1817 grant by Congress of some 90,000 acres to the French Emigrant Association. It earned its unique name because of a stipulation in the grant that the settlers cultivate grapes and olives, a pointed attempt to make crystal clear the scheme's agricultural nature rather than a potential military operation that might aim to return Napoleon to power in Europe or allow him to assume power somewhere else. In part, Congress made the deal owing to the established presence of the Spanish on the young nation's Southwestern frontier, hoping an organized influx of former French soldiers would bolster the United States' presence in the region and put even more pressure on Spain to relinquish its shaky claim on Florida. Although many of the grantees never made it to the banks of the Tombigbee, with many choosing instead to sell their lots and settle in New Orleans or Mobile, between 100 and 200 French families (many actually from the French colony of Haiti and not France itself) established the town of Demopolis on the granted lands. When a survey revealed the city had been created on land just outside the acreage granted to them, however, they abandoned that community and established the towns of Aigleville and Arcola a short distance away, within the designated tract approved by Congress. Despite high hopes and the best of intentions, the colony never developed as planned. Within a decade, almost all of the original settlers had departed the area for various reasons, with the handful who stayed being swept into the tide of American settlement of the region, ultimately having lent little more than a name and a legend to the area's cultural development.[20]

Though they had no choice in the matter, slaves were also a pivotal part of the migration to the Old Southwest that would help define the social and economic development of early Mississippi. While not all white settlers who moved to Mississippi in its formative years owned slaves themselves, involuntary servitude nonetheless became central to the visions of how the land might be utilized to greatest advantage by the great majority of the new arrivals. About 100,000 bondsmen were imported into Mississippi in the decade between 1830 and 1840 alone, ultimately increasing the enslaved population in the state by an astounding 197 percent during the decade. This continued a trend that resulted in Mississippi's black population doubling between 1810 and 1820 and again between 1820 and 1830. Slavery had a long history in the land that became Mississippi by the time of the migrations that populated the state in its formative era, having been part of French, British, Spanish, and even Native American societies, but never had it assumed so central a role on so massive a scale as it did during the first decades of the nineteenth century. The institution of slavery became a defining characteristic of Mississippi society during these transformational decades and, as will be discussed in later chapters, would further entrench itself during the remainder of the antebellum era. But for that to happen, its practitioners had to first make their way to the new state, and that process proved to be anything but a simple change of address for most.[21]

CHAPTER 4

New Beginnings

The American settlement of Mississippi during its foundational period is in some respects the defining event of the era, because without people seeking to take advantage of what the land offered and their understanding of how to realize individual and collective visions of a thriving society, there would be no story to tell. The people who settled in Mississippi in its territorial and early statehood years came from near and far via trips that were commonly arduous and marked an abrupt turn in the course of their lives. The waves of immigrants did not arrive evenly in terms of chronology or geography, but they nonetheless shared so many basic commonalities that they can best be understood as an essential shared experience. If we are to make sense of how and why Mississippi developed as it did, it is essential that we understand the process of migration and the establishment of a new home within its borders.

"By horse, by wagon, by boat, and by foot the flood of humanity poured in," Charles Lowery, a leading authority on the migration into the Mississippi Territory, has observed. While Lowery was making specific reference to the peak of an early wave of resettlement in Mississippi, the process of the settling of the territory and early state would have indeed appeared as a deluge washing over the region's landscape to witnesses at almost any given point in the state's early history. This steady wave of immigrants arriving in Mississippi between the 1810s and the 1830s slowly but steadily brought in free settlers and enslaved people from all directions and transformed the region in a single generation from a remote wilderness backwater into one of the most vibrant emerging corridors for travel and trade in the American South.[1]

The new arrivals came in almost as many forms and fashions as there were individuals. While lone travelers could be seen on the roads, emigrants most often traveled in groups; frequently one family made its way westward alone but sometimes several from the same vicinity made the trip together for safety and companionship. For almost all of them, regardless of when it took place, the trip was a very long one. According to one estimate, the average distance of a migration to Mississippi was around five hundred miles along haphazardly maintained trails through the wilderness. For a smaller number, the trip involved floating down one of the region's major waterways to their destination. Travelers throughout the era under discussion usually departed in the fall when the roads were generally in their best condition—hard and dry—and the numerous creeks and rivers that needed to be crossed, for the most part without the aid of bridges, were less susceptible to flooding. Caravans commonly made their way over these routes at the rate of fifteen to twenty-five miles per day, depending on the size of the party and the conditions encountered. For most, the journey involved a few weeks of travel at minimum and for some a month or more.[2]

In the words of one observer, they traveled with "all their worldly possessions packed in wagons, while their women rode atop the baggage or in four-wheeled carriages or two-wheeled carts, depending on the economic status of the family." Others with less means carefully packed their possessions into hogshead barrels and rolled them mile after weary mile to their destination via mule power. Whatever cattle and hogs the emigrants laid claim to were driven along the road with them. The whole process bore the appearance of one continuous, slow-moving, discordant assemblage of men and beasts passing through the forests and fields of the region. An exceedingly small number, mostly individual travelers, occasionally stopped for the evening at one of the area's few roadside taverns, but for the overwhelming majority the only stops were to make nightly camps where they cooked whatever food they had and gathered around the fire for warmth and conversation before getting some sleep under the stars. They slept fitfully, for newcomers could routinely hear wolves and large cats howling in the distance and innumerable rustlings in the woods made by the region's native wildlife.[3]

Emigration involved expense and all too often endangered health. For a single man, the trip west might cost him between $100 and $200 in supplies and miscellaneous expenses; for an average family with a few slaves the cost could be well over $1,000 at a time when most people counted themselves fortunate to earn that amount over the course of a year. Provisioning these people as their caravans creaked and groaned through the wildernesses of the Old Southwest during the territorial period spurred an industry unto itself among enterprising individuals. Legendary figure Sam Dale, hero of the "Canoe Fight" during the Creek War of 1813–14, became one of dozens who recognized the immigrants as potential customers, contracting with some for transportation or as a guide to the Mississippi Territory from as far away as Savannah. Dale moved to provide individually a service much in demand by hundreds of travelers by attempting to secure food and provisions that would allow them to complete their journey. A surprising number came to the region inadequately supplied, and hundreds more without means to obtain necessities even if they could be found—and with regional trading centers scattered and isolated, commonly they could not. "Bread was the first demand" of travelers, noted Dale. "With tears, with persuasions, even with threats they demanded it. Human nature was not proof against such distress. . . ." Later arrivals, taking advantage of better roads and more frequent points of supply, had a less daunting experience in some respects, but travel over long distances throughout the period inherently involved a degree of suffering. Supplied or not, the vicissitudes of travel, exposure to the elements, and lack of access to prompt or adequate medical attention could make the journey a harrowing experience. Many became sick along the way to their new home, and an unknown but substantial number perished in the process, their forgotten graves ironically lying along the now-overgrown trails that were to serve as their path to a better life.[4]

Regardless of the high hopes for the future that fueled emigration to Mississippi from elsewhere in the United States or abroad, leaving one place to make a new home in another involved a certain degree of uncertainty, a temporary upheaval, and often a permanent sense of loss for early settlers. Whether starting out for this new land in the latter years of the eighteenth century when it had just come into American ownership, or in the heady days of the mid-1830s when it seemed to offer an easy path to wealth for enterprising planters, nobody contemplating a move could know definitively what their future held. A move westward was a gamble fraught with danger and potentially disastrous consequences. Despite the seeming flood of migration the region witnessed, there were many reasons that kept countless numbers from ever making the journey including fear of failing to find economic success, having one's health compromised due to rugged conditions on the frontier, or simply being unable to leave loved ones. This worry over the destruction of the family contained an element of harsh reality in those times that those living today can scarcely appreciate.[5]

Emigration tore families apart throughout the period. For free white settlers, visits to relatives would thereafter be infrequent and very difficult; for many leaving for Mississippi it would be the last time they saw some family members. Realizing this at best tempered the excitement of a fresh start and at worst consumed the thoughts of some emigrants with dread. Women especially seemed to fear migration because of the ways separation from familiar surroundings particularly would affect them. Many contemplated with perfect horror attempting to raise children alone in the wilderness without the networks of support and companionship friends and family provided. "The fear of being forgotten by relatives ran like a dark undercurrent through the correspondence of many women in the Southwest," notes Joan E. Cashin in *A Family Venture: Men and Women on the Southern Frontier*. Even letters, a poor substitute for actual visits, were unreliably delivered, especially in the territorial years when simply locating a post office could be a problem.[6]

A Slave-Coffle passing the Capitol.

Figure 4.1. Depiction of slave coffle. (Courtesy of the Library of Congress)

Of course, for the slaves who accompanied many early settlers, the sense of irreversible separation proved even more real. "Searing farewells" took place in slave quarters as families prepared to start for the west, as tearful goodbyes were exchanged among the extended nuclear family which made up the only home that most slaves knew. In an era in which slaves rarely had a chance to travel beyond the borders of their home county, much less to another region of the country, emigration must have been viewed by them with an even greater sense of finality. These separations inordinately affected slave families, for the trade with the Upper South which brought so many bondsmen to the nation's southwestern frontier focused on young men and women of prime working age—what historian Ira Berlin has called the "shock troops of the cotton revolution"—and ripped apart whatever family life many immigrating slaves experienced before being sent south.[7]

In contrast, family units formed the core of the wave of white settlement that washed over Mississippi during its formative period. Often two or more households of close kin traveled together. While some households made the trip west as a unit, many came in two or more waves, frequently delineated by generation, with the first serving as scouts to locate suitable tracts of land for the rest. Early settler James Tait, for example, came to the region in 1819 with very specific instructions from his father Charles, who intended to join him after he found the right spot. He challenged James to locate land that had

> . . . a stream near at hand for a mill and machinery—a never failing spring at the foot of a hillock, on the summit of which a mansion house can be built in due time . . . have an extensive back range where our cattle and hogs can graze and fatten without the aid of corn houses, that on the right and left there is an extensive body of good land where will settle a number of good neighbors and from whom the pleasure and benefits of society will soon be realized.[8]

If Tait's instructions sounded as if he might have been searching to duplicate a situation at home with which he had familiarity, they were far from the exception. Settlers of early Mississippi commonly migrated along regional isothermal lines sharing similar climate, geography, and vegetation, not necessarily seeking the richest lands in the region as much as "the richest of the particular type of land to which they were accustomed back in the East." After all, any familiarity they could find in their new home on the frontier would be both a comfort and a practical advantage in seeking economic success. Emigration remained a risk no matter how comfortable settlers might be with their surroundings, and they looked for anything that would improve their odds.[9]

We have no specifics whatsoever about the journey undertaken by the overwhelming majority of immigrants, but a few detailed accounts survive that enlighten our understanding of exactly how they traveled and how they lived immediately after arrival. One traveler visiting southeastern Mississippi, for example, recorded having met a man whose family had been among the first wave of settlers of the region and who reported that they had come from Georgia with only a one-horse cart, a feather bed, an oven, frying pan, two pewter dishes, six plates, some spoons, a rifle, and three dogs. Doubtless dozens of others arrived in similar fashion if even that well-equipped, but their stories will, for the most part, be forever lumped into cold statistics.[10]

A particularly lucid firsthand account of the trip to Mississippi was written by Gideon Lincecum of his early settler family who moved to Mississippi from Georgia in 1818. Lincecum's narrative cannot speak for the hundreds if not thousands of others similarly situated, but it offers a colorful glimpse into the physical and emotional experience of emigrating west that allows these sojourners to become more human. Lincecum's family made their trip, like so many others, after his father had previously explored and found acceptable the lands on which they were to make their new home. "Altogether, it was the wildest, least-trodden, and tomahawk-marked country he had ever explored, and the soil was rich enough. His description put me in a perfect transport. I told him that I owed nobody anything. I had nothing to hinder me from starting in two days. . . ." According to Lincecum, the family immediately entered into "a perfect ecstasy over the prospect of a wagon journey through a roadless wilderness," and eagerly gathered supplies for the trip. Lincecum stated that they believed their wagons were "the first that had ever traversed that unhacked forest," and they had to open a space sufficient for them to pass in many places, taking advantage of natural clearings and openings in the forest whenever they could. He noted that owing to the regular clearing of underbrush by Indians in the area, their trip through even the most densely wooded areas they traversed was not as arduous as they had expected. The exception came when they attempted to negotiate the many unbridged waterways of the region, which they accomplished with great difficulty. Along the way they gathered any wild fruits and nuts they found, and hunted deer, turkey, ducks, and wild pigeons, which they cooked in their nightly camp as they were serenaded by wolves. "The entire trip was delightful beyond description," Lincecum summarized; a thrilling wilderness experience even for people who already made their living off the land.[11]

For early settlers, the real work began once they arrived at the spot where they intended to live. They immediately set to work constructing housing for themselves and their family, often throwing up a simple wooden cabin for temporary shelter before constructing a more substantial home. Many lived in tents in a camp similar to those they had known nightly on their journey in this interim, which could be for days or weeks depending on the number of laborers available. A single-room log cabin, measuring approximately twenty feet by sixteen feet, became something of a standard for early arrivals. The work required to produce these simple homes could be intensive and demanded a certain skill. If settlers arrived at an area with neighbors were close enough by, they were invited to assist in the house-raising. In many cases the entire experience turned into a multi-day community event of sorts, the work "being lightened by jest and laughter and by the anticipation of a good dinner."[12]

Regardless of the number of hands, the basic process followed a similar plan. Settlers first felled trees by axe, cut them into the appropriate size logs by saw, and notched them with an adze to fit together like so many puzzle pieces. They then rolled them into place and the frame took shape. Settlers attached a roof of barked slabs, laid like shingles, and applied clay chinking to gaps between the log walls to keep out the elements. This chinking could be knocked out in the summer to allow in cooling breezes and reapplied in the winter months. Eventually, many of these early homes would have split clapboards for siding as they were added to or otherwise modified. A simple wooden door, usually hanging on wooden hinges, served as the entrance while any windows were sealed with

Figure 4.2. The dogtrot was the typical housing style used by the vast majority of frontier settlers. (Courtesy of Mississippi Department of Archives and History)

a curtain, glass being a luxury virtually impossible to obtain in the early days of settlement. Depending on the degree of permanence with which they viewed the structure or the resources and time available, cabins might have puncheon or split log floors, but most at first had dirt floors. The whole process might take place with surprising speed, as one settler reported:

> Three days after we came there I began to prepare for building me a house. I got the clapboards in one day, cut the logs in a day, hauled them together in a day; and the next day, by the aid of my brothers and Jos. Bryan, raised and covered it. The next day I floored it with linwood puncheons, and the day after I made a wooden chimney to it. We then left our camp and moved into it.[13]

For the great majority of families, a one-room structure such as this would serve as home for at least the first year of their existence in this new territory while they focused their attention on clearing land and raising their first crops. In subsequent years as time allowed and the family grew, the one-room cabin would commonly be enlarged by adding additional "pens" with a breezeway running between them to form the ubiquitous dogtrot. Noted religious figure and early settler William Winans observed with candor the omnipresence of that particular form of vernacular architecture in frontier Mississippi, stating that after his first simple cabin had been completed, he later duplicated its construction to form a dogtrot and double his family's living space. Thus sheltered, he believed himself "fully as well-housed as nine-tenths of the citizenry."[14]

Winans became one of many to comment on the makeshift nature of the housing of most early Mississippi settlers. In his autobiography he related his opinion that most of his pioneer neighbors built "mere shelter" in place of real homes, because their paramount concern "was to bring their lands into cultivation, that they might provide subsistence for themselves and those dependent on them." This simplicity stood in stark contrast to the appearance of established communities most had known back east, and visitors scarcely knew what to think of them. Travelers to Mississippi noted the "uniform neglect of the homes and the grounds," in the words of one historian of the era, while famed period travel writer Joseph Holt Ingraham characterized the homesteads he encountered in early Mississippi as being "suffered to remain in their pristine rudeness." Others were even less generous in their assessments, as one northern visitor disdainfully observed that even the region's planters at first occupied "log huts in the wilderness" as they devoted "their whole time and attention" to agriculture. This visitor went on to note that "when they became lords of a domain and a hundred slaves . . . many retain their cabins even till then" and only at that time "razed the humble cabin, and reared upon its site the walls of an expensive and beautiful fabric." Territorial-era Mississippi did have a few columned mansions, and it certainly had its share of affluence, but even those with the deepest pockets usually started off in a simple house that often belied their true means.[15]

Furnishings inside these early homes could be extremely sparse. "I have seen houses in this place . . . scarcely furnished beyond the first stage of civilization, when a few boards nailed together have served for a bedstead, and a mattress covered with a few blankets for a bed, when there has been scarcely a chair to sit down upon, or a table to place anything on, but everything in the greatest confusion and disorder about the room," observed one visitor. Countless numbers of early Mississippi homes featured only a scattering of the most humble homemade furniture, with beds commonly simple board boxes stuffed with Spanish moss. Puncheon floors partially covered with animal skins were a common sight, with a few iron pots, an assortment of glazed crockery, and gourds equipping the kitchen. Virtually every home contained a rifle, a vital tool for obtaining meat, which could of course be used for defense and, not infrequently, sheer entertainment. Tallow candles, oil lamps, or sometimes the fireplace alone lit their dim interiors. Just about anything else settlers needed they or their slaves made by hand, from clothing and quilts to tools. A European visitor marveled at the ingenuity of early residents, recording in his journal: "A washtub, piggin, or water pail was often made with no other tools than a broad-ax and a scalping knife . . . much of the work done by the natives looked so simple, that we thought we could easily do it. We soon learned that every trade and occupation requires a certain skill." Just about everyone used tobacco. Spitting boxes, spittoons, or cuspidors graced almost every establishment, public or private, from hotels to churches to homes.[16]

Early Mississippians were generally well-fed, but their meals were of limited variety. Meat from both wild and domesticated animals formed the centerpiece of the early settler diet, with residents filling their pots with a variety of the plentiful game. This was only in part because of the abundance of protein to be found in the forests that surrounded pioneers; it took time for orchards to grow, chickens and cows to mature, or hogs to be fattened. While still present in numbers that allowed them to be hunted in the first decades of the nineteenth century, bears became a prized delicacy with their hide and oil used as valuable by-products within the household. Turkeys, geese, and an assortment of freshwater fish frequently graced dinner plates in settler homes. Venison served as the primary game staple; deer were abundant and readily hunted at virtually any time of year throughout the territorial and early statehood years. Night hunting became the easiest way to ensure success. The quote-worthy Gideon Lincecum described this common, if unsporting, process as it manifested itself in the woods of northeast Mississippi where he and his family settled:

> The quantity of game that was found in that dark forest and the canebrakes was a subject of wonder to everybody. My brother Garland and I . . . would go out nights on horseback, taking a big bag of nicely cut, rich pine and a frying pan tied on a stick, to burn the pine in. This pan full of pine, set on fire and carried on the shoulder, produced sufficient light to enable us to see the eyes of a deer 80 to 100 yards away. And with a big old shotgun that we had, we killed plenty of meat. . . .[17]

Corn served as the staff of life in early Mississippi, and one of the first tasks when setting up a new homestead involved clearing a patch of land for its cultivation. Many Mississippians ate corn virtually every day—off the cob, in mush, ground into meal, and baked in varieties of cornbread with such colorful names as cornpone, ashcakes, hoecakes, johnnycakes, or fried as a corn dodger. The observations of many visitors—such as James R. Creecy, that save for corn production "few, indeed, of the early settlers gave a thought to gardens or vegetables"—and the assertions of later historians that "fruits and vegetables were, strangely enough, met with rather infrequently" were both based in fact, but neither tells the whole story. Varied vegetables were not as a whole a prominent part of all early Mississippians' diet, but as the state developed in the early statehood years certain foods that could be easily cultivated did become staples. The list of the most common vegetables sounds familiar to us even today: turnips, okra, peas, and sweet potatoes. Indeed, so common were sweet potatoes in some sections of the state that they were known simply as "potatoes," and describing any other less common variety required further explanation. The ubiquitous tubers could be easily grown even in poor soil, and multiple bushels could be produced with little tending on very small patches of land. The frequently quoted passage found in J. F. H. Claiborne's entertaining narrative of life in southeast Mississippi, "A Trip Through the Piney Woods," describing his visit to the house of a family in the region, is often used by historians in a humorous fashion to communicate the simplicity of early settler life, but it illuminates the Mississippian diet in unique fashion:

> The repast was abundant, excellent and scrupulously neat—but almost every dish was composed of *potatoes* dressed in many various ways. There were baked potatoes and fried potatoes—bacon and potatoes boiled together—a fine loin of beef was flanked round with potatoes nicely browned and swimming in gravy. A hash of wild turkey was garnished with potatoes mixed up in it. A roast fowl was stuffed with potatoes, beside us stood a plate of potato biscuit, as light as sponge; the *coffee*, which was strong and well flavored, was made of *potatoes*, and one of the girls drew from the corner cupboard a rich potato pie.[18]

A sampling of other accounts of life in early Mississippi that discuss diet, gathered from journals, letters, newspapers, and reminiscences, paints a slightly more balanced portrait of regional food and drink. Mississippians ate a lot of pork; bacon, salt pork, ham, and pickled pigs feet were among the numerous foodstuffs derived from the ubiquitous animal that in some manifestation formed the centerpiece of many meals throughout the antebellum decades. Many visitors, such as James R. Creecy, expressed disappointment with the indigenous menus they encountered, his notes on dining experiences allowing us a candid look into a typical kitchen: "in all my previous life I had never fallen in with any cooking so villainous. Rusty salt pork, boiled or fried . . . corn-meal dodgers, rarely a vegetable of any description, no milk, butter, eggs, or the semblance of condiment—was my fare often for weeks at a time."[19]

Creecy's personal experience aside, most Mississippians washed all this pork down with a limited number of beverages that were readily available. Decent water and milk could usually be obtained in most places, but coffee was exceedingly scarce and often exorbitantly priced when available. If there could be said to have been an official beverage for early residents, it would have been whiskey, for a bottle seemed to appear on every table at virtually every meal in private homes and public inns. The "favourite beverage" of residents encountered by one traveler, Creecy claimed all he met "present [it] to the stranger with one hand, while they give him a chair with the other."[20]

The people seated around those tables would have been dressed plainly, many in homemade clothes. Simple dresses, homespun trousers, and white cotton shirts predominated, and especially in the earliest years of the territory prior to statehood, the hunting shirt. For years "universally worn," according to one noted historian of the Old Southwest, this loose-fitting, rugged, all-season frock and the accompanying buckskin leggings were inspired by Native American dress. The Native American influence extended literally from head to toe among early settlers, as many also wore moccasins. With the rise of urban communities and the assumption of wealth among portions of the population as the state developed, such humble attire gradually fell out of fashion by any who could afford anything better. By the 1830s the dress of rural farmers stood in remarkable contrast to that of polite society. Visitors commented on the widespread wearing by the common folk of "a coarse linsey-woolsey, of a dingy yellow or blue, with broad-brimmed hats. . . ." In contrast, a young John A. Quitman noted with incredulity in his memoirs that wealthy young men in 1820s Natchez and those abiding on the plantations of the hinterland routinely ordered several expensive custom suits per year from tailors in the North and accessories from Europe. Later, in the height of the famed "flush times" when cotton famously enriched a portion of Mississippi's population, observers noted men wearing "dark suits," "long trousers," and "long blanket coats of white, or green, or blue, trimmed with a broad selvage and gathered at the waist with a wide belt," all topped with a fine, wide-brimmed hat. Such refinement, copied to the degree it could be with less expensive outfits among those in the countryside, caught the eye of observers throughout the antebellum period for its relative extravagance.[21]

Early settlers proved remarkably self-reliant in obtaining most of the items necessary for day-to-day living, but it must be remembered that throughout the territorial period and well into Mississippi's statehood, many residents traded with Native Americans for a variety of things that eased the burdens of the pioneer family and sustained an active commerce. Until their first crops were harvested, many American settlers obtained quantities of corn from neighboring Choctaws. Many engaged in small-scale trading for a range of other foodstuffs, including beef and pork from Native American herders. Early Mississippians learned to appreciate many staples of the Native American diet as a consequence of these trade-based exchanges. They learned how to store and prepare wild nuts and oils, how to make corn-based soups and mushes, where to find and how to use certain wild fruits, and even how to prepare certain dishes featuring wild game. Some even consulted their Native American neighbors for medical advice when family members became sick, tapping into the extensive indigenous knowledge of medicinal plants. A few enterprising individuals turned this concurrent Native American abundance and American settler need into thriving businesses that formed an important part of the frontier economy. "I bartered with them for every kind of produce," remembered Gideon Lincecum, "consisting of cowhides, deer skins, all kinds of fur, skins, buck horns, cow horns, peas, beans, peanuts, pecans, shellbarks, hickory nuts, honey, beeswax, . . . bacon and venison hams and big gobblers. . . ." Lincecum brought these items to a trading company in Mobile, where they were exchanged for supplies such as groceries and dry goods that were sold to settlers for cash. This combination of cooperation, kindness, ingenuity, and seizure of opportunity, as historian Christopher Morris has observed, allowed "families who arrived with little more than a gun, an axe, some corn and pumpkin seed, and the clothes on their backs to become prosperous farmers, herders, and eventually even cotton planters."[22]

Many indeed arrived in the condition Morris outlines, and in the humblest of fashions through their labor or that of their slaves laid the foundations for an organic, agriculture-based society that underlay the social, cultural, and economic trajectory of the state for generations. Having claimed their tract of land and erected upon it a cabin, settlers and slaves went about the arduous process of converting patches of wilderness into farms. Sometimes this became a degree easier by settling near an old Indian field, which, while not cleared as thoroughly as an American agricultural plot, would take relatively less labor and time to prepare. Most settlers, however, opened up land that had never been tilled on which to plant crops. Depending on the size of the family and the number of hands engaged in the endeavor, the process of opening a sizable plot to farm might take a few weeks or an entire season and continued for successive years until an area adequate to sustain large-scale crop production had been prepared. Settlers used fire extensively in this process, burning away underbrush to clear an area and provide a precious layer of fertilizer for soon-to-be fields. They girdled trees with an axe, killing them slowly but much more efficiently than chopping each one down; new fields were called "deadenings" as a result. It might be the second year of such clearing before they could plow these crude fields, relying on parents and family back east for financial support in the interim. Settlers called on neighbors for help with "log-rollings" to help get the dozens of fallen logs rolled out of the way so that planting could begin. It must be remembered that "neighbors" is a relative term, as rural frontier communities of a few dozen families might extend over dozens of square miles. In areas subject to inundation, especially along the Mississippi River, neighbors pooled resources to construct some of the state's first levee systems. These piecemeal, localized efforts eventually became standardized and interconnected through regulation; but haphazard as they were, they enabled early settlers to put under cultivation some of the state's richest lands in selected areas otherwise impractical to farm.[23]

Few of the "intensely individualistic" settlers who came to carve a living from the wildernesses of the Old Southwest viewed the dispersion of homesteads as an inconvenience. Many arrived not only expecting but desiring a degree of isolation that those back east they left behind could not fathom. One resident remembered rather romantically the simple motivations of an early settler from Georgia he encountered in the state's southeastern "Piney Woods" by noting "The turpentine smell, the moan of the winds through the pine-trees, and nobody within fifty miles of him, was too captivating a concatenation to be resisted, and he rested here." In the words of a contemporary resident of Natchez, Mississippi, backwoodsmen were simply "a different people," reveling in their seclusion and the autonomy it allowed. A British traveler recorded a conversation with a man from Kentucky who had come to Mississippi seeking his personal version of freedom, which illustrates the mindset of many:

> Driven from place to place by dislike of neighbours, he had, several years ago, settled on the banks of the Mississippi, in hopes that its reputation for unhealthiness would deter emigrants from approaching these regions; but the prospect of lucre from the supply of steamboats with wood was too tempting to be resisted by poor Irish emigrants. They came within a distance of about one hundred miles of our Kentuckian. He could not possibly bear the intrusion. . . . "I have no elbow-room" he said. "I cannot move about without seeing the nose of my neighbour sticking out between the trees. Thou dost not understand, stranger, what liberty is; don't meddle with it."[24]

The commitment and ability to live lives largely independent of traditional systems of societal infrastructure perceived as burdensome animated a great deal of the free white settlement of early Mississippi. Rather than a willful escape from governmental or societal restraint (though in some cases it certainly was), settlers were motivated by a pursuit of unfettered opportunity. At the time "self-made" men were held in particular esteem, the phrase being imbued with a notion of individual enterprise, ingenuity, and ability that can scarcely be imagined today. A large percentage of the population throughout Mississippi's foundational era built their own houses, raised their own food, and made their own clothes, after all. To stand out as exceptionally self-determining in that environment took extraordinary effort.[25]

In any discussion of early Mississippi, it is important to keep in mind the fundamentally transitory nature with which settlers commonly viewed the homesteads and communities they founded. The people who comprised the "Great Migration" commonly continued their movement after arrival in Mississippi, either moving elsewhere in the state or continuing their journey further westward, constantly in search of better land and more promising opportunities. "Few persons in this country consider themselves fixed," noted one resident at the time, "hence the motives to making solid improvements . . . and forming those kindly relations which constitute the main charm of social life, operate but feeble here. This accounts for the general unembellished condition of the country. . . ." One family of which we have record moved no less than nine times to various locales in the Old Southwest between 1808 and 1820, their mobility being closer to the norm than to the exception. Early Mississippians were, in the words of John Hebron Moore, "almost unique in history" because their propensity to move made them "farmers largely devoid of that deep and abiding love for the land." In certain situations, moves were triggered by things settlers discovered not to their liking shortly after establishing a home in a given area: the arrival of neighbors uncomfortably close by, the unexpected recurrent flooding of a nearby river or stream, disappointment with the productivity or topography of the land they attempted to farm, or a host of other inconveniences they deemed best remedied by relocation. Often, however, moves came about simply "for the mere love of moving." One visitor to the region who interviewed an exceptionally mobile frontier family in the 1820s found they claimed they "have been doing so all our lives": "Just moving from place to place—never resting. As soon as ever we get comfortably settled, then it is time to be off to something new."[26]

For a large number, Texas became that "something new" by the 1830s. The lure of opportunity further westward inexorably drew American settlers, and those who came to Mississippi believed in a tangible version of Manifest Destiny long before the phrase became common. They never specifically contemplated the appropriateness of settling the deserts of Arizona or the rocky Pacific coasts of California as some sort of patriotic duty. Rather, they possessed a basic unshakable faith that new lands, only found further and further west, held the promise of elusive opportunity. As Mississippi matured as a state and settlers slowly inhabited its every region, many residents turned their gaze to Texas for the next land bonanza. Especially in the wake of the national depression in the 1830s, which struck Mississippi particularly hard, dreams of favorable prospects in the nascent republic a few hundred miles to the west consumed those with wanderlust, financial shortfalls, legal problems, or no apparent outlet for their talents—in short, a good deal of the total population. As early as the 1820s, the Mississippi state legislature noted with some alarm that "swarms of American citizens" were departing for Texas "to avail themselves of the flattering prospects which are held out in the Mexican Dominions." At the height of the difficulties of the Panic of 1837, "GTT"—Gone to Texas—became a common phrase of summary explanation for departures. Noted historian of early Mississippi Bradley Bond states that perhaps "the greatest emigration from Mississippi occurred in the decade after 1837," in large part spurred by the depressed economy. Many abandoned whatever improvements they had made to their lands and moved westward, leaving homes to rot and cleared lands to revert to wilderness in a sort of melodramatic last act in the early statehood drama. For a small number, Texas in the end proved only a brief sojourn, as they moved again or even in some cases returned later to Mississippi having failed to find the prosperity they envisioned. Most of those who left, however, never looked back.[27]

Even with these departures, Mississippi experienced dramatic population growth during its territorial and early statehood periods. When first organized in 1798, the Mississippi Territory had a total population of less than 5,000 Americans, the great majority living within the city of Natchez. By the late 1830s, over 375,000 whites and blacks called the state home. It was a relatively young population throughout the era, with as much as half of the total inhabitants being children in the early territorial years and only a slightly smaller percentage by 1840. Families, often with many children, formed the backbone of the "Great Migration" and laid the groundwork for early Mississippi society.[28]

The state experienced all this population growth rather unevenly. The Natchez region and large portions of both southern and northern Mississippi claimed large and growing populations by the second decade of statehood, while other areas languished or remained frontiers well into the antebellum era. The Natchez area, for example, as late as 1830 laid claim to 34 percent of the total population of the state (and 65 percent of all its slaves), accounted for 69 percent of state taxes collected and owned a telling 78 percent of the property value. Northern and eastern Mississippi by 1830 each had become almost as populous, but far less wealthy, accounting together for only about a quarter of the total tax revenue base and less than 20 percent of the total property value. While there were pockets of settlement in all regions, large areas of the Delta and extensive tracts of southeastern Mississippi's "Piney Woods" remained largely unsettled until the time of the Civil War or later. Some of the particular factors influencing this pattern of development, notably involving the piecemeal cession of Indian lands and the sudden shifts those compacts wrought on the state's maturation, will be discussed later. Regardless of the area of the state in which one resided in 1840, Mississippi would have been viewed as a still-developing region that, within the span of a lifetime, had been transformed from raw wilderness to an established part of the American union with remarkable potential for even further explosive growth.[29]

CHAPTER 5

War on the Frontier

No other event impacted the Mississippi Territory more than the interconnected Creek War and War of 1812. The results of these conflicts forever altered the political and economic landscape in the Territory and did more than all the previous activity to pave the way for statehood. Although most of the actions of these conflicts took place in the present-day state of Alabama, their impact dramatically shaped the course of future Mississippi, and therefore deserves a detailed examination. These battles produced horrific combat, spectacular displays of courage and leadership, and devastated a powerful Native nation. In order to understand their consequences, it is important to grasp how and why the Creek War occurred, its relationship with the larger War of 1812, an understanding of the battles and campaigns themselves, and how both affected the Mississippi Territory.

For decades prior to the outbreak of the Creek War, Americans, Creek Indians, and the Spanish had maintained an uneasy truce as they each claimed portions of the Gulf South. Pressure on this shaky arrangement steadily mounted during the early nineteenth century as the region witnessed increased American migration, strained efforts at cultural adaptation on the part of the Creeks, and international intrigue associated with the Spanish and their newfound allies, the British. When violence finally erupted, it quickly spiraled into a cataclysmic war that would become a turning point in American history.[1]

Creek lands were in the center of the hotly contested Old Southwest in the early 1800s. The Creek Nation occupied territory located primarily in the eastern section of the Mississippi Territory and Georgia. To their west and north lay the lands of the Choctaws, Chickasaws, and Cherokees; further north lay the state of Tennessee. To the east, Creek lands were bordered by the state of Georgia, and to the south lay Spanish-controlled West Florida. As a consequence of their location, the Creeks had long been courted by both the Americans and the Spanish, and previously the French and British, for economic and military alliances.

While Americans jealously looked upon rich Creek lands as perfectly suited for large-scale agriculture, the Spanish simply hoped to use the Creek Nation as a buffer to American encroachment into their territory.[2]

As each party pursued its own interests, conflict inevitably resulted. Spanish efforts to win the loyalty of the Creeks angered Americans, many of whom suspected the Spanish of deliberately inciting Indians to violence on their unprotected frontier settlements. Further, many viewed the continued illegal British trade with the Creeks, much of which was carried on in Spanish territory with colonial officials seemingly unable or unwilling to halt it, as a glaring threat to American safety. Just as importantly, settlers throughout the Old Southwest had longstanding misgivings over the fact that Mobile Bay and the Alabama-Tombigbee River system, potentially one of the easiest routes of invasion into the southern United States, lay in the hand of a foreign nation demonstrably committed to preventing American expansion in the region.

These concerns only grew worse over covert British attempts to undermine the safety of the American Gulf South frontier with the outbreak of the War of 1812. Though many of the provocations listed by President James Madison in his call for war, including the longstanding British policy of impressing US sailors and Britain's refusal to evacuate forts on American soil per the terms of the treaty ending the Revolutionary War, were only peripheral concerns of most residents of the Mississippi Territory, the threat of a British-Spanish alliance that would enlist the support of Southern tribes was one of the settlers' greatest fears. The British were believed to have instigated Indians to violence against American settlers in the Northwest, and their increasingly close relationship with the Spanish on the southern frontier caused considerable alarm.[3]

Concerned over this foreign complicity in growing Creek hostility and desiring to end once and for all a decade-old territorial dispute with the Spanish, the United States finally ordered General James Wilkinson to seize Spanish Florida west of the Perdido River in the spring of 1813. Americans had argued for years that this territory was rightfully part of the United States by virtue of the terms of the Louisiana Purchase, and through a combination of armed uprising and political maneuvering, to be discussed in more detail later, had already acquired portions of the colony in piecemeal fashion. Realizing the futility of continued resistance, the overmatched Spanish garrison at Fort Charlotte (Fuerta Carlota) in Mobile surrendered without a fight on April 13, 1813. The United States immediately annexed the area into the Mississippi Territory.[4]

Caught in the middle of this international intrigue were the Creek Indians, who had been the special focus of a concerted American effort at assimilation since the 1790s. From his agency on the Flint River, federal agent Benjamin Hawkins spearheaded the United States government's effort to convince the Creeks to adopt tenets of American society in place of traditional practices. Essential to this plan was the undertaking of staple agriculture in place of hunting; the rationale being that the Creeks would need less land to live on and vast expanses of their former hunting grounds could therefore be opened to American settlement. The plan, based on cold economic considerations as much as any altruistic motives, ultimately served to highlight growing divisions in Creek society. The Creeks who embraced the plan were forced to completely reject their ancestral way of life. Furthermore, adoption of the plan by only portions of the Creek population caused previously nonexistent divisions in tribal society to develop.[5]

Further straining Creek-American relations was the construction of the Federal Road. A government-sponsored route through the heart of Creek territory, the road connected central Georgia with Mississippi Territory settlements north of Mobile. The road had been designed as an essential link in a road system that would ultimately connect the nation's capital with the vital port city of New Orleans. Many Creeks watched with growing apprehension as thousands of white settlers and their slaves made their way through their homeland over the route.[6]

Members of the Creek Nation were divided over what course of action to take regarding continuing American interference in their way of life and encroachment on their lands. The Creek Nation was a loose confederacy of many smaller tribes representing dozens of towns, politically aligned by geography into "Upper" and "Lower" towns. Many Upper Creeks, living in what is today north-central and northeast Alabama along the Coosa and Tallapoosa River systems, gradually began to perceive allowing Americans to pass through or trade in their territory as part of an acquiescence in a wholesale destruction of their culture. Relatively lacking regular interaction with Americans and less assimilated with their culture, Upper Creeks felt increasingly isolated in their struggle to retain their cultural and territorial identities. The Lower Creeks occupied land stretching from central Georgia to the lower reaches of the Chattahoochee River and its tributaries. They generally believed it was in their best interest to befriend Americans and negotiate with them to maintain their territorial integrity. Complicating matters, Creeks had intermingled and intermarried with Americans and Europeans for decades to the point that many could claim as much European as Indian ancestry. Many were, in fact, living an "American" lifestyle, operating farms and plantations and even enslaving African Americans.[7]

Into this tense situation in 1811 entered the Shawnee chief Tecumseh, the proverbial spark that ultimately ignited the smoldering tinderbox that was the Old Southwest. Claiming familial ties to the Creeks, Tecumseh hailed from the Great Lakes Region and had become a leading figure in Native American resistance to American settlement in the Old Northwest. Along with his brother Tenskwatawa (The Prophet), Tecumseh believed an Indian confederacy held promise as the only way to ensure the survival of native tribes in the face of mounting encroachment by Americans. Assisted by prophets who helped transform his political vision into a religious crusade, he called for a halt to American encroachment and a return to traditional ways of life. In the summer and fall of 1811, he traveled throughout the Southeast in an attempt to rally the Chickasaws, Choctaws, and Creeks to his cause. He proved largely unsuccessful with the Choctaws and Chickasaws due to the efforts of Choctaw Chief Pushmataha, who counseled his fellow Indians not to be deceived by Tecumseh's message. Cautioning them to "listen to the voice of prudence," he urged them to not "rashly act" and join Tecumseh's movement.[8]

Tecumseh found a more receptive audience with the Upper Creeks, many of whom he addressed at the Creek annual council meeting at Tuckabatchee on the banks of the Tallapoosa in the eastern section of the Mississippi Territory. While no transcript of his speech survives, evidence strongly suggests that he urged abandonment of "American" styles of agriculture and a return to traditional folkways, even if to do so might lead to armed conflict with the United States. Regardless of the exact wording, the message was clear for those inclined to agree with his call. Pointing to the appearance of a comet which glowed its brightest just as he arrived, those encouraged by what he said became even more supportive when his prophecies regarding the occurrence of an earthquake seemed to be fulfilled shortly after his visit. He had warned that he would shake down the houses of those that failed to heed his call to collaboration by stamping his foot when he returned to his home. Just a few weeks after his presentation at Tuckaubatchee, the famous New Madrid earthquake rattled much of the Midwest and South. Creeks who supported Tecumseh and were swayed by these events became determined to halt further American settlement in their territory and the adoption of American ways of life among their tribe.[9]

Heightened tension between the Red Sticks, or those who were prepared to take up the symbolic red stick of war, and Creeks friendly to American interests soon erupted into a civil war that fractured Creek society and eventually led to conflict with the United States. In the coming months, Red Sticks began threatening Creek leaders who opposed their vision of tribal sovereignty. Many took their talk a step further, destroying the livestock that was a hated symbol of Creek accommodation with the "plan of civilization." Ultimately, scattered armed conflicts between the two factions took place. With such a state of affairs, it was only a matter of time before American frontier settlers became entangled in this struggle over the future of the Creek people.[10]

Violence between Red Sticks and American settlers first erupted in the spring of 1812. During that year, Red Sticks launched several attacks on American settlers living in isolated frontier communities in the Mississippi Territory and beyond. Residents flooded Governor David Holmes with concerns of danger from "hostile Creeks" who pleaded with US military and government officials for help. With open warfare seemingly inevitable, Holmes and other officials within the

Mississippi Territory began to mobilize forces to respond in case of emergency by the summer of 1813.[11]

Nowhere did this state of alarm appear more pronounced than in the southwestern portion of Creek territory north of Mobile. This area, centered near the confluence of the Alabama and Tombigbee Rivers and featuring some of the richest agricultural lands in the Territory, was a virtual island of American settlement. It contained a large population of mixed-blood Creeks who were increasingly viewed with contempt by the Red Sticks. The nearest sizable town, Mobile, lay well to the south. More importantly, it was separated by several hundred miles of wilderness from the seat of the Mississippi territorial government in Washington in Adams County near the Mississippi River. Keenly aware of their precarious situation, area settlers began to construct a series of stockades for their protection as they prepared for what they believed was an inevitable conflict.[12]

Long-simmering tensions erupted into open conflict between American and Red Stick forces in July 1813. On July 10, a large group of Red Stick warriors headed for Pensacola, where they hoped to obtain arms and ammunition from the Spanish. Their mission soon became general knowledge among the Tensaw area settlements after they burned the plantation homes of prominent fellow Creeks along the way. A state of alarm prevailed once settlers realized they might use any supplies they received to attack Americans instead of other Creeks. Without awaiting instructions from Mississippi territorial militia commander Ferdinand L. Claiborne, Colonel James Caller, the ranking officer in the local militia, hastily called out his command and set out in search of the Red Sticks.[13]

Caller's force of about 180 troops attacked the Red Stick encampment on the morning of July 27, 1813, near a small stream known as Burnt Corn Creek. Although the Red Sticks initially scattered, the Indians soon rallied and counterattacked while the militia stopped to inspect the packhorses they had just captured. The American militia fled in terror; they straggled back home and disbanded. The troops were in such disarray on their retreat that even Caller himself became lost and was not found until over two weeks later.[14]

This victory gave the Red Sticks a newfound confidence in their martial abilities. Simultaneously, American forces had been embarrassed and humbled. According to George Stiggins, who wrote one of the very few accounts of any part of the war from the Creek perspective, the victory at Burnt Corn Creek gave the Red Sticks "an exalted opinion of their own valor and prowess and a most contemptible opinion of the Americans, who, they were confident, were touched by a cowardly spirit." Aware of the defeat of Caller's force, many terrified residents fled to the safety of their makeshift forts and awaited the probable Red Stick offensive. What happened next at Fort Mims sent shockwaves through the nation and seared the volatile situation in the Mississippi Territory into the nation's consciousness.[15]

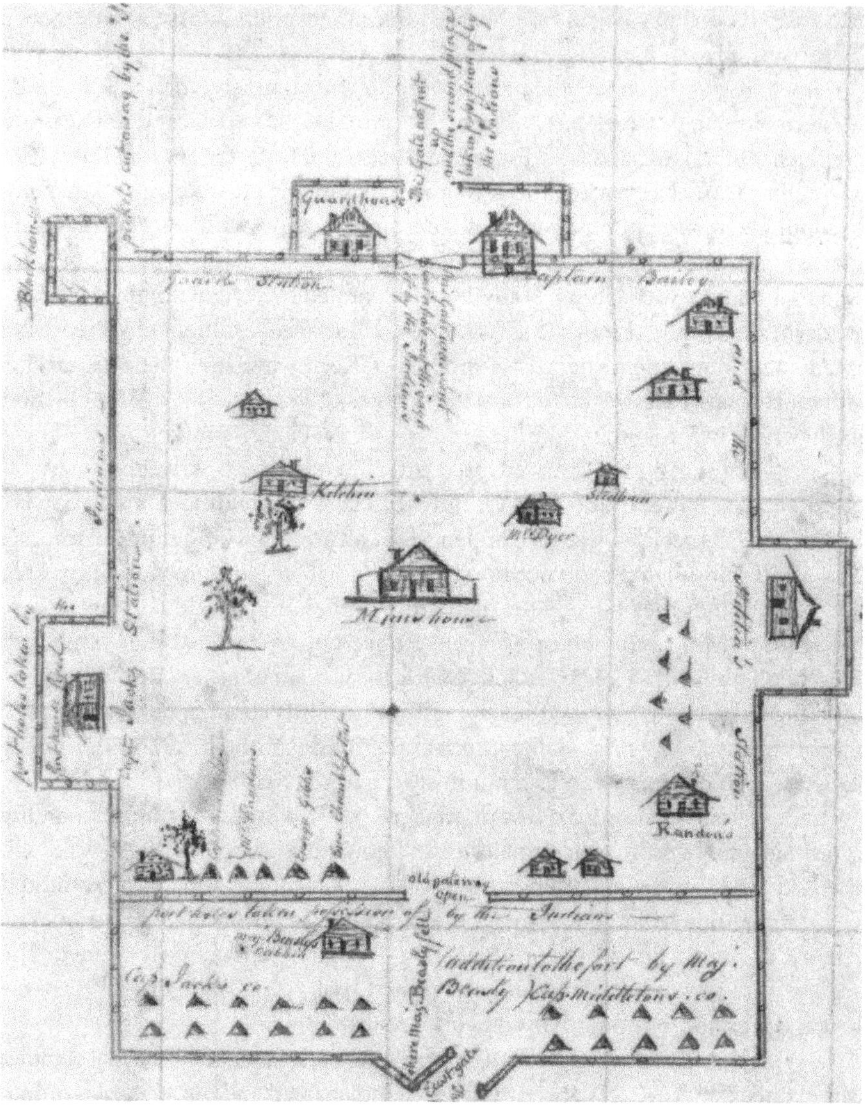

Figure 5.1. Contemporary hand-drawn map of Fort Mims showing location of site that ignited Creek War. (Courtesy of Alabama Department of Archives and History)

Fort Mims had been built around several structures on the plantation of planter Samuel Mims. It featured split log walls, two gates, and a partially constructed blockhouse in addition to the Mims's plantation outbuildings and several rude cabins constructed by area settlers who had come there for safety. By the end of August 1813, the fort held approximately 250 settlers, just over one hundred troops of the territorial militia, and about forty local militiamen under the overall command of Major Daniel Beasley.[16]

Seeking revenge for the surprise attack at Burnt Corn, the Red Sticks targeted the fort in large part because of the many Creeks living there that had either assisted Caller's troops or simply refused to join their cause. A group of approximately seven hundred Red Sticks advanced on Fort Mims, and though several individuals detected their movement and reported it to Major Beasley, he refused to believe that Red Sticks were planning an attack on his post. As a consequence of his false sense of confidence, the fort lay totally unprepared for the attack.[17]

The Battle of Fort Mims began at noon on August 30, 1813. Hundreds of Red Stick warriors, hidden a few hundred yards from the fort, rose and ran silently toward it at the command of one of their leaders. They went unnoticed until within a few steps of the stockade and took those inside by complete surprise. Major Beasley became one of the first casualties of the battle, being struck down as he desperately tried to close the fort's open eastern gate. The occupants of Fort Mims were nearly overwhelmed and forced to flee to the interior structures of the fort to organize a defense. They finally managed to stem the initial Red Stick onslaught, but the attackers launched a second assault that spelled doom for Fort Mims.[18]

In the massacre that followed, Fort Mims was destroyed and the great majority of its occupants were killed. Almost immediately, the Red Sticks began to set fire to the structures inside the fort, and the garrison was gradually corralled into one bastion. Red Sticks brutally murdered and scalped hundreds of men, women, and children as the fighting wore on. Only a handful of those in the fort, no more than thirty, managed to make a desperate escape. The fighting ceased around five o'clock in the afternoon. The Red Sticks had won a stunning and complete victory.[19]

News of the Red Stick strike stunned the nation. Americans were horrified and indignant at the scale of the atrocity, and many suspected Spanish or British interlopers as the masterminds of the assault. To the thousands of troops immediately raised to put down the rebellion, however, the name "Fort Mims" became a rallying cry for revenge.

Genuine fear swept throughout the Southwest frontier regarding what the strike portended for American settlements. In few places was that fear more pronounced than in the Natchez area, still the economic, cultural, and population center of the Mississippi Territory. Though far removed from the scene of the fighting, rumors ran wild that the area had been targeted by Native Americans for an attack similar to that at Fort Mims. During this brief "Mississippi Panic," runners were sent from town to town in the region advising settlers to seek shelter, and many families in rural areas gathered up their belongings and headed toward the relative safety of towns such as Port Gibson. A small number of temporary stockades, similar to those in the Tensaw region, were hastily thrown up for the safety of groups of these refugees who were deathly afraid from an imagined combined Creek and Choctaw advance. In mid-September, a committee of leading citizens of Port Gibson organized "for the purpose of taking measures for the public safety," but sheepishly reported back that from what it could learn, "the late alarm of invasion on the frontiers of this county by a savage enemy, has been groundless and unfounded." Nevertheless, so consuming was the preoccupation with the Red Stick rebellion that in October, Governor David Holmes suspended the General Assembly in recognition of "the disastrous events that have happened upon the eastern frontier of our Territory." Closer to the area where actual fighting raged, in Wayne County, a mere sixty miles or so from Fort Mims, at least two forts were established around the community of Winchester. Further north near modern-day Columbus, at Plymouth Bluff on the Tombigbee River, Fort Smith was erected shortly after the outbreak of hostilities, at the request of the US interpreter for the Choctaws John Pitchlynn, to serve as a base of supply for operations in the Black Warrior River area.[20]

Almost before the victims of the Fort Mims attack had been buried in early September, official plans for reprisal were put in motion. Armies from the Mississippi Territory, Tennessee, and Georgia would simultaneously converge on Red Stick territory from different directions. Besides engaging Red Stick forces, these troops would also burn villages and crops and other supplies, forcing the hostile Creeks to give up the fight. Governor Holmes was especially active, rallying his residents in the face of the crisis and organizing the militia for action. For instance, he specifically gathered a force of 200 cavalrymen under Thomas Hinds from the counties surrounding Natchez and sent them to the front, although many were fearful this would place those communities closer to home at risk. He even accompanied the troops in person to see for himself the state of affairs at the front.[21]

The Mississippi Territorial militia, under the command of Ferdinand Claiborne, became the first army to be engaged, portions having already been involved in the fight at Fort Mims. In the fall of 1813 Claiborne's soldiers sought out Red Sticks throughout the Alabama River region, engaging in several small skirmishes and a pitched battle at a place called the Holy Ground, a home for Red Stick prophet leaders as well as a base of supply and place of refuge for warriors. On December 23, 1813, Claiborne's force of volunteers, militia, and friendly Choctaws destroyed the Holy Ground-and scattered its defenders. It would be the last significant battle in that theater of the war, as the focus of attention soon turned to the east and north.[22]

General John Floyd commanded the main Georgia army raised in response to the Red Stick threat, composed of over 2,300 volunteers and militia. Advancing from central Georgia to the banks of the Chattahoochee on the Mississippi Territory's eastern border in the fall of 1813, Floyd's men constructed Fort Mitchell as a supply base and launched two major offensives against the Red Sticks in this theater. The Georgia troops destroyed the village of Autossee on November 29, 1813, killing about 200 Red Sticks in the fighting. On January 27, 1814, as Floyd's army made its way toward another principal Creek population center, Red Stick forces fell upon it in a devastating surprise attack near Calabee Creek. Floyd's army narrowly escaped destruction, beating back the attackers and retreating to Fort Mitchell. Before they could reorganize for another expedition into enemy territory, the short-lived war would be over.[23]

The third, and most consequential, theater of the war featured campaigning by Tennessee volunteers and militia, regular army troops, and a number of Indian allies in the northeastern and central-eastern portions of the Mississippi Territory. These campaigns and the leadership of Andrew Jackson brought the war to a sudden close in the spring of 1814. Already among the foremost spokesmen for the interests of the West, Jackson saw in the massacre of Fort Mims an opportunity to eliminate European influence on the Gulf Coast and acquire from the Creeks valuable land for the growing country.[24]

Jackson had already acquired a military reputation in the War of 1812. In early 1813, he had led a force of Tennesseans to Natchez to take part in the defense of the Gulf Coast against a threatened British attack. His dreams of early glory were quickly dashed, however, when his men were dismissed before seeing action. Jackson swallowed his pride and led his men back to Tennessee via a long, exhausting march up the Natchez Trace back to Nashville. Having nonetheless earned the respect of his men and the acclaim of the citizens of Tennessee, the *Nashville Whig* declared "Long will the General live in the memory of the volunteers of West Tennessee" upon his triumphant arrival back home. His soldiers began calling him "Old Hickory" for his toughness. Jackson would soon have the opportunity to live up to that nickname and more.[25]

Upon arriving back in Tennessee, Jackson was given command of one of two forces of Tennessee militia raised in response to the attack on Fort Mims. Jackson's men attacked with a vengeance. They laid waste to the Creek village of Tallushatchee on November 3, 1813, and less than a week later moved on the village of Talladega, where Creeks allied with the United States lay besieged by Red Stick forces. Jackson's men shot down the Red Sticks in droves on November 9 and might have killed all within it had his army been able to encircle the town as planned. Jackson desired to continue on his path of destruction in the winter, but ended up spending more time trying to simply keep his army intact and supplied than plotting military strategy. Many of his volunteers desired to return home immediately when their terms of enlistment were up late in the fall of 1813, and it proved exceedingly difficult to obtain enough food for the troops over the lengthy supply line stretching across the rugged wilderness from Tennessee into the heart of Creek country. When finally reinforced in January 1814, Jackson again took the offensive.[26]

Jackson targeted a Red Stick force then gathering at the village of Tohopeka, located in a bend of the Tallapoosa. The Creeks called the one hundred-acre plot of land Cholocco Litabixee, or "the horse's flat foot," but the Americans simply called it Horseshoe Bend. Jackson was delayed in his approach, however, by two well-planned surprise attacks. On January 22, 1814, at Emuckfau Creek and on January 24 at Enitachopco Creek, his army suffered serious setbacks inflicted by Red Stick forces which forced him to retreat, regroup, and secure additional reinforcements. With an army now composed of over 5,000 men, Jackson headed toward Tohopeka again in March 1814, finally arriving on the 27th.[27]

At Horseshoe Bend the American army found 1,000 warriors under Menawa lying in wait behind an impressive fortification that spanned 350 yards across the neck of land in the curve of the river. The barricade consisted of logs stacked five to eight feet high and situated in a way that subjected attackers to crossfire. Though formidable, Jackson saw that the Creeks had essentially trapped themselves behind their fortification. He dispatched General John Coffee along with his Indian allies to the opposite side of the river to block the Red Sticks' only avenue of escape and made plans for his attack.[28]

Jackson began the decisive battle at 10:30 a.m. with an artillery bombardment. With the Red Sticks shouting defiance, Jackson's artillery ineffectually poured shots into their barricade. During the bombardment, Coffee and his Indian allies entered the fight. Several Cherokees crossed the river and captured the Red Sticks' canoes to prevent them from being used to escape, and then pressed on into the village, eventually setting it on fire. When Jackson saw the smoke from the fires of Tohopeka and realized the ineffectiveness of the artillery bombardment, he ordered an all-out frontal assault.[29]

The soldiers charged energetically and scaled the fortifications in a matter of minutes. Once the barricade had been breached, the battle turned into a slaughter in which more Indians would die than in any other battle in United States history. Jackson's men counted over 550 Red Stick bodies on the field after the battle, and officers estimated the total killed to be upwards of 900. Jackson's army, on the other hand, had less than fifty killed and about 150 wounded. Though scattered pockets of Red Stick resistance remained to be eliminated, their power had been shattered.[30]

Jackson did not know the extent of his triumph at the time, however, and next targeted the Hickory Ground at the confluence of the Coosa and Tallapoosa Rivers, an area known to be a major gathering spot for hostiles. On April 17, Jackson arrived at the site of the old French Fort Toulouse, which had been designated as the gathering point for the armies. Soldiers built a new stockade on the site and named it Fort Jackson in his honor. Soon hundreds of starving Creek refugees, many of them allies, made their way into the army's encampment. Even the principal Red Stick leader, William Weatherford, surrendered to Jackson, claiming he had no more warriors to continue fighting. As refugees continued to pour into the camp, it soon became obvious to all that the war was indeed over.[31]

Tennesseans greeted Jackson as a hero on his return to Nashville. At a time when the War of 1812 had been going badly for the country, he had destroyed his

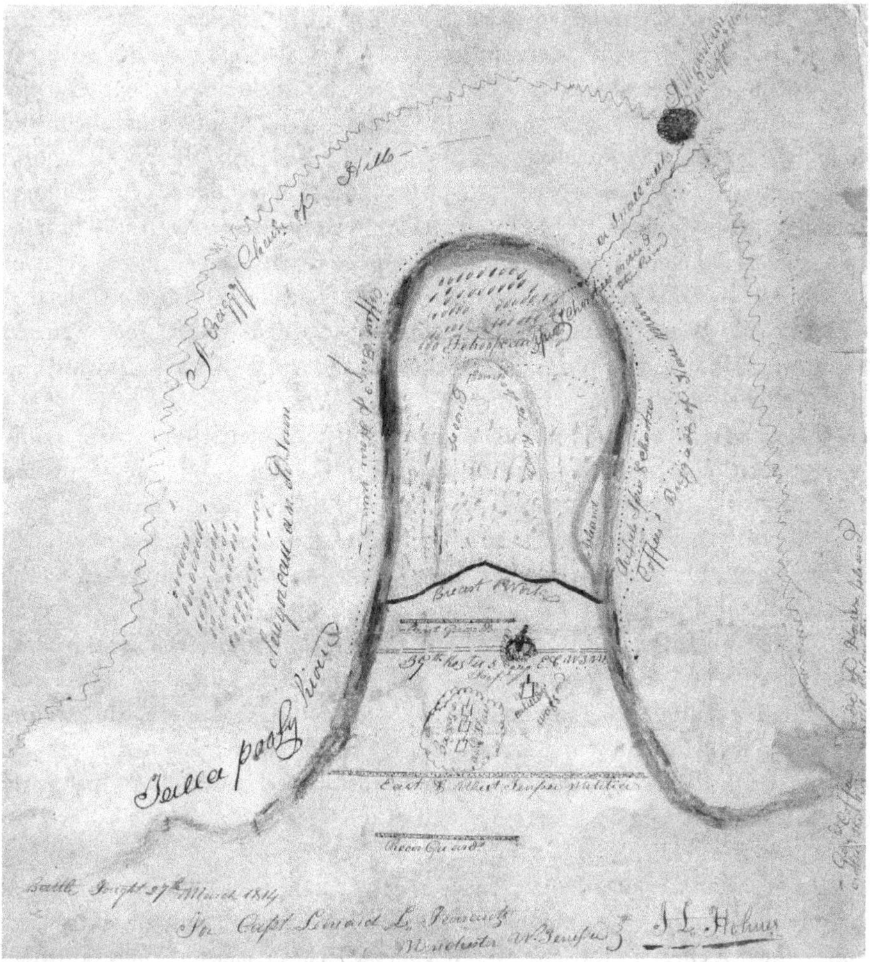

Figure 5.2. Contemporary hand-drawn map of the climactic battle of Horseshoe Bend, which effectively crushed the Red Stick resistance. (Courtesy of Alabama Department of Archives and History)

enemy on the battlefield and earned the respect and admiration of the nation. The War Department acknowledged his hard-earned status as the country's foremost military leader by offering him a major generalship. On June 18, 1814, Jackson became a major general in the US Army, responsible for the Seventh Military District, comprised of Louisiana, Tennessee, the Mississippi Territory, and the Creek Nation.[32]

A daunting task awaited him. Secretary of War John Armstrong ordered Jackson to report to Fort Jackson and assume control of treaty negotiations with the Creek Nation. Secretary Armstrong had originally assigned General Pinckney and Creek Indian agent Benjamin Hawkins to negotiate the peace treaty with the Creeks, but their demands were far too lenient for Jackson's taste. An advocate for land-hungry westerners, Jackson expected the Creeks to pay dearly for the war. Since he also wanted to prevent the Creeks from having contact with the Spanish and British, he viewed removing the Creeks from the border region as necessary to national security. Altruistically, he felt the Creek way of life so incompatible with that of whites that removal was the only way for the Indians to survive. In the end he required the cession of twenty-three million acres of land, one-half of all Creek Territory to the United States. Jackson also insisted that Creeks cease all interaction with the British and Spanish. If the Creeks refused these terms, then they could take their chances and simply move southward and join the rebels in Florida.[33]

Jackson's terms shocked the allied Creeks in attendance. They expected only the Red Sticks to bear the brunt of the cost of the war. While they expected to lose some land, they did not expect their ally to repay them in this way for their service. They pleaded with Jackson about the fairness of his terms, but Old Hickory gave the Creeks no real choice in the matter, stating, "Your rejecting the treaty will show you to be enemies of the United States—enemies even to yourself." This land amounted to almost three-fifths of the future state of Alabama and one-fifth of Georgia. Jackson chastised all the Creeks for allowing the war to occur. He claimed they should have arrested Tecumseh and other instigators and prophets when they first arrived in the region. The Creeks had no choice but to sign the Treaty of Fort Jackson on August 9, 1814. Ironically, of the nearly three dozen chiefs who signed on behalf of the Creeks, only one is believed to have been a Red Stick.[34]

The ink had not yet dried on the Treaty of Fort Jackson when Old Hickory focused his attention on those he thought were the real instigators of war, the British and the Spanish. As head of the US Seventh Military District, Jackson knew of British plans for an offensive as well as their intention to utilize Red Sticks in the effort. He had also heard that thousands of veteran British soldiers would soon arrive from Europe to assist in operations on the coast. In late August, Jackson moved his headquarters to Mobile, closer to the developing threat, and began strengthening Fort Bowyer, located on Mobile Point, in order to better guard Mobile Bay.[35]

Containing twenty guns and 158 men under the command of Major William Lawrence, Fort Bowyer constituted the primary line of defense for Mobile Bay and the city itself. On September 12, 1814, 250 British soldiers and Indians landed near the fort to assault it from the rear, while a naval squadron of four ships moved into position to bombard it from Mobile Bay. Despite British superiority in numbers and firepower, the American defenders repelled both the British land and naval forces. The British had no choice but to limp back to Pensacola, which they had earlier established as their base of operations, and rethink their plan of attack.[36]

Figure 5.3. Based on an earlier painting by Charles Bird King in the 1820s, this modern portrait of Pushmataha depicts the Choctaw chief around the age of forty wearing clothing that would have been typical of a Choctaw chief of the time period. Pushmataha fought alongside US forces during the Creek War and War of 1812. (Collection of the Museum Division, Mississippi Department of Archives and History, 1999.17.1)

Angered at Spanish complicity in the British offensive, Jackson planned an attack against Pensacola. Admitting in a letter to Secretary of State James Monroe that "I act without the orders of the government," he explained his reasons for invading Spanish Florida with confidence that the administration would eventually justify his actions. Jackson arrived outside Pensacola on November 6, 1814. Wasting no time, Jackson's force attacked on November 7. Within a matter of minutes, Governor Mateo Manrique himself sought out the Americans to surrender. Yet the limited resistance provided the British enough time to destroy Fort

Barrancas, the key fort protecting Pensacola Bay, and to retreat from the area. At a cost of less than twenty casualties, Jackson had delivered a severe blow to British plans on the Gulf Coast. His mission accomplished, and with Pensacola no longer defensible due to the loss of Fort Barrancas, Jackson returned the town to Spanish authorities.[37]

Quickly learning of British intentions to attack New Orleans, Jackson next moved to counter that threat. He organized the forces at his disposal, which included local militia, a company of free blacks, some Choctaw warriors, and two US infantry regiments. Jackson also had at his disposal a cavalry unit led by Thomas Hinds of the Mississippi Territory. He eagerly awaited the arrival of additional Tennessee and Kentucky militia that he had earlier requested to bolster his numbers. Despite first refusing the services of "pirate" Jean Laffite, he reluctantly accepted his aid and that of his "hellish banditi," in large part because of the arms and ammunition that they could provide. Laffite, as leader of the outlaw group based near Barataria Bay on the Louisiana coast, had earlier entertained overtures from the British before ultimately deciding to side with the Americans. His support would prove critical to Jackson during the coming battle.[38]

The lead elements of the British army arrived outside of New Orleans by December 23 after brushing aside a small American naval presence at the Battle of Lake Borgne nine days earlier. Jackson moved to attack the intruders that night in a combined army-navy operation. Technically a draw, the confused fighting in darkness and fog did little serious damage to either army but bought Jackson invaluable time. It halted the British advance on New Orleans and allowed Jackson's men to establish a defensive position at Chalmette along an old millrace known as the Rodriguez Canal, a four-foot-wide and ten-foot-deep rampart that stretched nearly three quarters of a mile from the river into a swamp. Although neither army knew it at the time, diplomats in Europe had already drafted the treaty that would end the war. On December 24, 1814, British and American representatives signed the Treaty of Ghent. Word would not arrive on the Gulf Coast until after the contest for the Crescent City.[39]

The fateful British assault took place on January 8, 1815. Beginning their attack with the launch of a signal rocket, the British columns surged forward in a fog soon blown aside by the wind. Jackson's men greeted the attack with artillery and musketry. "Give it to them, my boys," Jackson cried. "Let us finish the business today." Artillery and rifle fire tore holes in British lines as they moved across the open field, and attacking infantrymen and their officer corps fell by the hundreds. In less than two hours of fighting, Jackson's army had inflicted more than 2,000 casualties on the British forces: 291 killed, 1,262 wounded, and 484 captured. Jackson lost less than twenty men in one of the most lopsided victories in American military history. On Jackson's way back home months after the battle, Mississippi hosted one of the first celebrations outside of New Orleans lauding the general, the nation's new preeminent military hero, for the triumph in a gala in the territorial capital of Washington. The British, meanwhile, had retreated back to the Gulf but made another attempt to take Mobile. They actually captured Fort Bowyer in a second assault on that outpost on February 11, 1815, before getting word of the signing of the Treaty of Ghent.[40]

The results of these conflicts profoundly affected the Mississippi Territory's development. The Treaty of Fort Jackson ended the Creek War and provided to the United States government over twenty-three millions acres. The great majority of this land was located in the eastern section of the Territory, and scores of land-hungry white Americans and their slaves moved in rapidly. The path toward statehood now seemed certain. Simultaneously, the campaigns of the War of 1812 on the Gulf Coast had allowed American forces to at last secure possession of Spanish West Florida and incorporate portions of the former colony into the Mississippi Territory. Through the remarkable victory on the plains of Chalmette, they had ended forever any European interference in regional affairs. Statehood and the form it might take had been the paramount questions in territorial politics almost from the formation of the Mississippi Territory in 1798. Those questions would soon assume even more unprecedented urgency.

CHAPTER 6

Twentieth Star on the American Flag

Mississippi's entrance into the American union as the twentieth state is a landmark event in its history and one of the defining events of the roughly forty-year period under discussion. While much of the story of the Mississippi Territory's development can be understood as preparatory to that milestone goal, competing visions of how it could best be achieved made Mississippi's road toward statehood a sometimes contentious and at times divisive issue. Sectional rivalries, uneven regional paces of development, and international intrigue all became major factors in determining where and when the borders of the state as we know it today were placed.

The root cause of perhaps the most pervasive of all political disagreements in the Mississippi Territory's long road to statehood could be traced to simple geography. On the eve of statehood, the Territory stretched from the Mississippi River in the west to the Chattahoochee in the east and from the Gulf Coast in the south to the Tennessee state line in the north. Encompassing an enormous frontier area, it featured relatively isolated pockets of American settlement with vastly divergent interests and populations. In one form or another, each community believed it should become the paramount trading and political center of the new state and worked assiduously to advance its own interests at the expense of the others.

The Natchez region was by far the most populous, wealthy, and influential area throughout the territorial period. Eastern section residents—meaning almost anyone living east of the Pearl River—continually felt overlooked and underrepresented in the functioning of the territorial government. Part of the blame for the situation unquestionably lay with the federal government, which set out specific requirements for territorial eligibility for statehood while admitting new states in a seemingly arbitrary manner, as it kept a careful eye on maintaining a balance between slave and free states in Congress. A share of the blame for the rocky course toward statehood must also go to the delegates the Mississippi Territory sent to Washington to represent its interests, both official and unofficial. With no clear consensus on the matter at any point in time, the elected delegates—Dr. William Lattimore and George Poindexter—were virtually required to act independently and in the manner they thought best for their constituents at the moment. The last-minute presence of an unofficial, high-profile delegate representing the wishes of a shifting faction in the decade-and-a-half-long fight, in the form of territorial judge Harry Toulmin, only complicated matters.[1]

As early as 1803, a mere five years after its creation, settlers in the lower Tombigbee River region requested Congress divide the Mississippi Territory. In a petition by the "Inhabitants of the Washington [County] District," they exposed the clear fault lines in the territory's already pervasive east-west sectional rivalry by laying out a host of grievances that they believed could only be remedied by formal separation from the wealthy and remote Natchez area where the territorial government was headquartered. They observed that as things stood, the nearest center of law lay hundreds of miles away, "all of which distance is a howling wilderness with its usual inhabitants of Savages and beasts of prey." As a result, communication with the territorial government routinely proved difficult and sometimes impossible. On a related note, they brought to Congress's attention the fact that circuit-riding legal officials appointed by the territorial government often did not appear in the eastern section of the territory when they were supposed to, if at all, rendering any attempt at maintaining law and order in the region difficult. In a more philosophical vein, they expressed their belief that the ". . . settlements on the Mobile Tombecbee and Alabama rivers are composed of people different in their manners and customs, different in their interests, & nature appears never to have designed the two countries to be under the same Government." While summing up concisely the complaints of the eastern portion of the Mississippi Territory both then and far into the future, the petition appears to not have been given much consideration in Washington. In the end, the only practical result of the effort was the creation of a new judicial district for the Tombigbee region.[2]

The issue festered among the eastern section inhabitants in the ensuing years, and they seemed only to grow more estranged from the more populous and affluent settlements of the Natchez District as time progressed. In 1809, as talk of how the Mississippi Territory might enter the union began in earnest, they again requested division of the territory via a petition by "a Convention East of Pearl River" made up of representatives from several settlements in the Tombigbee/Alabama River basin and what is now the Mississippi gulf coast. Again claiming to be "Detached from all other American settlements," the petitioners stated in no uncertain terms that they did not want to be a part of any proposed state "on the Mississippi": "A change of names will not bring us nearer to the seat of Government; it will not bring our Public Officers nearer to us: it will not give to the Mississippi Legislature any greater knowledge of us, any greater sympathy with us, any greater zeal for our security, for our interests, or for our rights."[3]

Working proactively, they further questioned the reasoning behind any potential plan to create a single state from the immense territory, observing that administration of justice in such an expanse would inherently always be "lax and feeble." They pointed out the existing shortcomings in their current situation as proof, citing in addition to the previously noted issues with the territorial government their frustrations at its ineffectiveness in helping them deal with their alternately feared and despised neighbors—Native American tribes and the Spanish in West Florida. Spanish territory proved to be a sanctuary for runaway slaves and outlaws, and goods shipped into or out of the port of Mobile (the region's only practical outlet to the Gulf of Mexico) were subject to exorbitant Spanish taxes.[4]

The settlements along the lower reaches of the Alabama and Tombigbee Rivers, just north of the port of Mobile, would come to occupy a key role in the sectional rivalry of the Mississippi Territory. If Natchez served as the capital of political, cultural, and economic life in the western section of the territory, the Mobile area gradually assumed a similar, if less centralized, position in its eastern section. The city of Mobile itself officially lay in Spanish hands until the War of 1812, but the American settlements within the American boundary just to the north of it became the only other concentrated point of American settlement in the entire region for the first half of the Mississippi Territory's existence. Into Mobile Bay drained most navigable rivers south of the Tennessee and east of the Pearl. The region quickly became an important center of settlement and trade that coalesced politically around issues of access to this vital transportation route. So central did the Mobile area stand in eastern section residents' thoughts that as part of their 1809 plea for division of the Territory, they suggested that a "Mobile Territory of the United States" be created.[5]

Rather than spurring any congressional action, though, the primary effect of this effort ultimately proved to be the galvanizing of the residents the western section of the territory to lobby more aggressively for their own interests. Most political leaders in the Natchez area had opposed the idea of division of the territory when it was first proposed by easterners, and had matter-of-factly assumed the Mississippi Territory eventually would become one state. While the 1803 effort did not garner much serious attention along the Mississippi, the 1809 campaign brought the matter front and center. After learning of what was afoot, the Territorial House of Representatives on July 5, 1809, passed a resolution in response to the proposal for division that expressed its unanimous "marked disapprobation [to] the objects and views of said Petitioners." Keenly aware of

Figure 6.1. George Poindexter, early statesman of Mississippi who served a variety of roles including United States Representative, senator, and state governor. (Collection of the Museum Division, Mississippi Department of Archives and History, 1978.347.1)

the economic and political dominance of the Natchez region in the territory's affairs, westerners had no intention of relinquishing their position. They also were concerned that division might indefinitely delay statehood for either section owing to the slow population growth in the territory as a whole. In 1809 the Mississippi Territory's total population fell well shy of the 60,000 required for admission as a state; dividing it would mean neither section would have more than half of the needed total. Accordingly, Natchez resident and territorial delegate to Congress George Poindexter soon began a concerted effort to have the Mississippi Territory admitted to the union as a single state. His attempts sparked the first serious debate over the conditions of statehood throughout the Mississippi Territory and in Washington.[6]

Poindexter's first proposal for admission of the territory as a single state began with a memorial approved in November 1810 by the Territorial General Assembly and reviewed by the US House of Representatives in January 1811. Referred to the committee of the whole, it got no farther before Congress adjourned. In late 1811, Poindexter tried again. This time he recommended attaching to the Mississippi Territory portions of the formerly Spanish-held province of West Florida (how and why to be discussed below); this would give the territory adequate population to apply for statehood and add to it choice lands that drained several of its rivers. In March 1812, he got the House to pass a bill authorizing the Mississippi Territory to form a single state government within its existing boundaries, which including the recently acquired portion of West Florida stretching from the Perdido to the Pearl Rivers. To Poindexter's dismay, the Senate committee that reviewed the proposal determined that the proposed state would be "disproportionate to the size of any of the largest states which now compose our confederation," and in its report proposed division of the territory. It recommended the eastern boundary run along the Mobile River, then due north until it intersected Bear Creek near the Tennessee state line, roughly dividing the territory in half via a north-south border. The committee pointed out, though, that before any final decision could be made in the matter the Georgia legislature had to give approval, since that state had in 1804 formally relinquished longstanding claims to much of the Mississippi Territory on the condition that a single state be formed from it in the future. Before this approval could be obtained, Congress declared war on Great Britain and laid aside the issue of statehood for the Mississippi Territory for more pressing business.[7]

The years between Poindexter's efforts toward statehood and the war with Britain nonetheless were marked with significant events that ultimately would bear tremendous influence on the arrangement of Mississippi's borders. Just to the south of the Mississippi Territory's pre-1812 border and to the east of the Orleans Territory (the forerunner of the state of Louisiana, established in 1804) lay the Spanish colony of West Florida. The effort to rid the Gulf Coast of Spanish rule would temporarily overshadow the pervasive east-west sectional rivalry that otherwise defined regional politics, as residents throughout the area and in neighboring Orleans were briefly if loosely united in a common desire to rid the Gulf's sunny shores of European influence.

For Americans living along the border between the Mississippi Territory and Spanish West Florida, foreign control of the Gulf Coast region through which most of the area's major rivers emptied was a festering source of tension from the moment the territory had been organized. Practical economic considerations combined with a growing sense of what would soon be termed Manifest Destiny and a resentment of the interference of a decrepit colonial power in local affairs all worked together to eventually make the issue of control of the Gulf region one of the foremost concerns for the territory's populace and a centerpiece in the conversation about its future development. As a result, the Mississippi Territory's southern border became a region of continual intrigue, scheming, and plotting that taxed officials attempting to keep order for the better part of the decade and a half.[8]

At the root of much of this turmoil lay the fact that, in the terms of the 1803 Louisiana Purchase, the eastern boundary of the region being acquired by the United States had been rather vaguely defined. The terms of the agreement made reference to the borders of the colony of Louisiana being the "same extent that it now has in the hand of Spain, & that it had when France possessed it." Louisiana, as originally organized and administered by the French during their hegemony in the region (1699–1763), extended along the Gulf Coast all the way to the Perdido River. American officials later used this as a convenient excuse for assuming control of a region that they very much wanted but were not necessarily prepared to go to war to obtain. The Spanish—to whom the French ceded the colony in 1763 and who had maintained it among their possessions until 1802, when they returned it to the French—had a different view of things. They asserted that the colony of Louisiana bordered the Mississippi River in the east, and viewed the lands in question to the east of it, beyond the river, as part of the colony of West Florida, which they had captured from the British during the Revolutionary War. The inflated claims of the Americans were not a major issue for either country at first, but as the Mississippi Territory began to develop, particularly in the settlements around Natchez and in the Tombigbee District, it began to loom larger in international affairs and became a point of significant concern locally. Americans came to feel that Spanish control of the Gulf Coast retarded the growth of the Mississippi Territory by artificially restricting its expansion.[9]

Most onerous of all to settlers along the lower reaches of the Mississippi, Alabama, and Tombigbee Rivers—the very regions experiencing the most marked population increases in the territory—were the fees seemingly arbitrarily placed on shipping through West Florida to the Gulf by the Spanish. Americans seeking to do so were subject to a 12 percent ad valorem tax on all imports or exports, a relatively exorbitant fee that they believed threatened unnecessarily to restrict economic development in a region rich with potential. But the Spaniards would not budge on the issue despite pleas from every quarter, refusing to make an exception even for the supply of the Choctaw factory just north of the boundary that had been established after the Treaty of Mount Dexter in 1805. Spain had planned for the fees to discourage settlement in the border zone and perhaps forestall pressure on it to relinquish its Gulf lands, but it only accentuated the controversy by highlighting the mounting discord. "Are we Americans or Spaniards?" railed one petition from settlers in the region, exposing a rising level of frustration that only grew as time passed. No less a figure than Secretary of War Henry Dearborn publicly decried Spain's perceived belligerence in denying Americans free use of rivers they believed they had as much as right to as the Floridians, bellowing that "those rivers which empty themselves out of the U. States into the ocean through a small part of the Spanish Territory, are common highways. . . ." Meanwhile, President Thomas Jefferson chimed in that Spanish intransigence was becoming a stumbling block to the transformation of the Tombigbee region "from its present haunt as a refuge for the destitute and profligate into a haven for the virtuous and industrious." Jefferson sought a way around Spanish dominion of the coveted river outlets by getting Congress in 1804 to pass an act to set up a custom district within the contested area of West Florida (the Mobile Act of 1804), only to have Governor Vicente Folch warn Orleans Territory Governor William C. C. Claiborne that Spain would resist the measure with force.[10]

It was a situation rife for intrigue, and there proved to be no shortage of individuals willing to stir the pot. Most settlers found the apparent lack of federal action to remedy the situation, coupled with the obvious weakness of Spain, discouraging indeed. Feeling isolated, neglected, abandoned, and with festering discontent, many felt encouraged to contemplate taking matters into their own hands. It would be in the district of Feliciana, a relatively densely settled and prosperous area just below the border containing a majority American population, that the first homegrown efforts at disrupting the status quo would arise.[11]

A trio of brothers, Reuben, Samuel, and Nathan Kemper, would be front and center in the scheming and become forever linked with the tumult on the West Florida border. The brothers had moved to the Feliciana District in 1802 as agents of United States Senator John Smith of Ohio as part of a land speculation scheme whose centerpiece project was the creation of a planned community he called New Valentia. The Kempers envisioned the city would spring up just south of the international border. They soon ran afoul of their sponsor, however, and after mismanaging his affairs badly, were separated from Smith's employment. The brothers settled in Pinckneyville in 1804, a crossroads community in the Mississippi Territory virtually lying on the border with West Florida. They promptly became involved in a number of disturbances of the peace, some of which are believed to have been instigated by other speculators based in New Orleans and elsewhere. All these plans were aimed at the seizure of West Florida from the Spanish.[12]

In August 1804 Samuel and Nathan, with a group of about thirty armed men they had recruited in the Mississippi Territory, entered Feliciana intending to kidnap the commander of the fort at Baton Rouge and use him as collateral to obtain the Spanish governor's consent to grant independence to West Florida.

During the implementation of this half-cocked scheme, the Kempers' band of ruffians raised a gaudy flag containing seven white and blue stripes with two stars, presumably the banner of the new republic they planned on founding. They beat a hasty retreat before the 150 or so volunteers the Spanish had quickly assembled to restore order, however, with little of consequence having taken place. Far from chastened, the Kempers continued to agitate along the border throughout the next year. By September the Spanish authorities had had enough. They put up a bounty of $1,500 each for the capture of the brothers. A nearby family with which the Kempers had long feuded jumped at the offer. On the night of September 3, 1805, a group of some twenty men, comprising members of the Horton family and their friends and a few of their slaves, succeeded in capturing all three of the targets of Spanish wrath. They promptly whisked them across the boundary to a waiting guard, and from there on to a barge lying in the river on which they were to be transported to Baton Rouge. The wily captives managed to alert American troops at the small outpost at Point Coupee that they passed along the route, however, and a detachment from the outpost immediately set out in pursuit. The Kempers were ultimately freed as a result of the military's pursuit but placed under peace bonds. Authorities realized that while another potentially inflammatory crisis had been narrowly averted, it was only a matter of time before another would flare up.[13]

Though tensions over the possible independence of West Florida or its acquisition by the United States subsided in the aftermath of the Kemper scheme, it would indeed be rekindled with a fury only a few years later. The administration of President James Madison proved every bit as determined to wrest the Gulf Coast colony from the Spanish as had been that of Jefferson, and the steady growth of the region's pro-American populace gave impetus to clandestine efforts to undermine Spanish authority. President Madison countenanced surreptitious support of a rising separatist movement in West Florida at the beginning of his term of office, and knowingly allowed Orleans Territory Governor Claiborne to offer encouragement to the rebels just across the American line. The epicenter of the renewed spirit of expansion again sprang from the Feliciana district, and more specifically in the city of Baton Rouge. Mounting pressure on the weak and increasingly outnumbered Spanish authorities there had resulted in their allowance of the restless American sympathizers some limited self-government in the district through chosen representatives by the summer of 1810. Yet the extension of such privileges served as but the prelude to what the rebellion-minded instigators of the privilege had planned. A full-blown insurrection took place.[14]

On September 23, 1810, a party of rebels launched a surprise attack on the weakly defended Spanish fort at Baton Rouge under cover of dark. After a short but intense firefight, they gained possession of the post and raised a flag bearing a single white star on a blue field—the lone star flag which would become the iconic artifact of the short-lived rebellion. The insurgents drew up a declaration of independence and moved quickly to organize a government of their own in nearby St. Francisville. They elected Fulwar Skipwith as president, organized a legislature, and called a convention for the drafting of a constitution. The convention created a governing document modeled on the United States constitution and authorized the raising of a small army to put down any rebellion against its authority in the environs. It also sanctioned additional forces to head east to secure control of the rest of the colony as far as Mobile, which they aimed to include in the independent state of West Florida. Alarmed but unsure exactly what his response should be, Mississippi Territory Governor David Holmes sent troops to the southern border to monitor the situation, and Judge Harry Toulmin commenced a thorough investigation.[15]

Rumors of the hostile intent of the upstart West Florida government and its alleged alliance with local insurgents soon swirled throughout the settlements of the Tombigbee region and into the offices of the Spanish leadership of the city of Mobile. A vaguely described "Expedition of Mobile" or a so-called "Mobile Society" was alleged to have formed, its aim the forcible seizure of the town. Representatives of the West Florida convention had indeed been dispatched to the Mobile area. Reuben Kemper was in the van and working in coordination with Joseph P. Kennedy, under the assumption men would flock to the call to rise up and overthrow the yoke of the Spaniards and join the new republic. Yet the inflated numbers reported to be in this phantom army—in some accounts credited as 1,600 or better—were pure fantasy. Still, the fears of a possible clash sent an already troubled region into a frenzy of panic. Unknown to all at the time was the fact that the Madison administration, upon receiving word of the successful rebellion in Feliciana, had officially annexed all of West Florida between the Mississippi and the Perdido into the United States on October 27, 1810. How such an act would be enforced and to what American territory or territories the colony would be attached to was unclear at the moment.[16]

Spanish authorities alerted American military officials at Fort Stoddert almost immediately after getting word of the extralegal force supposedly heading their way, imploring the United States to put a stop to the insurgents' schemes and preserve international peace. The brazen rebels went as far as to directly solicit those same authorities for support in their filibustering mission. They were given little attention, in part due to the hard work of Judge Toulmin, who did his level best to put out all the fires of discontent the had kindled in the region. The judge also labored diligently, per the orders of Governor Holmes, to warn the residents of the lower Tombigbee region of the danger posed by the unauthorized meddling of the brigands and enforce law and order. In the meantime, he worked quietly to feel out Governor Folch about helping lessen the tension by a relaxation of the hated duties on shipping at minimum or even perhaps a voluntary evacuation. Folch proved receptive, agreeing to a relaxation of fees and duties if Americans would repudiate the extralegal West Florida Convention. He also hinted in cryptic terms that he might be forced to leave Mobile altogether unless his superiors reinforced him.[17]

In November, Reuben Kemper, Kennedy, and their small army of sympathizers—no more than 100 in all—gathered opposite of Mobile. They chose as their rallying point a bluff along the Blakeley (Tensaw) River called McCurtin's (or Fisher's) Bluff but which they referred to as "Bunker's Hill" in an overt reference to the supposed revolutionary mission they believed they were undertaking. There they raised the new republic's lone star flag on Sunday, November 25, 1810, and went about the motions of preparing for a hostile takeover of Mobile through the rallying of a pro–West Florida military force. But the actions of Kemper's men were marked by considerably more bluster than substance. They began by demanding the surrender of Mobile and calling for the eastern districts of the new republic to elect delegates to the newly formed government in St. Francisville. Nobody seemed to know exactly what to do next, however, especially after Judge Toulmin ordered them to disband. The unofficial convention army, more ragtag rabble than organized freedom-fighting force and counting only a few dozen men among its number, could only wait for additional men and supplies to arrive. Save for a boatload of whiskey, neither would ever appear in considerable quantity. On the other hand, Spanish officials, themselves of doubtful military strength and unwilling to provoke action at that time, watched the unruly expedition with unease as November wore on. Cold rains, uncomfortable quarters, and weeks with no activity or direction threatened to dispel the mob as effectively as military action. By early December the rebel camp found itself riven with dissension and in-fighting.[18]

This would-be expeditionary force, now losing members fast and its cohesion even faster, broke down into factions with conflicting objectives. A few dozen of the adventurers moved their base across the Mobile-Tensaw Delta to where a small stream called Saw Mill Creek joined the waters of the Mobile River just north of the city. Meanwhile, Kemper and a few horsemen began a long ride north, around the Delta, to join them. Once there, the roughly thirty disorganized rebels still remaining had little to do other than break into the small supply of whiskey that had recently arrived and bloviate about future plans. While they reveled and boasted, Spanish forces in Mobile decided to take action. Governor Folch authorized a force of some 200 troops to head to the encampment on the evening of December 10, 1810, intent on breaking it up. The men arrived a little after midnight, where they found the erstwhile rebels in the middle of a drunken frolic. They advanced on them, and in a brief exchange of gunfire killed at least four men and captured ten more, scattering the remainder in disorder. Two Spaniards fell dead in the melee. The American prisoners were rounded up and sent to Castle Moro in Cuba. Meanwhile Judge Toulmin arrested a handful of other individuals belonging to the expeditionary party further upriver, but a grand jury assembled to hear the charges made against them refused to indict.[19]

Unrest was not confined to the Mobile area, however. Just to the west, near the small, isolated, and predominantly French settlements along the Pascagoula River, a man named Sterling Dupree led another party in allegedly taking action to bring about the transfer of West Florida into American hands. Dupree possessed a commission in the Convention army, but his actions under the guise of that title had nothing to do with the interests of the republic. His men were unabashed raiders and marauders, bent on taking advantage of the unsettled situation and plundering whatever they could. They set upon farms and plantations almost at will, occasionally engaging in small-scale skirmishes but for the most part running roughshod over the frightened populace. Fortunately for the residents of the region, Dupree's rampage would prove to be one of the last acts of violence in the long struggle to bring West Florida into the federal domain. When American officials arrived in Feliciana to disband the independent government there and assert United States control over the territory per President Madison's October order, officials grumbled but offered no resistance to annexation.[20]

Although on paper Madison had annexed into the United States all of West Florida from the Mississippi to the Perdido, Spanish troops would continue to occupy Mobile for the time being. The first official American attempt to extricate them came in December 1810, when Secretary of War William Eustis sent Colonel Thomas Cushing with troops to garrison any posts in West Florida abandoned by the Spanish. Cushing arrived just in time to maintain the peace, as the commandant at Fort Stoddert, acting at the urging of the governors of Orleans Territory and the Mississippi Territory, had sent an emissary demanding Spanish forces immediately evacuate Mobile under threat of attack. Rumor held that Governor W. C. C. Claiborne had even considered extralegal action similar to that of Kemper's filibusters to assert American control of Mobile when the commandant failed to act. Cushing helped quash such hostile actions, but it remained to be seen how long he could postpone an outbreak of violence as American patience grew thin in waiting for the Spanish to leave as the New Year dawned.[21]

In January 1811 Secretary of State Robert Smith dispatched John McKee and George Matthews to Mobile to accept the transfer of the city to the United States. President Madison even offered to assume some of the expenses associated with the Spanish evacuation. In late February, however, Governor Folch reneged on his original pledge to peacefully leave if not reinforced, suddenly claiming that he did not have authorization to evacuate his post. The delay left the Madison administration in a delicate situation, as the federal government had already taken actions necessary to bring West Florida into the Union, including the appointing of certain public officials, and continued to make plans for its future disposition into one or more states.[22]

Throughout 1811 and into 1812, various plans for attaching the territory to the Mississippi or Orleans Territory were bandied about locally and within official circles in the nation's capital. Mississippi Territory delegate George Poindexter worked hard to arrange a deal wherein all of West Florida between the Pearl and the Perdido might be attached to the Mississippi Territory, with the area between the Mississippi and the Pearl becoming a part of the Orleans Territory. Orleans would then be put on the fast track for statehood. The plan was both politically expedient and practical, for the area west of the Pearl closely associated itself with New Orleans, and the areas east of it aligned to a great degree with Mobile. On March 5, 1812, Congress approved the admission of the Orleans Territory with these proposed boundaries into the Union as the state of Louisiana, with statehood becoming official on April 30. In May, the United States asserted jurisdiction of the section of the colony stretching between the Pearl and the Perdido. Spain, however, continued to garrison troops in Mobile and no American officials could bring into actuality their nation's assertion of control of the region without risking a potential altercation. Renewed violence seemed all but certain.[23]

A few months after the admission of Louisiana into the union, the United States found itself at war with Great Britain. It seemed the perfect time to take military action, as Spain served as an open ally of Britain and could easily be complicit in arranging for British invasion of the southwest. In the fall of 1812, President Madison requested Governor Willie Blount of Tennessee to raise a force of militia to allegedly defend the region against potential British action in that theater. Its real purpose was to lay the groundwork for an invasion of West Florida. Congress, however, balked at the scheme and refused to sanction the proposed action. When the army the governor had raised, under the command of Andrew Jackson, finally reached Natchez after a long journey from Tennessee, officials ordered it summarily disbanded. While "Old Hickory" led his troops back home in a legendary saga that would help launch his fame, the administration was left to devise other means to finally assume control of the province it had claimed jurisdiction of for almost two years.[24]

In February 1813, Secretary of War John Armstrong ordered General James H. Wilkinson to take formal possession of Mobile through military force. Wilkinson arrived in April with some 600 men and several gunboats, with an additional 400 troops from Fort Stoddert set to join him. He demanded the Spanish leave what he boldly proclaimed to be the territory of the United States. Fort Charlotte commander Layento Perez, outnumbered, outgunned, and with no promise of support forthcoming, surrendered without a fight on April 13. Wilkinson allowed the garrison to march out with dignity and evacuate to Pensacola two days later. Perez could only mumble something about legitimate jurisdiction being a matter to be decided by the commanders' respective governments. Thus, with a whimper rather than a bang, the long-sought area finally came into actual American control. It would be the only territorial acquisition made by the United States during the War of 1812, and was quickly incorporated into the Mississippi Territory.[25]

In the interim before the matter of statehood for the Mississippi Territory was taken up again in November 1812, the territorial legislature sent notice to Congress that it "most respectfully and solemnly" disagreed with the contemplated division of the territory "or any diminution of its original limits." It further disavowed "any instructions to their Representatives in Congress to obtain the consent of the Legislature of Georgia to have this Territory divided." Almost simultaneously, however, the United States House of Representatives on November 18, 1812, passed an enabling bill authorizing the people of the Mississippi Territory to form a constitution and state government when expedient, but required a division of the territory into two states once the population east of the Tombigbee River reached 60,000 and Georgia gave its blessing. That long-awaited approval finally arrived via an act of the Georgia legislature, read before Congress on January 4, 1813, recording its assent for one *or more* states to be formed from the territory at the proper time. Before any action could be taken, however, another round of memorials arrived in Washington from the territorial legislature and groups of citizens in the Natchez area. While noting the potentially positive effects of statehood on the development of the region, these memorialists, aware of the building momentum toward division of the territory in the nation's capital, now counseled postponement of statehood owing to the expense and difficulty involved in forming a new government during a time of war. Residents of the western section of the Mississippi Territory had long feared the inordinately heavy tax burden statehood might impose on their section, anyway, given the relatively less developed nature of the eastern section.[26]

The situation became even more confusing in the coming weeks. In 1812, in the midst of all these machinations, William Lattimore had for a second time won election to the post of territorial delegate to Congress and had been sent to Washington to replace Poindexter (he had first served in that position from 1803 to 1807). Besieged by contradictory pleas on the matter of division, Lattimore found it difficult to determine the proper action to endorse upon arrival. While the General Assembly in Natchez collectively petitioned him to not consent to division, he simultaneously received correspondence from individual members in favor of doing so. In the meantime, various memorials advocating both positions continued to be sent to the nation's capital by groups of private citizens. Lattimore found himself at a loss to sort out these conflicting pleas. Many people in Huntsville and fast-growing Madison County, for instance, a rising population center in the northeastern section of the territory which had barely entered the minds of territorial officials in 1803 when this debate began, now entered the fray in favor of division. For his part, Lattimore simply counseled patience, at least until the confusion in overlapping land titles dating back to grants made within the area by three successive European nations prior to American control could be better resolved.[27]

The Senate committee evaluating all these "sundry memorials" advocating for and against statehood or arguing over boundaries could not decide on a clear course of action any more than Lattimore could. On February 26, 1813, it reported that its members "have not been able to form a conclusive opinion on the subject." Citing the "embarrassed situation of the land titles in that territory, the want of numbers in its population, and the great division that exists amongst the inhabitants in relation to the question of its being made a state," the committee recommended debate be postponed to the next session of Congress.[28]

A number of distractions, especially the continued waging of the War of 1812 against Great Britain and the fighting against the Red Stick faction of the Creek Nation in the Creek War of 1813–14, delayed serious talks on the issue of statehood for over a year. The fact that the latter conflict took place almost entirely within the eastern section of the Mississippi Territory only highlighted the disconnect between the territorial government on the banks of the Mississippi and the now fast-growing eastern section, as settlers on the exposed frontier perceived a slow response from their territorial government to the crisis. By the time the matter of potential statehood again came to the attention of federal officials, changes were taking place on the ground in the Mississippi Territory that significantly affected those discussions and essentially reversed the original positions taken by the eastern and western sections.[29]

As a result of the Creek War, millions of acres of choice agricultural lands were ceded by the defeated Creeks to the federal government and plans put in motion for them to be opened to American settlement. Hoping to capitalize on the situation and the potential to more heavily influence any new state of which they were to be a part by virtue of a certain regional population boom, many eastern section residents soon began to evaluate the benefits that might fall to them should the territory be admitted as one state. Some of those in the western section, however, fearing the future diminishment of their economic and political influence the cession foreboded, similarly began to countenance division. They could not help but note that nearly three quarters of Indian claims to lands in the eastern section of the Mississippi Territory had been extinguished and that the area would soon be flooded with American settlers, while a majority of lands in the western section remained legally in the possession of native groups and hence not available for American settlement. A switching of the longstanding imbalance in population and wealth in the eastern and western sections of the Mississippi Territory appeared on the immediate horizon.[30]

The US House of Representatives took up the issue once again in February 1815, having continued to receive still more memorials from the territorial legislature and private citizens asking for consideration of their concerns. While the representatives were as much at a loss as ever in determining the true wishes of the majority of the residents of the territory, they did begin to consider the length of time that the area had held territorial status as a major factor in their debates: at seventeen years, the Mississippi Territory's existence had been the longest territorial period of any eventual state to date. A House committee called at the persistent instigation of Delegate Lattimore stated it could "perceive no good reason why its enlargement should still be deferred." On February 23, 1815, the committee recommended authorizing the forming of a single state and its citizens "to assume such name as they shall deem proper. . . ." The bill was read before the House but with no consensus on the matter in that body as a whole, legislators tabled the committee's report. While many southern congressmen were anxious to see the admission of an additional state (or states) and the political spoils, especially protections for the institution of slavery, its representation might entail, many northern and eastern political leaders were of course hesitant for the same reason. With sectional rivalry in the territory and political intrigue in the nation's capitol, the status quo regarding Mississippi's potential statehood remained.[31]

In the winter of 1815, additional memorials poured in to Washington urging Congressional action and generally complaining about the form and functioning of the territorial government. In one of these messages, the territorial House asked why the Territory was still being held in a "state of probation," and pointed out that other territories with smaller populations had been granted statehood previously. Containing a majority of eastern section residents, the territorial House assumed the position formerly taken by its western counterparts and urged Congress to consider that "vast tracts of country lying within its [Mississippi Territory] limits are not habitable by reason of its sterility, and on that account, the population of this Territory must ever be vastly inferior to that of some of the states already in the Union." Division, therefore, would be, in their opinion, "most calamitous." Representatives from the western section disagreed, of course. A group of private citizens of the eastern section of the Mississippi Territory, meanwhile, expressed their increasing frustration with the inactivity in general in a petition that arrived in Washington in December 1815. Stating that they desired statehood in short order, they again called attention to the "political evils" complained about for a dozen years. Exasperated about "the imperfect form of a Territorial Government" under which they lived, they resented as much as ever that its capital lay a mere six miles from its western limit in a territory some 350 miles wide.[32]

Seemingly impassable divisions of opinion over the issue of statehood were as deep as they had ever been in 1816 and no clear path toward statehood appeared in sight. Taking matters into their own hands, influential citizens from the eastern section of the territory in October 1816 called a special meeting at the home of prominent minister and government official John Ford along the Pearl River in

Marion County to determine how they might most effectively push the issue of statehood forward. Seventeen delegates from fifteen of the Mississippi Territory's twenty counties met in this "Pearl River Convention" between October 29 and 31, 1816. Not surprisingly, the assembly overwhelmingly consisted of eastern section residents and its agenda to recommend action favorable to that section was clear to all. While a majority of territorial counties were represented, those western counties notably absent from the gathering contained well over half the population and wealth of the Mississippi Territory as a whole. Regardless of this inconvenient fact, the "Convention of the Delegates of several Counties of the Mississippi Territory" drafted a memorial to Congress pointing out the inefficiency and inexpediency of dividing the territory on practical, legal, economic, and political grounds. They urged the federal government to disregard the "statements made and petitions extended from a small section of our Territory." It was the wish of the inhabitants that division occur, they stated, because much of the territory could be described as such a "waste of pine barren" with a "climate . . . so oppressive that our population will never be much condensed" that dividing it would be foolhardy. Neither side would meet the population requirements for statehood soon, if ever, according to their calculations. They also called attention to a host of other concerns mitigating against division, including that the territory bordered a foreign country, that Georgia had agreed to forming a state from its former claims as soon as possible, that forming one state was inherently more economical than creating two, and, gauging the direction of the political winds in Washington, that a large Southern state might "counteract the imposing influence of the large northern and middle states." The convention sent notice to those counties that had not sent delegates to the Pearl River gathering expressing regret at their absence, informing them of its results, and stating its hope that they would have local meetings discussing "that evil resulting from a division of the territory."[33]

The convention went one step further and sent a representative to Washington, DC, to request admission of the Mississippi Territory as a single state. It selected Superior Court Judge for the Tombigbee District Harry Toulmin, one of the most influential political leaders in the eastern section of the territory. Toulmin had his finger on the pulse of affairs in the region he served and had achieved a reputation as a capable administrator and spokesman for eastern section interests. Members of the Pearl River Convention hoped Toulmin would be able to work with territorial delegate Lattimore in Washington to pursue single-state admission. Unwritten in his official instructions clearly lay a charge to achieve that goal with or without Lattimore's approval. Convention members knew that even if they could not keep the territory intact that Toulmin could at least lobby for a line of division that best suited them.[34]

Lattimore, at the time of the convention already working diligently with Congress to move the territory toward statehood, viewed Toulmin's presence as

Figure 6.2. John Ford Home in Sandy Hook, Mississippi where delegates discussed Mississippi's entry into the Union. (Courtesy of Mississippi Department of Archives and History)

unnecessary interference with his duties as delegate and attempted to ignore him. Finding it impossible to follow the contradictory opinions of all of the territory's citizens with which he had been bombarded, Lattimore had already determined to request division. A westerner himself with sympathies for the concerns of the Natchez region, he objectively knew that Southern senators would probably support the plan since, other issues aside, it would mean there would be four new senators from the region instead of two and thereby strengthen the South's representation in Congress. Members of the territorial legislature residing in the western section aided his efforts in this regard by sending, ironically almost simultaneous with Toulmin's arrival, an additional memorial declaring that "nature never intended the present limits of this Territory to be embraced in one state," and pointing out that the single-state plan would "unfitly" force the two very different sections together. Members of the territorial legislature residing in the eastern section quickly sent a counter-memorial dismissing these arguments and claiming three quarters of the population desired a single state to be formed. Hence, in Lattimore and Toulmin the Mississippi Territory now had official and unofficial lobbyists advocating divergent plans for statehood and openly arguing with each other over the future of the region they represented.[35]

Figure 6.3. Assembly Hall, located in Washington, Mississippi, hosted sessions of Mississippi's territorial legislature. The building burned in 1993. (Courtesy of Mississippi Department of Archives and History)

Lattimore's efforts to have the territory divided clearly had found traction, however, by the time of Toulmin's arrival. The Judge confided in a letter to a friend on January 16, 1817, that it appeared both houses were poised to endorse division. Even as he attempted to counter Lattimore's proposal in a petition read before the Senate, he subtly began to change tactics behind the scenes by offering that in the event that Congress should elect to divide the territory, settlers along the Pascagoula River desired to be placed in the eastern, or "Alabama," section. Acknowledging this position would necessarily make the state formed from the eastern section larger, he justified the request by claiming it to be an appropriate trade-off for the much better lands along the Mississippi that would belong wholly to a future western, or "Mississippi," state.[36]

A wearied Congress had long prior made up its mind to follow the original recommendation for division that had been set out in the 1812 Senate report. On March 1, 1817, Congress approved and President James Madison signed the enabling act that granted admission to the Union of the western section of the territory as the state of Mississippi. Two days later it approved an act creating the Alabama Territory from the eastern section, with a provision that the territorial government it authorized become effective as soon as Mississippi formed a constitution and state government. In other words, should Mississippi fail in that regard, Alabama's statehood stood in jeopardy as well.[37]

That provision proved to have unintended consequences, for controversy threatening the entire plan arose immediately over the line of division chosen between the new state of Mississippi and the Alabama Territory. One of the chief aims of easterners in sending Judge Toulmin to the nation's capital had been to secure a border to their liking, and the line proposed by Lattimore and agreed to by Congress was far from optimal in their opinion. The border started at the Gulf about ten miles east of Pascagoula, ran north to the northwest corner of the boundary of Washington County, then northeastward along the Choctaw boundary to the point where Bear Creek emptied into the Tennessee River, then down that river to the southern border of Tennessee. Designed as a compromise between western and eastern section residents allowing both access to the Gulf, it suited neither. Many viewed it as arbitrary and in blatant disregard of the needs and wishes of those in the Mobile area. Discord centered on the jurisdiction in which lay the Mobile area and surrounding associated settlements, including those closely affiliated communities along the Pascagoula River. Eastern section residents had long been adamant about their need to have Mobile in any proposed state of which they were to be a part, while westerners had long desired to have the entirety of the Tombigbee basin.[38]

Barely had word of the enabling act reached the Territory before Toulmin drafted a petition on behalf of eastern section residents asking for a revision of the line, stating that "the people of the Alabama Territory do not consent. They revolt at the idea of being united to the Mississippi State, unless the whole Alabama Territory could be united to it. . . ." Meanwhile in the west, prominent officials including Poindexter and fiery political leader Cowles Mead expressed disbelief that Lattimore had allowed Mobile to be given to the Alabama Territory and threatened to have the entire matter brought before Congress again. The election of delegates to the constitutional convention called for in June itself turned into a referendum of sorts on the proposed border in some areas, as whether to proceed forward toward statehood as proposed or fight for a new line of division became a subject of heated debate. Even as steps were eventually taken toward forming a state constitution and government in Mississippi as outlined by the congressional act, the issue did not die. In one of the first debates during the constitutional convention, delegate Cato West requested the convention approve a resolution that it was "not expedient" to form a state government at the moment for those people living in the western portion of the territory. Debate over the appropriateness of moving forward with the drafting of a constitution consumed the next two days and involved multiple votes. Ultimately, a majority voted in favor of proceeding, but certain members nevertheless went so far as to independently draft a memorial to Congress asking to extend the boundaries of Mississippi eastward to encompass Mobile Bay.[39]

In the end, none of these efforts yielded a change in Congress's specifications. The majority of Mississippians, east and west, in effect agreed to compromise on the compromise, realizing that further fighting would only delay admission to the union. The line Congress suggested remains the boundary of the states of Mississippi and Alabama today with one minor change. In the 1819 congressional act authorizing the Alabama Territory to form a state government, officials ordered the lower border redrawn to run slightly southeast from the northwest corner of Washington County, Alabama, to the Gulf of Mexico because surveyors determined the original north-south running line had infringed slightly on the eastern borders of Wayne, Greene, and Jackson counties in Mississippi.[40]

Mississippi's constitutional convention gathered on July 7, 1817, in a Methodist church on the grounds of Jefferson College in Washington. The venerable George Poindexter chaired the committee that drafted the document, and much of its wording can be credited to him. Meeting for six weeks during the height of a hot and humid summer, the convention's forty-seven delegates representing Mississippi's fourteen counties (one delegate did not attend) assisted in hammering out the document by which the new state would be governed. Their backgrounds indicated affluence—twenty-one had served in the General Assembly and thirty-one were either lawyers, planters, or both—and the constitution they adopted was a decidedly conservative document. While it granted voting rights to all white males who had lived in the state for a year (and their voting district for six months), it also required that they pay state or county taxes or have served in the militia. In line with other state constitutions written at the time, it had a bill of rights guaranteed to state citizens. In response to the longstanding contempt for the perceived excessive authority that had resided within the territorial executive office, the convention clearly established the legislature, the branch directly responsible to the voters, as the most powerful branch of state government. Further, it made the offices of governor and lieutenant governor elected directly by the people. The convention attempted to address persistent complaints of inadequacies within the territorial judiciary by creating new and independent court systems. The constitution also carried provisions allowing the legislature to pass laws pertaining to manumission of slaves and requiring slaveholders to treat their chattel humanely. While there may have been some humanitarian impulse behind such legal codification, there was without doubt an overarching practical motivation from the standpoint of slaveholders obsessively concerned about the possibility of slave rebellion. Egregiously mistreated slaves were presumed to be much more willing to instigate insurrection or spread disaffection among the enslaved community.[41]

That the constitution compared well with other state constitutions of the era was no coincidence, as its framers borrowed entire sections almost verbatim

Figure 6.4. Rare twenty-star naval flag produced upon Mississippi's entry into Union as twentieth state. (Collection of the Museum Division, Mississippi Department of Archives and History, 2001.31.1)

from the constitutions of the recent "western" states of Tennessee, Kentucky, and Louisiana. Most offices carried life tenure and were to be appointed by the legislature, and property and even religious qualifications existed for office holding. Virtually all the language pertaining to protection of slaves *allowed* legislation to that end to be drafted at some future date; the new constitution clearly set out the institution of slavery as a fundamental part of the new state's social and economic structure. It gave only lip service to support for education, and left the amendment process largely in the hands of the legislature alone instead of the citizenry. Highlighting the cultural environment in which the delegates lived, a motion to include a provision outlawing dueling sparked much debate but in the end failed to garner enough votes to pass.[42]

Perhaps not surprisingly, the issue that brought about the most lively discussion involved apportionment of representation in the state legislature and the location of the state capital. These debates exposed anew the old fault lines of sectional rivalry that had been key factors in territorial politics and would continue to be so in state affairs for years to come. Over two-thirds of the total population of Mississippi resided in the seven "river counties" in the Natchez region, and representatives of eastern counties, many of whom had never wanted to be included in Mississippi anyway, had serious reservations about their status in the new state legislature with such an inherent western dominance. River county representatives desired to use the federal ratio for calculating representation in the legislature, by counting white males and a portion of the slave population. Easterners, with less total population and dramatically fewer slaves, desired apportionment based on

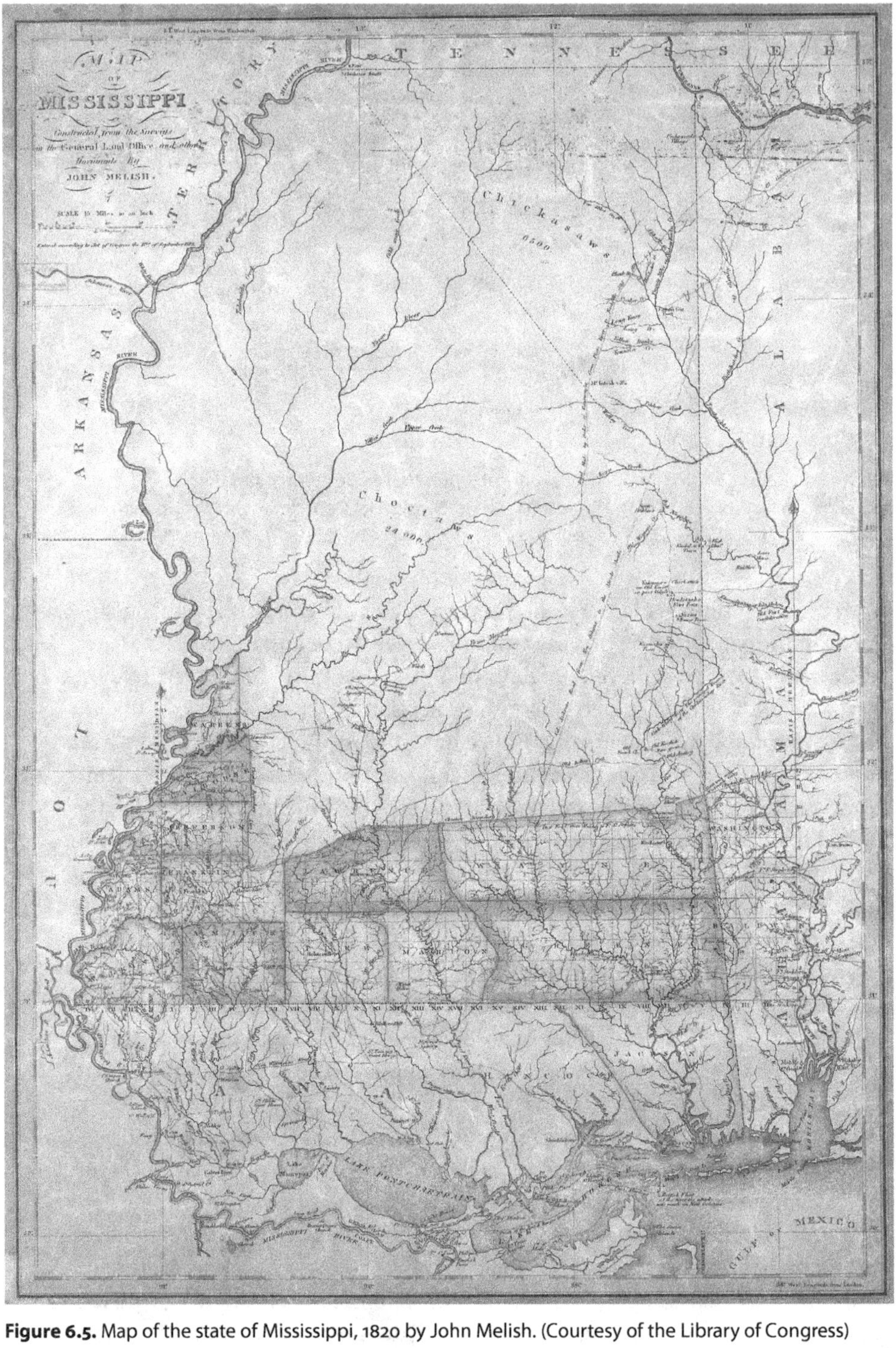

Figure 6.5. Map of the state of Mississippi, 1820 by John Melish. (Courtesy of the Library of Congress)

the free white adult male population alone. The final compromise allowed each county to be represented by one senator in the upper house, and representation in the lower house to be calculated by the total number of taxable inhabitants. In a closely related matter, the location of the state capital proved equally contentious. Legislators bandied about several proposals for a location in the eastern section of the state, but with no consensus among easterners as to a specific option and given the strength of the western county delegations, the convention reluctantly chose Natchez as the temporary seat of government until a future change "as may be directed by law." Neither compromise would prove to be permanent, but each played a critical role in completing a draft of a constitution and moving toward statehood. Although the framers of the constitution entertained a motion to have the state named Washington in honor of the nation's first president, the already more traditional name of Mississippi carried the day.[43]

The convention adopted the constitution on August 12, 1817, and forty-five of the forty-seven attending delegates signed the document on August 15. On cue, a cannon placed just outside the doors of the convention hall boomed a salute to announce the moment. The constitution did not undergo scrutiny by the voters, but rather, the convention sent it directly to Washington for federal approval. The Senate approved the constitution on December 3, and the House on December 8. President James Monroe signed the act admitting Mississippi as the twentieth state on December 10, 1817. David Holmes, the last territorial governor and president of the constitutional convention, won election without opposition as first governor of the new state, while Walter Leake and Thomas Hill Williams took their seats in the US Senate and the venerable George Poindexter took his in the House. The long, tortuous road toward statehood behind them, Mississippians now turned to face the even more daunting challenge of establishing the physical and political infrastructure of a state.[44]

CHAPTER 7

Land and Labor

The acquisition of land for agricultural purposes and access to labor to bring it under production were critical to the economic operation of the new state of Mississippi. The income derived from the cultivation of cotton would come to be the driving force in Mississippi's economy in the state's developmental years. While not all Mississippians would become slaveholders, the institution of slavery that facilitated cotton's ascendancy would be critical to the finances of planters and yeoman farmers across the state. It would also become completely intermeshed with all levels of early Mississippi culture and society. But slavery's rise in the Magnolia State was predicated on settlers gaining possession of the hundreds of thousands of rich lands that, with only a few notable exceptions, still lay in Native American hands at the time of statehood. Any discussion of how and why the state developed as it did must include an understanding of the process by which Mississippi's Native Americans became dispossessed of their land and the simultaneous flourishing of the "peculiar institution" within their former homeland. The dramatic rise of slavery and its influence on Mississippi society is quintessential to the time period and the most important theme of the era.[1]

By the end of the French and Indian War in 1763, only two major tribes remained in what would become Mississippi. Controlling millions of acres of much sought-after land, the Choctaws and the Chickasaws, in the eyes of the vast majority of whites, served as a roadblock to growth and prosperity in Mississippi. Although the two nations had their differences, they shared many similar traits. Cultivation of crops had become the dominant cultural feature for both tribes and led to the establishment of towns. Hunting remained an important endeavor; it provided not only meat but its by-products supplied material for tools, clothing, and weapons. Skilled craftsmen forged intricate pottery for cooking and storage. Religion pervaded both societies and helped explain the mysteries of life and was instrumental in the instruction of children. But Native American life was undergoing a radical change. One Choctaw man in 1829 discussed how children used to be taken to the banks of the river to learn the customs and manners of their ancestors and that now, many Choctaws sent their children to Protestant missionary schools. This particular Choctaw gentleman correctly sensed "great changes had taken place among the Indians."[2]

The Choctaw ranked as the largest nation in the future state, consisting of nearly 20,000 individuals residing in nearly fifty villages scattered across its central sections. The nation was divided into three districts (western, eastern, and southern), with each containing a principal chief elected by men of the district. A national council consisting of these three chiefs, as well as others who would meet to decide issues, ruled the nation. For years, Choctaws (and Chickasaws) had hunted for pelts to obtain necessary items from trade, but the deer population had dwindled to the point that many had recently taken up farming. This push toward agriculture had also introduced the institution of slavery into Choctaw life, with nearly 2,000 African slaves being owned in the districts.[3]

The smaller of the remaining tribes, the Chickasaw, occupied the northern section of the state with a population around 4,000. While farming and cattle ranching played important roles in their society, the Chickasaw placed more emphasis on military prowess. In fact, the Chickasaw (or at least their ancestors) had been the ones to confront de Soto militarily during his expedition.[4]

Generations of French and British traders living among both tribes had intermarried and created long-lasting change with regard to the economic, social, and political lives of the natives. The matrilineal nature of their societies played a huge role in the consequences of this interaction; descent traced through the female helped explain how children of these unions took on leadership positions within the tribes. These children could not help but alter Native American life. Trade with whites eventually led natives to become dependent on trade goods that decimated Indian independence. Mixed-bloods acknowledged and accepted these lifestyle changes. Natives soon lived in cabins, wore Anglo-American clothing, herded cattle, and used modern implements like plows for agricultural purposes. And as indicated, they even owned slaves. These new leaders welcomed or at least tolerated new "civilization" policies of the American government in hopes of holding on to their land, status, and autonomy.[5]

The national government took the lead in establishing relationships with the sovereign Native American nations. Initially, the paramount concern centered on keeping peace and establishing clear boundaries between these Indian nations and the growing United States. President George Washington and presidents who followed quickly pivoted to a policy of "civilizing" the Native Americans. This basically meant teaching them how to become yeoman farmers and ranchers as well as other basic skills to help them acclimate to the white man's way of life without a need for large amounts of land to hunt upon. To accomplish this, the government established agents who were authorized to interact with tribes and fulfill a number of duties including enforcing Federal laws with regard to intruders, traders, and contraband. They also helped settle disputes and, of course, assisted in "civilizing" the natives by teaching them certain arts and skills.[6]

The underlying idea was that once Indians became farmers, they would not need as much land to hunt, and therefore would willingly cede their domain to the rapidly expanding United States. To push this process along, President Thomas Jefferson promoted the factory system. Factories were basically government-operated or sponsored trading houses that provided Indians with various goods, sold mostly on credit. When Indian debts got too large, the United States could liquidate those debts with land cessions. Jefferson explained his intentions rather clearly when he wrote, "Establish among the Chickasaws a factory for furnishing them all the necessaries and comforts they may wish (spirituous liquors excepted), encouraging them and especially their leading men, to run in debt for these beyond their individual means of paying; and whenever in that situation, they will always cede lands to rid themselves of debt." Interestingly enough, alcohol had long played a huge role in the lives of Native Americans. Throughout the century prior to America winning its independence, European traders had swapped alcohol for deerskins in the backwoods of the Southwest, leading many natives to economic ruin.[7]

This tactic led to several early land cession treaties as the Indian trade fostered indebtedness of enormous amounts. For instance, those Chickasaw to whom Jefferson alluded gave up 2.25 million acres to pay off their debt to traders in the 1805 Treaty of Chickasaw Nation. The Choctaw owed double what their brethren to the north owed at that time, leading to several treaties. By signing the Treaty of Hoe Buckintoopa in August 1803, the Choctaws gave up over 850,000 acres of land in exchange for various items including some blankets, a few rifles, gunpowder, and a saddle. Two years later they surrendered an additional 4.1 million acres in the Treaty of Mount Dexter.[8]

The use of missionaries became another key component in the civilization policy. Besides teaching the Gospel to Indians, missionaries were used to provide basic education for Native American families as well as provide additional vocational training to further the civilization policies of the federal government. The impact of missionaries and Indian agents made it extremely difficult for those Indians hoping to hold on to their traditional ways of life.[9]

James Monroe continued down this same path with his presidency. In his first message to Congress, he stated "it is our duty to make new efforts for the preservation, improvement, and civilization of the native inhabitants. The hunter state can exist only in the vast uncultivated desert." Basically, Monroe intended to continue the policy to civilize the Indians while also not allowing them to control more land than observers believed they could reasonably cultivate. As

Monroe's secretary of war, John C. Calhoun of South Carolina would take the lead role in guiding this policy.[10]

Calhoun advocated a policy of moderation regarding the treatment of Native Americans. He placed emphasis on education and hoped for a peaceful integration of natives into society. In a report he wrote, "By a proper combination of force and persuasion, of punishments and rewards, they ought to be brought within the pales of law and civilization." But, all the while, he advised Indians about remaining in their ancestral homeland and questioned how they could survive while pressured from the white encroachment from the surrounding states. He encouraged them to move west where they could live their own lives without pestering from whites. Through the use of treaties, Calhoun hoped for a peaceful removal, while still advocating education and individual ownership of land. In hindsight, Calhoun's pushing both methods seemed contradictory because either it made sense to remove the Indians so they could practice their traditional ways of life or simply to educate them and incorporate them into "mainstream" society.[11]

While the national government determined methods of dealing with the Native Americans, Mississippi's leaders had their own opinions. The territorial governors faced this concern even at the Mississippi Territory's beginnings. Winthrop Sargent constantly complained of the Indians; W. C. C. Claiborne believed they were in need of "humanization" and supported teaching young Native American girls to spin and boys to become blacksmiths. David Holmes, Mississippi's last territorial governor and first governor in statehood, looked at the issue from another perspective. He saw the development of the state and necessary internal improvements as being reliant upon tax revenue garnered from the sale of Indian lands. Building new bridges and roads could only be done with an expanded tax base made possible by large Indian cessions.[12]

Mississippians as a whole, however, were rapidly distancing themselves from any idea of civilizing the natives in favor of removing them altogether. Longtime politician George Poindexter, who headed a congressional committee to study the feasibility of relocating the Choctaw west of the river, would not accept Choctaw and Chickasaw ownership of millions of acres of choice land. When he became governor, he continued to push the federal government to purchase the Indian lands. The *Mississippi State Gazette* reiterated the annoyance that the governor, legislature, and citizens were having with the ongoing Indian land ownership issue and exclaimed that the Choctaw still retained land "which they hold to the great detriment of this state." Echoing these beliefs was the person who would become most responsible for Indian removal in the state, Andrew Jackson.[13]

Jackson had become more and more critical of the national government and its delays in dealing with this perceived Indian problem. He had grown tired of the "civilization" policy and pushed for removal. Calhoun finally agreed that it was time

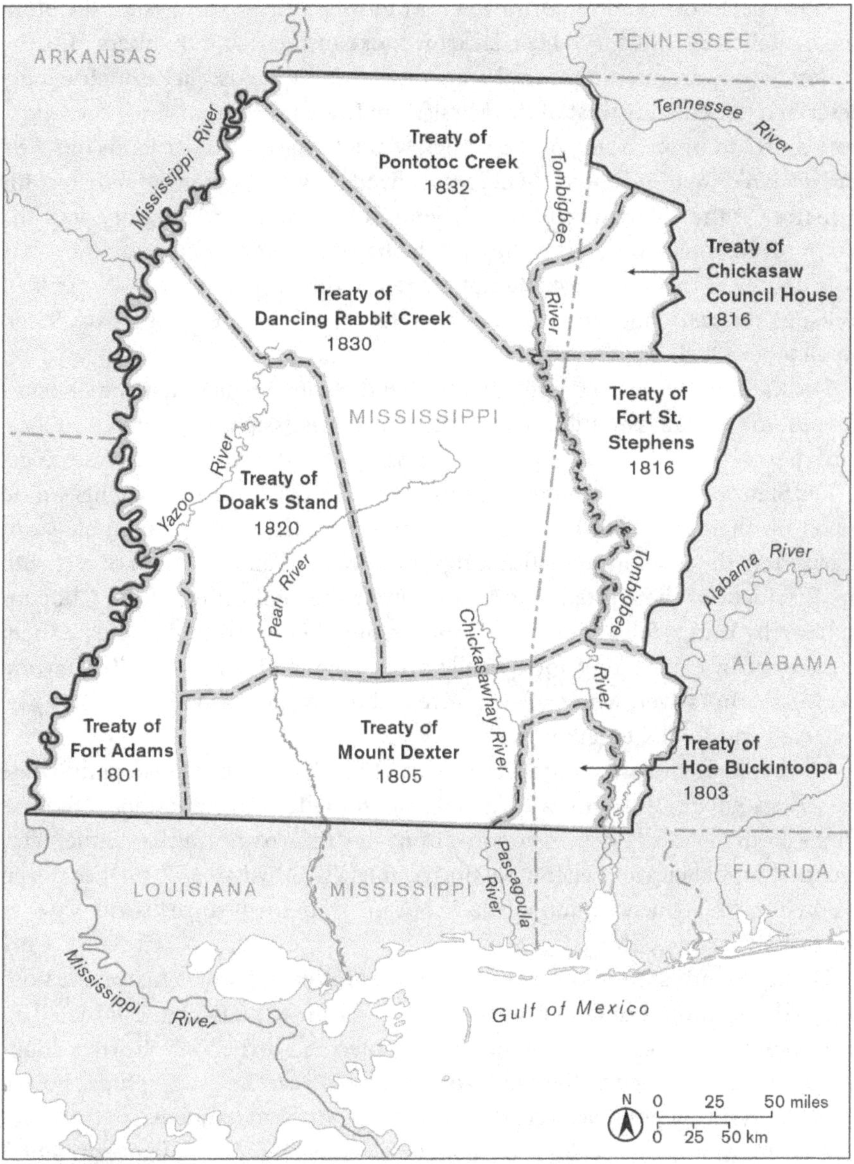

Figure 7.1. Indian land cessions in Mississippi. (University Press of Mississippi)

for more treaty negotiations with the Choctaw and appointed Jackson as one of the commissioners, but gave strict orders that the Native Americans be treated fairly. Congress even appropriated $20,000 to cover the costs of treaty negotiations.[14]

Negotiations started in September 1820 on the Pearl River at an inn on the Natchez Trace known as Doak's Stand. For weeks prior to the talks, Jackson supplied beef, corn, and liquor in an effort to soften the Choctaws for the blunt and brutal discussions to follow. Jackson spoke of the rising numbers of white settlers who were moving into the area demanding lands. Jackson glowingly described better lands west of the Mississippi River that would allow the Choctaws to live in peace. Many of the Choctaw chiefs knew of those lands out west and declared them inferior to where they lived now. Jackson eventually lost his patience. "If the Choctaw children of your father the President will adopt the measures here recommended, they will be happy; if they should not, they may be lost forever. This is the last attempt, we repeat that will be made. . . ." Fearful of Jackson's threats, Choctaw leaders reluctantly signed the Treaty of Doak's Stand on October 18, 1820.[15]

Doak's Stand became a model for future land cession treaties. In it, the Choctaw gave up more than five million acres in central Mississippi for thirteen million acres beyond the Mississippi River. Each man who moved west was also to get a rifle, blanket, kettle, ammunition, and corn. Schools, stores, and agents would be set up there just like they were in Mississippi. The treaty's preamble summarized up the government's thinking: "Whereas it is an important object with the President of the United States, to promote the civilization of the Choctaw Indians, by the establishment of schools among them; and to perpetuate them as a nation, by exchanging, for a small part of their land here, a country beyond the Mississippi River; where all, who live by hunting and will not work, may be collected and settled together."[16]

Most Mississippians praised the treaty. The Mississippi House and Senate passed a joint resolution praising Jackson and fellow commissioner Thomas Hinds. Both men were forever honored by having their names affixed to the state's eventual capital city and encompassing county. The *Mississippi Republican* even claimed the treaty negotiation was Jackson's finest moment since his victory over the British at New Orleans.[17]

Doak's Stand is a monumental turning point in the state's history. It both doubled the amount of land available for American settlement and initiated an erosion of the political power of the elitist planters in Natchez and the river counties. This eventually led to the capital being moved near the geographic center of the state, granting political ascendency to those who had long been in the backwoods and tipping the scales toward a more democratic form of government.[18]

The ink on the details of the treaty was not yet dry when several Choctaw chiefs traveled to Washington seeking to have some of its provisions rescinded. The Choctaw had discovered to their dismay that the land promised them across the river had already been taken by many whites, and begged to have the matter of their exchange of land reconsidered. Continued talks led to a new treaty in early 1825 that clarified boundaries, established annuities, and cancelled the tribe's trading factory debt. Unfortunately, two of the chiefs died due to this long journey to obtain relief and justice for their tribal members. One was the celebrated Pushmataha who had fought with General Jackson in the Creek War. Jackson characterized him as "the greatest and bravest Indian" he had ever known. Interestingly enough, finalizing the future Choctaw land deal meant very little, as fewer than fifty Choctaws emigrated across the Mississippi as a result of Doak's Stand.[19]

Mississippians were pleased with the results from the Treaty of Doak's Stand, but it was not enough to quench their thirst for hegemony over Choctaw territory. There would be no stopping the removal movement until all Native American land in the state was opened for white settlement. Congressman William Haile of Woodville wanted missionaries to continue to promote removal, and United States Senator Thomas Reed of Natchez went even further by saying the Choctaw Nation and Mississippi could not exist side by side. Reed alleged that the Choctaws could not be civilized and that it would be better if they simply surrendered their lands and went west. As early as 1826, Governor Gerard C. Brandon supported a bill to abolish tribal ownership of land and extend state law into Choctaw and Chickasaw claims. The removal movement was gaining such steam that anyone who talked of moderation was ignored and pushed aside. This onslaught could do nothing but affect leadership within the tribes.[20]

After Doak's Stand, Choctaw leadership held several meetings to devise methods of dealing with the United States government. Since the early 1800s, the Choctaws had signed several treaties that had clarified boundaries, allowed for the construction of a federal road through their territory, and had ceded millions of acres. Up to this point however, few Choctaws had emigrated west, and they still held precarious ownership to the vast majority of their ancestral lands. The Choctaws wanted to resist further concessions, but a feeling of despair and a sense of absolute fatalism with regard to the inevitability of removal hung heavy in the air. Eventually, full-blood chiefs were forced out and mixed-blood chiefs such as David Folsom and Greenwood Leflore began wielding more and more power. Some hoped that these men's mixed-blood ancestry would allow them to better negotiate with the American government. Both men hoped to speed up the civilization process so the Choctaws could better conform to white society while still remaining in full opposition to removal. In time, Leflore played both sides as he worked behind the scenes with US officials on a possible treaty while steadfastly standing against any further land cessions when speaking to members of his people. By 1830, Leflore was named chief of the entire Choctaw nation, a title that had never before been bestowed on anyone.[21]

Up to this point, the Chickasaw were also desperately holding on to their possessions. Like the Choctaw, they had signed several treaties in which they had given up much land in Kentucky, Tennessee, and Alabama, but they still held the vast portion of their primary ancestral land in Mississippi. But circumstances had sent most full-blood Chickasaws into a state of depression. Many withdrew and spent time hunting like their ancestors had before them. Interaction with whites had basically reduced this once independent nation to nothing more than wards of the US government. Leadership transferred to mixed bloods, specifically the Colbert family, who had fully adopted white society and were fully accepting of the civilization policies of the United States as evidenced by the statement issued by the Colberts avowing that "Our father the President introduced missionaries to come amongst us to advance us to a state of civilization; we accepted them, and are making all the progress that people can; we have also been providing means for the support of the missionaries, to enable us to go on with the education of our children and to have them enlightened. Industry is spreading amongst us." Chickasaws were putting all their hopes of holding onto their land on changing their way of life and conforming to the white man's ways. In the end, it did not matter.[22]

Two major events marked the death knell for the Choctaws and Chickasaws in Mississippi. Andrew Jackson, who was inaugurated president in March 1829, quickly let it be known what his priorities would be. Although he claimed he wanted to give "humane and considerable attention to their [Indians'] rights and their wants" in his inaugural address, he later told Congress that to prevent disaster for the Indians, land must be set aside in the west where the Native Americans could be free of the white man. If they stayed, they would be subject to the laws of the states. Congress followed Jackson's lead by passing the Indian Removal Act, which Jackson signed in late May 1830. This landmark legislation authorized the President to exchange land in the west for Indian-controlled land east of the Mississippi River.[23]

After Jackson's election, Mississippi's state government quickly passed an act that eliminated Native American sovereignty within its borders. This January 1830 act extended Mississippi laws "over the persons and property of Indians resident within its limits." Punishments and other fines would be levied on anyone who claimed to be a chief of their Indian nation. Although its enforcement was problematic at best, passage of the law provided all the proof necessary that Mississippians would no longer tolerate Native Americans in their state.[24]

The Choctaw would be the first nation to fall. Treaty negotiations began in September 1830. Nearly 6,000 Choctaws began gathering around Dancing Rabbit Creek in present-day Noxubee County. As with previous treaty negotiations, gamblers, saloon keepers, rowdies, prostitutes, and others anxious to see the Indians get separated from their money and possessions arrived on the scene. US negotiators John Coffee and John Eaton were Jacksonian in their tactics. They demanded the natives either move west or fall under the control of the state. It would have been hard to find a single Choctaw in favor of ceding land, but on September 27, 1830, 172 Choctaw leaders signed away their remaining ten and

Figure 7.2. Chickasaw Baldric, Native American baldric given to Dr. John Miller by Chickasaw Chief William Colbert when he left for Indian Territory around 1830. (Collection of the Museum Division, Mississippi Department of Archives and History, 1960.68.1)

a half million acres in Mississippi for thirteen million acres out west. Several chiefs, including Greenwood Leflore, got gifts in recognition for wielding their special influence in obtaining the desired result. Three received a reservation of over 2,000 acres to keep or sell.[25]

Besides granting land across the Mississippi River, the treaty also stipulated other things to be provided by the United States. The Choctaw were to receive assistance in making their move, and as a group receive $20,000 a year for twenty years. Article 14 of the treaty stipulated that any Choctaw who wanted to stay could do so, with heads of families receiving 160 acres. All the tribal members needed to do was to register with their agent, William Ward. Unfortunately, Ward failed in his duties either through incompetence or impudence. He kept poor records, lost records, and was later accused of corruption and drunkenness. Settlers soon swarmed the area in rapid numbers, heedless of any prior legitimate Choctaw claim. Little was done to remove these trespassers. David Folsom stated, "Our doom is sealed. There is no other course for us but to turn our faces to our new homes toward the setting sun."[26]

The Chickasaw proved more difficult to come to terms, but it was only a matter of time. They asked Jackson to save them from Mississippi laws, but Jackson replied, "To these laws you must submit; there is no preventive—no other alternative." And in two years, Chickasaw leaders signed away their lands just as had the Choctaw. On October 20, 1832, representatives from both nations signed the Treaty of Pontotoc Creek in which the Chickasaw surrendered their remaining six million acres of land in Mississippi. The United States agreed to pay the Chickasaw the funds from the sale of these lands, minus the costs of surveys, as well as the tribe's expenses in relocating westward. The treaty's racist preamble stated the Chickasaw's only option: "This Chickasaw nation find themselves in their present situation, by being made subject to the laws of the States in which they reside. Being ignorant of the language of the laws of the whole man, they cannot understand or obey them. Rather than submit to this great evil, they prefer to seek a home in the west, where they may live and be governed by their own laws." Similar to what had occurred in Choctaw territory, whites prematurely settled on Chickasaw land; surveyors, speculators, auctioneers, and interpreters swarmed quickly looking to acquire land and make money.[27]

Unfortunately for the Chickasaw, no future home had been pre-established at the signing of the treaty. Shortly afterward, Chickasaw leaders roamed the trans-Mississippi territory to find a new home but had little success. Not until 1837 did the Chickasaws sign an agreement with the Choctaws in the Treaty of Doaksville where the Chickasaw agreed to pay their fellow tribesmen $530,000 to acquire over three million acres of their large land tract.[28]

Although more commonly associated with the Cherokee, the Choctaw and Chickasaw experienced their own "Trail of Tears." Mismanagement and outright corruption botched the process. Inadequate supplies, miscommunication, sickness, and disease, worsened by inclement weather, made the arduous journey by land and by sea a literal hell on earth. Exact figures of how many lives were lost are unknown but it must have run into the hundreds. George Gaines, a Choctaw Indian factor, remarked that this removal was "truly painful to witness," and another observer of the Chickasaw removal said "Much money could not compensate for the loss of what I have seen. . . ."[29]

Not all Native Americans chose to move westward. Some stayed, trying to forge a life for themselves under dramatically different circumstances. Lacking any state citizenship, they held few if any rights. They lived along the outer fringes of Mississippi society, scraping by through subsistence farming and hunting. Members of the current Mississippi Band of Choctaw Indians are descendants of those who refused to abandon their homeland. But for those who did journey westward, historian Arrell Gibson has stated bluntly that they "had to overcome the trauma of exile from the land of their ancestors and face up to the problem of building a new life in the southwestern wilderness."[30]

With millions of acres of land now available upon the removal of Native Americans, all varieties of fortune seekers swarmed into Mississippi. The decade of the 1830s witnessed unparalleled population growth, a 175 percent jump, the largest in state history. Settlers and speculators, opportunists and entrepreneurs flooded the landscape as new lands for cultivation were sold. "King Cotton" was taking shape, and the proverbial "Flush Times" were coming to pass. "This [removal] freed the slave States from an obstacle to their growth and prosperity, and left them free to expand, and to cultivate, to the full measure of their ample boundaries," exclaimed Missouri senator Thomas Hart Benton. Of course, "Flush Times" is a relative term: Native Americans and African American slaves reaped no benefits from the sudden influx of money as Mississippi assumed a key role in the international cotton trade.[31]

Ironically, one of those who became wealthy in similar fashion to white planters was Greenwood Leflore. By the 1850s, Leflore had become a wealthy planter himself, amassing over 15,000 acres and 500 slaves. He also eventually became a member of the Mississippi State Senate. His mansion, Malmaison, near Greenwood, stood as the envy of Mississippians everywhere. But Leflore was by far the exception,

Figure 7.3. Greenwood Leflore, Choctaw Chief who remained in Mississippi after removal and became a state senator. (Courtesy of Mississippi Department of Archives and History)

not the rule. Having lived in Mississippi for thousands of years, Native American dominion had suddenly ended. The unyielding pressure of impatient settlers and the state and national governments had been simply too much for the tribes to withstand. Whites simply saw Native Americans as an obstacle to overcome and remove as a precursor to the introduction of slave-based agriculture.[32]

"Just as the varicolored frontier eclipsed the ancient nations," as two of the more prominent historians of the age have stated, "the peculiar institution eclipsed the frontier of the Old Southwest." Slavery stood at the center of the new way of life that the removal of Native Americans hastened in early Mississippi. Much of its economy would literally be built on the backs of enslaved African Americans and virtually every aspect of the state's culture and society was influenced in some way by the presence of bondsmen.[33]

Importing slaves to labor on the newly acquired lands in early Mississippi became big business as, in the words of noted historian Ira Berlin, the "Second

Middle Passage" "washed thousands of black men and women across the continent, expanding slavery westward." Demand for laborers spiked as hundreds of thousands of acres of some of the best cotton lands on the continent came under American jurisdiction after years of Native control, and the pace only accelerated as the state developed. While some slaves were purchased through traders operating out of New Orleans, throughout Mississippi's territorial years and first decade of statehood, coffles served as the primary means for bringing in slaves to local markets. Coffles were essentially walking groups of individuals chained together and overseen by accompanying white men, all stopping at intervals to camp for the night. The coffle ranked as the cheapest way to get slaves between the Upper South and the Mississippi Valley until well into the steamboat era. A great majority of early Mississippi's enslaved population arrived in the state through this method of transportation. Most made the weeks-long trek between early fall and late spring, with many following the Natchez Trace. The weather was more conducive to travel in the cooler months, planters had money in their pockets for purchases after the sale of crops, and a fall or winter purchase would allow time to have crews ready to work on planting a new crop in the spring. Many sickened and died along the way, regardless. These "gangs" seldom failed to elicit a reaction from travelers, who were struck by the uniqueness of the sight of these unusual caravans. They could often be heard before being seen, such as the one encountered by Joseph Holt Ingraham on his visit to Mississippi in the 1830s: "a sudden clanking of chains startled our horses, and the next instant a gang of negroes, in straggling procession, followed by an ordinary looking white man armed with a whip . . . Each negro carried slung over his shoulder a polished iron ball, apparently a twenty-four pounder, suspended by a heavy ox chain five or six feet in length and secured to the right ankle by a massive ring." Coffles remained a feature of Mississippi's roads until well into the 1830s, although by the 1820s transit of slaves for market by ship between Virginia and New Orleans, and then upriver to Natchez, became more common. Crowds sometimes turned out to witness the arrival of slaves aboard steamers at the city wharf, observing them march up the hill:

> each with his bundle, under the charge of their temporary master or conductor, toward the city in a long straggling line, or sometimes in double files, in well-ordered procession, gazing about them with curiosity and wonder upon the new scenes opening before them, as they advance into the city, and speculating upon the advantages afforded as their home, by the beautiful country to which they find themselves transplanted. . . .[34]

Itinerant slave traders plied their trade throughout Mississippi during its early statehood years, and permanent markets operated in most of Mississippi's larger towns during the antebellum era, with active establishments in locations including Vicksburg, Jackson, Woodville, and even Aberdeen. Natchez claimed by far the largest markets; the city contained several "pens" at different points in time during the territorial and early statehood era, and by the early 1830s had well over two dozen traders operating in the city. The infamous market at the intersection of Liberty and Washington Roads about a mile east of downtown Natchez, locally known as the "Forks of the Road," eventually became the primary one for the city, the state, and to some extent the larger region. The Forks' origins can be traced to the formation of a partnership between traders Isaac Franklin and John Armfield, who bought the land on which it sat around 1819 with an eye toward supplying the rapidly growing market for slaves in Mississippi and Louisiana by importing bondsmen from Virginia and Maryland. Prices were escalating in the former territories, as new arrivals seeking to make fortunes cultivating cotton were scrambling to secure the necessary labor and driving up prices due to a limited supply, while in the eastern states there existed a surplus of labor and slaves could be purchased relatively cheaply.[35]

Originally, Armfield managed most of the buying from Alexandria, Virginia, and Franklin handled most of the selling in Natchez and New Orleans. The partners later brought a man named Rice Ballard into the partnership, forming Ballard, Franklin and Company. At their market were sold as much as two-thirds of all the slaves brought into Mississippi between 1819 and 1834. As many as 750 slaves at a time were housed there in assorted old buildings and tents during its peak activity, with purchases being made daily.[36]

Visitor Joseph Holt Ingraham understatedly described the market at the Forks as a "scene of novel character," and left this poignant description:

> A line of negroes, commencing at the entrance with the tallest . . . extended in a semicircle around the right side of the yard. There were in all about forty. Each was dressed in the usual uniform of slaves . . . consisting of a fashionable shaped, black fur hat, roundabout and trowsers of coarse corduroy velvet, precisely such as are worn by Irish labourers . . . good vests, strong shoes, and white cotton shirts. . . . This dress they lay aside after they are sold, or wear out as may be; for the negro dislikes to retain the indication of his having recently been in the market. . . . With the exception of displaying their teeth when addressed, and rolling their great white eyes about the court—they were so many statues of the most glossy ebony. . . . The entrance of a stranger into a mart is by no means an unimportant event to the slave, for every stranger may soon become his master and command his future destinies.

This surreal scene of human beings being inspected and sold as cattle varied little from market to market in frontier Mississippi.[37]

Not all slaves were bought directly from the markets in this manner. A large percentage of slave sales occurred in transactions conducted between two private individuals for an agreed-upon price. Many others were sold in that most notorious of spectacle of the time and place—the auction. Humans were sold to the highest bidder in town squares across early Mississippi both by traders and by the order of legal authorities to settle estates and administer wills. Frequently the persons to be auctioned were prepared for the event by being washed, dressed in new clothes, having any gray hairs plucked, and on occasion "blackened" by being rubbed with solutions that would give them a "sleek" and healthy appearance. Customarily the person being auctioned stood on a box or some type of elevated platform, often only partially clothed, where they could be viewed and closely examined by the prospective buyers crowding in around them. Questions about temperament and disposition abounded, though it is difficult to imagine sellers describing slaves at auction as anything but naturally subservient. As the auctioneer called for bids and hands were raised or voices shouted out their willingness to pay, the slave looked on helplessly as his or her destiny hung in the balance. With the cry of "sold" the slave stepped down and a new slaveholder took possession. While some buyers and sellers did attempt to keep slave families together in sales—usually meaning mothers and children only—their motivations were as a rule practical rather than altruistic, as family units were perceived as more manageable and less likely to attempt to escape. Slave marriages held no legal standing and few attempted to keep husbands and wives together, and such nuclear family units as existed were divided as a matter of course. "Oh, such crying and weeping when parting from each other!" recorded one witness to such arbitrary separations.[38]

Despite slavery's ubiquitous presence throughout early Mississippi, most citizens viewed the actual process of buying and selling of slaves as a somewhat unsavory necessity with which they preferred not to be confronted on a daily basis. Most people desired that markets be located outside of town limits and out of sight of residents and the visiting public whenever possible, commonly listing as reasons that the overcrowding in them invited disease. Occasional outbreaks of deadly illness in the confines of pens were a grisly reality within some of the larger trading establishments. Even in Natchez, the hub of early Mississippi's slave trade, efforts were made to move all of its slave pens outside of town between the late 1820s and early 1830s. In addition, and with no small degree of irony, the public often held in low esteem the slave traders that trafficked in human flesh for the manner in which they made their living. The very nature of their business spoke to a flagrant lack of concern for human life of which some preferred not to be reminded.[39]

Part of this situation undoubtedly can be traced to disgruntled buyers in every corner of the state who, when a slave they recently bought became ill or otherwise did not perform to expectations, commonly lashed out at the traders with whom they had done business. Many traders in fact did go to great lengths to make the slaves they sold appear as healthy, young, and capable as possible at the time of sale as they could to drive up the price, helping create an overall air of suspicion of traders as inherently untrustworthy. Further, many buyers suspected traders of bringing into the state some of the least desirable slaves from the Upper South, whose punishment for being rebellious or lazy was to be sold "down the river." Even though both the original state constitution of 1817 and the second constitution of 1832 explicitly made slavery a fundamental part of Mississippi's legal fabric, the latter took legal measures to curtail the interstate slave trade out of both a growing fear that troublesome bondsmen might overwhelm the state and a desire by some to drive up slave prices. The 1832 constitution allowed settlers to bring their slaves with them until 1845, but specifically prohibited trade after May 1, 1833. The state doled out few penalties for violations of the statute until the later 1830s, going so far as to tacitly sanction the continuance of the practice by taxing imported slaves. Subsequent legislatures ended up backtracking on the issue entirely in the 1840s when the easy availability of enslaved labor Mississippians had long been accustomed to turned into a shortage. Ultimately, the fact that traders operated in what one scholar has described as a "moral vacuum," measuring the worth of individuals only in cold dollar figures, and recorded their deaths as mere business losses. Occasionally some even sold kidnapped legitimate free blacks back into slavery. Such actions made for unsettling visceral demonstrations of the stark realities about slavery which many preferred not to witness and would rather their guests not see.[40]

The lucrative financial returns of the profession lured men into the business, social taboos and all, as it assumed its place as one of the largest commercial enterprises in the region. Slaves might bring as much as $1,000 at auction, with most selling for between $400 and $900 during the frontier era; women might bring prices of around $600 on average and men in the neighborhood of $800. In a revealing commentary on some of the most awful aspects of slavery, attractive young females, sometimes marketed as "fancy girls," might bring in as much as the most capable male laborers. Traders made profits of as much as $200 on each sale, and became very wealthy in the process.[41]

From the moment of purchase, or birth on a plantation, slaves were subject to the absolute authority of slaveholders. While some treated their chattel relatively humanely under the circumstances, many egregiously abused their power and treated slaves brutally. The unquestioned right of slaveholders to physically punish slaves for violations of expected codes of conduct, outright disobedience, and a variety of other infractions of rules by beating them with whips or other devices served as the most tangible reminder of subservience in frontier Mississippi. At their discretion, masters could have slaves stripped, bound, and cruelly whipped with hundreds of lashes. They could keep them locked in chains like animals if they had attempted to run away. In some cases, they might actually have slaves

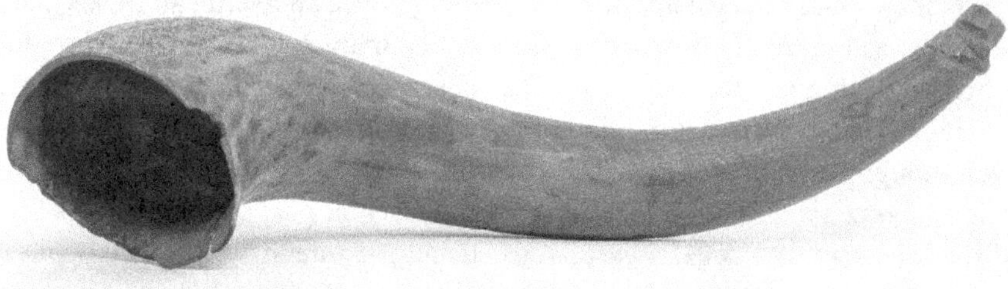

Figure 7.4. Slave horn used to awaken slaves on plantation in Boliver County. (Collection of the Museum Division, Mississippi Department of Archives and History, 1986.52.1)

branded like cattle. Regardless of how often such measures actually might be employed, the threat remained ever present.[42]

While the state's first constitution provided that the state could sell the slaves of a cruel master, such half-hearted inducements to treat slaves well, even if in part meant to suppress rebellion, carried no weight in practicality, especially with poorly paid overseers charged with enforcing discipline on plantations. Few men took the job when they could find work elsewhere. Overseeing, like slave trading, was looked down upon in polite society. Individually tasked with forcing as many as fifty slaves to work against their will, overseers often felt special motivation to be feared on the plantation, and were quick to make an example of slaves who defied them.[43]

While numerous details of slaves' lives varied from location to location, their experience generally followed certain contours statewide regarding basic work patterns, housing, food, and medical care. Slaves customarily worked six days a week in early Mississippi, with Saturdays often being a half day of labor at certain times of the year. While slaves worked "just about anywhere there was manual labor to be done," in the words of one historian, the rhythms of the plantation became the experience of most. Workdays commonly began at or before daylight with the blowing of a horn signaling the start of the day. Work ended at dark. Everyone had a task; children as young as five might be charged with carrying water to older slaves in the fields, while elderly slaves might help prepare food. Some slaves later reported seeing nursing mothers take breaks to feed their babies while in the field. By the 1830s, most attended some sort of church service on Sunday, either on the plantation grounds or at a community church where they might sit in a balcony. Depending on each slaveholder's prerogative, a few holidays allowed for all work to be halted; Christmas Day was nearly universally observed in this manner, but at some places Independence Day and New Year's Day were as well.[44]

Slaves were roughly clothed, their attire usually being made of coarse, durable fabrics marketed as "negro" cloth or "linsey-woolsey." Enslaved women usually wore simple dresses and frocks, men plain trousers and shirts, and young children a one-piece lengthened shirt. The small minority of slaves who worked within the plantation house as domestic servants might appear dramatically better dressed than field hands, sometimes being attired with not only better clothing, but accessories such as vests, jackets, and hats similar in style and fashion to that worn by elite white society. Whereas these "house slaves" might eat food similar to that of their masters, the great majority of slaves in early Mississippi were as roughly fed as they were clothed. Food was generally abundant if not varied, with rations of corn meal, salt pork, and molasses nearly ubiquitous and flour, rice, peas, meal, and on occasion various other meats. This monotonous fare could be supplemented, however, with small vegetable plots and chickens which by custom slaves were allowed to keep for themselves, along with fish, possums, rabbits, and other small animals that might be obtained in the nearby woods. Bondsmen ate with the simplest of plates and utensils, and sometimes children were fed in a trough much like animals. Slaves lived in humble, sparsely furnished wooden cabins as a rule, almost invariably with no floors and often no daubing between the split timber logs. They slept on simple corn shuck mattresses or directly on the floor, and in good weather sometimes on the grass underneath the stars. Local physicians who made periodic visits to plantations provided what little medical care slaves received outside of herbal remedies composed within the slave quarters. In a few of the state's larger cities slave infirmaries operated where the most serious debilities might receive attention if a master proved willing to pay for the service.[45]

The slaves' daily existence contained reminders of slaveholders' authority at every turn. Strict prohibitions stood against slaves learning to read and write, even though many managed to do so surreptitiously nonetheless. Elaborate series of rules contained within the state's legal code proscribed their behavior, providing for official enforcement of basic tenets of bondage that leaders wanted to ensure were everywhere observed. Slaves dared not use abusive language toward whites or assault them in any way, both being offenses punishable by a certain number of lashes on the "bare back, well laid on." Slaves could have their hand burnt if they were found guilty of a felony. If convicted of raping a white women or burning plantation buildings—specifically including both the slaveholder's house and the outhouse—they could be put to death. A host of other regulations governed virtually every circumstance in which slaves might find themselves. Given all the effort placed in legally outlining their status, slaves occupied a precarious position if ever involved in courts, and ended up relying more on the good will of whites who knew them than any concept of fair legal standing before the law.[46]

But the legalization of oppression was only half the story of subjugation, for masters held total control over their chattel in practicality despite weakly enforced provisions in law for humane treatment. Few aspects of this totalitarian structure of governance more poignantly revealed the complete power of discretion residing with masters than the numerous children of slave women they fathered. Not every slaveholder raped attractive female slaves, but enough did that the occurrences must be mentioned in any discussion of slavery. So must slaveholders' arrangement of marriages among the enslaved in an attempt to orchestrate the production of children they deemed likely to possess desired physical attributes. Enslaved for life by simple virtue of being born or sold into the system, bondsmen could only hope for legal emancipation in the rare circumstances that the state worked to more narrowly define as time progressed. Perceiving no other recourse for relief from their situation, many slaves ran away. Organized plans for escape to the North, or occasionally to return to a place they had previously known and been forcibly removed from, existed and were sometimes (although rarely) successfully carried out. Most slaves, however, who fled the plantation had no solid notion of where specifically they were going or how to get there. They simply had tolerated all they could at a particular location. Running away could be as much a statement of dissatisfaction as a genuine attempt to find freedom, which must have seemed almost an impossible dream for most Mississippi slaves. Slaves were well aware that "troublesome" bondsmen were the first to be sold to another slaveholder. It was not uncommon for some runaways to hide out for short periods of time and voluntarily return, the punishment they received being deemed as a fair exchange for a brief taste of independence or the expression of frustration for which they had no other outlet. However, a large number of runaways had no intention of ever returning, and flight remained part and parcel of the institution of slavery throughout Mississippi's early years. Some slaves, such as William J. Anderson, who later left a harrowing written account of his life in bondage, attempted escape, only to be turned in for the reward offered for his capture by a white man who had befriended him. He actually attempted to flee multiple times afterward because, in his words, "the spirit of freedom still burned within me."[47]

It is difficult to find any issue of a major newspaper in the early statehood years that does not contain a mention of runaway slaves. The largest number of flights seem to have occurred at the height of work on the cotton crop, in the summer and early fall, but judging from the posting of notices, attempts at escape took place year-round. The advertisements reveal much about the slaves as individuals, who might otherwise never appear in the historical record as anything more than "male" or "female" on a census return. They also demonstrate how intimately slaveholders and slaves were acquainted with each other. For example, notices offering cash rewards for the return of slaves in an 1806 edition of the *Mississippi Herald and Natchez Gazette* informed readers that "Frank" might be heading back to Virginia, that "Toby" spoke some French, and "Murray" had a few white spots on his chin and worked as a blacksmith by trade. An 1807 issue of the same paper carried a notice of a "likely Mulatto girl" wearing a red fluff jacket and white cambric petticoat having run away, while an 1827 issue of the *Natchez Ariel* asked for help apprehending "Bill," who was "fond of spirits and forward in conversation." Issues of that paper in 1825 carried notices of runaways such as "Henry," a "yellow boy . . . rather reserved in his manners and taciturn"; "John," "a native of Cuba, speaks the Spanish language fluently, but the English very imperfectly"; and John's wife "Ann," "shrewd and sensible, bold and impudent in her address." All of these fugitives were likely hunted with dogs, and their presumed routes of escape tracked energetically, with neighbors and law enforcement officers enlisted in the effort even as accomplices in the slave quarters of their own and nearby plantations did what they could to assist them in clandestine fashion. Slaveholders captured a large percentage of runaways through these means near home, but many who were captured would have their flight ended in communities through which they were passing as strangers, having been observed by locals and apprehended when they could provide no believable reason why they were there. We simply do not know how many runaways successfully found permanent liberation through flight.[48]

In far less dramatic fashion than escape, slaves back home engaged in a more enduring, low-key but bitterly serious tug of war with slaveholders to define the borders of servitude. Despite the carefully laid out and diligently monitored parameters in which they lived their lives, slaves managed to resist doing more work than they deemed acceptable, to form their own communities, and even to express themselves as individuals. All of these efforts represented a subtle resistance of authority and facilitated a concept of dignity that played no small part in making their plight emotionally bearable. None were more vital in slave self-assertion than the creation of their communities and the enjoyment of a type of family life. Slave neighborhoods, sometimes comprised of residents of several adjoining plantations, were important parts of early Mississippi's social scene, and helped give enslaved peoples a sense of identity and a complex notion of place. The concept of family, even if many relationships within it were fictive, remained a vital organizing force in the slave community. Nuclear families did exist, sometimes at the encouragement of slaveholders, but slaveholders often viewed slave families as consisting of only a mother and children and proved all too willing to separate even these groups if financial considerations made it expedient. Since slaveholders commonly encouraged marriages of slaves living on nearby plantations and allowed husbands to travel to visit wives on a regular basis, overnight visits became an enduring part of family life. "A negro is a great night-walker," declared one early Mississippi resident. "He will, after laboring all day in the burning sun, walk ten miles to a frolic, or to see his 'Dinah,' and be at home and at his work by daylight next morning." Slaves understood their familial relationships much more elaborately than the narrow version self-servingly sanctioned by slaveholders. Slaves recognized aunts, uncles, and other extended kin, creating a community within a community that promoted a sense of belonging and helped organize a social network that gave a degree of stability and control utterly lacking outside of the slave quarters. On larger plantations, they even understood themselves as living within a class system in which field workers were not infrequently looked down upon by those charged with other duties such as working within the plantation house, driving carriages, or working at skilled trades. Slaves seized any opportunity to take ownership in their physical appearance regardless of their status whenever they had an opportunity, sporting unique hair styles, accessories, and customized manners of wearing hats and clothing whenever possible.[49]

Bondsmen clung even more tenaciously to the continuance and even expansion of minor privileges, such as opportunities to earn small amounts of money, tend their own gardens, trap game to supplement diets, engage in Saturday night dances and holiday feasts, and other measures of a degree of autonomy traditionally granted them by planters. Under the complex and unwritten rules of slave management that has come to be defined as "noblesse oblige," slaveholders took pride in displays of magnanimity that allowed them to be seen as generous to their chattel, reinforcing a belief that well-treated slaves were loyal slaves. As a consequence, slaves gladly played along when it suited them, enjoying momentary opportunities for revelry, community bonding, and respect that they came to view as rights and seeking to hold on to them through strategically orchestrated pace and quality of work and care of equipment and supplies. Slaves were sometimes allowed to participate in the market economy, for example, selling chickens, vegetables, cakes, brooms, mats, and other merchandise they grew or crafted. In special circumstances, slaves might even be allowed to perform "overwork" for small amounts of money. Such practices were widespread but not universal, and allowed certain slaves opportunities to collect modest sums of money, which they used to purchase desired goods, sometimes in clandestine trade with willing whites. They facilitated more work than otherwise might be accomplished, and in some cases even offset the burden of providing for slave needs by slaveholders. More common were the regular Saturday night gatherings in slave quarters across the state where musicians, customarily fiddlers, played tunes while those gathered around clapped, sang, or danced. These events became treasured moments of joy that slaves viewed as "their time."[50]

Slaveholders did occasionally grant slaves small respites from their duties. At Christmastime, slaveholders sometimes gave small gifts and feasts at which slaves might enjoy some of the best food they would be given all year. According to observers, the Christmas holiday might be ". . . for a week or ten days . . . a protracted festival for the blacks." Fourth of July barbecues, large wedding celebrations, and even attendance at funerals followed by fellowship all came to be opportunities for the forging of a community that, at least temporarily, enjoyed a measure of dignity and independence. John Anthony Quitman found the revelry commonly exhibited on such occasions remarkable, noting the incongruity with which bondsmen were transformed into "the most arrant coxcombs and aristocrats in the world." He noted with incredulity and condescending humor how he witnessed blacks at celebrations "addressed as governors, generals, judges, and doctors. . . . The 'gentlemen' sport canes, ruffles, and jewelry, wear boots and spurs, affect crape on their hats, and carry huge cigars. The belles wear gaudy colors, 'tote' their fans with the air of Spanish senoritas . . ." For Quitman, as for many slaveholders at large, such occurrences were proof of the slave's inherent frivolity, their contented status, the appropriateness of their subjugation, and the success of traditional slaveholder management techniques. Slaves may have known or suspected as much, but they heartily enjoyed the opportunities given them to wrest a moment of pleasure from a degrading system and wield it to their greatest advantage under the circumstances.[51]

Slaves found both evidence of oppression and opportunities for solace in religion. Even if slaves were sometimes coerced into its practice, Christianity gave hope of a glorious release from their condition in the future, and allowed the enslaved to focus their attention on eternal rather than immediate concerns. It allowed for another form of individual expression and the elevation of a unique type of community leader—the slave preacher—who held sway within a sanctioned forum where the troubles of life and the meaning of brotherhood in Christ could be openly discussed and assuage daily angst. Yet religion could also be among the most striking aspects of the authority under which bondsmen lived, as slaveholders attempted to edit those same messages and have them packaged in a way that reinforced the existence of slavery rather than pointing out its inequities. It proved a difficult line to walk for both parties, and religious instruction and spirituality became a front in the struggle over the parameters of slavery. Especially in the later years of the period under discussion, church attendance in mixed congregations became more and more a part of the fabric of slavery in Mississippi. Blacks participated in the state's early camp meetings, and commonly worshipped as part of its congregations throughout the antebellum era. They sometimes even outnumbered whites in church settings. Many slaveholders forced slaves to attend services at local churches, but others assembled in makeshift chapels on the plantation grounds. In either case, during the territorial period and the first decades of statehood, a significant portion of slaves would have been ministered to by a black preacher in an all-slave congregation, often built and encouraged by an affiliated white church. Increasingly in the 1820s and into the 1830s, following sensational cases of rebellion elsewhere, whites began to place restrictions on slaves' worship and most were forced into biracial congregations where what they heard could be more closely monitored.[52]

Deep, abiding fear lay at the heart of the administration of the institution of slavery. Regardless of what masters might publicly say or want to believe about the system of bondage they oversaw, they knew slaves were not always happy living under such conditions. Slaveholders worried what this situation might mean both to their bottom lines, and, occasionally, even their lives. "We repose on a volcano," observed an editor of the *Vicksburg Register*, noting with uncommon forthrightness the precarious nature of life within the slave regime. Even early in the territorial years, Governor David Holmes had confided in a letter that "Scarcely a day passes without my receiving some information relative to the designs of those people [slaves] to insurrect." In order to prevent slaves from plotting against them in various ways, slaveholders attempted to carefully monitor and proscribe almost every activity by their slaves off the plantation grounds, presuming such scheming less unlikely to occur within the sight of slaveholders. They set up an elaborate series of laws meant to facilitate control, which in theory would both restrict opportunities for slaves to engage in undesired activities and force their fellow slaveowners to observe agreed-upon practices and procedures. While permitted to travel on errands for their masters, for example, slaves were legally required to have in their possession a pass from their slaveholder stating the purpose of their business when out on the roads. Enforcement of a patrol system proved extremely ineffective, but its existence demonstrated a deep suspicion among slaveowners of unsupervised slaves. Equally revealing were strict prohibitions placed on virtually any gathering of slaves outside of their residence except for attendance at church. Even whites who were caught with slaves at an unlawful assembly could be severely punished, as their presence would have suggested some nefarious scheme being plotted.[53]

Slaveholders lived in utter fear of slave rebellion. The mere discussion of insurrection struck terror in Mississippi's white community, and led to constant, and at times almost irrational efforts to suppress it before it started. Many whites believed that organized slave uprisings were possible, indeed even likely. This perhaps reveals much about white citizens' true understanding of the slaves' situation and their capacities. Actual events provided more than enough fuel to stoke the fire of hysteria, for slaveholders were keenly aware of famous slave rebellions such as the German Coast Uprising near New Orleans (1811), the plot by Denmark Vessey in Charleston (1822), and Nat Turner's Rebellion in Virginia (1831). They also heard enough about isolated local instances of slaves resisting masters with force or scheming for their harm to be sensitive to the slightest sign of uprising. The excitement around the famed fictitious insurrection manufactured by a gentleman named Virgil Stewart demonstrated how quickly rumor could spark widespread panic.[54]

The affair began in 1833 when Stewart became involved in an effort to apprehend a known criminal named John Murrell who had been suspected of stealing a slave in Tennessee. In large part due to Stewart's testimony, Murrell was convicted and sentenced to ten years in prison. In 1835, Stewart published a highly fanciful account of his experience under a pen name as *A History of the Detection, Conviction, Life and Designs of John A. Murel* [sic], *The Great Western Land Pirate*, in which he claimed Murrell to be a criminal mastermind in charge of a regional secret society known as the "Mystic Clan," which was bent on organizing a massive slave rebellion that would destroy Southern society. The tale sparked incredible fear throughout Mississippi and much of the Southwest, leading to violent attempts to purge gamblers (specifically named as accessories in the supposed plot) from several Mississippi towns and contributing to a particularly sordid affair in Madison County that took on the air of a witch hunt. People in the vicinity of the community of Livingston became so convinced that a plot associated with Murrell was underway in their community in the wake of a visit by Stewart, who came attempting to sell his publication, that they actually apprehended a number of slaves and beat them until they confessed to being a part of a hazy plot. Evidence suggests that a few local slaves may indeed have had designs on harming some white persons in the community, or at least fantasized about doing as much, but any association with their discontent and Murrell was pure fabrication. The speed with which this isolated incident came to be believed as proof of a larger, region-wide violent uprising was shocking even for the time. Vigilance Committees quickly formed and canvassed the region for suspects, assuming guilt and certain they would discover a well-organized plan to murder the white population. Multiple searches and interrogations ultimately led to dozens of whippings, a few white men being banished from the area, and as many as eight whites and twenty slaves being hanged. The reverberations of the affair spread across the state, and in the end this and similar affairs played no small part in a wholesale redefinition of the institution of slavery by white society.[55]

During the decade between 1830 and 1840, Mississippians, along with other Southerners, changed their public stance on slavery from defending it as a "necessary evil" to advocating for it as a "positive good." From the time of Mississippi's organization as a territory, there had been some level of internal moral struggle about the institution of slavery among its leaders and most influential citizens. These people certainly were not abolitionists by any stretch of the imagination, but many regarded bondage as an unfortunate necessity in their society. The state was born in the era of the Enlightenment, and few of the most informed people proved willing at the time to link ideal societal advancement and human bondage as forever inseparable. They openly acknowledged the imperfection of the practice even as they grounded their justification for its continuance in racist theories, and sometimes even countenanced its inevitable end at some point in the distant future when a better labor system could be determined. This equivocation, at turns strained moral justification and postponement of effecting any sort of change, manifested itself throughout early Mississippi society. Both elected officials and clergy at times openly questioned and denounced the institution.[56]

Acceptance of the institution proved infectious despite the occasional debate over its appropriateness; few people of any means could avoid either being associated with it in some manner or partaking in the financial opportunities it presented. One Mississippi preacher, Thomas Griffin perhaps said it best when he noted with a touch of sarcasm the remarkable philosophical transformation of northerners who came to the state during the early statehood years. In a letter published in a Natchez paper, he observed that "when they first come among us, it seems as if they could see us all damned and double-damned, rammed, crammed and jammed into a forty-six pounder and blown into the fiery vaults of a deep damnation for being connected with slavery! . . . But in twelve months time they became a leetle [*sic*] smoother on the subject, and if they contemplate a permanent stay . . . are sure to form alliances with our slave-holding families . . ."[57]

Griffin might have been as harsh on his fellow clergy, as they were among the most hypocritical in explaining slavery's place in their society. Religious leaders were the most vocal in the admittedly limited efforts decrying the imperfection of the institution, but they could not bring themselves to advocate any measure that might in reality lead to its eventual extinction. Leading religious figure William Winans epitomized this position by acknowledging that, while not in favor of slavery, he believed that emancipation would "ruin them [slaves] absolutely, and . . . endanger the very existence of the Nation." Political leaders who dared to raise any concern about the institution during Mississippi's early statehood years sounded much the same. Popular statesman Seargent S. Prentiss decried the institution as a "great pest" to Southern society for having rendered it "disgraceful for a white man to do any kind of hard labor." But he could see no way to ever end the system. The Mississippi legislature, in an 1826 report on slavery spurred by emancipation efforts in other states, gave as the state's position on the institution a description of involuntarily servitude as a "national evil" that circumstances had regrettably rendered "inevitable." "The Southern states," the legislature observed, "who suffer and are compelled by circumstances to endure the evil, ought to be the best judges of the remedy; and as soon as they can concur in any expedient for their relief it will be time enough to adopt it." Until such time, if it ever arrived at all, "the right of property in slaves" would continue "sacred and inviolate." Even Governor Gerard C. Brandon referred to the institution as "an evil at best," and requested that the legislature prohibit the introduction of slaves for sale in the state, as the institution "invariably operated oppressively on the poorer classes of every community." Yet citizens held neither Brandon nor the state legislature in suspicion of harboring abolitionist sentiments at the time.[58]

Within a few years such language from state leadership would be unimaginable. The supposed Murrell conspiracy and other unrest during the decade, deemed the result of abolitionist agitation, forced a reevaluation of slavery in its society. These events and trends left Mississippians extremely touchy about any apparent attempt to call into question the appropriateness of slavery or any action that might be viewed as an effort to persuade slaves they might better their lot outside of bondage. It was entirely a defensive position, with no creditable moral argument in favor of the institution of slavery. Eventually finding one in a peculiar evangelical worldview, they ensured Mississippi's societal trajectory would place it at odds politically with much of the rest of the nation.

The move toward the sanctification of slavery in Mississippi had many points of origin, but its most mature expression can be found in a debate over the propriety of slavery in a Christian society among the leadership of the Presbyterian Church. In 1835 Rev. John P. Vandyke of Chillicothe, Ohio, sent a letter to Mississippian's Presbyterian establishment pointing out the hypocrisy of church members in the South owning slaves. Claiming the practice would divide the church, the letter pointed out the incompatibility of slavery and Christian teaching. While many in Mississippi were enraged by the accusations contained within the letter as well as its condescending tone, few were prepared to offer an intelligent response based in religious scholarship.

Rev. James Smylie of Port Gibson, Mississippi, became the individual who put into words the philosophy that would allow Mississippians to promulgate an argument that slavery was a benefit to whites and blacks. Smylie had drafted a philosophical reply to the letter from Chillicothe in 1836 that managed to both defend southern Christians and provide a moral argument for slavery that would allow evangelicals to embrace the institution as part of God's plan. Smylie, himself a plantation slaveholder who owned dozens of slaves, found throughout the Bible evidence of slavery he used to develop his response. In his view, and that of a growing number of others at the time, bondage could be justified by an interpretation of the disputed "Curse of Ham" (a son of the patriarch Noah) referenced in a passage in the book of Genesis. For an act of sin by Ham, his son Canaan, and his descendants, widely understood in the nineteenth century as a reference to people with black skin, are described as being relegated to the status of "a servant of servants." Armed with this and the knowledge that slavery could be understood as an integral part of societies discussed throughout the Bible, many reached the conclusion that it must be part of God's plan for mankind.[59]

Smylie's response went a step further than merely pointing out historical references. He equated the master-slave relationship to that of a parent and child, and stressed the reciprocal responsibilities of slaveowners and the enslaved as equal instruments of God's plan. In this new social gospel, slavery was both natural and righteous, part of a divine order for society that Christians decried at their peril. Smylie first advanced this position in public in a sermon delivered in Port Gibson. Even there, among his closest friends, the reception was initially a little frosty. The argument at first seemed a little too bold for many, who for decades had been apologizing for slavery as an unfortunate part of the human experience. Promulgated in a pamphlet that ultimately enjoyed wide distribution throughout the state and region, however, Smylie's reasoning gradually gained traction in a society awkwardly searching for just the type of justification it provided. Crucially, the thought process that slavery might be a "positive good" caught on among many evangelical leaders, who found convincing Smylie's emphasis on the primacy of scripture and his outline of God's plan reassuringly compatible with the world in which they lived. Within a few years, the argument contained within "Smylie's Pamphlet" came to dominate religious thought on the topic of slavery across the Deep South and soon became promulgated in pulpits across the region. The position originally advanced by Smylie allowed slavery's practitioners, so long on the defensive, to take the offensive against the abolitionists in the North.[60]

Mississippi's pro-slavery evangelical stance had the unexpected side effect of spurring robust activity within the state chapter of the American Colonization Society (ACS). Founded in 1816 in New Jersey, the ACS sought to "return" free blacks in the United States to Africa on the premise that American society held no place for them. The group created the colony of Liberia on the African continent and began sending freed slaves there in 1820. A curious alliance of liberal-minded thinkers on race and diehard slaveholders across the nation supported the concept, for very different reasons. The former believed removing former slaves to Africa would offer them the best chance to lead dignified lives, and some among them held out hope it might even be a first step toward a broader resolution of the divisive issue of slavery domestically. The latter endorsed the plan as a way to free the country of unwanted free blacks whom they viewed with a jaundiced eye as at best encouraging slave discontent and at worst fomenting outright rebellion. In Mississippi, several prominent leaders became active in the organization, including Stephen Duncan, Dr. John Ker, Cowles Mead, Governor Gerard C. Brandon, and a host of ministers throughout the region including William Winans. Not coincidentally, the group's support within Mississippi came predominantly from the Natchez region, which in 1830 contained about half of all free blacks residing in the state and where slaves outnumbered whites nearly two to one.[61]

While there had been members of the ACS working in Mississippi as early as the mid-1820s, the group began its most energetic work in 1831 in the wake of a visit by the organization's agent Henry B. Bascom. By 1832 the Mississippi Colonization Society, the state chapter of the ACS, working with local county-based auxiliary organizations, began sending free blacks to Liberia. The group's well-heeled supporters, sensing an urgency to their mission in the wake of news of slave revolts elsewhere and rumors of other plots, raised a substantial amount of money for the scheme and made Mississippi one of the most active ACS state chapters in the nation. By 1835 the Mississippi chapter of the ACS had financed the founding of a separate African colony, "Mississippi in Africa." While most active prior to 1837, the Mississippi Colonization Society ultimately sent over 500 free blacks to Africa, more than any other Deep South state except Georgia, and accounted for one in every twenty sent by the ACS in general. Perhaps the most noted endeavor the ACS became associated with in Mississippi actually concerned the purchasing and sending to Africa of a bondsman named Prince Abdul Rahman Ibrahima. An African prince who had been captured and sold into slavery in the late 1700s, Ibrahima was discovered in an incredible coincidence on a plantation near Natchez by an Irishman who knew him and verified his true identity. Through the help of President John Quincy Adams, in 1829 the ACS facilitated the repatriation of the man who has been called "Mississippi's most famous slave."[62]

While the efforts to relocate people of color form a colorful sidelight in Mississippi's formative era, they of course involved an extraordinarily small portion of its populace. By 1840 Mississippi claimed some 375,000 inhabitants—over 195,000 of them enslaved—and just a scattering of Native Americans who had managed to evade removal. The lives of virtually all were tied in some way to the unique pattern of development the state had pursued since its territorial days. It was a course of growth heavily reliant on agriculture and in large part facilitated by the dispossession of Native Americans of their ancestral lands and the forced labor of enslaved blacks.[63]

CHAPTER 8

An Agricultural Economy

Mississippians have notably been tied to the land for much of the state's history, and the story of its early development cannot be told without an understanding of the agricultural practices that underlay its economy and consumed the working lives of a large portion of its population. That historic dependence on agriculture, heavily influenced by the cultivation of a single crop—cotton—almost to the detriment of any other enterprise, first took root in the frontier era. Development of Mississippi's agricultural economy within the time period therefore established patterns and practices that would not only impact its course at the time, but hold sway in the state for generations.

While cotton production eventually became the undisputed focus of agricultural pursuits within the state, its dominance did not appear a foregone conclusion at the time of the formation of the Mississippi Territory. Contrary to common assumption, the primary agricultural pursuit of a substantial portion of early Mississippians at the time was herding, not cotton production. Herdsmen were "the typical southern pioneers," in the words of historian Frank L. Owsley, and usually formed the vanguard of western migration to the Old Southwest. Commonly of limited means and unable to afford the choice river lands upon which would be built the foundations of Mississippi's future cotton kingdom, these early agriculturalists happily occupied less desirable tracts from which they extracted a modest living from large herds of semi-wild cattle and hogs. They collected these animals for sale yearly via a "round-up of the sort familiar to all admirers of cowboy fiction." Herding had certainly taken place within what became Mississippi during its colonial years, but herding as a profession did not explode in the region until the formation of the Mississippi Territory.[1]

The huge swaths of open land made available to American settlers in the Mississippi Territory happened to be suited perfectly to open range grazing. It became a way of life for several generations. Surveyor Andrew Ellicott, who traced the line demarcating US and Spanish territory when the region transferred to American control in the 1790s, noted that he found "the cattle in the settlement of Natchez . . . are extremely numerous, and it is not uncommon for the wealthy planters to possess from one to two hundred head and sometimes more." By the late 1820s the Choctaw Nation within Mississippi alone laid claim to over 43,000 cattle. Claims filed for damages during the Creek War of 1813–14 reveal widespread herding activity among small farmers during the territorial days, as numerous claimants had the largest portion of their wealth tied up in cattle and hogs. Dozens owned herds of 300–500 head of cattle, and most claimants owned smaller but substantial numbers of hogs. Samuel Mims, whose modest estate became the scene of one of the war's most bitter and famous contests, himself owned over 400 cattle and 200 hogs. Travelers commonly observed herds of over 2,000 belonging to individual families on their journeys in the region throughout the territorial and early statehood periods. By 1840 hogs and cattle outnumbered people four to one in most counties of the state, and in a few counties that ratio approached over a dozen to one. The roughly twenty counties of southeastern Mississippi's "Piney Woods" region served as the epicenter of the state's herding activity. Longleaf pine country was largely unsuitable for cotton culture, but it contained enormous tracts of public lands perfectly suited for grazing and within easy reach of coastal markets.[2]

Herding remained a principal industry in much of Mississippi throughout the period prior to 1840 due to its simplicity and the demand for its products. With little more than a block of salt and some occasional supplemental corn, its practitioners could allow huge herds to graze freely in the sparsely settled countryside and earn a living with considerably less risk and labor than farmers. The fields and forest abounded with grasses, reeds, roots, nuts, and other forage necessary to sustain hogs and cattle, seemingly free for the taking, and the demand for beef and pork proved constant. Planters devoted their time and resources almost exclusively to the cultivation of cotton and hence were more than willing to purchase meat from herders, while urban centers including New Orleans, Natchez, and Mobile had large and growing populations prepared to pay for fresh meat.[3]

While few who herded for a living became wealthy, the vast majority earned enough to sustain themselves comfortably. Other residents of Mississippi, such as lawyer and author William Henry Sparks, tended to look down on these people as "careless of the comforts of the better reared," and many visitors observed with some contempt the hordes of apparently slothful "poor whites" lolling about their crude houses and unkempt yards in the Mississippi countryside, surmising them to be indigent. They noted the small, ragged patches of gardens where they grew just enough quantities of fruits and vegetables for sustenance and deemed them lazy at best and profligate at worst. "In no country that ever I have seen," recorded one disdainful observer, "is so little attention paid to comfortable living, as among the common people of Louisiana and Mississippi. . . . The men are generally idle, devoted to hunting, and the attention of their numerous herds. . . ." While there may have been some truth in these observations, many settlers undoubtedly enjoyed the herder lifestyle and its demands for merely occasional exertion.[4]

Most of the labor associated with herding involved the yearly or semi-yearly drives to major markets. In roundups that sound more like something out of the American West than the Gulf South, herds were collected in temporary pens, fattened with corn, and branded before being driven long distances into trading centers for purchase. Drives, which often lasted several weeks, involved teams of whip-cracking men on horseback traipsing through the countryside guiding hundreds of animals toward their destination. Upon arrival at a market, frequently a Gulf Coast port city, prices were negotiated with traders and the animals slaughtered for fresh meat. Surplus hides and tallow were packaged and shipped elsewhere, often to the West Indies.[5]

In his colorful description of the cattle drives of southeastern Mississippi, J. F. H. Claiborne calls up visions of the wild west of American lore:

> Half a dozen of them [herders] assemble, mounted on low built, shaggy, but muscular and hardy horses of that region, and armed with raw hide whips of prodigious size, and sometimes with a catching rope or lasso, plaited of horsehair. They scour the woods in gallant style, followed by a dozen fierce looking dogs; they dash through swamps and morass, deep ravines and swim rivers, sometimes driving a herd of a thousand heads to the pen, or singling out and separating with surprising dexterity a solitary steer which has become incorporated with another herd. In this way, cheering each other with loud shouts and making the woods ring with the crack of their long whips and the trampling of the flying cattle, they gallop thirty or forty miles a day and rendezvous at night at the stamping ground. Here they "bivouac" in the open air, a fire of light wood logs is soon kindled, that flings its blaze far into the depths of the forest; a young steer, or perhaps a fat buck that has been killed during the ride, is speedily cut into stalks and set upon sticks before the fire to broil . . . after a . . . little chuckling over the accidents of the day, they stretch themselves around the blazing fire on skins or blankets, contented, happy and at peace with all the world.[6]

As the population of Mississippi continued to rise in the 1820s and 1830s and farms appeared in every corner of the countryside, herders found themselves gradually restricted in their activities, and scenes such as the one Claiborne witnessed became increasingly rare. There were simply fewer and fewer tracts of available public lands on which to graze their animals as time progressed, and those that could be utilized quickly became overgrazed. As a consequence of this combination of factors, the once-thriving enterprise of herding entered a rapid decline by 1840 and soon became a forgotten way of life.[7]

Cotton production eventually supplanted herding, and any other agricultural pursuit, in virtually every corner of the state. Efforts to establish a cash crop in colonial-era Mississippi had a long and checkered history by the time the area came under American control. Tobacco, indigo, and other crops had been attempted, but none achieved long-lasting success until the widespread cultivation of cotton on Mississippi soil combined with the tools necessary to harvest and process it profitably. "The economic history of Mississippi, more than that of any other state, is the history of cotton," John Hebron Moore observed candidly in his landmark study *Agriculture in Ante-Bellum Mississippi*. Already on the rise as a cash crop in the region prior to the assumption of American control, cotton came to pervade every aspect of life in the state within a matter of a few decades, commanding the bulk of its labor, a substantial portion of its capital, a large percentage of its land, and animating the activities, thoughts, and even dreams of the majority of its residents. From being a nominal producer of the crop in the 1790s, Mississippi became one of the largest cotton producers in the nation by 1840. "Cotton," wryly but tellingly noted a visitor in one of the more celebrated accounts of travel within the antebellum state, became "the constant theme—the ever harped upon, never worn out subject of conversation among all classes."[8]

Cotton had been grown on a small scale in what became Mississippi as early as the 1720s by European settlers and even longer by native groups, but it did not begin to become a staple crop until the convergence of two successive developments in the early territorial years; the introduction of a hearty strain relatively easy to cultivate and the invention of the cotton gin. A modest amount of cotton had been grown during Spain's control of Mississippi, almost all of it in the vicinity of Natchez, but varieties available to planters proved highly susceptible to disease and required enormous amounts of labor to prepare for market. A variety known as "Georgia Sea Island" had been the standard throughout Mississippi's colonial years, but its small bolls and the difficulties involved in cleaning it (separating lint from seeds) kept it from being grown on a large scale. Other varieties such as "green seed," "Georgia Upland," and "Tennessee Upland" were cultivated to varying degrees of success prior to about 1810. All of these gave way virtually overnight to a strain generally known as "Mexican" cotton, which seemed to combine the best of all known varieties—it demonstrated resistance to the cotton crop-killing fungus known as "rot," grew fast, had large bolls that could be easily picked, and yielded itself to much easier cleaning. Experimented with and adapted to Mississippi's particular circumstances by enterprising agriculturalists, this Mexican cotton, eventually known as "Petit Gulf" in honor of the area of southwestern Mississippi where it was perfected, quickly became the standard in the state, and eventually in the American South as a whole.[9]

The story of the introduction of Mexican cotton into Mississippi is engrained in state lore. It all began when a man from Natchez named Walter Burling, an associate of the infamous Aaron Burr and General James Wilkinson, traveled on a special mission to Mexico City in 1806 on behalf of would-be separatists during the height of the intrigues over their rumored schemes to carve an independent nation out of the American southwest. Somehow gaining an audience with the Viceroy of New Spain, Burling allegedly delivered a letter from Wilkinson, already a secret agent for Spain, requesting money for persuading Burr to not include Spain's holdings in Mexico in the scheme. Rebuffed, Burling nonetheless managed to leave Mexico City with something that would unexpectedly change the course of state history. Burling had noticed stands of a particular type of cotton being grown in Mexico during his travels and had attempted to obtain a quantity of the seed to take back home to the Mississippi Territory. Although such exportation was illegal, the viceroy allowed him to take several seed-stuffed handmade dolls with him as "souvenirs." The details of how Burling distributed this seed upon arrival at home are lost to history, but soon several planters in the vicinity of Natchez were experimenting with the new variety of cotton he had introduced. Dr. Rush Nutt, of the community of Petit Gulf (later Rodney), became particularly active in working with the seed. Through a series of trials, experimentation, and cross-breeding of carefully selected seed, Nutt succeeded in developing a strain of cotton that proved to be the catalyst for the lion's share of Mississippi's agricultural enterprises for over a century.[10]

"Cotton mania" soon swept over Mississippi. As early as 1799, planters such as William Dunbar were exulting over the change the crop had already wrought through early experimentation, proclaiming cotton ". . . by far the most profitable crop we have ever undertaken in this country. The climate and soil suit it exactly, and I am of opinion that the fiber, already so fine in quality, will be still better when our lands are well cleared and the soil properly triturated." The lands were indeed cleared and prepared for cultivation throughout the state in short order, and production progressively skyrocketed. In 1800 around 2,000 bales of cotton were produced in Mississippi; in 1816 about 24,000 bales; in 1820 around 49,000; in 1836 over 300,000; in 1840 over 500,000. Observers such as Joseph Holt Ingraham, writing in the 1830s, noted with only a slight degree of sarcasm that not until the state became "one vast cotton field" would the cotton craze, which had "entered into the very marrow, bone and sinew of a Mississippian's system, pass away."[11]

To know the process by which Mississippians grew and harvested cotton is to understand the daily rhythms of labor for a large portion of the population of all classes, especially the enslaved, and the special skills they acquired. The cultivation of the fiber demanded almost year-round activity, especially so when it involved new fields that had to be cleared of trees and undergrowth early in the year before planting. Using mules and sometimes horses, fields were plowed in preparation for planting in the spring, usually around early April. If the field had been previously cultivated, furrows would be run between those of the prior year, approximately three feet apart. Seeds would be placed in these furrows at regular intervals of about four feet, and a light harrow run to cover them. Once the seedlings began to emerge, the fields would be "scraped" to clear them of any grass that might have begun to grow and later "chopped" or "thinned" so that the young cotton plants stood about a foot apart in the rows. In early summer, the fields would be chopped and thinned a second time to allow only the heartiest plants to grow to maturity. In mid-summer, the soil around the remaining plants would be loosed with a hoe and the crop "laid by." From then until harvest, occasional scraping would be performed to keep any grass from growing. The first bolls opened around September and picking began in earnest by October. The work got progressively heavier deeper into the season as more and more bolls ripened, usually well into November across the state and into December and even January in some places.[12]

While representing only a portion of all early Mississippi farms, plantations and the planters who operated them came to dominate the cotton economy. Slaves performed the great majority of the backbreaking labor involved in cotton production on larger farms and plantations throughout the state, often in large work gangs but sometimes in smaller groups of just a few people. Its drudgery consumed lives as it wore down human frames and crushed spirits regardless of the size of the working group. During the peak cotton picking season in the fall, work on some of the larger plantations might begin hours before daylight and continue until dark had enveloped the fields. Slaves stooped over harvesting the crop that greased the wheels of the state's economy in the hot sun of late summer, in the cool, damp mornings of fall, and in the frigid afternoons of early winter, frequently under the watchful eye of an overseer more than willing to apply the lash should there be an appearance of slacking. Gathered in sacks at the end of rows, the cotton was weighed, often multiple times a day, before being emptied into wagons to be hauled to a gin. Conditions of course varied from plantation to plantation, but if ever there was a line of labor that demanded the working of one's fingers to the proverbial bone, it was cotton production. Thorny bolls occasionally pricked fingers, and the sheer repetitive nature of the enterprise wore down those digits and painfully taxed arms, legs, and backs. Early in the territorial period, before the introduction of the Mexican cotton strain, a laborer might pick anywhere from fifty to eighty pounds of the fiber per day working in this manner, depending on the variety being grown. Once the Mexican variety came under widespread cultivation, production skyrocketed. Slaves could commonly pick 150 or even 200 pounds of the fiber per day, and in some circumstances up to 300. Planters deemed four to eight bales per hand per season to be productive.[13]

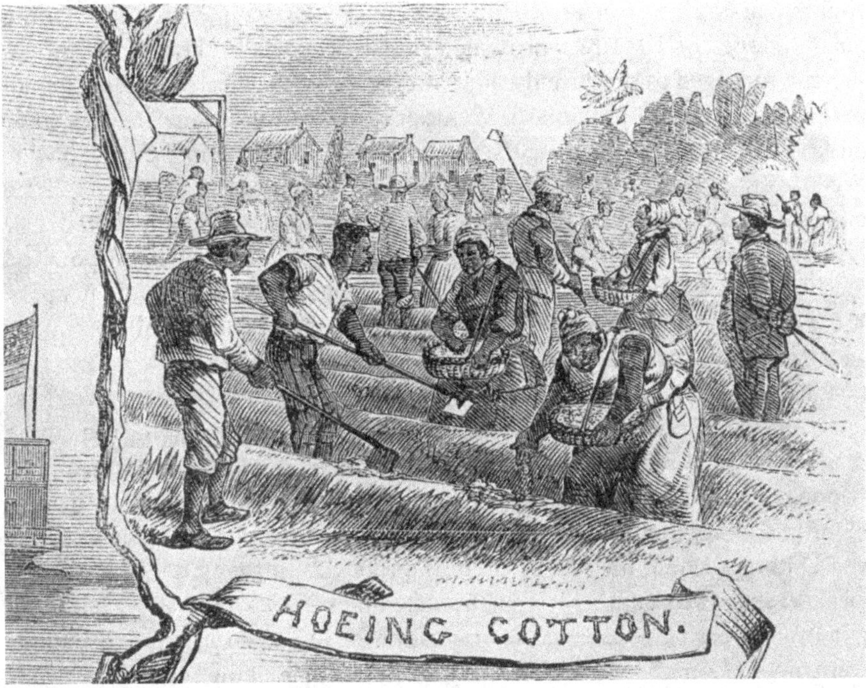

Figure 8.1. Slaves performing tasks associated with cotton agriculture. (Courtesy of Mississippi Department of Archives and History)

Innovations in the tools used by laborers steadily increased the amount of cotton that could be grown on any given plot of land. A number of horse-drawn implements developed specifically for cotton production were introduced to Mississippi cotton fields prior to 1840, including a variety of plows, harrows, sweeps, cultivators, and scrapers that allowed for maintenance of larger and larger stands of cotton. Regardless of any mechanical advancements, workers cultivated the overwhelming majority of crops throughout the period with hoes and picked every one of the bolls by hand. Under normal conditions, planters could expect every cultivated acre to yield from 1,000 to 2,000 pounds of cotton a season—about 250 to 500 pounds cleaned and ready for market.[14]

The process of cleaning all this cotton, or removing the multiple small black seeds from each boll, was inherently a tedious, labor-intensive endeavor. The time and expense required to do so by hand would probably have prevented cotton from becoming a major cash crop without a technological breakthrough, regardless of the variety grown, because of the impracticality of ever producing the quantities required for substantial trade by any but the wealthiest of planters. That equation changed almost overnight with the invention of the cotton gin by Eli Whitney in 1793. There had been many efforts at creating a reliable machine that could separate cotton seed from lint predating Whitney's innovation, including one developed on the Krebs plantation near Pascagoula in the 1770s. Whitney, though, managed to produce the practical and easily replicated gin that would revolutionize cotton processing. Variations of Whitney's gin, produced after observing his patented models elsewhere, arrived in Mississippi during Spain's occupation of what would become the Mississippi Territory. The first machine built on the Whitney principle to be used in the state was demonstrated near Natchez in the fall of 1795. Featuring rotating wire "fingers," the hand-powered machine drew cotton bolls into narrow slits through which seeds could not pass. A series of brushes swept the seeds away as it operated. As a small committee gathered for the demonstration looked on, the machine cleaned a reported eight pounds of cotton in less than fifteen minutes. The effect must have been electric, as those observers could not have helped but realize they were observing something that had the potential to change the economic future of the region immediately. "Upon the whole," they reported, "we are of opinion that this invention will prove of infinite utility to this Province, and has very far surpassed our most sanguine expectations." Under the best of circumstances, cleaning cotton by hand might yield seventy-five pounds per day. The gin could easily clean 500.[15]

A major reason for the sudden success of the gin lay in its relatively simple construction. A number of enterprising locals throughout the South successfully copied Whitney's invention within a few years of its introduction. In Mississippi, planter Daniel Clark is generally credited with being the first to produce a version of Whitney's gin on his Sligo Plantation near Fort Adams. A small team of workmen were apparently involved in the process, in one version of the story interestingly including a slave named Barclay. Little is known of the exact design or appearance of the machine other than that its builders utilized hoe blades in producing hand-cut saws that mimicked those of Whitney's design as understood through drawings, produced by a traveler from Georgia. Other planters soon copied Clark's homemade gin, and its pattern became something of an ad hoc standard in early Mississippi. Variants of this early design underwent later modification for service in larger and larger machines powered by horses and mules, water wheels, and eventually, steam engines. Much of the entire enterprise occurred in direct violation of patent rules, but such technicalities would not have deterred the homegrown engineers in the territory even had they fully understood them. By the time of the transfer of the region from Spanish to American control in 1798, several planters had homemade gins in operation in the Natchez region. For instance, David Greenleaf had begun a gin production business prior to that time and later built the first public toll gin at Selsertown. Production of a variety of sorts and sizes of gins became a small but important industry in southwest Mississippi in the early territorial years, with noted ginwrights—a new professional avocation—such as Eleazer Carver at the forefront. By 1800 virtually every

Figure 8.2. Drawing of large cotton press, 1870s. (Courtesy of the Library of Congress)

large plantation in the Natchez District had a gin, and as time progressed, large gin operations could be found in just about every crossroads community in the state where multiple plantations could be found. They grew larger as they became more numerous, with two-story gins eventually becoming the norm.[16]

Ginning served as a key cog in the complicated system of the cotton economy in which growers, ginners, wagoners, commission merchants, and shippers all played a role. After being ginned and baled, cotton was transported to warehouses in regional trading centers, where commission merchants negotiated a price and arranged to have it eventually shipped on to ports in America or Europe. In the territorial years, this first step usually involved transportation via keelboat, flatboat, or steamboat to New Orleans or Mobile, where agents of the larger trading houses were located. Later, cities such as Natchez, Port Gibson, and Vicksburg became large cotton markets in their own right, connected via the mighty Mississippi to worldwide markets. Cargoes of thousands of bales, valued at well over one million dollars each, were not unusual. Commission merchants in trading centers, who generally charged a fee of about 2.5 percent of the total sale on each transaction, determined when to sell the crop at maximum profit. This process often required holding the cotton in the warehouse for sale at a later date. Until the sale to trading houses in such places as Liverpool, England, they extended credit to the planters with which they did business, facilitating the purchase of supplies needed for the production of the next year's crop such as blankets, bagging and rope, hoes and plows, and a variety of clothing and food for enslaved workers. A few adventurous planters did attempt to arrange for direct shipment of their crops to European ports from Mississippi, desiring to cut out the proverbial middleman. However, these efforts generally failed, and the system established early on prevailed throughout the period and well into the nineteenth century.[17]

All this ginning activity wrought a sea change not only in the way planters marketed their product, but also became a fundamental component of Mississippi's economy. Because of the backlog at many gins, cotton began to be sold while still in the possession of the ginner, positioning ginning operations as a sort of middleman in the trade of the staple. Early large-scale ginners commonly charged a fee amounting to one-tenth of the total unprocessed crop for their services. They calculated a quarter of the total raw cotton being cleaned lint and were aware that ginning more than doubled, at least, the value of cotton and guaranteed its sale. During Mississippi's territorial years, seed cotton generally traded for about $4 per hundred pounds, whereas cleaned cotton sold for $25 per hundred pounds. Early on, receipts from ginners became accepted as a form of currency; such receipts represented a sort of promissory note on the certain cash return on any given load of cotton. These financial instruments were in use in some places prior to 1800, and by the 1820s had become so ubiquitous that the state legislature took measures to regulate their circulation. As early as 1807, the territorial legislature pronounced them legal tender. Negotiable by law, they were accepted by merchants for purchases of goods, and even traded with a value of $5 per hundred pounds of cotton delivered to the gin for processing.[18]

"Cotton money" associated with ginning served such a vital role in early Mississippi's economy because it operated largely without actual circulating tender of any other sort. Items were traded rather than bought in many instances, since hard money could be scarce. As Mississippi's steady economic growth turned into a boom in the second decade of statehood, complex financing of larger and larger land sales, the building of homes and businesses, and the buying of slaves demanded amounts of capital that receipts for a year's crop of cotton could not supply. Consequently, when Mississippi entered the banking era, it did so with a vengeance. A sudden proliferation of banks in the mid-1830s all hedged their bets for success on perpetual economic growth.[19]

A lone bank served all of Mississippi's needs for over two decades—the Bank of the State of Mississippi. Chartered in 1809 as the Bank of Mississippi and renamed in 1818 to reflect a revised charter that allowed it to function as an instrument of the state, the institution received official permission from the legislature to operate with a monopoly on banking within the state until 1840. Headquartered in Natchez, it also operated branches at Port Gibson and Woodville. The failure to extend its physical presence into eastern Mississippi or even make many loans outside of the Natchez region led to much criticism from the most rapidly growing sections of the state, and as early as 1821, the institution came under both popular and political attack. Sound almost to a fault, in truth the bank operated so conservatively that it became viewed as actually restricting, rather than facilitating, economic growth in the state. In an attempt to expand credit and more equitably spread it around the state, as well as to ensure the state would continue to be a major player in banking even if a branch of the Bank of the United States eventually opened in the state at the time, the legislature in 1830 chartered the Planters' Bank of Mississippi. This action stood in direct contradiction to the charter of the Bank of the State of Mississippi, which had guaranteed no other bank in the state for another decade. The state's dynamic growth and spiking demand for credit required additional banking services, however, which would allow planters to acquire and put under cultivation more and more tracts of the state's rich cotton lands. The state asserted its involvement in the Planters' Bank from the start, by owning a majority of its stock and appointing a majority of the members on its board. Within a year of its establishment, it had acquired the assets of the Bank of the State of Mississippi. The Bank of the United States did open a branch in Natchez in 1831, but there was plenty of business to go around for both institutions. Together, these two banks allowed unprecedented access to capital during one of the most robust periods of economic growth in the state's history.[20]

The 1830s, in the words of one resident, "may be called the golden days of Mississippi": "It was a time of fullness of life and activity, and boundless possibilities seemed to await the hand that was adventurous enough to seize them. Cotton was the great staple. Credit was universal. . . ." Likened to a gold rush by historians of the era, the cotton-fueled economic boom the state experienced transformed its economic landscape with astonishing speed. With cotton production soaring and its prices high, land plentiful and cheap, emigration at an all-time high, and numerous and growing markets for slaves, demand for credit exploded. Its extension by those who had the money to lend proved a simple calculation, as the booming economy promised great returns for both creditor and borrower. In what one historian has described as a "frenzy of finance," no less than two dozen banks were chartered in Mississippi between 1832 and 1837 alone. These "wildcat" institutions operated on optimism and paper notes rather than sound fiscal policy and carefully measured reserve ratios, overextending themselves as a matter of course. There were a few individuals who expressed concern over the banks' shaky foundations. Some pointed out, for example, that the value of the 1834 cotton crop, upon which many if not most of these banks' loans were secured at the time, was valued at around fifteen million dollars. At the time there were only about six million dollars on deposit in financial institutions across the state. Such voices were drowned out by the bustle of unchecked growth.[21]

Overwhelmingly, the credit extended by the banks facilitated the buying of land on which more cotton could be grown and the purchase of more slaves who would tend and harvest the crop. Mississippi had experienced robust land sales since the territorial period, but the 1830s ushered in an era of land purchasing unlike anything ever seen in the state. In 1832 three Mississippi land offices sold over 260,000 acres, an impressive amount dwarfed in 1833 by the 1.1 million acres sold following the opening of former Choctaw lands in the central portion of the state. Mississippi led the nation in revenues from land sales paid into the federal treasury in both 1834 and 1835, and land offices at Mt. Salus (Clinton) and Columbus were the busiest in the country from 1833 to 1835. During that remarkable three-year period, over eight million acres of Mississippi land entered private hands from the public domain, over three million in 1836 alone. "The people here are run mad with speculation," reported one resident. "Money is scarce, but credit is plenty, and he who has no money can do as much business as he who has."[22]

The booming economy made many very wealthy in short order. "No men grow old or gray in their profession if at all successful," observed one visitor, noting how the opportunities for making money as planters surpassed any other vocation in Mississippi. With the exception of occasional short-lived economic downturns, the price of cotton generally made a steady rise throughout the early statehood years. Healthy profits encouraged more and more planters to cultivate increasingly larger crops, even though aware cotton production lay subject to the vicissitudes of nature and large financial returns were not always guaranteed. Floods, disease, insects, and drought periodically destroyed crops throughout the early statehood era, and occasional hard winters negatively impacted yields. Still, throughout the 1820s the fiber generally sold for between fourteen and eighteen cents a pound, topping twenty cents in the early 1830s and reaching a high of thirty-one cents in 1836 on the eve of the cataclysmic depression that fundamentally altered economic life in the state and much of the nation. Even that calamity could not dethrone cotton's growing stranglehold on the Mississippi economy. Already home to some of the richest planters in the South by 1840, on the eve of the Civil War Natchez famously boasted more millionaires per capita than any other city in the United States, and the state of Mississippi ranked among the wealthiest in the nation by some measures. This wealth became concentrated intensely among the state's elite and highlighted a growing income gap that foretold of future problems.[23]

Cotton, slaves, and wealth became inextricably linked during Mississippi's frontier era, and almost all who could pursued more of each. Joseph Holt Ingraham recorded the simple rule-of-thumb way he learned to gauge the wealth of planters from locals in the journal of his travels, *The Southwest, By a Yankee*:

> The southern farmer . . . works on his plantation a certain number of slaves, say thirty, which are to him what the sinewy arms of the Yankee farmer are to himself.

> Each slave ought to average from seven to eight bales of cotton during the season, especially on the new lands. An acre will generally average from one to two bales. Each bale averages four hundred pounds, at from twelve to fifteen cents a pound.... Deducting two thousand and five hundred dollars for the expenses of the plantation, there will remain the net income of eleven thousand dollars.... Incomes of twenty-thousand dollars are common here. Several individuals possess incomes of from forty to fifty thousand dollars, and live in a style commensurate with their wealth. The amount is generally expressed by the number of their negroes, and the number of "bales" they make at a crop. To know the number of either is to know accurately their incomes. And as this is easily ascertained, it is not difficult to form a prompt estimate of individual wealth.[24]

Only a small percentage of Mississippians could be categorized as large planters, but those who were held an inordinate share of wealth in the young state. The concentration of affluence among the burgeoning ranks of Mississippi's newfound planter elite proved remarkable and remains the stuff of legend. "The planters ... ride fine horses, [and] are followed by well-dressed and very aristocratic servants ...," observed a young John Anthony Quitman shortly after arriving in Natchez in the 1820s. "They live profusely: drink costly Port, Madeira, and sherry, after the English fashion, and are exceedingly hospitable. Cotton-planting is the most lucrative business that can be followed." Describing real-life scenes that helped give rise to the "moonlight and magnolias" version of the Old South, he wrote in letters to his family of visits to the homes of wealthy planters. On one sojourn in 1823 he recorded:

> Mint-juleps in the morning are sent to our rooms, and then follow a delightful breakfast in the open veranda. We hunt, ride, fish, pay morning visits, play chess, read or lounge until dinner, which is served at two P.M. in great variety, and most delicately cooked in what is here called the Creole style—very rich, and many made or mixed dishes. In two hours afterward every body—white and black—has disappeared. The whole household is asleep—the *siesta* of the Italians. The ladies retire to their apartments, and the gentlemen on sofas, settees, benches, hammocks, and often, gipsy [*sic*] fashion, on the grass under the spreading oaks. Here, too, in fine weather, the tea-table is always set before sunset, and then, until bedtime, we stroll, sing, play whist, or croquet. It is an indolent, yet charming life, and one quits thinking and takes to dreaming.[25]

On other visits he observed dinner tables set with "green peas, lettuce, radishes, artichokes, new potatoes, and spinach, grown in the open air, and roses, jessamines, jonquils, and pinks in profusion," all set within a mansion surrounded by "stately oaks" within an "extensive park" bordered by a "vast, undulating sweep

Figure 8.3. Concord plantation in Natchez, built in 1789, served as home to Spanish governors and was one of several large plantation homes built in region. (Courtesy of Mississippi Department of Archives and History)

of cultivated fields." Contemporaries elsewhere recorded multi-course dinners and dessert in the homes of the wealthy Natchez planters, with slaves standing behind every chair to provide prompt individual service.[26]

Indeed, extravagance became a hallmark of the planter lifestyle. Well-off planters conspicuously consumed European fineries that only a tiny fragment of the population could afford. Such goods were being imported directly to Natchez even during the territorial period in surprisingly large quantities. An 1801 manifest of a ship bound for the Natchez market, for example, hints at the high standard of living of the elite at an early date. Included in the cargo were 720 caskets of claret, 2,400 bottles of red wine, fifteen pipes of brandy, seventy dozen men's white silk stockings, 312 dozen kid gloves, reams of wall paper, and a variety of fine linens. Observers reported on the ubiquity of well-trained hounds and stables of horses kept on the grounds of the larger plantations, as the expensive sport of fox-hunting became both a pastime and a symbol of status.[27]

Astounded observers of such displays of wealth could not help but comment. Of his travels in southwest Mississippi, Joseph H. Ingraham noted "the extraordinary number of private carriages, clustered before the doors of the most fashionable stores, or millineries, rolling through the street, or crossing and recrossing it from those by which it is intersected, nearly every moment. . . ." None other than famed actor Tyrone Power, among the most famous and well-traveled gentlemen of his day, remembered seeing the dapper dress of the Natchez "nabobs" while on his visit to Mississippi in the 1830s. The nickname had become synonymous with great wealth and came to be applied to the top tier of the state's elite. "A finer set of men I have rarely looked upon . . . they were mostly clad in a sort of tunic or frock, made of white or grass-green blanketing, the broad dark-blue selvage serving as a binding, the coat being furnished with collar, shoulder-pieces, and cuffs of the same colour, and having a broad belt, either of leather or of the like selvage; broad-leafed white Spanish hats of beaver were evidently the mode, together with high leather leggings. . . ."[28]

Not all of the wealthy lived in well-appointed and columned mansions surrounded by well-tended grounds. Such structures, many of which survive today, existed in copious numbers in those days, but contemporaries noted that many of the richest planters lived in homes "not better than those of our common farmers." Seargent S. Prentiss recorded in his memoir on life in frontier Mississippi that planter homes were often located "two or three miles distant from each other, and each one surrounded by some ten, twenty, or thirty negro cabins, which are the very pictures of misery and filth." Others reported that while some planters "inhabit a building that would grace an English park," their grounds "are suffered to remain in their pristine rudeness." Featuring little ornamentation and often doubling as grazing lots for horses, the grounds of many early frontier-period plantations remained more unkempt than might be assumed.[29]

In addition to creating a wealthy upper class who enjoyed lifestyles few Mississippians would ever experience, generally soaring profits from cotton and an obsessive concentration on making more of both brought about a somewhat ironic circumstance: one of the nation's leading agricultural states became a net importer of food. The seemingly insatiable demand for cotton caused planters in early Mississippi to "abandon all pretense of economic self-sufficiency," in the words of one historian, as they devoted themselves wholly to the cultivation of cotton and purchased just about any provision needed from outside vendors. "A great majority of the planters, large and small," observed one traveler, "obtained their supplies on the nearest rivers from the upcountry flat boats. . . . All the industry was employed in the production of cotton." Another noted with incredulity that "although this place is surrounded by an excellent and well-cultivated country yet it wholly depends on produce from up the river, which can be had much cheaper, and for this reason the farmers do not raise corn, wheat, &c." Cotton plantations operating in this manner sprung up by the 1830s wherever the soil allowed it, which proved to be the great majority of the state. Only a few planters, such as Samuel Gibson, namesake of Port Gibson, purposefully raised everything used on his plantation with the exception of sugar and coffee. He cultivated a variety of fruits and nuts, supplied his own milk, butter, and cheese, and his wife supervised the production of slave clothing. Such thrift stood in marked contrast to the great majority of plantations in the state. Even in the territorial days, Mississippi imported much more corn, salt pork, wheat, and flour than it produced. This is not to say other crops were not cultivated, for corn and sweet potatoes were grown widely, and orchards could be seen adjacent to almost every plantation of any size. By the 1840s, for example, Mississippians grew over four bushels of sweet potatoes per capita. But owing to its mania for cotton and the food requirements of its large slave labor force, Mississippi ended up relying on outside sources for a large portion of its food prior to 1840.[30]

The seemingly heedless and accelerating rate of cotton-fueled economic growth in Mississippi proved unsustainable. When a nationwide depression struck in 1837 and stalled that progress, it devastated the state. Some form of a check on the wild speculation, too-easy credit, and spiraling inflation might have been inevitable in due time, but the brake ended up being applied abruptly by the federal government. President Andrew Jackson, in an effort to curb runaway speculation in western lands and rein in the loosely operated banks of which he famously was skeptical, issued the famed "Specie Circular" in 1836. The act required that all government lands be purchased with real money rather than paper script issued by local banks. A bursting of the proverbial bubble took place almost immediately, as the entire system of land sales undergirded by the extension of credit suddenly became unstable. Concurrent actions taken to regulate the banking industry nationwide exacerbated a difficult situation. In the Deposit and Distribution Act, the federal government placed reserves in selected local banks across the nation in a proportional formula based on representation in Congress, diverting specie from some of the largest trading centers along the east coast and consequently slowing down the pace of their lending. When New York banks suspended specie payments to investors in May 1837, the first domino fell in a chain of events that would soon reach the banks of the Mississippi. The economic crisis that ensued was felt in different regions at different times and with varying intensities, but generally persisted until the mid-1840s and represents one of the most pervasive and debilitating depressions in United States history.[31]

The gubernatorial administration of Charles Lynch (1836–38) dramatically illustrated the sudden nature of the crisis and the extent of its repercussions. When Lynch took office in January 1836 at the height of a robust economy, he did so in an elaborate inauguration ceremony that featured a formal escort to a joint session of the legislature and an installation as "the governor and commander-in-chief of the army, navy, and militia of the state of Mississippi." Lynch launched into his duties by, among other endeavors, seeking to reform the state's outdated criminal code—derided as the "Bloody Code" owing to its imposition of death as penalty for many offenses—and recommended the establishment of a state penitentiary. Only a year later all such progressive legislation was put on hold as the state attempted to deal with the disastrous consequences of the unexpected economic downturn.[32]

The wheels of Mississippi's economy came to a screeching halt in the spring of 1837. In a cascading wave of disasters, real estate values plummeted, unemployment skyrocketed, and people went bankrupt by the score. Banks, unable to cope with the run on their reserves, suspended operations, and for a time the state functioned almost entirely without them. For residents, it seemed as if the world had ended, for the very foundation of their economic life had suddenly shattered and no one appeared to have a solution. "We had no currency . . . ," according to Reuben Davis, "All the state banks were buried in . . . ruins. Commerce was suspended. Insolvency was the rule, and judgments accumulated against nearly all citizens. . . . Despair was in all faces." In more florid fashion, Joseph Glover Baldwin captured the moment by describing the crash "as if the ribs of nature broke, and a scattering like the bursting of a thousand magazines, and a smell of brimstone. . . . Men worth a million were insolvent for two millions; promising young cities marched back again into the wilderness. . . . The frolic was ended. . . ." When coupled with a gradual downturn in cotton prices, which collapsed in 1839 and only slowly improved in the early 1840s, neither planter nor yeoman farmer could turn a profit. "Gone to Texas" or "GTT" became a catchphrase in the popular lexicon, as disillusioned people by the hundreds, with no way to pay collectors for mortgages and little hope to find money anytime soon, simply packed up and moved west en masse, one step ahead of creditors.[33]

The Mississippi legislature's attempt to deal with the crisis only worsened the problem. Recognizing the inability of existing cash-strapped financial institutions to serve the needs of the state, the legislature authorized the creation of yet another bank in 1838—the Union Bank. Five million dollars in bond sales financed the start-up of the bank, enabling it to begin making loans immediately. Outside investors bought millions of dollars' worth of these bonds, enabling rare specie to suddenly flow back into the state. The first major delivery created no little excitement under the circumstances, and crowds gathered to witness the guarded caravan of bullion as it made its way from Vicksburg, where it had arrived by steamer, to the capital in Jackson. It was, however, too little too late. The five million dollars of bonds represented a drop in the proverbial bucket, because the state's banks were capitalized pre-panic at several times that amount and rarely dealt in hard money anyway. It soon became apparent that the state had another failing institution on its hands and millions more dollars for which it was pledged that it could not pay. "Our poor state is nearly at the bottom of the hill," observed a despairing citizen from near Natchez named Horatio Eustis, who spoke for many at the height of the disaster. "In two months we shall probably have no circulation but the bills of other states."[34]

The amusing saga of a charismatic visitor named Shocco (Joseph Seawell) Jones, who visited the state in the worst year of this financial drama, underscored both the relatively lax nature of bank regulation at the time and the ineffectiveness of officials to deal with crisis. Pretending to be an agent of both the federal Treasury Department and a North Carolina bank, Jones toured several Mississippi cities in 1839 to allegedly check on federal deposits and seek investment opportunities. With nothing more than his engaging personality, a bundle of papers, and some boxes supposed to contain cash, he managed to ingratiate himself into society in Jackson, Vicksburg, and other places during a whirlwind tour of the state. He fooled leading political figures including Seargent S. Prentiss, and even managed with his phony credentials to get a bank in Columbus to name his stepfather, a resident of the town, as the bank's president in addition to securing an unknown amount of investments. He may have swindled more cash, apparently for sheer sport, had the state's financial institutions not been utterly bankrupted at the time. The point is not that Mississippi's banking officials and political leaders were rubes; they functioned within a system precariously founded, inadequately vetted, and easily thrown into disorder.[35]

The financial and political aftershocks of the crisis would affect Mississippi for years. Citizens generally regarded the banks as having brought about the disaster and helped fuel widespread resentment against them. Democrats seized control of the state in the 1839 elections with a public mandate to rein in bank operations. Leaders soon enacted a series of measures designed to regulate banks more carefully within the state, including placing specie reserves under state supervision, limiting the issue of any bank to three times its hard money capital, requiring regular reporting on specie in deposit, and ending the practice of securing loans with cotton. Response to the disaster, however, extended far beyond legitimate regulation of the banking industry. The political backlash over the issuance of bonds to finance the Union Bank during the depths of the depression hung over the state like a pall for years to come, and whether or not to repudiate them became a central issue in state politics. The matter became a defining issue of the administration of Governor Alexander G. McNutt (1838–42), who had the misfortune of leading the state during some of its most challenging economic times. Many Democrats contended the bonds had been illegally issued, in part as a convenient excuse to avoid their repayment. The position lay grounded in a technicality in the legislation over the establishment of the Union Bank, which had required two successive legislatures to vote to create the institution and, in theory, the same measures to be taken for capitalization. These provisions had not been followed to the letter of the law. Whigs and a minority of Democrats, on the other hand, argued that the bonds represented a moral obligation and to repudiate them would reflect poorly on the state and cripple outside investment. The debate raged off and on throughout the 1840s, ultimately engulfing other clearly legitimate bond issues by the Planters' Bank, which became associated in the public mind with those made by the Union Bank. In the end, Mississippi never paid bondholders of either institution, seriously damaging the state's fiscal reputation and creditworthiness throughout the antebellum era.[36]

Mississippi's extreme dependence on cotton contributed to both the depth of the problem of its depression and the slow recovery it experienced. By the time the depression struck, decades of intensive extractive agriculture were already devastating the most productive tracts of the state's land, which most early planters treated like an expendable resource to be recklessly exploited. B. L. C. Wailes, a leading intellectual during the early statehood years who spearheaded the establishment of the Mississippi Historical Society, noted the unsustainable pattern of land use within his lifetime: "We seem to have inherited from the pioneers of the land the principle of destruction, which they brought with them into the wilds which they invaded to conquer and subdue." Early on, planters commonly cleared land and grew crops on it for only a few years during its peak productivity before moving on, leaving eroded, depleted fields in their wake. Anticipating the decline in fertility, many planters with the means sent slaves to clear new lands even as operations were winding down in others, working two plantations simultaneously so as to prevent any interruption in production. Lands in southwest Mississippi where farmers first engaged in large-scale farming were also some of the lands most susceptible to erosion, Writing in the 1830s, a visitor observed "yawning chasms" of erosion scarring the landscape in the vicinity of Natchez, noting that the city itself had become "nearly isolated by a deep ravine." With little incentive or commitment to reinvestment, continual cultivation of a given tract of land under these conditions could render it useless in a decade. Thus, the spread of cotton fields in early Mississippi from an ecological perspective "resembled nothing so much as a cancerous growth spreading death and desolation across the face of the earth."[37]

The utter lack of self-sufficiency and the worn-out soils left in the aftermath of cotton cultivation did cause many to wonder about the sustainability of such practices. Inefficiency demonstrably harmed the land, but infinitely more importantly to most farmers, it hurt bottom lines. For pecuniary reasons alone, some individuals began to experiment with diversification and improved production techniques that might yield higher profits while simultaneously more effectively utilizing the soil which provided their livelihood. Any serious talk of diversification in crops ended up being placed on the back burner throughout the early statehood era as long as the price of cotton trended upward. Setbacks such as the temporary decline in prices during the War of 1812 initiated a few rumblings over innovation, but subsided shortly afterward when the price matched and then quickly exceeded prewar levels. Serious efforts at crop diversification did not begin in Mississippi until well after the 1830s. It was the contraction of the global textile trade that forced cotton planters' hands. With economic conditions demanding a higher degree of self-sufficiency, corn production temporarily skyrocketed between 1838 and 1840. The depression actually spurred an unprecedented effort at improving agricultural practices across the board, launching an era of experimentation and study that would influence land use in Mississippi for generations afterward. In the words of one historian of the topic, "modern agriculture in Mississippi had its beginning in 1839."[38]

In that year in the town of Raymond, a man named Martin W. Phillips unofficially inaugurated a largely grass-roots effort within the state aimed at agricultural reform by persuading a number of planters to join in organizing the Agricultural Society of Hinds County. Philips and his compatriots hoped to encourage long-needed collective diversification and experimentation with the security and strength of collaboration. The formula proved infectious, especially arising as it did during challenging economic times. Similar societies on varying scales soon sprung to life, some of which engaged in the publishing of journals, such as the *Mississippi Farmer*, which served as both an outlet for agricultural news from throughout the region and nation as well as forums for discussion about more provincial concerns. In their pages were the latest news on the merits of cast iron as opposed to wrought iron plows, new uses for cotton seed and other agricultural by-products, the most efficient ways to farm various types of terrain, and experiments with breeds of hogs and cattle to identify the best yields of meat. This late-blooming reform effort made only brief and halting headway in diversification during the era. Instead, it served primarily to improve cultivation of the undisputed king of crops in the state—cotton. Its success effectively served to prohibit serious investment not only in alternative agriculture but in any other commercial enterprise, especially manufacturing.[39]

Of the state's relatively miniscule and late-starting industrial efforts prior to 1840, lumber and the manufacturing of wood products were by far the most widespread and successful. But even they languished in Mississippi until the building boom of the 1830s kick-started the industry on a substantial scale. Several scattered sawmills did exist, some dating to the territorial period. A steam-powered sawmill operated in Natchez prior to 1810, and by the 1820s the city had become the center of the state's nascent lumber processing industry. Several steam sawmills sprang to life throughout Mississippi in the 1830s, becoming the forerunners of what would become a mainstay in the state's economy for decades. It would not be until later that the famously vast tracts of longleaf pine in the state would be tapped. "Miles on end untouched by man," this unbroken forest of giant pines, accurately predicted the insightful J. F. H. Claiborne, would soon become "the great source of wealth in this country." A smattering of other industrial enterprises also opened for business in the early statehood years. One of the state's few iron foundries opened in Holly Springs in the late 1830s, specializing in the production of sawmill and plantation machinery. Entrepreneurs dabbled in textile manufacturing in the state beginning in the 1830s as well, catering to the needs of planters by producing such items as cloth for use in slave clothing and blankets, as well as cotton bagging. No large-scale textile enterprises operated in Mississippi until later in the antebellum era. Near Pascagoula, a small community of professional shipbuilders plied their craft as early as 1838 in what soon became a hub of such activity in the state. As in the cases listed above, only in later decades would shipbuilding be conducted on a substantial scale in the region.[40]

Work and economic life in Mississippi remained overwhelmingly tied to the soil, rooted for the most part in a mode of staple crop production dictated by circumstance and geography. This fact both shaped daily life for residents and underlay motivations for immigration by new arrivals. This situation set in motion the distinctly agricultural pattern of development that long stood as a Mississippi hallmark not only in the first decades of statehood but well beyond.

CHAPTER 9

Dying (and Living) in Early Mississippi

Mississippi developed on the fringes of more established sections of America. Its frontier location and circumstance heavily influenced its cultural development, highlighting life's fragility and encouraging the formation of its hallmark rough-edged, self-reliant, and insular culture. In contrast to the consuming and sometimes monotonous work that defined how Mississippians earned their livings, a variety of ad hoc amusements and raucous diversions added color and texture to daily existence. The roughly four decades of the territorial and early statehood years witnessed the birth of a special society that helped set the stage for decades of future cultural development, but this fact cannot be fully understood without some examination of the realities of life on the frontier and how early Mississippians chose to spend their free time.

The first judge of the Superior Court of the Mississippi Territory, Ephraim Kirby, left us with a colorful, if unflattering, description of his impression of the inhabitants of the region to which he had been sent in 1804. He observed that the area had long been the refuge of criminals and assorted outlaws who deemed it beyond the reach of legal authorities, or in Kirby's wording those "who prefer voluntary exile to the punishments ordained by law." He went on to provide a sweeping indictment of the frontier culture he encountered:

> The present inhabitants (with few exceptions) are illiterate, wild and savage, of depraved morals, unworthy of public confidence or private esteem; litigious, disunited, and knowing each other, universally distrustful of each other.—The administration of justice, imbecile and corrupt. The militia, without discipline or competent officers.[1]

Kirby's judgment may have been a harsh overgeneralization, but it contained an element of truth worthy of notice for anyone attempting to understand life in early Mississippi.[2]

Regardless of its untamed nature, family stood at the center of frontier life in early Mississippi. "The rural environment of the Old South where the whole family worked together, hunted together, went to church and parties together, and expected to be buried together and to come to judgment together on the Last Day, helps explain the closely knit family group," proclaimed Frank Owsley in his landmark study *Plain Folk of the Old South*. Many white households of Mississippi's formative era contained large extended families: grandmothers and grandfathers on occasion, but more commonly aunts, uncles, cousins, nieces, and other especially beloved friends. These family groups frequently formed close-knit quasi-independent communities that provided mutual assistance with everything from socialization and education to child rearing. In the unfortunate circumstance that a family member locally or elsewhere passed away and left orphaned children, the young ones were "without question adopted as a matter of course," in the words of one historian. Family-centered life did not always translate into domestic tranquility any more than it does today. Besieged with requests for divorce from both men and women, the territorial government in 1803 passed the first of several acts codifying how marriages might be dissolved by listing no less than six justifiable reasons for divorce: consanguinity, impotency, bigamy, adultery, desertion, and cruelty.[3]

Long stays by visiting family were the norm in early Mississippi, perhaps explaining in part why hospitality became a hallmark of the culture and the subject of no little commentary by out-of-state visitors and even native travelers. "Hospitality and southern planter are synonymous terms," remarked noted visitor Joseph Holt Ingraham, who like many wondered at the lavish welcomes received by visitors at the homes of the wealthy. But even among the yeoman farmer class, hospitality ranked, in the words of Mississippi resident J. F. H. Claiborne, a "cardinal virtue" where "all are alike kind and attentive to the stranger."[4]

Life on the frontier was inherently precarious. Crude living conditions and limited medical knowledge, primary among several factors, combined to make life expectancies much shorter in early Mississippi than those of today. This situation contributed to an acute awareness of the fragility of life that permeated daily existence. Part and parcel of living in Mississippi during its territorial years and the first decades of the statehood era were either immediate or lurking confrontations with illness and death that colored experience, outlook, and expectation.[5]

The suddenness with which illness, often mysterious in origin, could strike and debilitate its victims kept people on edge. Peggy Dow, wife of famed itinerant preacher Lorenzo Dow, wrote of the quick onset of an undiagnosed life-threatening fever in the span of a few hours. Within the course of a day the Dows were both bedridden, "unable to help each other to as much as a drink of water . . . nor walk without assistance . . . Lorenzo appeared to be fast approaching to eternity. . . ." Many living in the region at the time could readily identify with the Dows' experience, for various and vaguely described "fevers" or "agues" carried away people on a regular basis in the early statehood years and were a near-constant threat to health. One Mississippi planter noted that a wave of unnamed fevers killed twenty-four of his slaves in one season, overwhelming local ability to properly deal with the emergency or attend to normal burial customs; dry goods boxes were used as coffins and newspapers substituted as shrouds. Other even less specific but equally rapidly advancing maladies stalked Mississippians. "You will be much astonished to hear of the death of old Col. Sessions," wrote one resident to his sister, for example, informing her that the gentleman passed away in less than forty-eight hours from an attack of "pleurisy" suffered "as he was returning home from his plantation, and was taken suddenly ill." Others were suddenly stricken with "paralytical shocks," "consumption," and a host of other illnesses they were at a loss to detail specifically, which in short order sent them to their graves. In what became an all-too-common occurrence, one resident recorded in his memoirs the quick, mysterious, and heart-rending death of a child who became sick one day, "fell asleep early in the evening, and breathed her last in the latter part of the night." Children were naturally particularly susceptible to certain quickly debilitating, undiagnosed diseases and families with multiple children almost invariably lost one to sickness before the age of five. Mothers passed away during childbirth at an equally alarming rate. Due to the relatively primitive state of medical knowledge at the time and difficulties accessing the care that did exist, the process of having a child could be anything but routine. With disheartening frequency mothers, and very often their babies, died during or shortly after childbirth.[6]

The state of travel and communication made every brief separation from loved ones potentially the last. Business trips or visits to family elsewhere in the South could easily take weeks, and letters written by travelers might take several days to several weeks to arrive at their destination—plenty of time in the interims for folks to contract and succumb to disease without anyone back home having the slightest clue. Consequently, every delivery of mail during a family member's absence had the potential to bring bad news. A man named Thomas Roddy, for instance, wrote one of these grim reports to his brother in 1823, informing him of "the painful Inteligence of the death of my Father . . . during my absence to South Carolina after an illness of about ten or twelve days." Sometimes a letter never arrived at all. Rebecca Ruth Hogg Young, writing in 1838, relayed to her sister in rather straightforward terms the unfortunate circumstances surrounding the death of an acquaintance: "Mr. Ellis . . . I am sorry to inform you died of Pleuresy [*sic*]. . . . his wife . . . knew nothing of his illness, until he was brought home a corpse. . . ."[7]

In addition to the relatively routine threats to health, epidemic diseases periodically swept through the state and carried off dozens and sometimes hundreds at a time. The foremost threat among these, yellow fever, proved particularly devastating. "Yellow jack," as it was known, is a viral disease spread by mosquitoes. After a short incubation period it manifests itself in a variety of unpleasant ways, including fever, headache, nausea, muscle pains, and the telltale yellowish tint to the skin caused by liver damage. Many of those who contracted the dread illness died within a matter of days—sometimes even hours. No cure existed, and as medical experts of the day did not grasp its cause, the limited efforts at prevention were only minimally effective. The fever usually struck in the late summer or early fall in the years it made an appearance. The closely packed riverside population and trading center of Natchez proved to be a perfect host and experienced some of the deadliest outbreaks in the state. Authorities there did what they could to contain them and shorten their duration, such as enforcing quarantines on boats arriving at the city's port, but, with no understanding of how the disease spread, most measures taken were ineffective.[8]

A case of yellow fever in the state's largest city could bring business to a standstill and render the community a ghost town in short order. Those who could often fled the city for the supposedly healthier environs of the countryside while the epidemic raged, but dozens of people might already be on the verge of death from the quick-striking disease before they had time to react in this manner. Excerpts of letters written by leading citizen John Anthony Quitman during an outbreak of the disease in 1823 provide a particularly enlightening window into the turmoil yellow fever caused both in and out of the city. Quitman apparently fled the city as a "refugee" in August at the onset of the crisis, planning for an extended sojourn. On October 1, he wrote that he did not plan to return until December when frosts and cooler weather allowed the epidemic to subside. He reported bluntly: "Whole families there have been exterminated. I have lost several warm friends. . . ." During his time away from town, he was struck at how the "awful pestilence in the city brings out, in strong relief, the peculiar virtues of this people." He observed approvingly how "mansions of the planters are thrown open to all comers and goers free of charge. Whole families have free quarters during the epidemic, and country wagons are sent daily to the verge of the smitten city with fowls, vegetables, etc., for gratuitous distribution to the poor." Upon his return a few months later, he related how it "was painful to see the desolation of the streets. . . . A gloom and sadness pervaded the whole place, and when friends met they pressed each other's hands in silence, or averted their faces and burst into tears. There was a chasm in every family, and ah! how many bleeding hearts!"[9]

While not as common as yellow fever in the state's first decades, cholera proved equally deadly. Cholera is an intestinal infection generally caused by poor sanitation and frequently spread by drinking contaminated water. Mississippi was struck with an especially vicious outbreak of cholera in 1833 during a wave of a global pandemic of the disease. In Vicksburg, for example, nearly forty new cases per week were reported during the height of the crisis. Most residents evacuated the capital city of Jackson during the chaos, but recently elected Governor Abram Scott refused to leave. He apparently showed the first signs of illness on the evening of June 12, 1833, and died from the rapidly advancing disease at eleven o'clock that night. The disease struck children especially hard. "The hand of Providence has fallen heavily upon me in these last three days," mournfully wrote John Anthony Quitman in May. "Our beloved little Edward, who had never before had a moment's illness, was for about a week affected . . . , and his pure spirit left this world for a better on the morning of the 18th." The Quitman family's suffering had just begun, as the next day he reported that "my beloved, my beautiful, noble, and affectionate little John was seized with the fatal scourge, without any premonitory symptoms, and in six hours the little angel left this world for a better one."[10]

In such an environment, health concerns and the fragility of life naturally weighed heavily on the minds of Mississippians. Updates on health status, especially when illness had occurred, filled many letters. "The past winter my health has been very indifferent," wrote one resident to his family, while another wrote his brother that "My health has been very poor. I have had two spells of fever. . . ." Yet another observed that "sickness preys on my frame," while someone else reported that he and his wife "both came very near dying of fever two or three times." Thousands of similar examples appear in the surviving correspondence from those living in early Mississippi.[11]

The reputations for the relative healthiness or unhealthiness of various locales could determine in part their prosperity and significantly impact their future. As a result, characterizations of the healthiness of cities could become something of a contentious point of public discussion during the time period. At times such debate carried on within the pages of regional newspapers. The Natchez-based *Mississippi Republican*, for example, in 1818 took issue with circulating claims of the city's unhealthiness. "The health of our city continues to be unusually fine," the editorial staff observed, drawing attention to the fact that "There are but few cases of indisposition among us, and these are chiefly confined to strangers." He noted that the editors were "particular in noting the good health of Natchez, because of the monstrous folly and idle loquacity of the *State Gazette*, operating upon the timid and credulous, have succeeded in creating considerable alarm as to the danger to be apprehended in this city." Such public debates had not only lives but fortunes in trade at stake between competing communities. Traveler Henry Fearon, writing of his visit to Natchez about the same time as the *Republican*'s editorial, recorded an instance of how personal such debate could become:

> Two young men . . . had been warmly engaged in a debate; one was a resident in Natchez, the other not so; their subject of controversy was the healthiness of the city; the latter contended that it was sickly; his friend could not endure so foul an aspersion upon his native town; the other explained that he did not mean any thing personal, but he considered Natchez was sickly, and as a strong proof that his opinion was correct, he pointed to the church-yard, in which one-fourth of the late population had been entombed in the course of five weeks.

Of course, throughout the period the open air of the rural countryside was perceived as inherently more healthful than urban environments no matter the location—a perception that seemed to be borne out with the rapid spread of disease in cities when epidemics struck.[12]

Home and natural remedies, superstition, and the kindness of loved ones provided the only defenses against illness for most people. Herbs, extracts from roots, and poultices derived from certain plants commonly sufficed as frontier medicine. Good diets and moderation regarding alcohol and tobacco were advised as preventative measures for a host of troubles. A wide variety of manufactured "snake oils"—questionable proprietary concoctions with outrageous claims regarding healthfulness—proliferated. For those who could afford it or had the time, mineral springs were popular as treatments to ward off or even supposedly cure illness. The reputedly healing waters of springs such as Brandywine and Bankston in central Mississippi or other retreats along the coast were said to "act favourably upon most of the diseases of the climate, such as affections of the liver, bowels, cutaneous and chronic diseases, congestive and bilious fevers, debility, and numerous other ills. . . ." For just about anything beyond the scope of the already mentioned treatment methods, a sick person might be "bled." The widespread belief was that imbalances and impurities in the circulatory system were at the root of many maladies and could only be addressed through the purging of blood. Regardless of what ailed them, most people received medical care from family and friends. "My wife," recorded one early settler who spoke for a large portion of the population, became "the physician, nurse, and servant of the family" when illness struck. "In less than two years, she had apparently rescued every member of the family, more than once, from death."[13]

Professional medical services, such as they were, did exist. Licensed, and even more unlicensed, doctors operated in communities throughout the state, making house calls to attend to the sick and the wounded both slave and free and distributing the medicines common at that time. Some even administered inoculations against diseases such as smallpox. Larger cities sometimes boasted of hospitals or "infirmaries" where, in the words of an advertisement for one of these institutions, all "curable shall not go away unhealed." Given the primitive state of medical knowledge in general and the professional training demanded of them, the quality of the care doctors and hospitals provided varied greatly from place to place. They helped many of their patients, but they seem to have sometimes done them more harm than good.[14]

Early settler Gideon Lincecum experienced the best and the worst of nineteenth-century medicine and provides a case in point. In his autobiography he somewhat humorously recalled his rather serious encounter with doctors when he had an apparent cardiac episode, observing that their

> opinions and prescriptions were as varied as their faces. Some were of the opinion that it was enlargement of one of the oracles; others, that the symptoms indicated aneurism of the arch of the aorta; others, that it was enlargement of the heart itself. One thought that it was a softening of the substance of the heart. So one and another of them, first and last, suggested treatment for all the heart complaints known to the faculty. Bleeding was the remedy most universally believed in by them. And I also had more faith in it, so I bled myself every day. In 20 days I had taken 22 ½ pounds of blood . . . the depletion by the lancet and mercury had laid me pretty low.

Observing all this activity, Lincecum's wife matter-of-factly observed that it was not the ailment but the treatment that might ultimately kill him.[15]

Lincecum's experience aside, early Mississippi did have its capable doctors and even some leading lights in the practice of medicine. Foremost among these stood John Wesley Monette. Trained as a physician at Transylvania College, Monette was a man of many talents and interests. He conducted some of the first and most intensive studies of yellow fever undertaken by medical professionals, researching appearances of the dread disease in Washington and Natchez in the 1820s and 1830s. He first reported his findings before local intellectuals prior to ultimately publishing an insightful summary in the *Southwestern Journal* under the title "Observations on the Epidemic Yellow Fevers of Natchez and the Southwest from 1817 to 1839." His recommendations for new methods of quarantine helped revolutionize the way communities fought the epidemic. Monette went on to publish several other articles in noted medical journals in the 1840s. Despite all his acclaim for medical research, however, he is probably best remembered today for his work in history. His *History of the Discovery and Settlement of the Valley of the Mississippi* remains a landmark study of the region.[16]

Another threat to health, perhaps for a smaller but particularly visible portion of the population, was violence. Bertram Wyatt-Brown (*Southern Honor*) and other scholars who followed him have conveyed the exaggerated sense of personal honor that inspired so much of the social interaction on every level of society in the antebellum South. While historians such as Thomas D. Clark and John D. W. Guice have argued that violence was probably no more common in the early

American Southwest than in other sections of the country, the peculiarly touchy nature of sensibilities in the region, which led to rapid escalations of individual aggressive acts, startled observers at the time and has become engrained in legend about the era. The slightest perceived insult could provoke an altercation among men, who in the estimation of one resident, were "virile, aggressive, ambitious, quarrelsome, energetic, explosively independent, and enormously self-confident." They expected to settle disagreements themselves, as in their eyes part of proving one's manhood lay in not allowing others to insult or take advantage of you. Besides, the nearest center of law enforcement on the frontier might be several days away. Acceptance of violence could also be tied to the presence of slavery and the clear hierarchy of power and subservience it presented. As one historian of early Mississippi has observed, "In a society in which mastery meant the ability to use force and masters were used to having their will obeyed, petty disagreements could become bloodbaths." Such affairs escalated swiftly owing to the fact that in many locations men might be seen openly "garnishing . . . his person with pistols and bowie-knife." When combined with what one author has termed the region's characteristic "daredevil masculinity" and its emphasis on physical prowess, the recipe for confrontation is obvious.[17]

On his journey through Mississippi in 1839, traveler James Silk Buckingham stood aghast at how "the papers of Natchez . . . literally teemed with the records of excesses of all kinds; murders, duels, affrays, acts of incendiarism, and crimes which would make up a calendar too large for a month in any country but this." Others noted with alarm the frequency with which tarring and feathering, beatings, lynchings, and others habits of "forestalling and improving upon the decisions of the courts, by taking the execution of the laws into their own hands" occurred. This independent administration of justice sometimes even extended to the very officials charged with carrying out the laws. One visitor to the state illustrated the point by relating how he saw a man jailed for allegedly murdering his wife, only to be released by a judge to a crowd who "invited him to take a walk." "He was taken quietly to the suburbs of the city, stripped, whipped most severely, tarred and feathered, and then marched back into the city, with a fife and drum playing the 'rogue's march.'" Political leaders set no better example, frequently becoming embroiled in bitter personal disputes that involved violence.[18]

Even when legal authorities did try to enforce the law, they sometimes encountered bold mobs that defiantly challenged them. In 1817, for example, "ruffians" in a dispute with city law enforcement officials in Natchez engaged them in an open gun battle that ultimately required militia, armed with rifles and cannon, to calm. Similar affairs occurred well into the statehood era. In 1837 a group of river traders operating in the city flatly refused to pay a tax on flatboats that had been levied to fund a hospital. When authorities moved to seize the boats of the recalcitrant rivermen, they were met with an obstinate display of force that required the support of local militia to suppress. The same thing occurred under very similar circumstances in Vicksburg about the same time in an episode that became known as the "flatboat war." While none of these disturbances necessarily are evidence of any unique trends of disrespect of authority in early Mississippi, they are illustrative of a general willingness to challenge its existence both individually and collectively during the period in which the state acquired its cultural identity.[19]

In such an environment, dueling became viewed as a legitimate way to settle disputes between gentlemen. While the practice seems both barbaric and ridiculous to modern observers, social mores of the time virtually mandated the issuing and acceptance of such challenges by men of standing. "No individual could have refused a summons to the field of honor without being consigned to permanent discredit and coldly shut out from all intercourse with gentlemen," candidly recalled noted political leader Henry S. Foote. Another, Seargent S. Prentiss, explained simply that "when a man is placed in a situation where if he does not fight life will be rendered valueless to him both in his own eyes and those of the community, and existence will become a burden to him; then I say he will fight and by so doing, will select the least of two evils." Prentiss and Foote ironically found themselves facing off in a duel over a disagreement during a trial in which the two lawyers opposed each other. They met twice to settle their differences in a field in Louisiana across the Mississippi from Vicksburg, both times leaving one man wounded. Pride intact, they carried on with their careers. No less a figure than political luminary George Poindexter found himself engaged in duels during his long career, infamously killing a rival in an affray that would haunt him by serving as fodder for his detractors for the duration of his life. Governor Hiram G. Runnels also participated in a duel that resulted from an altercation with a Jackson newspaper editor. Despite their notoriety, relatively few duels actually ended in death to one of the opponents. Such were the elaborate rituals of challenge and procedure involved in these contests that multiple opportunities were afforded to resolve confrontations with reputations intact. Public letters of retraction might be issued, agreement on terms—such as time, place, weapons, or rules—never reached, or by mutual consent purposefully errant shots might be exchanged. Any of these tactics or others might enable adversaries to save face without either man being branded a coward.[20]

Duels involving the wounding or death of one and even on occasion both participants did take place. In addition to the principals, these affairs commonly involved seconds who handled the preparation of the weapons and ensured all protocols were followed. Handguns usually were the weapons of choice, though rifles were involved on occasion. The contestants faced each other at an agreed-upon distance measured in paces, and at the signal raised their guns and fired. Custom allowed for the repetition of these steps until the challenger was satisfied or one of the participants disabled. These vainglorious contests usually occurred just outside of communities at some nearby rural location. In Natchez and Vicksburg, the Louisiana shore of the Mississippi opposite those cities hosted multiple encounters. "These affairs take place every month or two, in plain sight of all Vicksburg," recorded one resident of that city in his memoirs, adding that "people here talk of going over to get a near view of them." Perhaps the most legendary of all Mississippi duels, the infamous "sandbar fight," took place opposite of Natchez in 1827. Although the principals, Samuel Wells and Dr. Thomas Maddox, ended their exchange of missed shots with neither man so much as wounded, several of their seconds, including Jim Bowie wielding one of his famous knives, got into a scuffle that left two men dead and two others seriously wounded. The areas near the cities of Clinton and Jackson also became hotspots for duels. The most notorious duelist in the state, Alexander McClung, resided in the capital. The "Black Knight of the South," as he is remembered, reputedly killed ten men in duels in the span of about twenty years. The prominence of some of the individuals who participated in deadly encounters, even more than their frequency, ensured dueling would be remembered out of all proportion to its actual occurrence. Leading judges, Congressmen, and even ex-governors found themselves squaring off with adversaries at measured paces in early Mississippi.[21]

As early as 1803 the Mississippi Territorial General Assembly passed measures to restrict dueling, and in 1807 officially outlawed the practice, calling it "barbarous and savage conduct." Aware of the ineffectiveness of the territorial government's efforts to curtail dueling, the state legislature in 1822 declared that those who killed opponents in duels could be tried for murder, even if the death occurred as many as three months later as a result of wounds received in these affairs. For a few years anyone holding elected office in the state had to swear they had not engaged in a duel. Governor Walter Leake (1822–25), who pushed for the abolishment of imprisonment for debt in Mississippi among other legal reforms, became an advocate for the eradication of dueling during his administration. He believed the practice antithetical to civilized society. Such arguments and their associated legal prohibitions and restrictions still did little to prevent dueling. It did not help anti-dueling efforts that even some of the most vocal critics of the practice themselves sometimes became involved in these contests. John Anthony Quitman served as president of an anti-dueling society but himself served as a second in a duel. Lorenzo A. Besancon, the outspoken editor of a leading Natchez newspaper, campaigned against dueling for years in the pages of the paper, yet accepted a challenge on the field of honor in which he killed his adversary. "Thus sternly denounced by law but recognized by society," a leading historian on the subject has observed, "the duel continued to flourish."[22]

Perhaps ironically because of the general fragility of life on the frontier, early Mississippi residents relished opportunities to engage in entertainments that diverted their focus from the routines of daily life. These ranged from the urbane to the frivolous. Surveyor Andrew Ellicott, whose services proved essential in the transfer of the region from Spanish to American control in 1798, complimentarily characterized the people he encountered as "generally a sprightly people, and appear to have a natural turn for . . . painting, music, and the polite accomplishments." Artistic endeavors, literature, and the performing arts were indeed enjoyed with gusto by a certain portion of early Mississippi population, especially in urban communities. Every city seemed to have a theater, and no fashionable home could be considered complete without art and a library. Dancing became such a popular pastime that schools in the state's larger cities taught the newest dances for social functions. Music assumed a central place in just about any recreational gathering regardless of class. The playing of the pianoforte entertained guests in the homes of the wealthy, while fiddle playing sparked revelry among even the humblest gatherings of both free and enslaved.[23]

For the great majority of the citizenry, a variety of community events relieved the tedium of isolation on farmsteads. Political rallies frequently assumed the trappings of carnivals, where in addition to the appearance of candidates to address crowds on the matters at hand, there were community-wide barbecues, large dances, footraces, shooting contests, and even wrestling and boxing. One resident recalled how, during the 1840 presidential election, a local group in support of the William Henry Harrison–John Tyler ticket painted up a wagon and, equipped with a barrel of hard cider and coonskin caps, traveled the roads of the neighborhood, "stopping at every cross-road to meet the people. . . . Wherever we tarried, there was music and speaking. The men brought out their best liquors, and the women their choicest dainties, for our refreshment." Circuses traveling from town to town with clowns, trained monkeys, performing bears, wax figure exhibits, and a variety of stunt performances proved very popular. Minstrel shows, vocal and instrumental concerts, and even magic acts all graced stages to popular acclaim. Dog and cock fighting drew interested crowds in certain communities. Weddings could spark raucous community-wide celebrations with music, drinking, and dancing. In truth just about any organized event might be considered spectator entertainment during the era; people were even known to travel long distances to see public hangings of criminals merely for the spectacle.[24]

Discussing news and politics became among the most popular pastimes in early Mississippi, providing fodder for conversation around dinner tables, sidewalks, and campfires across the state. Next to word of mouth, newspapers served as the primary source of information about current events in early Mississippi. Many of the papers that circulated in the territory and state were actually published elsewhere, as residents with the means to do so often subscribed to a variety of newspapers, magazines, and journals printed in places such as New Orleans, Philadelphia, and London. This situation vexed editors attempting to establish newspapers during the era, as agents for these larger newspapers were a common site in the state's larger communities. By some estimates, as late as 1835, circulation of out-of-state papers equaled that of state-based publications. As the population steadily grew in Mississippi, its homegrown press similarly took shape. There were four newspapers published in the Mississippi Territory in 1810, by the mid-1820s six in the state of Mississippi, and by 1840 some thirty papers were being published within the state's borders. These statistics are a little misleading, however, for newspapers were as a matter of course exceedingly short-lived. Many lasted merely a year or less, and those that persisted longer frequently changed name or even location from time to time. Even with this caveat, the growth in press activity clearly reflected the uneven regional growth of the population; Natchez and the surrounding area served as the epicenter of the state's nascent publishing industry until well into the statehood era. While towns in the Natchez area along the Mississippi River, such as Port Gibson and Grand Gulf, might host two papers each at any given time, there were virtually no newspapers being published in the eastern section of the state until well into the 1830s.[25]

Frontier newspaper content did not always resemble news in the traditional style, and editors frequently presented it with a clear bias. Local news occupied very little of the space within these often single-sheet periodicals—perhaps owing to the fact that in small communities residents already knew current events well enough that they disdained paying to read about it—and the news they did carry came in the form of articles reprinted as desired from other newspapers. According to one resident of Mississippi during the territorial and early statehood periods, early newspapers "were filled with Napolean's [*sic*] exploits, sometimes to the complete exclusion of news about current local elections." Information on national and even world events did occupy significant column space, but so did poetry, recipes, advertisements for merchandise or services, notices about runaway slaves, and editorials expressing opinions on a range of issues. As the paramount issue of public discussion usually involved politics, it should come as no surprise that many early papers were less news-reporting institutions than they were straightforward political organs published for the express purpose of advancing a party or candidate. The first newspaper to be established in the territory, the *Mississippi Gazette* (1800), carried a bent that soon ran afoul of the territorial administration and quietly disappeared. When *Green's Impartial Observer*, perhaps the second paper in the state, attempted to live up to its name and allow opinion from all political persuasions, it instead became derided by all sides. Surviving on circulation subscriptions from jealous partisan groups, several of the state's early newspapers can be likened to modern membership organization newsletters more than newspapers in format and scope.[26]

Even in the best of times newspaper editing did not prove to be a lucrative profession in early Mississippi. Most editors were young, poorly paid, overworked,

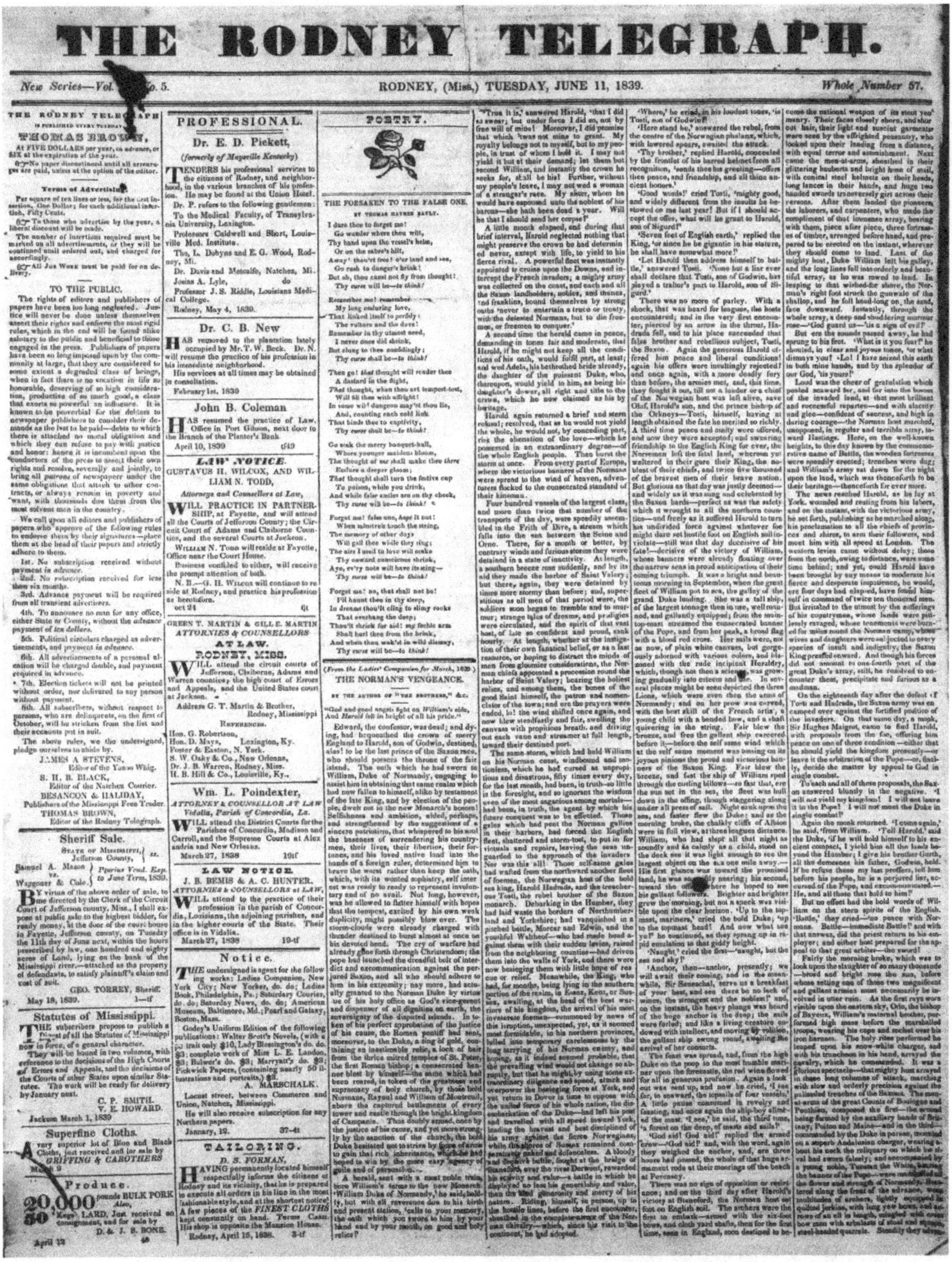

Figure 9.1. *Rodney Telegraph*, June 11, 1839, edition is just one of dozens of newspapers published during the time period. (Courtesy of Mississippi Department of Archives and History)

and surprisingly inexperienced. Famed frontiersman Sam Dale, who tried his own hand at editing at one time, summed up the life of newspapermen thus:

> A printer in the South usually lives in a little box of a house, not big enough for furniture; his pictures and statues are his wife and children; his office is a mere shanty, stuck full of glue and paste; and all sorts of traps; he works in his coat-sleeves, with the assistance, sometimes, of a little, ragged, turbulent daredevil of a boy; he toils night and day, often never paid and half starved, making great men out of small subjects, and often receiving for it abuse and ingratitude . . .[27]

Mississippi's first publisher, Andrew Marschalk, struggled as much to survive as any other in his situation. As a reward for his attacks on political foes he was jailed and even chased through the streets. Marschalk's interesting story as a publisher in Mississippi begins in the 1790s at the military outpost of Fort Nogales at Walnut Hills (modern Vicksburg) where he was serving as a lieutenant at the time of the formation of the Mississippi Territory. Working on a small mahogany press he had bought and learned to use, Marschalk began tinkering with publishing while off duty, likely angling for a job in publishing with the new territorial government. The scheme worked, for shortly after the publishing of a short piece entitled "The Galley Slave," which is believed to be the first piece of literature published in Mississippi, officials asked him to print the laws of the Mississippi Territory. Incidentally, Marschalk is also credited with publishing the first book in Mississippi, *Paine Detected* by John Henderson of Natchez, in 1799. After the printing of the laws, Marschalk launched his career as a newspaper editor, publishing the *Mississippi Herald* in 1802 and eventually going on to a long career in the industry that lasted into the 1830s.[28]

A lot of what might be classified as entertainment to frontier settlers involved work. Activities associated with clearing fields for planting, such as log-rollings, might include neighbors from miles around, which could turn the labor into a series of spirited contests over the course of several days. The primary responsibility of the host, aside from helping with the work, would be to feed the volunteers and often provide some music—usually the fiddle—to dance to when the workday was done. In a similar manner houses were raised, corn crops shucked, apples pared, wood chopped, quilts stitched, and so on. As hunting could be equal parts sport and chore in early Mississippi, a variety of activities associated with guns and game proved popular. Marksmanship contests with handsome prizes frequently drew large crowds, and gander pullings (where contestants on horseback would attempt to pull the head off of a greased goose while at a gallop) could provide an excuse for spirited gatherings. Simple story-telling, perhaps the most ubiquitous form of entertainment on the frontier, would have been engaged in during just about any of these events. The sharing of tales of experiences and legends became part and parcel of campfire and dinner table conversation throughout the region.[29]

Gambling may have been the unofficial state sport in Mississippi's formative years. "Gambling is carried to the greatest excess, particularly horse racing, cards and betting—a wager always deciding every difference of opinion," remembered one shocked visitor. Citizens and visitors routinely whiled away their idle time in all manner of games of chance including cards, roulette, dice, and faro. They placed bets on horse races, cockfights, and practically any sort of contest where the outcome seemed undetermined. Games of chance proved popular even among Mississippi's native Choctaw. At "ball-plays," in which teams of as many as 100 on either side squared off in a forerunner of modern stickball, whole villages turned out to witness the spectacle. Onlookers placed bets on the outcome of the contest, according to witnesses involving wagers on "skins, furs, trinkets, and every other imaginable thing that was part and parcel of Indian wealth."[30]

For good reason, steamboats and gambling remain closely associated in the minds of many people even today. Not only were games of chance popular with passengers in passing the time traveling up and down the Mississippi, but it is estimated that as many as 1,500 professional gamblers plied their trade on steamers operating between New Orleans and St. Louis in the 1830s alone. These particular tradesmen operated primarily in small groups, making a career of fleecing unwary travelers. They usually pretended to be on business of some sort, striking up conversation and weaving elaborate tales of their seemingly legitimate reasons to be heading to a given destination. Using both raw skill and a variety of infamous tricks including marked cards and loaded dice, they separated their unassuming victims and their money with surgical precision. Little law enforcement infrastructure existed on the steamboats to monitor or prohibit their activities, and those in ports of call such as Natchez and Vicksburg habitually looked the other way until these "sharpers" tangled with more respectable businesses and residential areas in their respective towns or caused some excessive amount of disorder.[31]

This latter type of incident proved to be not as much a question of if but when, especially once gamblers inevitably left the boats to visit some of the many quasi-legal portside gambling establishments. Altercations over the results of games and accusations regarding cheating flew fast and furious when people lost money, and occasionally violence occurred. "They had not long been at the table when a violent quarrel took place," observed one traveler who visited one of Mississippi's riverside entertainment districts and in short order found himself in the middle of a typical fast-developing scrape:

> I saw a man snatch or grab a handful of bank notes from the table with one hand, and a pistol, near him with the other; and then I noticed several other pistols and

> bowie-knives on the table. . . . And simultaneously I heard the clicking of several pistols as they were cocked. My back was to the table. I looked round, and there were certainly six or even seven pistols pointed at me and the man against the wall, and as many bowie-knives uplifted and glittering in the fire light. . . .[32]

A particularly chaotic episode in Vicksburg became exactly the scenario many who objected to gambling had long prophesied could happen if the practice continued unchecked. Remembered by contemporaries as "the liveliest gambling place in the whole Southwest," Vicksburg featured a sort of red light district known as Kangaroo that offered opportunities for gaming "in log-cabins, board houses, canvas tents and in flatboats." In 1835 events gone awry surrounding a Fourth of July celebration in the city shone a spotlight on all this gaming activity and became a cautionary tale throughout the state. It all began when a lone rowdy gambler interrupted a military company holding a celebratory barbecue. Arrested but released, the now-enraged man came back armed and belligerent later in the day. Upon this second brush with authorities, he was whipped, tarred and feathered, and ordered to leave the city immediately. This treatment apparently upset the man's fellow gamblers, and some talked of seeking revenge. Whether in reaction to a specific or supposed threat is unknown, but following a public meeting sparked by the affair, officials decided to order all gamblers to leave town and organized raids on known gambling establishments. Both militia and a few eager citizens at large joined these raids. Perhaps inevitably, the affair devolved into a free-for-all with destruction of property, burning of furniture and gambling equipment, and even some gunfire. Many of the targets of this vengeance naturally fled as fast as they could. A few unlucky or intransigent gamblers found themselves cornered in a house and a firefight ensued in which a prominent local physician who had volunteered to participate in the raid was shot. At least five gamblers were captured and later hanged.[33]

Such disorder, albeit generally on a smaller scale, had long been the bane of more polished society and posed a real threat to the businesses and reputations of riverside communities. "In Morals we are low overrun with Gambling . . . ," complained one Mississippi resident to a relative, voicing a complaint of many who viewed unrestricted activity of this sort as a problem that demanded remedy. In 1839 those with similar concerns were finally able to get the state legislature to pass measures to officially discourage gambling. New laws going into effect that year made it illegal to bet on cockfights, duels, or the result of elections, with monetary fines for first and second offenses. Such relatively halfhearted efforts did little to curtail such activity, and gambling remained a popular fixture of life in Mississippi throughout the antebellum period.[34]

Horse racing rivaled gambling in general interest in early Mississippi. No less than thirty-three racetracks existed in the state prior to 1840, each being the site

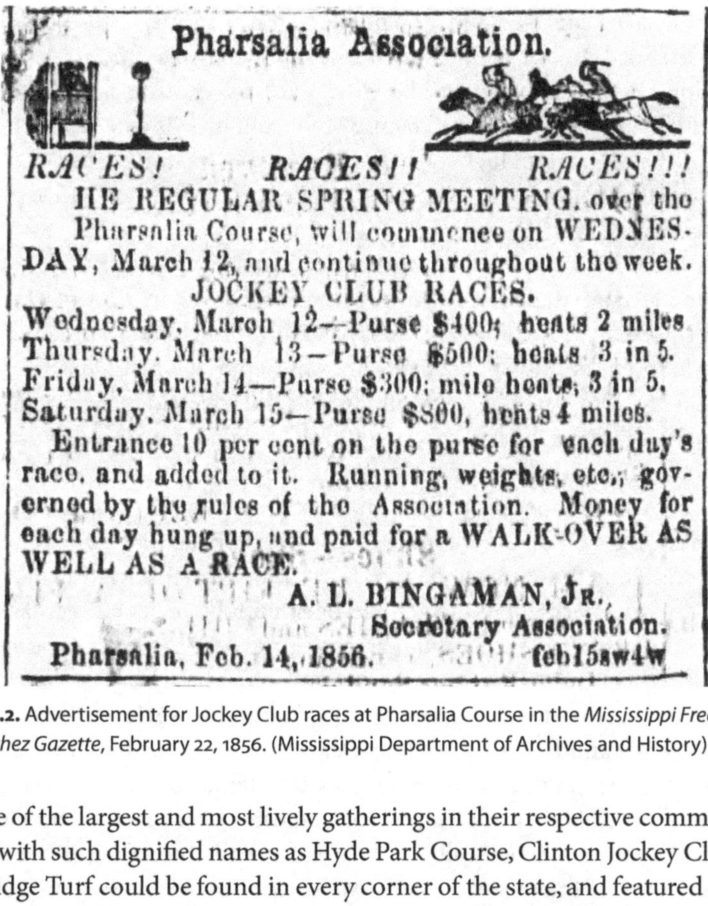

Figure 9.2. Advertisement for Jockey Club races at Pharsalia Course in the *Mississippi Free Trader and Natchez Gazette*, February 22, 1856. (Mississippi Department of Archives and History)

of some of the largest and most lively gatherings in their respective communities. Tracks with such dignified names as Hyde Park Course, Clinton Jockey Club, and Toll Bridge Turf could be found in every corner of the state, and featured regular racing events that served as Mississippi's most popular spectator sport. Natchez alone had multiple tracks in its vicinity, including the famed Pharsalia Course, the "capital of antebellum racing in Mississippi." City newspapers routinely carried articles discussing the latest happenings in the world of racing. One (the *Natchez Ariel*) in the 1820s even included a standing section devoted to horse racing in the area called the "Sporting Intelligence"—the equivalent of a modern-day sports section. Races drawing large and boisterous crowds might take place on a single day or, especially at the larger facilities, over as many as three days. The first day would feature the longest race, commonly up to four miles, the second day a three-mile heat, and the final day, two- or even one-mile contests. Each day's contest had a cash prize to be won.[35]

The planter elite dominated the inner workings of the sport. Having the finest horses, and being willing and able to lavish the resources on them, became one of the many unofficial measures of status among the wealthy in early Mississippi. Slave jockeys were the norm, as carefully selected and trained as the horses themselves. In the concise estimation of one leading historian of the period, horse racing "provided an outlet for planters to publicly display their self-assertion, their competitiveness, and their liberality." Exclusive private clubs dedicated to the breeding, buying, selling, and racing of thoroughbreds sprang to life around the sport. The Mississippi Jockey Club of Natchez, for example, was a gentleman's association that functioned as both a statement of social status and outlet for racing passion.[36]

The theater also proved immensely popular in Mississippi from an early date in the territorial period. Some of the earliest performances of plays in the Old Southwest were held in Natchez, with a touring company's staging of *The Provoked Husband* in the City Tavern in 1806 reputedly being the first. As was the case with so many other cultural pursuits, the riverside metropolis quickly became the center of thespian activity in the region. Touring companies and local talent staged performances as short as one night and sometimes as long as several days at a number of locations in Natchez during the first decades of the nineteenth century. Some took place on the "showboats" that passed the city on their travels along the Mississippi. A Natchez Theatrical Association had formed by 1808, the first permanent theater had been built by 1813, and regular seasons were scheduled by 1817. Soon local newspapers devoted as much space to discussion of the theater as horse racing, with critical reviews of plays appearing as early as 1818. "The costumes were unrivalled," raved one reviewer about a play in the 1830s, while another critiqued that a lead character appeared "rather too stiff in his movements on this occasion, and his countenance wanted a little more of expression." Several other Mississippi cities, especially Port Gibson and Vicksburg, claimed lively theater activity albeit on a smaller scale. According to one scholar's intensive study of the theater in early Mississippi, between 1806 and 1840 over 1,600 performances on 1,100 nights were staged in southwest Mississippi alone. This number includes at least 400 actors and no less than 450 plays.[37]

Frontier theaters were not always sophisticated places of entertainment. Frequently crowded and featuring crude sets, dim lighting, and all too often, mediocre talent, they could on occasion prove every bit as raucous as any other entertainment option. One resident of early Mississippi who wrote of his experiences remembered an episode he witnessed in Copiah County that illustrates one of the many forms of disruption that became part and parcel of play-going during the era. During one performance he saw a drunken man wander in and sit near the stage. He was soon asleep and snoring loudly. "It was very hot," the author observed, "and the perspiration and other fluids were flowing freely from the person of Uncle Billy, irrigating much of the barren space around him." Soon an altercation over this behavior erupted between the leading actor and the drunkard, the end result being that the curtain came down and the show abruptly ended. A Natchez newspaper review of another play recorded an equally disruptive but notably more dangerous development during a play that involved a "lion" briefly appearing on stage. "I am happy to see that my favorite [actress], Miss Russell, has consented to tarry a little while with us," he wrote, "but I would advise her 'as a friend' not to appear upon the stage until all the animals are removed from it."[38]

As is the case with any location, early Mississippi's society was heavily influenced by the time and place it took shape. The daunting challenges of life on the frontier, the fierce pride in reputation, the determined pursuit of leisure activities, and access to information that helped residents understand their place in the larger world were not unique to Mississippi as factors contributing to cultural development. Their special arrangement in the state's formative period, however, did heavily influence the quality and character of life for a large portion of its citizens and played a major role in shaping its singular cultural environment.

CHAPTER 10

Nurturing Mind and Spirit

Opportunities for learning and worship were fundamental to the stability and nurturance of early Mississippi society. The ways in which these endeavors were undertaken reveal important details about the hopes, dreams, and worldviews of those who inhabited the state during its developmental era, as well as something of the wherewithal of its citizens to create institutions they believed important to civilize society. The slow growth of both therefore helps us understand the raw frontier in which Mississippi emerged and the remarkable transformation of the few decades between its founding and its antebellum maturity.

Early Mississippians saw value in learning as a practical component of overall societal improvement. They also agreed with the appeals of national leaders that an informed citizenry was necessary for the realization of American liberty, but they were hard pressed for the resources to bring these lofty goals into reality. Although Mississippi's first constitution proclaimed that "schools and means of education shall be forever encouraged in this state," the legislature actually did precious little toward that end in the first years of statehood. Empty promises regarding state support for education already had become something of a tradition. Throughout the state's territorial years, a sixteenth portion of each surveyed section of land technically had been reserved for schools; but, in the words of one noted historian of the era, "the allotment . . . proved far more magnificent in the wording of the act than in the realization of the future." While neither the territorial nor the first state legislatures had the means or desire to attempt to create a true system of public education, the idea did have its advocates.[1]

In 1820 Governor George Poindexter began the first serious efforts at funding public schools in Mississippi. Observing in a flourish of optimism that "the brightest Luminaries of intellect and virtue, often burst forth . . . from obscurity to add renown to his country, and adorn the page of history," Poindexter urged the legislature to invest in the state's educational infrastructure. Preparatory to his final recommendations, he canvassed the state to learn of the status of schools in each county. His survey revealed that some counties had between five and ten schools teaching the "rudiments of the English Language" and some had none at all. Further, there were virtually no standards regarding curriculum, grading, or length of school year from county to county or even community to community. In 1821 Poindexter authorized the creation of the Literary Fund to help address these inconsistencies. The fund directed for educational purposes a portion of state monies gathered from escheats (intestate estates), and certain confiscations and forfeitures. While entirely inadequate to the task, this well-meaning effort had even less effect than it otherwise might because it got buried in the bureaucracy of state government. Without a champion once Poindexter left office in 1822, the Literary Fund languished and apparently became forgotten within a few years.[2]

During his second term in office, Governor Gerard C. Brandon (1826–32) looked into reviving the Literary Fund by appointing a commission to investigate potential means of subsidizing a state system of education. During its 1829–1830 session, the legislature passed several acts that earmarked money for education. In addition to reestablishing the Literary Fund, it diverted proceeds from a small tax toward the fund and adopted a proposed constitutional amendment authorizing the establishment of schools in each surveyed township reserved for that purpose. Further, money from rent of other lands within those sections was earmarked for the schools. Even these acts quickly proved insufficient to raise and manage the revenue needed for a true educational system worthy of the title. Governor John A. Quitman (1835–36) addressed what had become a glaring shortcoming in the state during his short term in office. In somewhat dramatic prose comparing republican and monarchical governments, he asked why the "elements of knowledge" should not be communicated to "those who are to become the rulers of their destinies. The means of a plain practical education should be extended to every free child in the country, cost what it may. . . ."[3]

Despite Quitman's rhetoric, substantive action regarding education of the state's citizenry did not come until the administration of Governor Alexander G. McNutt (1838–42). In 1839 the state legislature passed measures providing for public education and the establishment of a series of academies and directed that court fines be added to the list of sources of revenue for schools. Owing to these and a variety of other local efforts, including lotteries, between the opening of the first free public school (Franklin Academy in Columbus) in 1821 and the year 1840, approximately 300 public schools began operation throughout Mississippi. Many of these schools held classes as little as three months of the year, and most offered only the most basic instruction in reading, writing, and arithmetic, but they formed the foundations of Mississippi's state-run educational system.[4]

While there may have been precious little state support for education in Mississippi's territorial and early statehood years, there were nevertheless many schools.

The real story of education in early Mississippi is one of private enterprise and local initiative. Perhaps the most basic component of privately funded education during the era did not involve a traditional school at all. Wealthy families commonly hired private tutors to educate their children in their homes. These tutors usually contracted with parents for room and board and a fee based on the number of children to be taught. The great majority of these instructors were from elsewhere, having been lured from many northern states with relatively generous salaries and other amenities that allowed for both a decent standard of living and excellent opportunities for professional advancement on the burgeoning Southwestern frontier. Noted Mississippi lawyer and statesman Seargent S. Prentiss, for example, initially came to Natchez as a tutor from his native Maine. He contracted to teach five children of the Shields family (and later those of a few neighbors) for $300 per year. He received board with his hire, had free use of Mr. Shields's well-stocked library, as well as use of one of his horses and any guns and ammunition he needed for hunting. Daily lessons averaged between three and four hours, and the rest of his time he spent "studying law, reading and gunning." Not all tutors labored in such advantageous conditions, and a common complaint of the trade involved disciplining the privileged children of the wealthy without offending benefactors.[5]

The majority of the children who received any structured education in early Mississippi did so in private academies. Between 1817 and 1860 nearly 200 such schools were chartered in the state, having been brought about by the wishes of parents desiring high-quality education for their children and well-meaning civic leaders wishing to enhance their communities. The 1840 census showed just over 2,500 students attending some seventy-one schools. Their existence followed an already thoroughly established pattern of development throughout the nation at the time. It became a mark of progress for communities to have academies where children were taught the basics of reading and writing. Between the efforts of churches and those of other private groups, most early Mississippi communities of any size featured schools, even if a relatively small segment of the population could afford them. Many were unimposing single-room establishments. While rarely exorbitant, the price of tuition nonetheless prohibited the majority of families from participation. At the time of statehood, average tuition for schools in the Natchez area stood at about fifteen dollars per quarter; by the late 1830s that figure had risen only to about twenty dollars. Wide variation existed within schools across the state, with some charging one or two dollars per week for basic instruction and others offering a-la-carte instruction, charging a certain amount per month based on the courses selected. Inspired by the classic civilizations of Greece and Rome, the curriculum the students received for these rates could be far more sophisticated than one might assume. In addition to reading, writing, arithmetic, geography, and grammar, schools commonly taught Latin and Greek languages, algebra, astronomy, philosophy, chemistry, and rhetoric.[6]

Early Mississippi schools were a reflection of the society in which they existed. Hence, school curriculums might include almost as much instruction aimed at developing proper moral character and providing a guide for social etiquette as lessons in grammar or arithmetic. Even in the first real effort at establishing a college in the Mississippi Territory, the debate centered on the need for a place of learning "Science & Virtue." Although schools at every level were understood to serve an important societal function through practical and academic education for the entire student body, this understanding of the role of education in society became especially evident in the establishment and functioning of the state's several "female academies." Schools for girls existed in the Mississippi Territory as early as 1801, and several were founded in the early statehood years. Women's education at the time centered on their role within the home, and parents generally expected that any education girls received beyond the most fundamental worldly knowledge be applicable in making their daughters better equipped to function in polite society, secure a husband, and eventually be a good wife and mother. Schools for girls advertised their ability to improve both morals and minds, and often placed as much emphasis on instruction in music, dancing, drawing, and needlework as grammar and composition.[7]

While Mississippi may have been fundamentally conservative in its approach to education of its female population overall, it assumed a position in the vanguard of the movement for higher education of women. Elizabeth Female Academy, among the first schools of its kind in the nation, was incorporated in February 1818 a few miles east of Natchez. Organizers built the privately administered institution, affiliated with the Methodist Episcopal Church, on land donated by Mrs. Elizabeth Roach. Exceptional in the South at the time, the school operated for over a quarter of a century with an average enrollment of about thirty students. Its ambitious curriculum included literature, Latin, French, English, geography, astronomy, arithmetic, grammar, composition, geography, and moral and natural philosophy. With a nod toward women's role as homemakers, girls were taught "such parts of chemistry as are applicable to domestic and culinary purposes." As further proof of its somewhat less than egalitarian nature, the school did not offer instruction in science, allegedly because the male-dominated board believed women could not comprehend the subject. Students began their school day at sunrise, and it concluded with an evening prayer at 8:00 p.m. The school granted hundreds of advanced degrees to women at a time when there were few such opportunities anywhere in the country. Incidentally, Mississippi College in Clinton is generally regarded as having been the first coeducational institution in the nation to grant an advanced degree to a woman in 1831.[8]

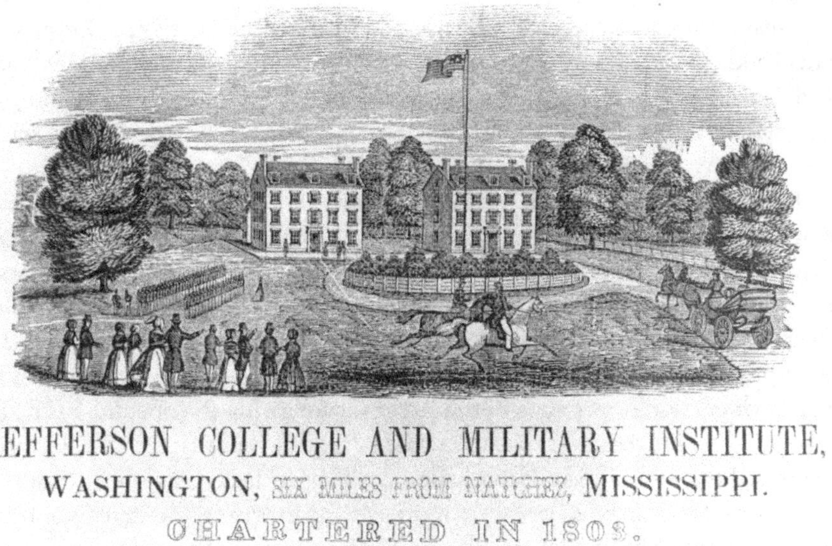

Figure 10.1. Jefferson College was the first institution of higher learning chartered in the Mississippi Territory. (Courtesy of Mississippi Department of Archives and History)

Elizabeth Female Academy's success aside, Mississippi's path toward establishing colleges and universities proved even more tortuous than its halting steps toward a system of public education for children. As early as 1802 Governor William C. C. Claiborne had called for a "Seminary of Learning" to be established at some central location for the benefit of the entire Territory. The territorial legislature approved the proposal on May 13, 1802, and on paper established Mississippi's first institution of higher education—Jefferson College (named in honor of President Thomas Jefferson). Owing to continual arguments, first over where exactly the college would be located and then how it should be funded, it took nearly a decade before the school actually opened in 1811. Enrollment rarely topped seventy-five before 1840, and attracting and keeping qualified instructors proved to be persistent problems for the college's board. By 1837, however, Jefferson College offered as many as forty courses to a slowly growing student body for tuition of about sixty dollars a year. Classes included the study of math, history, science, engineering, and philosophy, with special courses on foreign languages and the writings of Virgil, Homer, and Horace. Despite its fragile existence in its early years, Jefferson College helped chart the course for the establishment of additional colleges in the state.[9]

Protestant churches played a significant role in the establishment of Mississippi's early institutions of higher education. Baptist Church–affiliated Hampstead Academy (later Mississippi College) was incorporated in January 1826 and held its first class as Mississippi Academy in 1832. The Presbyterian Church founded the "Institution of Higher Learning under the care of the Mississippi Presbytery," later Oakland College, near Rodney in 1830. The Methodists founded Centenary College at Clinton in 1839, but it soon relocated to Brandon Springs and then Louisiana. They were also closely associated with Sharon Female College, which opened in Madison County in 1837.[10]

Establishment of an official, publicly supported state university took considerably longer than the relatively short period from proposal to construction of these private ventures. Efforts at creating such an institution date to the earliest years of statehood, but did not gain serious momentum until the 1830s. In typical fashion, the process became mired in sectional rivalry, and no less than seven host sites were proposed and debated. Ultimately, the population boom occurring in the northern portion of the state in the late 1830s following the opening of the last Choctaw and Chickasaw lands in the state swung the momentum. The legislature chartered the school in 1840, and commissioners selected Oxford in Lafayette County as its home by a narrow margin. For the first time, the state established a major state institution in its northern section.[11]

The number of colleges and universities does not tell the whole tale of interest in scholarly pursuits in early Mississippi. Individuals interested in intellectual enterprises found outlets in a number of private organizations that devoted themselves to the study of literature and science and to the advancement of educational institutions. Among the first of these was the Mississippi Society for the Acquirement and Dissemination of Useful Knowledge, which is often credited with being the first cultural organization in the state. Founded early in the territorial years with an eye toward providing a forum for discussion of politics as much as philosophy, its incorporators included such leading lights as William C. C. Claiborne, William Dunbar, and David Lattimore. It eventually outgrew its early partisan nature to become a true literary society that lent vital support to Jefferson College.[12]

In Greenville (Jefferson County) a Franklin Society was organized to channel support for the establishment of an academy there, and in 1809 the Natchez Mechanical Society was founded by those interested in fostering opportunities for adult education in the city. In Port Gibson in 1817, the Literary and Library Company was chartered for the purpose of establishing a local library. By the 1820s Wilkinson and Amite counties had Debating and Literary Societies, and Library Societies existed in Greene and Pike. In Winchester, literary activities were advanced by a Philomathean Society that was organized in 1825. Athenaeums, or private, membership-based libraries or literary clubs, arrived in Mississippi during the territorial years with the establishment of the Natchez Athenaeum. Other athenaeums soon opened outside the city, with the one in nearby Washington apparently the first.[13]

The lyceum movement also influenced the development of intellectual life in early Mississippi. An outgrowth of the concepts of lifelong learning first prominently expounded by Josiah Holbrook of Massachusetts, lyceums were privately funded societies for "Mutual Education" designed to provide opportunities for public learning. Activities varied from region to region, but most engaged in staging lectures, dramatic performances, debates, and demonstrations of practical science. The first and most active lyceum in Mississippi appeared in Adams County in 1832, but several similar organizations were founded during the brief period of the movement's heyday in the antebellum era. The Washington Lyceum became especially active, holding its meetings at Jefferson College and publishing the *South-Western Journal*, a novel frontier publication that aspired to be a "Magazine of Science, Literature and Miscellany" for the edification of the people of the region. Within its pages could be found essays ranging from investigations of school curricula and overviews of the latest advances in medical science to poetry, meteorological charts, and thoughts on "moral greatness." The efforts of a host of these committed groups, even if usually short-lived and decentralized, provided a critical outlet to intellectual interests in the early state, and played no small part in the founding and functioning of its fledgling institutions of higher education.[14]

At the heart of educational initiatives in early Mississippi were a fairly small group of well-read, inquiring citizens who exerted influence out of all proportion to their numbers. Only a very small percentage of people in the state had access to academic endeavors or the luxury of the time and means to indulge in them. We may never know how many common citizens attempted to edify themselves through learning independently of any formal system. One example of a common man who sought self-improvement was Ferdinand L. Steel, a farmer who recorded in his diary that he attached a book of Latin grammar to a plow to memorize as he worked his fields. There were a few notable intellectuals who merit mentioning for their particular influence or the way they exemplified a certain sophisticated segment of frontier society.[15]

William Dunbar stood as the unquestioned intellectual giant in early Mississippi. Referred to by J. F. H. Claiborne as "the most distinguished scholar in our annals," Dunbar is remembered as an exacting and pioneering scientist who brought a spirit of experimentation and examination to his many pursuits. He studied the plant and animal life of the region assiduously and reveled in its exploration and documentation. Dunbar became a wealthy and influential planter, making money on cotton and other staples but tirelessly searching for new and better agricultural products and production methods; at one point he became so fascinated with the processing of indigo that he went to area plantations engaged in the enterprise to "study the art." Dunbar also observed the stars and kept detailed records of the weather, and became an accomplished writer, political leader, and physician whose infectious curiosity and tireless work ethic helped make frontier Mississippi a most unexpected center of enlightenment. A personal friend of Thomas Jefferson, Dunbar arrived in the Southwest in the 1770s and spent most of his life in the Natchez area. While truly an exceptional mind by any measure, his most recent biographer observes that he ranked as "the personification of Natchez rather than its antipathy; William Dunbar and territorial Natchez complemented each other perfectly."[16]

The spirit of intellectual inquiry nurtured in the early Natchez region stood apart from any other portion of the Mississippi Territory and remained exceptional well into the first years of statehood. The city and its environs claimed several citizens who belonged to the prestigious American Philosophical Society, a preeminent scholarly organization based in Philadelphia. Men such as B. L. C. Wailes, founder of the Mississippi Historical Society, maintained private museums of fossils and Indian relics and conducted serious research into the region's past, while planter Levin Covington presented lectures on "experimental philosophy" and conducted elaborate astronomical observations in his spare time. Early Mississippi was no educational Eden, but it had more capable champions of intellectual investigation than might be expected in a frontier area where day-to-day existence quite literally consumed the minds and talents of most of the population.[17]

Ironically, the establishment of organized religion in Mississippi required similar extraordinary individual effort. While Mississippi eventually became firmly established as part of the "Bible Belt" in the South, religious institutions traversed a difficult road toward becoming a major influence in its society during the territorial early statehood years. By some estimates, as few as one in twenty Mississippians belonged to any church at the time of statehood, and religious institutions of the era in general played as little a role in the life of citizens of the state as at any point in its history. On his first visit to Natchez in 1803, famed itinerant Methodist minister Lorenzo Dow doubted that there were as many as three Christians in the town. Even by 1820, noted naturalist John James Audubon reported that he could only find "two miserable looking churches" in the city, both of which he observed appeared abandoned. Another traveling minister lamented that the people residing in the Natchez area were "in general . . . very rich, very proud and very polite . . . exceeding all others on compliments . . . but with little humility, little religion and little piety." A somewhat humorous observer of early Mississippi society who passed through the area in 1808 summed up the spiritual disposition of residents by noting: "The gentlemen pass their time in the pursuit of three things; all make love; most of them play; and a few make money. With Religion they have nothing to do; having formed a treaty with her, the principal article of which is, 'Trouble not us, nor will we trouble you.'" The story of how that situation dramatically changed in a few decades is a critical part of understanding how the territorial and early statehood years influenced the trajectory of societal development in Mississippi.[18]

The gradual expansion of the influence of organized Christian churches in early Mississippi largely mirrored the national rise of evangelical Protestantism in America. Spurred by the growth in religious enthusiasm brought about by the cultural phenomenon known as the Second Great Awakening or the Great Revival, the era of Mississippi's maturation occurred at a time in which evangelical Christianity rose to ascendancy in the nation as a whole. The era witnessed the adaption of Christian teachings to an unprecedented focus on individual spirituality by, in the words of one historian, recognizing "deepest spiritual impulses at face value rather than subjecting them to the scrutiny of orthodox doctrine." The masses of the state's common folk, those very people pushing America's boundaries westward and attempting to establish new societies on the frontier through their own exertions, found the emphasis on individualism especially empowering. It called into question the very concept of selfish material gain, which few could ever realize, and emphasized the power of self-determination on a rugged frontier in which self-reliance was already a way of life. A substantial portion of the entire population became caught up not only in this new mode of theological thinking and the emotional spiritual experiences it fostered but also in the optimism about ecclesiastical and societal synchronization it inspired. Churches gradually came to assume a role as a cornerstone community social institution that helped bring a particular type of order and direction to the state as time progressed.[19]

Among the first and most influential expressions of this newfound religious fervor in early Mississippi were camp meetings. A frontier phenomenon that persisted throughout the antebellum period and beyond in the South, these assemblies had their origins in 1700s England but acquired their distinct American form in the fields and forests of the Old Southwest. Physically, camp meetings were gatherings of hundreds of people in wilderness clearings assembled to hear gospel preaching by traveling ministers. They often lasted for several weeks at a time, and customarily occurred in the fall. Residents from throughout the area in which the meeting took place would travel long distances to attend them, and during the duration of the meeting its participants would live in "tent cities" and participate in worship services held in makeshift brush arbors and pole-framed pens several times a day. They were commonly the biggest event to occur in many of the isolated frontier communities in Mississippi, and quickly became among the state's premier social events.[20]

These rural gatherings had an electric effect on the spread of religion in early Mississippi. These meetings featured an impulsive spontaneity; living embodiments of the overtly democratic, relatively free-spirited mode of spiritual awareness swept into vogue by the Great Awakening's emphasis on personal piety. Further, they

Figure 10.2. Drawing of typical frontier camp meeting, where hundreds were first exposed to religious doctrine. (Courtesy of the Library of Congress)

offered a focused individualism that made spiritual enlightenment available to the masses on an unprecedented scale. The "pillared folk," as the leading scholar on religion in Mississippi, Randy Sparks, observes, hardly knew what to make of these decidedly unorthodox gatherings where men and women, black and white, young and old, well-to-do and poor, mixed freely. Further, the shocking physicality exhibited at camp meetings mocked the graceful manners of elite society. People in the throes of spiritual passion sometimes jerked, jumped, flopped, and shouted incoherently and simultaneously. The "falling exercise," in which an individual would become so consumed with religious emotion that they would fall to the ground and rise repeatedly, became a hallmark demonstration of spiritual rapture at early camp meetings. The half-spoken, half-sung sermons delivered by ministers in a "chanted" presentation that became characteristic of camp meeting worship services served as the catalysts for all these demonstrations and more. Rousing congregational singing of popular hymns played no small part in prompting transcendent spiritual experiences. Descriptions of nighttime camp meetings in progress, "when all the fire-stands are ablaze, and the multitude are assembled and singing," hover somewhere between eerie and surreal.[21]

Lorenzo Dow is credited with holding the first camp meeting in Mississippi in 1803 near Natchez. According to his account of the event, "about fifty were awakened, and five professed justifying faith, so that it may now be said, the country which was a refuge for scape-gallowses, a few years since, in Spanish time, is in a hopeful way. . . ." Camp meetings led by men such as Dow briefly served as the primary way in which a large percentage of frontier residents encountered organized religion. Their heyday came and went as fast as communities transitioned from rustic outposts to full-fledged cities, in the words of one scholar tracing the "advance and retreat of the frontier." Within the chanted sermons camp meetings featured lay a powerful call to spiritualism that resonated with early Mississippians, smacking as it did of anti-elitism and acceptance of all. Some of the state's most prominent Christian churches and organizations can trace their roots to these services.[22]

If camp meetings introduced a new type of popularized Christianity to Mississippi communities, the "circuit rider" and the itinerant minister often served as the first step in nurturing the spark they kindled. Circuit riders ministered to several communities within a defined area, visiting each to preach and help organize churches on some sort of regular schedule of visitation. Itinerant ministers roamed the countryside in similar style to traditional missionaries, seeking to take advantage of whatever opportunities for an audience presented themselves. These were anything but gentle clergy. Traveling largely alone through hundreds of miles of wilderness and braving the elements to serve an often ambivalent and not infrequently hostile citizenry, they could be on the road for weeks at a time. Circumstances required these men to have a certain toughness just to get to their appointed locations. "My life was sometimes endangered while crossing the deep waters in the Territory this year," reported circuit-riding minister Launer Blackman in a typical travel log from the period. "I consider I made a very narrow and providential escape with my life. I was led to believe that Satan had much to do in trying to afflict, drown, or otherwise kill the preachers who came to the Territory." Another complained that every day on his journey he had to "swim through creeks and swamps, and I am wet from head to foot, and some days from morning to night I am dripping with water. . . . I have rheumatism in all my joints."[23]

The arrival of a circuit rider or itinerant at any given place could be rather inauspicious. One itinerant named Jacob Young remembered that when sent to the Mississippi Territory in 1807, he stopped in a small rural community and asked if could stay the night in a log cabin. With permission granted, he asked if he might be allowed to "hold prayers" in the man's house. When he began, the slaveholder, "a very wicked old man," according to Young, "slipped out of the back door, and ran off till I was done." Other ministers encountered even less friendly welcomes. Officials allowed one minister on a visit to Jackson the use of the capitol building when no other space could be found. He preached "the best sermon we could to one man and four ladies," in the daytime and about a dozen that night. Another had his services interrupted by drunken rowdies who stood outside the building in which he preached and "began to yell and hoot, interspersed with loud 'amens' and other words used in religious worship." Yet another minister, attempting to hold worship services in the courthouse in Brandon, witnessed a group of local youths for their amusement fire blanks near the building to startle the congregants. In 1829 Rev. George Moore had his preaching interrupted by a group of drunken men who declared they had come to stop such "silly doings." Nonplussed, Moore took off his coat, strode rapidly toward the intruders, "and began to pummel them right and left." After the unwelcome guests unceremoniously fled from the premises, Moore calmly resumed his lesson. These and numerous other misadventures aside, traveling preachers made steady progress toward their goals in early Mississippi by planting the seeds of numerous congregations.[24]

Though operating on a very small scale, organized religion in Mississippi technically predated the arrival of camp meetings and itinerants. The first Protestant church in the state is believed to have been a Congregational church in Kingston, just outside Natchez, formed in the 1770s by Rev. Samuel Swayze. During Spanish rule, when Protestant worship was outlawed, its members met clandestinely in private homes. Although Catholicism had the sanction and encouragement of Spanish authorities in what became the Mississippi Territory, the Catholic Church never had an especially strong presence in the area, and the region witnessed a steady decline in Catholic influence after it came under American control. The Catholic faith did not begin substantial growth in Mississippi until late in the antebellum era. In 1798 only about a dozen Catholic families lived in Natchez, conducting intermittent services with traveling priests. By 1820 only one resident priest and two small organized Catholic churches, in Natchez and Bay St. Louis, could be found in the entire state. When Pope Gregory XVI established the Diocese of Natchez in 1837 (charged with working throughout the entire state) a lone organized Catholic church stood within the state's border. The overwhelming majority of churches in early Mississippi were Protestant evangelical congregations. This circumstance reflected both the backgrounds of early settlers and provided a commentary on the level of missionary activity of the various predominant Christian denominations in the region from elsewhere in the country.[25]

Three evangelical Christian denominations—Baptist, Methodist, and Presbyterian—captured the hearts and minds of the majority of those who affiliated themselves with any church during the frontier period. Baptist congregations were meeting clandestinely in the Natchez area as early as the 1780s, but the first organized congregation—Salem Baptist Church—appeared in 1791. A man named Richard Curtis is credited with founding the church. Curtis had moved to the area from South Carolina and soon ran afoul of Spanish officials for his evangelical zeal, being first ordered to cease "heretical psalm-singing, praying and preaching in public." He was arrested on at least one occasion. Once the territory came under American control, other Baptist churches appeared. By 1800 there were four in the Mississippi Territory, eighteen in 1813, and nearly forty at the time of Mississippi's statehood. Divided into Missionary and Primitive congregations over deep-seated differences of opinion concerning church government, support for missions, and educational requirements for ministers, the denomination overall experienced steady growth throughout the early statehood years. By the 1830s Mississippi Baptists claimed over 100 congregations organized into ten associations with some 5,000 members. The Baptist Church thrived among the most common of Mississippi's common folk, attracting large numbers of poor and middle-class citizens who found its emotional worship style attractive and its pronounced anti-elite bent empowering.[26]

Near the opposite end of the social spectrum in early Mississippi stood the Presbyterian Church, a denomination that drew much of its membership from the upper middle class. It, too, had humble beginnings during the Spanish colonial period. One of the first Presbyterian congregations in Mississippi prior to American control reputedly was called to worship by the blow of a cowhorn, which signaled no government officials were watching. Presbyterians first moved to establish themselves in the Mississippi Territory with the appointment of missionary James Hall in the Natchez area in 1800. Several preaching "stations" were established through his efforts prior to the arrival of early Presbyterian leaders James Smylie and Joseph Bullen, whose work in the 1810s laid the foundation for the growth of the church in the state. The first organized Presbyterian church, Pine Ridge (originally Salem), formed in 1807 near Washington. Mississippi's first presbytery, consisting of several early congregations growing out of the first missionary-established stations, formed in 1816. Mississippi's third-largest denomination throughout the antebellum period, the Presbyterian Church's growth trailed the others noticeably. As late as 1830, it had only some 630 members.[27]

The Methodist Episcopal Church, which drew its membership from the widest spectrum of citizens, became the largest religious organization in early Mississippi. Claiming over 2,000 members at the time of statehood, on the eve of the Civil War the Methodist Church had over 61,000 members. Regarded as neither as poor as the Baptists nor as well off as the Presbyterians, the Methodist message struck a popular middle ground among a cross-section of the lower- and middle-class population. An important component of the church's success lay in its effective use of camp meetings and itinerant ministers as missionary vehicles. Methodists sent more traveling ministers into the region than any other religious body,

Figure 10.3. Rodney Presbyterian Church, completed in 1832. (Courtesy of Mississippi Department of Archives and History)

creating a presence for the church in communities of every size and description across the state. The first Methodist missionary in Mississippi, Tobias Gibson, arrived in Natchez in 1799 and organized the first Methodist church in the territory a year later. By 1816 Methodists had formed their independent local conference. The exceptional growth of Methodism in the era was due in no small part to the tireless work of leading minister William Winans. Volunteering to come to the Mississippi Territory from Indiana in 1810 despite hearing rumors of its unhealthiness and lawlessness, he served in Mississippi until his death in 1857. Winans preached to crowds of blacks and whites throughout Mississippi in every place he could find, from a backwoods brush arbor to a steamboat, and served in prominent leadership positions within the Methodist Church and Conference for decades. He became not only one of early Mississippi's most visible Methodists but one of its most influential evangelical leaders in general.[28]

Religious groups other than these three largest churches existed in early Mississippi, but in much smaller numbers. Episcopalians were active in the area even during Spanish administration, but did not establish a permanent church until 1820 (Christ Church) through the efforts of Reverend Adam Cloud. In 1826 the four existing Episcopal parishes in the state organized as the Diocese of Mississippi. Despite its organization and the ties of its early leadership to more evangelical denominations, the aristocratic Episcopal Church remained a distinct minority in frontier Mississippi, its membership being drawn almost exclusively from the ranks of the planter elite. At least one Quaker congregation existed by the 1810s in Mississippi, and Cumberland Presbyterians became active primarily in rural areas of the northern portion of the state. Forerunners of the Church of Christ and Disciples of Christ (Christian Church) organizations, spawned by the teachings of nationally famous religious reformer Alexander Campbell, were first formed in the state in the late 1830s. There were a small number of Jews in the Natchez area as early as the late 1700s, and several Jewish families lived in the Walnut Hills settlement (forerunner of Vicksburg) during the territorial years. Reputedly, Jewish worship services were held there in private homes prior to statehood. A true Jewish community did not become a part of Mississippi society until later in the antebellum period, however, with the arrival of substantial numbers of them from Europe in the 1840s and 1850s.[29]

Although less than half of all Mississippians were official members of any church by 1840, the steady growth of the influence of evangelical Christian denominations in the state during its formative years inexorably became a more crucial part of its cultural fabric. Already a major force in the state's society at the time of the close of the frontier period, evangelicals increasingly exerted their influence in Mississippi's educational, social, and civic infrastructure as the antebellum era progressed. The doctrines they promulgated came to define both a theological worldview and a system of domestic social order that provided an impetus for community improvement when government resources were wholly inadequate to the task. Above all, the seeds of evangelical institutions that took root in the frontier era helped nurture a spirit of fierce self-determination that penetrated to the very core of early Mississippi society and foreshadowed the direction it took in the later antebellum era.

CHAPTER 11

Travel, Trade, and Urban Centers

Mississippi became progressively more interconnected and populous over the course of its territorial and early statehood years. During the span of just a few decades, it witnessed some of the most robust growth in its physical infrastructure of any era in its history. Road networks of progressive sophistication were developed, steamboat travel revolutionized the way goods were brought to market, and the new railroad technology pointed the way toward a radical new future for intrastate travel and trade. Mississippi's river towns became the early state's foremost urban centers in large part due to their strategic location along major avenues of commerce. Meanwhile small inland crossroads communities, whose primary impetus for being was sometimes simply their location along major travel routes, took root. Taken together, the development of early Mississippi's interconnected travel network and urban infrastructure played a vital role in determining where its people lived and how they connected with each other and the rest of the world.

Few aspects of Mississippi's early period witnessed as much change as its developing transportation network. At the time of the Mississippi Territory's organization, a few scattered wilderness roads traversed its interior, and virtually all economic activity was confined to a few key ports along the major waterways connecting the region with the Atlantic. By 1840 several new and improved roads crisscrossed the state, and every river capable of being navigated had steamers operating on it with some regularity. Finally, railroads were ushering in a new future in transportation that would change the very notion of how and where commercial trading centers in an agricultural region could operate.

Travel along early Mississippi's roads could be an adventure. The great majority of these trails were muddy and haphazardly marked and were often little more than narrow traces in the wilderness, many of which had no bridges at stream crossings. As a consequence, the recorded experiences of those attempting to travel any substantial distance overland seem filled with trials to the point of being almost comical. "I have had occasion to say a great deal about roads . . . ," one traveler who traversed a territorial period road in the eastern Mississippi Territory commented, "but I pronounce that along which our route lay on the present occasion, to be positively, comparatively, and superlatively, the *very worst* I have ever traveled in the whole course of my peregrinations." The writer referred specifically to a section of the Federal Road, but might have been speaking about any number of roads in frontier Mississippi. "In passing through the Chickasaw Nation," another traveler remembered, "we had a swamp to every creek and creek every few miles. These swamps are mostly of a clayey consistency; and . . . our wagons and horses frequently sunk in up to the body, and in several instances so firmly, as to become immovable . . . we were compelled to unharness the horses to extricate them from the mire; next to unlade the wagons, pry them up with levers, and roll them by hand to a place where the horses could stand. . . ." Another gentleman attempting to traverse the interior of the state in 1823 observed that "Our course, the whole day, was along an Indian path, about twelve or fourteen inches broad, through woods. . . . It was twice crossed by hunter's paths, a little narrower than itself; and we were admonished, that if we deviated into these, we should perhaps come to no habitation for 100 to 150 miles." In many sections of the territory and state, travel might not even be attempted in rainy seasons on account of the impossibility of making it through the mud or safely crossing swollen streams.[1]

While the state government worked to improve a few roads primarily around major commercial and population centers, the overwhelming majority of early transportation routes underwent no routine inspection or repair. What maintenance did take place usually came under duress from the travelers themselves when confronted with obstacles to their progress. Not infrequently, this meant slightly adjusting the route on the fly to pass by a particularly troublesome stretch, resulting in a series of meandering courses that could quickly become difficult to follow. The limited legislation aimed at road improvement that did get passed during the era usually attempted to compel male citizens to work on roads in their counties for a specified number of days per year, but inconsistent enforcement of such policies and the poor quality of work when completed did little to improve travel in the state. Governor Gerard C. Brandon made it a priority to advocate for the continued modernization of Mississippi's transportation infrastructure during his tenure (1825–32). Ambitious projects including roads, bridges, turnpikes, and even railroads were suggested, but lagging resources hampered any actual implementation of most of them at the time.[2]

Regardless of any road improvements, an assortment of ox and mule-drawn carts, horse-drawn wagons, and mounted and on-foot travelers, could be seen every day along the roads and byways in early Mississippi. The stagecoach reached its heyday in the era, becoming one of the mainstays in regional travel by offering, at least in favorable conditions, regular service between points within the state and beyond. Coaches provided travelers several other intangibles not to be taken lightly; companionship, the safety of numbers on their journeys, strong teams of horses and knowledgeable drivers that decreased the chances of becoming stuck or lost. These conveyances offered seating for up to six fairly comfortably, even though overland travel could be a bone-rattling experience where passengers might on occasion be called upon to move from side to side to keep the vehicle balanced on uneven terrain or actually get out and help push it through stretches of mire. Their arrival at the points to which they served, often grandly trumpeted via horn, could draw crowds, as they brought not only travelers who might need accommodations, but the latest news from other places.[3]

This matter is an important consideration, for at the time of the Mississippi Territory's formation, it could take as long for mail to travel from the nation's capital in Philadelphia to Natchez as to Europe. Through the efforts of hearty mail carriers and the use of the growing stagecoach system, Mississippians remained in contact with the outside world and, in no small measure, with themselves. A focus on improvement in mail delivery between nationally significant points indirectly benefited Mississippi during the era because of nearby New Orleans's strategic role in the country's transportation network. By the early 1800s, overland mail delivery time between Washington, DC, and the Crescent City—traveling through Natchez and interior Mississippi—had been reduced to a mere twenty days with multiple deliveries per week. The territorial hinterlands off this main corridor, however, could remain out of touch for extended periods of time. Even the regionally important commercial, transportation, and population center of St. Stephens, located north of Mobile, for example, received mail only once per month as late as 1816. The poor road system likewise restricted overland trade until well into the statehood era, when the lucrative profits promised by cotton crops grown in the interior finally spurred significant private financial investment in road creation and improvement.[4]

A few major transportation routes handled most of the long-distance traffic in Mississippi's early years. These roads were piecemeal assemblies of trails of varying quality that often merged with other more established routes over portions of their course. The closest thing to an exception to this rule might have been the "Military Road," also known as "Jackson's Military Road," which roughly followed the route of modern Interstate 59 and Highway 45 as it connected Madisonville, Louisiana, with more established road networks in the Tennessee River Valley. Suggested by Andrew Jackson after the War of 1812 as a more efficient route connecting Tennessee with New Orleans, by 1820 it featured over 300 miles of some of the most improved roadways in the region. The "Gaines

Trace," connecting the Tennessee and Tombigbee Rivers (and predating the modern Tennessee-Tombigbee Waterway System), was opened by its namesake George Strothers Gaines in 1810. The "Robinson Road," named after its surveyor, Raymond Robinson, opened shortly after Mississippi's statehood to connect the northern Tombigbee Valley (at Columbus) with the Natchez Trace. It quickly became one of the more important routes in the state, facilitating trade and travel between two of the state's primary population centers and, by extension, allowing increased access to the relatively remote capital city of Jackson in central Mississippi. In the southern section of the state, the "Natchez–Fort Stephens Road" and an assortment of other east-west paths generally connecting the Mississippi and Tombigbee River valleys, today often collectively remembered as the apocryphal "Three Chopped Way," remained vital transportation corridors throughout the period.[5]

One road, the famed Natchez Trace, looms as especially important in the era. The road is today commemorated as a 444-mile-long national park roughly following the original route. During Mississippi's territorial and early statehood years, it connected Natchez and Nashville, but it traces its history back to a time when neither city existed. It originated as a series of Native American footpaths and largely assumed its lasting route in the late 1700s. True work on improvement of the road to something more than a wilderness footpath began in 1802 after territorial governor Winthrop Sargent complained of the difficulty of communication with the area he governed and the more established states along the Atlantic Coast. The Choctaws agreed to allow the road to be widened and smoothed to accommodate vehicular traffic via the Treaty of Fort Adams in 1801. The next year troops, engineers, and Indian guides began work that continued intermittently in different areas until nearly the time of Mississippi's statehood.[6]

At the height of its use prior to the War of 1812, the Trace served as a primary route of travel and communication between the lower Mississippi, the Midwest, and the eastern United States. It existed for the most part as a one-way route, however. Thousands of traders who had traveled with the current down the Ohio, Tennessee, and Mississippi Rivers aboard flatboats laden with goods to be marketed in Natchez and New Orleans used the route for their return home. The boats these men arrived on themselves became a commodity, as upon arrival they were customarily taken apart for lumber and sold piece by piece together with the cargoes they had carried. The total value of the goods and boat generated a season's income for farmers from throughout a large area of the interior of the country. These traders used the Trace as the first leg in their long journey back home. Largely traveling on foot, they would frequently cluster together in groups for safety and companionship. These bands of rough-edged and weary travelers presented quite a sight, being described colorfully by ornithologist Alexander Wilson on a trip to the region in 1810:

Figure 11.1. Located along the Natchez Trace, Mount Locust was constructed around 1780 and represents many of the primitive stands or inns that served travelers during their journeys. (Courtesy of Mississippi Department of Archives and History)

> I passed . . . several parties of boatmen returning from Natchez and New Orleans. . . . These were dirty as Hottentots, their dress a shirt and trousers of canvas, black greasy and sometimes in tatters; their skin burnt wherever exposed to the sun; each with a budget wrapt up in an old blanket; their beards eighteen days old added to the singularity of their appearance, which was altogether savage. These people came from various tributary streams of the Ohio, hired at forty or fifty dollars a trip, to return back at their own expense.

Wilson estimated that in his fourteen days of travel along the Trace he met about fifty such boatmen every day.[7]

Although he could not have known it, Wilson was witnessing the last flickers of the Trace's brief heyday. With the invention of steam-powered navigation, which allowed for travel back upriver in a fraction of the time it took to go overland, the venerable highway suddenly became obsolete. By the 1820s, use of the road had already dramatically declined, and by the 1830s it had begun to fall into disrepair. While segments of the road continued to be used for regional travel well into the future, the route's role as a single, intersectional travel corridor lay in the past.[8]

The Trace has survived in our memory much longer than its period of use owing in no small part to the legends associated with criminals who lurked along its path. It acquired a reputation as the haunt of villainous gangs even during its time, its infamy embellished in the modern era with its history retold in such titles as *The Devil's Backbone* and a host of others referencing its supposed treacherous past. The stories are based to some degree in truth, for boatmen traveling through the wilderness on foot with half a year's earnings in their knapsacks, traders with cash from recent sales in saddlebags, or settlers with all their worldly possessions in tow, attracted no little criminal attention. The road's reputation as a dangerous route spurred many to take extra precaution in their travels, ranging from attempting to hide money in Bibles, sewing it into the linings of clothes or stashing cash somewhere away from their camps every night. Notices of actual robberies such as this one posted in a Natchez newspaper spread like wildfire, and became exaggerated with each retelling:

> On Monday evening . . . I was struck from my horse by some villain, by a violent blow on my head, which deprived me of sense for nearly six hours, on my recovery, I found that I was robbed of my pocket-book, containing a due bill signed by D.D. Elliott, for John Wilkins and Co for 1539 dollars or thereabout . . . a receipt given by Nicholls for 1100 dollars (or perhaps more) and several other papers. . . .[9]

No legend sparked as much conversation at the time or in later years as that of the Mason Gang, whose dark tale seemed to represent all that early travelers feared about traversing early Mississippi's frontier wilderness highways. A small criminal syndicate led by Samuel Mason, the group preyed on travelers along the Trace in the early 1800s and became arguably the most wanted and notorious men in the southwestern United States. Virtually every mishap, real or imagined, along the road came to be blamed on the Mason gang for a brief period of time, with the number and grisly nature of their misdeeds growing exponentially in the retelling. In truth they are known to have robbed several travelers, but were never conclusively linked to any specific murders. Regardless, the group and the fear of unchecked criminality they symbolized came to be a special focus of the citizenry of the Mississippi Territory, beginning with Governor William C. C. Claiborne. The $2,000 cash reward he offered for Mason's capture ultimately led to his undoing by his own associates, who murdered him and brought his head in a sack to a circuit judge in order to claim their bounty. Unfortunately for them, they had been so active along the Trace that they were instantly recognized as part of Mason's entourage and were promptly arrested, tried, and hanged. The demise of Mason coincided with a general decline of reported criminal activity along the Trace, perhaps giving credence to his alleged level of activity.[10]

Regardless of the route they took on Mississippi's early roads, travelers encountered rather rude accommodations. Widely scattered inns, also known as stands or taverns, charging nominal rates ranging from about fifty cents to a few dollars per night, were located along the state's major roads and infamously featured the minimum in comfort and little or no privacy. Guests customarily shared beds, which more than likely had dirty sheets and a variety of insects to boot. Food could be "pretty rough, and often too scarce," in the words of early Mississippi resident and traveler Howard S. Fulkerson. "The boarders would crowd around the door at the hour of meals, and not infrequently the first man in would be pushed forward so violently as to floor him. . . ." Many of these early inns along paths on land ceded by native tribes were owned and operated by Native Americans. Mixed-blood entrepreneurs such as David Folsom and Greenwood LeFlore ran profitable and well-known stands, while a variety of others sold food to passing travelers: "corn at two dollars per bushel, corn blades at a bit [twelve and a half cents], pumpkins for a quarter, and hickory-nuts, walnuts, hazel-nuts for a bit."

The best-appointed and most professional hotels well into the statehood era were naturally located in Natchez, which had acquired a reputation for hospitality unrivaled by any other city in the territory. With the maturation of the state, more and increasingly better hotels gradually came on line, especially in Mississippi's developing urban centers. Some of the best accommodations could be found at the state's various mineral springs and the coastal resorts along the Gulf Coast, which by the early 1830s were already developing into minor tourist destinations. Viewed as a healthy, "salubrious" retreat from the stifling summers in larger regional cities such as New Orleans and Mobile, resort hotels began to spring up in Shieldsborough, Pass Christian, Biloxi, Ocean Springs, and even Pascagoula as early as the 1810s. The famed Pass Christian Hotel, in particular, became well known in the 1830s as among the most posh of its type in the region, and its operators kept a booking office in New Orleans.[11]

Rivers were the primary highways in Mississippi. An incredible variety of types of boats serviced the river trade in the state's early years, bringing in a large portion of the imported goods its people purchased and shipping out a great deal of its agricultural products. "No form of water craft so whimsical, no shape so outlandish, can well be imagined, but what . . . may be seen lying to the shore, or floating on the river," observed one resident of early Mississippi. On any given day on the banks of the mighty Mississippi or along stretches of the state's other navigable streams one might see an assortment of watercraft: canoes, pirogues (essentially very long canoes); wide, flat-bottomed boats called skiffs; batteaus (especially large skiffs); a variety of simple rafts; and poleboats (open barges moved forward by means of long poles that made contact with the stream bed or bank). The mainstays of river trade in the pre-steamboat era were flatboats and keelboats. Coming in a wide spectrum of sizes, flatboats in particular were among the most numerous craft on the Mississippi in the period between 1800 and 1820. Essentially sturdy, square-ended floating boxes capable of carrying immense loads of cargo, they traveled with the current and were commonly broken up and sold for lumber upon arrival at their destination. Keel boats were also prevalent, but less common. These shallow-draft boats, averaging forty to

Figure 11.2. Flatboats were early form of transportation along the rivers of Mississippi. (Courtesy of the Library of Congress)

seventy-five feet in length, featured pointed prows at each end, and a central keel that provided stability. Much more manageable on the downstream journey than flatboats, they also could be operated in exceptionally shallow and winding waterways, which made them popular on interior rivers such as the Big Black and Pearl. To navigate upstream, keelboats could be pulled forward by crewmen using oars or long poles they stuck into the riverbed, or they could be "cordeled." Cordeling involved crewmen onshore pulling a boat with a rope or long cable or fastening one of these to a tree ahead of the boat and literally pulling it up its length, then repeating the process. Regardless of the method used, upstream travel on keelboats could be slow and laborious in the extreme.[12]

The advent of the steamboat revolutionized trade and transportation in frontier Mississippi, giving life to some of its largest communities in the period under study and influencing the rhythms to which its overall economy moved. The first steamer to operate on the Mississippi, the *New Orleans*, made its initial voyage in the winter of 1811–12, startling rapt onlookers with its ability to stem, albeit slowly, the river's powerful current. Other steamboats soon followed, ushering in a dramatic new era. The second boat to run regular routes between Natchez and New Orleans, the *Vesuvius*, made an especially memorable debut. Joseph Dunbar Shields left us with this memorable account of the boat's almost supernatural appearance in 1814 to Natchez residents, who at first could scarcely comprehend the novel machine that would soon transform their region:

Figure 11.3. A steamboat, 1833. (Courtesy of the Library of Congress)

> I was dozing quietly on my hill when I was somewhat startled by a loud, hoarse, cough, apparently from the lungs of a Mastodon. . . . I looked up and saw the most extraordinary monster that ever met my vision; the smoke fumed from its nostrils and it coughed at every step . . . oh my, how they (onlookers) all jumped and screamed when the engine blew off the steam.[13]

By the time of Mississippi's statehood, steamboats had become an everyday sight and entrenched in the regional trading network. In 1818 there were over thirty steamboats working on the Mississippi, and by 1820 steamers regularly traveled between New Orleans and Louisville. By the 1830s hundreds of steamboats plied the waters of the Mississippi and other regional streams, providing a pivotal link in emerging trading networks, reducing the time and expense involved in shipping goods to market, and helping entrench the cotton trade in the regional economy.[14]

Steamboat travel lay fraught with danger at every turn of the river. Tricky or tight turns, whirlpools, undercurrents, and sandbars could challenge even the most experienced pilots, while snags and all manner of floating river debris could pierce thin hulls. Nighttime navigation could be especially dangerous, as the dark concealed not only all these obstacles but other boats and on occasion the very channel itself. Temperamental boilers, if not monitored constantly by someone with intricate knowledge of their functioning, could become ticking time bombs. Riverwater silt clogged up valves, causing the machinery that powered steamers to quickly overheat and explode. As if all this were not enough, the extremely flammable cotton cargo Mississippi steamboats carried in ubiquity could engulf the entire boat in flames in mere minutes. "Thousands are the means employed by the Mississippi to attract its victims," wrote one candid observer. "If a month happens to elapse without a steamboat or some other craft being engulphed [*sic*] in the agitated waves, all at once you hear of the former having foundered, after striking against a snag, projecting from the bottom of the river, or of the boiler having burst, or the boat taken fire . . . on all these occasions, human lives are sacrificed." As a result of navigational hazards and wear and tear, steamboats had an exceptionally short average lifespan of only about three or four years.[15]

The potential profits from steamer operation made all these dangers worth the risk. While boats were expensive to build, easily costing upwards of twenty or thirty thousand dollars, most could turn a profit for slaveholders in as little as a year. Large boats could carry well over 1,000 bales of cotton by the 1830s, charging freight from Natchez to New Orleans alone at one dollar per bale. When combined with profits from passenger fares and the variety of other merchandise they transported from point to point, the lucrative nature of the boating business becomes obvious.[16]

Mississippi's namesake river served as the superhighway of trade and travel in its formative era both for the state and much of the nation as a whole. Over the river's roiling brown waters steamers transported all manner of merchandise that greased the wheels of regional economies. Everett Dick, who chronicled the development of the Old Southwest in *Dixie Frontier*, his sweeping look at the region, captured the diversity of the river-borne trade that gave impetus to the rise of steamers as for a brief time the most efficient means of transporting goods over long distances by noting the variety of river boats:

> bringing from southwestern New York lumber, from northern Alabama cotton, from Tennessee and Kentucky pork, flour, whisky, hemp, tobacco, and rope, from Illinois and various other places cattle and horses, from Missouri lead and pelts. Some boats were loaded with ear corn, others with barrels of apples or potatoes. There was frozen or boiled cider by the boatload, dried fruits, and every agricultural or manufactured product in the whole area. Roosters were crowing, cattle lowing, horses stamping in their stalls, and swine squealing. There were boats fitted especially for and loaded entirely with turkeys that gobbled furiously.

Virtually every commodity that could be traded, from soap to shoes, was for a time brought in and shipped out of Mississippi via steamer.[17]

Natchez served as Mississippi's primary port throughout the state's early years, virtually unrivaled until the ascendancy of Vicksburg as a chief competitor in the late 1830s. Arrival at the town served as a navigational milestone for steamer captains, it being the largest port between Memphis and New Orleans and a strategic location for resupply for the final leg of the run to the latter. The arrival of steamboats put the wheels of the Natchez economic engine in motion, and locals frequently heralded their appearance with the firing of cannon or the blowing of horns. Travelers could not help but be astonished at the number of boats they witnessed docked at Natchez. These "floating towns" consisting of all descriptions of watercraft, sometimes as many as 150, "loaded with the produce of the upper country." Thousands of boats stopped in the town annually, with local observers noting that at least two per day were seen passing by on their way to New Orleans in the 1830s. Steamboats operated on Mississippi's interior rivers as well, but in much smaller numbers. Operators made sporadic attempts to navigate on the Pearl as far north as Jackson as early as the 1820s. Even with the legislative appropriations for improving navigation on the shallow, winding river, however, it never became a practical route. The Tombigbee ranked as the only other river in the state that allowed for regular steamboat operation in substantial numbers. While the great majority of its length ran through Alabama, boats operated along its upper reaches in Mississippi as high as Columbus by 1822. In seasonal high water, the boats might ply even further up the river to Aberdeen.[18]

Travel aboard Mississippi steamboats could be quite luxurious for those with means. On some of the larger and better equipped boats, passenger cabins might be decorated with fine curtains and mirrors and feature attentive stewards who promptly took care of every need. Food was usually abundant even if rarely very good, according to traveler's notes, with large meals commonly served as many as five times per day.

For most steamboat passengers, however, river travel was anything but glorious or leisurely. Tight and uncomfortable quarters, long idle hours, a mad rush for the table at meals, the incessant noise of men and machines, and frequent stops at all hours of the day and night to take on passengers, cargo, or wood to fuel boilers could all make journeys something more to be endured than enjoyed. Early Mississippi traveler and minister George Rogers left this somewhat unflattering summary of steamboat travel, with which many could identify:

> Let the reader imagine an apartment twelve feet by twenty-five, with a huge stove in the midst, lumbered up with trunks, chests, articles for bedding, coils of rope, casks, cooking utensils, etc . . . and nearly every foot of the remaining space occupied by some half a hundred of passengers. Then let him imagine the fetor of an atmosphere tainted by so many breaths; by the continual frying of various articles of food; by the filth, of divers kinds, necessarily generated by the huddling together of so many persons and things in so small a compass; but chiefly by the vile tobacco juice continually spattering from nearly every mouth.[19]

Occasional violence added to the unpleasant realities of steamboat travel, much of it traced to the pervasiveness of gambling as a way to pass the time. While these confrontations were usually confined to occasional on-deck brawls sparked by a combination of tempers and alcohol, some altercations became much more deadly. One traveler aboard a boat that had docked at Natchez recorded how, upon pulling away from the wharf to continue its journey, "the crack of a rifle was heard, and one of the passengers, who had just gained the upper-deck after his shore-visit of an hour or so, fell dead, pierced through the head. The wheels were backed, the corpse laid on the nearest wharf by the captain, with an account of the manner of his death, and, this done, off went the steamer." Such episodes may have been highly unusual, but are illustrative of the unpredictability of travel during the era.[20]

Rivermen, who worked on the various boats and ports of call for a living, provided the most colorful aspect of river travel in Mississippi's formative years. Uniquely associated with riverine life, the legends associated with them have become part of the lore of the era. Few of those who left written accounts of life along the river failed to note the wild appearance, outrageous manners, and exuberant boastfulness of some of these men. Dirty, sunburned, and scruffy, professional boatmen were, according to one early scholar of the trade, the "epicure of excitement. Work no other man could do was his one luxury." Boatmen became famous for their braggadocio, delivered in the form of metaphors and similes as part of a witty but sometimes confrontational banter that filled abundant spare time and helped established chain of command. Christian Schultz's observations of travel along the Mississippi in 1808, *Travels on an Inland Voyage*, includes this colorful exchange between two boatmen he witnessed near Natchez:

> I am a man; I am a horse; I am a team. I can whip any man in all Kentucky, by G—d. The other replied, I am an alligator; half man, half horse; can whip any on the Mississippi by G—d. The first one again I am a man; have the best horse, best dog, best gun, and the handsomest wife in all Kentucky, by G—d. The other I am a Mississippi snapping turtle: have bear's claws, alligator's teeth, and the devil's tail; can whip any man, by G—d. This was too much for the first, and at it they went like two bulls, and continued for half an hour, when the alligator was fairly vanquished by the horse.[21]

The legend of Mike Fink, a largely apocryphal character but one based to a degree in truth as an embodiment of several personalities, is particularly well known. A braggart, notorious drinker, expert shot, ruthless brawler, and near superhuman worker with unrivaled depth of knowledge about the river, Fink—or his legend—became something of a folk hero. He supposedly met his end at the hands of a drunken friend who accidentally shot him while attempting to shoot a cup of whiskey off the top of his head. It served as a fitting end to the story of his reckless life, real or imagined, which only cemented his place in the culture of the river and highlighted the rollicking nature of those who labored along its path.[22]

Whereas steamboats performed their function with a degree of grace and glamour, railroads operated in a more straightforwardly utilitarian fashion and hence never acquired the same air of mystique. The clanging and banging of their smoke-belching engines and the chatter of squeaking wheels on monotonous iron strands of rails nevertheless ultimately became more vital to the economic life of the state. The railroads pointed the way to the future, promising to bring efficient trade to every corner of the state through which they passed and eliminating reliance on fickle rivers alone for trade. Ironically, water-dependent trade had become so fixed in the public mind that the first iterations of railroads in the region were conceived as merely a complement to steamboats. Some even featured cars pulled by horses over their short distances instead of steam-powered engines and operated exclusively to haul goods from an inland location to a previously inaccessible port. As the technology improved and investment poured in, railroads eventually revolutionized transportation in Mississippi and helped encourage settlement in the state's interior. As with steamboats, the revolution reached the state in its earliest stages. The first successful, albeit extremely short, rail lines in the United States began operation in the late 1820s, and Mississippi jumped into railroading with both feet in the decade between 1830 and 1840. Mississippi chartered its first railroad, the West Feliciana, in 1831 to run between Woodville and St. Francisville, Louisiana, on the Mississippi River. Regular service belatedly began in 1836, by which time plans for several other railroads had already been placed in motion.[23]

The explosive growth in Mississippi in the 1830s gave rise to dozens of railroad-building schemes. Between 1835 and 1839, the legislature approved the charter of no less than twenty railroads. Only a small portion, however, actually laid any track in that time. Railroad construction proved to be an enormously expensive and labor-consuming enterprise, requiring thousands of dollars of capital investment per mile and crews of hundreds of men. The logistical challenge alone precluded success of all but the most organized and determined. Further, with the demand for credit in the cash-strapped state so high in the mid-1830s, most railroad corporations spent more time pursuing lucrative bank-like lending activities than actual road construction. The financial depression of 1837 ended the operations of the great majority of the state's fledgling railroad operations before they had even begun. By 1840 a mere eighty-three miles of track had been laid in Mississippi, the majority of that only partially completing numerous planned routes.[24]

One, the Vicksburg and Jackson (Clinton) line, nevertheless augured the future of rail transport in Mississippi. Chartered in the early 1830s and in operation between the Mississippi and Big Black Rivers by 1838, the road easily became the most significant in the state by 1840. By that year, shortly after it had been completed to Jackson, it was already shipping thousands of bales of cotton from the interior of the state to the port of Vicksburg. The route demonstrated precisely the power of rails to transform trading networks and help spur cotton production along the routes through which they ran. It also played no small role in the unseating of Natchez as the economic capital in the state. In similar fashion in the coming decade, railroads would contribute heavily to both the settlement and economic ascendancy of the northern portion of the state. In every region of Mississippi, railroads would soon give sudden rise to "railroad towns," which tied their fortunes to locomotives every bit as directly as those of port cities had been linked to steamboats.[25]

Regardless of the impetus for their formation, Mississippi's widely scattered, relatively small, and predominantly agricultural and mobile population lent itself to the forming of few urban clusters in the territorial and early statehood years. With few exceptions, Mississippi's early towns were small communities that served as trading and legal centers servicing the surrounding countryside in which they lay. Several sprang up organically at the intersections of key roads, along bluffs overlooking navigable streams, or in other strategic locations. Many had a common history as a planned county seat or trading center, speculatively laid out and eventually taking root as much through fortunate geography as any inherent future value. "Various towns," reported one observer of town-building in early Mississippi, "were located . . . in various spots; and the proprietors of all had not the shadow of a doubt . . . that each and every one would, in a few years, contain a hundred thousand inhabitants, and that lots, seventy-five by twenty-five feet, would be worth at least twenty-five hundred dollars each. . . . Some of the embryo cities were removed by a single wagon to other locations which had their day, and were known no more forever." Joseph Holt Ingraham jotted in 1830 that "Small towns, with mighty names . . . are springing up here and there, like mushrooms, amidst the affrighted forests." Almost as many towns came and went during the era as survived past it, as they either were passed by in the flood of settlement of the state, overshadowed by an economic rival, decimated by an epidemic disease, or even left high and dry by a change in the course of a river.[26]

Most of Mississippi's early cities were dirty, rough-edged places that had little of the polish the term might imply. Built primarily of wood, they commonly featured a cluster of sometimes ramshackle structures forced together in random patterns. Through early city streets—muddy when wet and dusty when not—traveled a constant stream of dapper businessmen, roughly clothed farmers, petticoat-wearing housewives, coarsely dressed slaves, and a variety of dogs, cats, and livestock. The acrid smell of smoke from dozens of kitchens and hearths hung heavy in the air, along with other pungent odors such as an assemblage of men and beasts might generate in a hot and humid environment with no running water, no sewers, and no air conditioning. The clip-clop of horse hooves, the drone of wagon wheels traversing packed dirt, and the murmur of conversation and laughter formed the audible backdrop of these urban centers. They largely shut down at night, the occasional flickers of candles in windows or strains of music played on piano or fiddle sometimes the only signs of activity. These towns largely marched to the beat of the countryside they served, vibrating with activity in cotton-trading season or when courts held session, and often languishing in the periods between. Within their limits—and almost as important in the communities as the elected town governments—met a variety of associations, clubs, and fraternities that served as early settlers' collective efforts to bring a sense of order to the frontier and enhance community life. These included militia and fire companies, Temperance Associations, Anti-Dueling Societies, Debating Societies, Hibernian Societies, Sons of Temperance, Masons, Odd Fellows, Sons of Malta, and a host of others.[27]

Of the three primary population centers in the Mississippi Territory, two lay in what became the state of Alabama; the Mobile Bay area and the Tennessee River Valley. Each featured several small communities scattered over a wide region of relatively heavy settlement and a paramount commercial hub. The aged city of Mobile had been founded by the French in 1702, and by the time of its annexation into the Mississippi Territory had become a key trade and military outpost controlling Gulf access from the extensive Alabama and Tombigbee River systems. The city, an assortment of low-slung houses and businesses stretching along the flat, sultry waterfront at the head of the bay that shared its name, featured one of the more diverse populations of any community in the territory. French, Spanish, Creole, and American populations lived and traded there, including a substantial number of slaves and one of the greatest concentrations of free blacks in the Southwest outside of New Orleans. In the first decade of the 1800s, free blacks, often generically termed Creoles, formed as much as a third of its population and maintained militia groups and other social and civic organizations separate from those of their white neighbors. Despite its relatively small population, perhaps 1,000 at the time of Mississippi's statehood, Mobile's strategic location made it one of the most important settlements in the region. Just north of Mobile lay satellite communities known as the "Tensaw" and "Bigbee" settlements, which featured no large towns but a number of small villages (the eventual capital of the Alabama Territory, St. Stephens, being the largest, with a population of perhaps 500 people). Altogether, this closely interconnected area represented one of the most extensively settled regions in the entire Mississippi Territory.[28]

The boomtown of Huntsville sprang up in the northernmost reaches of the Mississippi Territory. Originally known as Big Spring, after the water source around which early settlers planned a community, the town traced its founding back to the arrival of John Hunt in 1805 prior to the official cession of the land by the Chickasaws and Cherokees. Within five years the fertile valley in which it lay had attracted a large number of settlers from Tennessee, North Carolina, and Georgia. By the time of the War of 1812, the town and the newly formed county of Madison had become one of the territory's most dynamic commercial and political centers. The town assumed the name of Twickenham in 1809, owing to influential early citizen LeRoy Pope's admiration of poet Alexander Pope (Pope called his home estate Twickenham). But in the days leading to the war the English-inspired name fell out of favor and locals changed it to Huntsville. Featuring a handsome public square consisting of a courthouse surrounded by numerous well-built homes and stores, the town gave the appearance of unusual refinement even during the territorial years. On the verge of Mississippi's statehood and the simultaneous formation of the Alabama Territory, Madison County had a population approaching 15,000 white and black people, and Huntsville stood among the largest cities in the region.[29]

The third relatively heavily settled area, and the one lying within what became the state of Mississippi, stretched along its western border on the banks of its namesake river. This oldest and most developed corridor of urban communities in the future state, featuring the city of Natchez and other noteworthy communities, had its growth fueled by trade along the continent's primary artery. Its geographic setting allowed the area a degree of wealth and influence found nowhere else in its early years. For most of Mississippi's frontier era, Natchez stood as the largest of these western communities, towering within the territory and state as its lone true city and primary hub of economic activity. It ranked, in fact, as the largest city between New Orleans and Cincinnati at the time of the formation of the Mississippi Territory in 1798. Established by the French as a colonial outpost near the villages of the Natchez Indians in the 1700s, the city had long been established as a primary trading center for an expansive region stretching hundreds of miles in every direction. Power, wealth, and the people that held both were clustered more tightly in the city and its hinterlands than any other place in the state until well into the antebellum era. Natchez proper, a compact concentration of homes and businesses spread along an orderly grid of streets laid out during the city's Spanish occupation, sat atop an unusually high and picturesque bluff overlooking the Mississippi. Consequently, the city presented a "most romantick [*sic*] scenery," in the words of one visitor, with its streets lined by "Pride of China" trees (chinaberry) and stunning vistas of the Mississippi and the lands beyond that its position afforded. Its heart and soul lay along the gritty riverfront below at the port that provided its economic lifeblood and connected it to regional and world markets. The city contained two distinct entities practically if not technically, Natchez and its port community, Natchez-Under-the-Hill, which together represented the best and worst of city living in early Mississippi. Exaggerated claims of the alternating cosmopolitan and hedonistic lifestyle each supported were, and continue to be, made by those attempting to understand the period in which they mutually thrived as the Magnolia State's dual-natured epicenter.[30]

Figure 11.4. Early twentieth-century view of the infamous Natchez-Under-the-Hill. (Courtesy of Mississippi Department of Archives and History)

The whole place bustled with activity. Carriages and wagons continuously ambled through crowded streets; throngs of traders and citizens wound their way in and out of well-stocked business establishments, inspecting imported goods of every description; and an exotic assortment of "Americans, French and Spanish creoles, Mulattoes and negroes" hawked meat, fish, and vegetables at the city's markets. The city's merchants ably served a relatively large and growing population, but relied on the steady stream of visitors daily arriving in town for business or pleasure for much of their commerce. They were especially reliant on planters or their representatives, who purchased goods needed on their plantations in bulk and usually on credit. On the riverfront, it seemed as if every hour a boat arrived or departed from the landing during the city's heyday as Mississippi's primary port. "Hundreds of arks, or flat-boats, loaded with the produce of the Western States, even from the interior of Pennsylvania, here line the landing for half a mile, often lying five tier deep," exclaimed an enthralled John Anthony Quitman in a letter to his father shortly after his arrival. "No part of the United States holds out better prospects for a young lawyer. Why did I not come here, instead of stopping in Ohio? Money is as plenty here as it is scarce there." Quitman should have felt right at home, because middle-class businessmen, including a large number of lawyers and an assortment of merchants unequaled anywhere in the Southwest outside of New Orleans, gave vibrancy to the city's robust commercial scene.[31]

Cotton provided the best gauge of its position of economic preeminence. Its centrality to the city, and the city's centrality to the state's trade, could not have been more obvious in the frontier era. Visitor Henry B. Fearon wrote a note of observation that could have been penned by hundreds of others, recording that he left Natchez "with little knowledge of its inhabitants . . . but with an impression of its comparative prosperity exceeding any town which I have ever seen. The streets are literally crammed with cotton bales for the Liverpool market." The city remained the state's leading cotton port by several times over until the emergence of other smaller but active ports of note in the 1820s. By the 1830s over 50,000 bales of cotton, as much of a sixth of all bales produced in the state as a whole, were annually shipped from the city.[32]

Natchez served as the early state's unquestioned cultural capital throughout the period. It hosted salons, balls, and dances, prided itself in having the state's most lively theater scene, and featured the best restaurants and hotels the state could offer. The city hosted some of the best schools and the most well-equipped libraries in the state, gave rise to a relatively flourishing press and a small but important printing scene, and laid claim to the most organized and sophisticated fraternal and civic societies of any community in Mississippi. Surrounding it were some of the largest and most elaborate planter mansions in the state, remarkable even for their time and some still standing as enduring testimony to the incredible concentration of wealth in the area. The presence of the well-to-do planters and the lavish lifestyles their wealth could support allowed for an assemblage of tradesmen such as silversmiths, painters, and musicians who could scarcely be found elsewhere in the state on any permanent basis until well into the statehood period. As a by-product of this concentration of affluence, the city held a position as the state's political capital throughout the territorial and early statehood periods. It only relinquished its virtual stranglehold on the functioning of state government and the occupancy of most of its highest offices in the 1830s, after demographic shifts brought about by the cession of huge swaths of Native American lands resulted in a dramatic change in the distribution of settlement and associated balance of political power in the state. Natchez's stature was such that on his celebrated visit to the United States in the mid-1820s, Revolutionary War hero Marie-Joseph Paul Yves Roch Gilbert du Motier, the Marquis de Lafayette, made the town the only stop in Mississippi during a whirlwind tour of every state in the nation at the time.[33]

Despite all these hallmarks of urban sophistication, Natchez remained a primitive city by eastern standards. It had few paved streets or sidewalks, and many travelers commented on the "filthy lodgings, exorbitant prices, mosquitoes, and crude manners" experienced during their stays. In its early years its architecture appeared surprisingly unimposing, featuring an assemblage of rather shoddily built wooden buildings and few brick structures until well into the statehood period. Its city council met in rented chambers for many years and even though it served as seat of state government after Mississippi's entry into the Union, it never had a state-owned capitol building or state office complex. Natchez never had quite as large a population as might be supposed from its position of influence in early Mississippi. It contained just 1,500 inhabitants in 1810 and little more than 2,000 at the time of statehood. It could boast of a population of only about 5,000 in 1840, modest enough by today's standards but the only city to claim that many residents in Mississippi until at least 1850. Still, it stood paramount in early Mississippi and exerted an influence significantly out of proportion to its actual size.[34]

Natchez's alter ego, Under-the-Hill, may have been the best-known urban entity in the state. It certainly holds the title as most legendary. Essentially a ramshackle village of businesses catering to a largely transient and river-borne clientele, it grew up around the wharves at the boat landing some 150 feet below the city's main streets on the bluff. The community became a place unto itself, offering gambling, drinking, and prostitution, located there out of a combination of convenient customer access and pressure to stay out of the city proper. Geography just made the boundaries more neatly defined, literally and figuratively.[35]

The place made quite an impression on visitors, many of whom claimed to be shocked and offended by the "profligate," "vile," "rude merriment" on open display. Despite their protestations of aversion, few could look away. Rather, they left some of the most colorful accounts of urban life in any part of early Mississippi. Joseph Holt Ingraham described Natchez-Under-the-Hill as viewed from the traveler's eye in a particularly detailed section of his book about his journey along the Mississippi:

> As we passed through the street—which we gained with difficulty from the boat, we picked our way to it as we could, through a filthy alley—the low, broken, half-sunken side-walks, were blocked up with fashionably dressed young men, smoking or lounging, tawdrily arrayed, highly rouged females, sailors, Kentucky boatmen, negroes, mulattoes, pigs, dogs, and dirty children. The sounds of profanity and Bacchnalian revels, well harmonizing with the scene, assailed our ears as we passed hastily along, through an atmosphere of tobacco smoke and other equally fragrant odors. . . .[36]

Others corroborated Ingraham's account by describing more straightforwardly a single busy street lined with "dancing-houses, tippling houses, houses of ill-fame, and gambling rooms," side by side with "ware houses, grogg shops, decayed boats proper for the uses of washer women." Many, such as Henry Ker, described it as the unsavory haunt of "the bold-faced strumpet, full of blasphemies" and the home of "the lowest orders of dissipation." Shortly after his arrival in Natchez, future Mississippi political and military leader John Anthony Quitman described the place with perhaps more insight in a letter to his father, explaining how "the river brings here the floating population of the whole West, and the wealth of the country entices adventurers from many lands. . . . Gambling and intemperance are carried to excess . . . and little jurisdiction is taken over their atrocities." Accounts of the outrageous debauchery and criminality in Natchez-Under-the-Hill must be taken with a grain of salt, for in all likelihood, it was never quite as wild or as large as legend might make it appear.[37]

Natchez's preeminence as Mississippi's primary urban center remained unchallenged until the 1830s. Several fast-growing towns either sprang up or matured in that decade and promised continued growth in the future as various sections of the state opened to American settlement. None looked quite as laden with potential as Vicksburg, which had developed from a humble village near the site of an old colonial-era Spanish fort to Mississippi's second largest city in the span of less than twenty years. Long before the city took shape, visitors noted that the land it occupied, a series of massive bluffs overlooking the Mississippi River long known as the Walnut Hills, was ideally situated for a settlement. A traveler passing through in the 1790s observed: "Walnut Hills is a beautiful situation for a town, and an advantageous one for a fort. . . . The few houses which are scattered around it [the fort], and the green bank on which they stand, surrounded with flowering, verdant, and lofty trees, presented at once a picturesque and romantic appearance to our eyes, fatigued with the uniformity of the prospect to which we had for so many miles been witness." In 1819 lots were laid out in and around the small village that had grown up on the spot where the bluff met the river, and in 1825 founders incorporated the town as Vicksburg in honor of early settler and Methodist minister Newitt Vick. By the end of the next decade, the rapidly developing town had a population of about 3,000. It included some fifty doctors and thirty lawyers, had dozens of thriving businesses, and boasted its own volunteer militias and fire companies, a Temperance Association, a Debating Society, a Hibernian Society, and several chapters of the Masons, Odd Fellows, and other fraternal groups. Most important as a factor in gauging its growth, it shipped annually from its port upwards of 30,000 cotton bales. Once rail service arrived in the city, it assumed a path toward overtaking Natchez as Mississippi's paramount center of trade.[38]

As in Natchez, population and economic growth did not necessarily translate into an urban paradise. While Natchez had Under-the-Hill, Vicksburg had Kangaroo, a riverside haunt of ruffians and gamblers that virtually formed its own community and whose activities were largely outside the reach of authorities in Vicksburg proper. "Never, positively, never was I in so rowdy a place in my life," observed one traveler who endured a rather unhappy stay in the frontier town and had nothing good to say about its people or its unusually hilly topography. "One half of the shops are drinking establishments and every bar seems thronged with customers. . . . A most singular place is Vicksburg! So broken into heaps and hollows is the ground, that your neck is in jeopardy, if you walk after night-fall; and the houses are built—Lord help me!—I cannot describe how. The ground floor is often on a level with the roof of its next neighbor! And after a rain, the streets are a paradise for ducks, geese, and other aquatics; but a perfect purgatory for horses and human bipeds."[39]

The venerable town of Port Gibson, nestled between the Natchez Trace and the Mississippi along a tributary stream known as Bayou Pierre, formed the third of the three river trading towns that comprised well over half of the state's frontier-era urban landscape. Approximately equidistant from the ancient commercial hub of Natchez and the developing one of Vicksburg in the early statehood years, it stood as perhaps the second largest city in the state when Mississippi entered the Union, and still ranked among the six largest in 1840. By the latter year it had acquired several flourishes of urban refinement, such as ornate churches, thriving stores, and several fashionable homes, eventually becoming a town that, according to popular legend, General Ulysses S. Grant claimed "too beautiful to burn" during the Civil War. But in the territorial period it had as rough and unpolished an appearance as any of the rude villages that passed for towns in the Mississippi Territory. A traveler on a visit there in 1808 observed that the "little town of twenty houses is the capital of Claiborne county, and is esteemed the most thriving place in the territory, notwithstanding it is extremely unhealthy, from the proximity of some stagnant ponds. . . . There is a very mean gaol [jail], and an equally bad court-house. . . . On the whole, Port Gibson and its neighborhood is perhaps the most dissolute as well as the most thriving part of the territory."[40]

The small town of Washington, which never contained more than 1,000 residents during the era, nonetheless came to play an unlikely but important role in defining what city life might be in early Mississippi. Remembered as the "Versailles" of the Mississippi Territory, it became the home of an unusually sophisticated society. One of the state's earliest historians claimed it was "the haunt of politicians and office hunters; the place of political intrigue; the point to which all persons in pursuit of land or occupation first came." When Mississippi was on the verge of statehood, Washington boasted at least three hotels, the first territorial public library, a newspaper, and the early state's premier institution of higher education, Jefferson College. Washington began life as an unassuming rural village a mere six miles northeast of Natchez. It suddenly became a place of prominence in the wake of the national election of 1800, which swept Thomas Jefferson's Republican Party into power and led to the ousting of territorial governor Winthrop Sargent in favor of William C. C. Claiborne. The General Assembly soon relocated the territorial capital from Natchez—perceived as a hotbed of the Federalist party—to the supposedly healthier environment of Washington. It was an act of political spite, but owing in large part to frequent outbreaks of yellow fever in Natchez, Washington ended up becoming the seat of government for the remainder of the territorial years. The town never had any public buildings despite this status, and remained an "indifferent looking little place in which scarcely one house was finished." The territorial legislature was forced to meet in various rented facilities while Washington remained capital, with a tavern owned by Charles de France, known as Assembly Hall, serving as the de facto capitol.[41]

Few cities of substantial size developed anywhere outside the river region in frontier Mississippi. Despite a relatively long period of American settlement, eastern Mississippi contained only one town of notable size, Columbus, by 1840. Actually one of the state's largest river ports by virtue of its location along the Tombigbee River, the town served as the trading center for a broad region and boasted a population of about 1,500. Cotton Gin Port, a small community located at the head of navigation of the Tombigbee, traced its origins to the establishment of a trading post serving the Chickasaw Indians in the early days of the Mississippi Territory. It received its unusual name from the cotton gin built there by the United States government. While it served as an important regional trading center throughout Mississippi's formative years, it never developed into a significant urban center. At its height in the 1840s it claimed at most 500 residents. On the Gulf Coast, where sandy soils made large-scale agriculture difficult, a widely scattered population consisting of several small and for the most part seasonally inhabited villages caught the ocean breezes, with only Pascagoula and Biloxi of the "Six Sisters" (Shieldsborough, Pass Christian, Mississippi City, Ocean Springs, and East and West Pascagoula) approaching the size of what might be termed actual towns prior to 1840. None had a population of more than about 500 at the end of this frontier era. In northern Mississippi, which remained officially in Native American hands until the 1830s, no sizable towns emerged until near the end of that decade. Those that did were a reflection of the dramatic population boom in the region that resulted following treaties with the Choctaws and Chickasaws that opened the area to American settlement. Holly Springs, the largest trading center in the northern section of the state in 1840 with a population of about 2,000, had only been in existence a mere three years.[42]

Mississippi's capital city of Jackson languished throughout the frontier era as a rather unpromising and artificial urban center. The town had been the site of a trading post operated by a Frenchman named Louis LeFleur prior to the War of 1812, but claimed only a mere cluster of homesteads when the state legislature directed that the state government be moved there in 1822. It incorporated the town and named it after Andrew Jackson. Its sole reason for being—that it lay near the geographic center of the state and was thus a suitable site for a capital—proved a predictably flimsy basis for community building. Laid out in a checkerboard pattern with several planned parks and wide streets, on paper it looked idyllic. In reality, though, it barely functioned as a city when the legislature adjourned in its early years. Unimpressed visitors from abroad derided the seat of government in the frontier city as "a kind of superior hay-loft" in which "the imitation of the forms of the British parliament was rather ludicrous."

Prior to 1830 it featured a small and transitory population, leading visitors to conclude alternately that it was either a "wretched village in a state of decay" or "a city springing up in the midst of the forest and as it were by enchantment. . . ." Most determined on the former, such as one visitor during the 1830s who found "buildings . . . scattered at long distances . . . of the plainest materials, and wholly devoid of architectural taste or design, and even then, wore the appearance of decay, though the town was in its infancy." Only with the decision to keep the capital in Jackson for an extended period of time, as a part of the 1832 constitution, did Jackson begin to assume the airs of a permanent city. By that time, Jackson finally had shown signs of developing into the thriving, centrally located city its founders envisioned and that it would eventually become.[43]

The Mississippi Territory began and ended its approximately two decades of life as a rather sparsely inhabited, poorly connected region full of more promise than practical means for economic and population expansion. The state of Mississippi, by contrast, ended its second decade of existence as a physically and economically integrated entity featuring several rapidly growing major urban centers at the heart of an increasingly sophisticated network of economic activity. The early statehood years laid the foundation for Mississippi's further development in the antebellum era and influenced the pattern of evolution it would experience far into the future.

CHAPTER 12

The Rise of Jacksonian Democracy

The development of Mississippi's political infrastructure during its first two decades of statehood proved every bit as important to its future as its physical maturation. As the state emerged from the faction-ridden, decentralized, and intensely local electoral system that characterized its territorial days, a new, party-based political system brought the young state into the realm of national affairs with remarkable speed. By 1830, national party alignment had already come to shape political debate in the state over everything from persistent internal sectional rivalry to broader issues such as states' rights and the scope and purpose of the federal government. Owing in part to the fact that Mississippians regarded the most prominent military and political leader of the era, Andrew Jackson, as one of their own, the state's politics came to be especially defined by his rise and all that he represented politically. By the end of the early statehood period, Mississippi had transformed from a frontier backwater region, disconnected from national affairs, to a central player in the defining political debates of the era.

Originally, the rugged self-sufficiency that characterized life in Mississippi's frontier era discouraged concern with politics in any broad sense for much of the populace. Governed by authorities that, in the words of one historian, were generally perceived as "remote and generally negligent," the average citizen had neither the time nor interest to ruminate on political philosophy or mull over the latest goings-on in the nation's capital. The majority of residents of the state in the frontier era hailed from other states or countries, and the relatively young political entity in which they found themselves living simply had not had time to nurture bonds of allegiance or affection. This thinking proved especially true during Mississippi's first two decades of existence, as the Mississippi Territory had not developed organically, and to most its government represented an amorphous political unit with which they could expect to have little official contact. The few government officials appointed to administer the territory generally arrived late and ill-equipped; the first judge in the Washington District, one of the primary population centers in the early Mississippi Territory, did not arrive until a full six years after its creation. Settlers such as Gideon Lincecum, who moved into the eastern section of the territory around the time of Mississippi's statehood and at first did not know for certain whether his settlement lay in the new state or the Alabama Territory, justifiably viewed themselves as "cut off from the law." In Lincecum's case, he remembered he had lived in Mississippi eighteen months before he saw a state officer of any kind. Even late into the frontier period, Mississippi's government had a strikingly small presence within the state. A county sheriff and district judge were generally among the few public officials with which most residents would have any actual dealings. Those first officers in many instances were thoroughly unprepared to carry out vigorous and effective government. Early judges often decided cases according to the laws of the various states from which they hailed, "so that the most amusing differences of opinion often prevailed." In such an environment few but intensely local concerns resonated as political causes worthy of attention. A relatively small percentage of the population even bothered to vote in most elections in Mississippi's first decades. To the degree that political ideologies formed among the general population, they coalesced around individual personalities who fashioned themselves as spokesmen for specific communities and outlooks as opposed to sophisticated elaborations on the size or scope of good government.[1]

Candidates for office rarely campaigned openly for their desired position until well into Mississippi's statehood years. Following the example set by esteemed national leaders such as George Washington, politics in the frontier era still functioned under a code of conduct in which the office allegedly "found the man." Aspiring office holders, however, worked assiduously to make the match apparent. Oratory ranked as the most powerful tool office seekers had in their arsenal for self-advancement. Nearly a prerequisite for holding public office in many cases, the ability to speak well in public could define campaigns and careers. Long-winded speeches at public gatherings might be the only opportunity candidates had to communicate their position on certain issues or their general suitability for office. As open campaigning increasingly came into vogue in the post-statehood years, public speaking became the centerpiece of political campaigns and a benchmark for performance in office. Seargent S. Prentiss emerged as Mississippi's most celebrated orator in the 1830s, setting a bar for eloquence on the campaign trail and in legislative halls that few could match. Remembered as "an orator of rare combinations," he could speak to audiences for over three hours at a time while evidently keeping their interest. By the mid-1830s, speeches had become the centerpiece of campaigns in which candidates for statewide office literally

Figure 12.1. Seargent Smith Prentiss, state senator, congressman, and famed orator. (Collection of the Museum Division, Mississippi Department of Archives and History, 1978.8.1)

might speak in every county in the state. At outdoor barbecues, evening balls, and from hotel balconies, office-seekers appealed to audiences large and small in what would usually be a highlight event for each community. Audiences came out to hear candidates speak out of genuine interest, but for many the arrival of a candidate in town simply represented a diversion from daily routines and an opportunity for merriment. Drunken disorder and fights among those gathered were not uncommon; candidates grew accustomed to simply waiting for the disorders to subside and then continuing their address.[2]

In an age in which personalities shaped politics more than policy, charismatic individuals rose to prominence in Mississippi and framed political discourse within the state. A few key individuals merit mention as examples of the form political leadership took in frontier Mississippi. George Poindexter stood as the very epitome of the elite ruler. Moving to the Mississippi Territory from his native Virginia in 1802, he soon became active in politics. In 1804, already serving as the territory's attorney general, he began a remarkable career by winning election to the territorial House of Representatives. Over the course of the next three decades, he served as a United States Congressman, in the US Senate, and as governor of Mississippi. Along the way Poindexter served as a volunteer aid to General William Carroll at the Battle of New Orleans, produced the first codified set of laws for the state of Mississippi, and helped author its first constitution. "The history of his career is, in fact," according to Mississippi's first prominent historian, J. F. H. Claiborne, "the history of the Territory and the State, so closely and prominently was he connected with everything that occurred." Outgoing and flamboyant but not personable, he had a "colossal vanity"—he presented a portrait of himself to the state shortly after his retirement along with a modest letter of explanation—and seemed to make enemies more easily than friends. For example, he killed a rival in a duel sparked by his outspoken politics; and his inveterate enemy President Andrew Jackson publicly accused Poindexter of being part of a plot to assassinate him when a deranged man tried to kill "Old Hickory" in Washington, DC, in 1835. Poindexter's famed opposition to the most influential man in American politics stood emblematic of his pronounced distrust of and even condescension toward the electorate he served. Aristocratic in both outlook and bearing, he could never bring himself to countenance the type of democracy Jackson and his supporters envisioned, and expressed that disagreement through a number of specific, often bitter personal fights over issues such as patronage and revenue distribution. Poindexter represented an era that had passed by the mid-1830s, and he seemed to know it. After defeat in his last bid for office, he quietly entered retirement.[3]

In stark contrast to Poindexter stood Franklin Plummer. Born in Massachusetts, Plummer moved to Mississippi around 1821 and lived in Jackson and Copiah counties before settling in Pittsburg, a town he helped found that eventually merged with nearby Tullahoma to form the city of Grenada. Enterprising, ambitious, and personable, Plummer made friends easily in his adopted state and by 1826 had won election to the state legislature. Plummer introduced a startling populist ethos to Mississippi politics, consciously styling himself as the champion of the working man and the small landholder while running for office under the slogan of "Plummer for the People, and the People for Plummer." In his campaigning, he articulated a view of society as comprised of two antithetical groups—the empowered and the disfranchised, understood in laymen's terms at the time to be Natchez and eastern Mississippi—and stressed that no party had the interests of the common person at heart. His modest background, "backwoods" Mississippi credentials, appeal to the rank and file, and political savvy proved to be a wildly successful combination for a short time. Taking "everything before him like a tornado," in the words of a contemporary, Plummer managed to win election to Congress by defeating an opponent supported by the Natchez establishment in 1830 despite no strong party affiliation. The unexpected victory sparked one newspaper editorialist to rave that "The East now dates political birth . . . it awakens our surprise to see how long it has bowed to the Aristocracy of the West." Though Plummer's star blazed brightly in 1831, by 1835 he found himself a man without a party at a time in which parties were becoming the vehicle for political advancement, and his sectional appeal proved increasingly less potent as over two dozen new counties altered the longstanding political landscape in the state.[4]

Two men who managed to transcend local politics and take leadership roles on the national stage during the frontier era were Robert J. Walker and John Anthony Quitman. Hailing from Pennsylvania and New York, respectively, both worked as Natchez lawyers in the 1820s and gained entry into the state's political scene soon thereafter. As a senator during the Nullification Crisis, Walker assumed special prominence as a Unionist and an expansionist who became one of the leading advocates of both the West and the institution of slavery in the Senate. He would go on to serve as the Secretary of the US Treasury and as governor of the Kansas Territory. Quitman became a force in the cause of states' rights and became especially visible in his opposition to the Jackson administration over the issue of Nullification and for his advocacy of the Mississippi's State Rights Party in its aftermath. In his own words "vigilant and jealous . . . of the reserved rights of the states," Quitman became passionately interested in the expansion of slavery in the 1830s. Following a brief tenure as appointed governor in 1835, Quitman ventured to Texas in an attempt to take part in the revolution there but arrived too late to have any meaningful participation. He would later go on to have a much more eventful experience during the Mexican-American War in the 1840s, when he served as a major general and then as military governor of Mexico City. Returning home and serving for a second time as governor in 1850, his term would be interrupted by his rumored involvement in a Cuban filibustering scheme.[5]

Men such as these rose to power in a bitterly partisan environment at first shaped more by geography and socioeconomics than philosophy. Sectional rivalry dominated state politics during the 1820s. The dissimilarity between the wealthy Natchez District and the eastern Piney Woods fueled the fires of antagonism, with the older, more established Natchez District featuring the majority of the early state's wealthy planters and businessmen and the Piney Woods populated primarily by subsistence farmers, herdsmen, and lumbermen. One resident of the state during the era remembered in his memoirs just how radically different the two sections were, observing that he could "fancy no country on earth of the same extent [that] presented a wider difference in soil and population, especially one speaking the same language and professing the same religion." As late as 1830 the river counties in the Natchez area contained a third of the population of the entire state, but owned two-thirds of its slaves, paid over two-thirds of its taxes, owned three-quarters of its assessed property value, and published four of its five newspapers, while the nine counties of the Piney Woods contained about a quarter of the population and paid a mere thirteen percent of its taxes. These differences manifested themselves in both commerce and a decided concentration of political power in Natchez that virtually everyone else in the state resented.[6]

Natchez aggressively moved to capitalize on its inherent advantages. The so-called "Natchez Junto," a group of affiliated, well-connected, and influential leaders in the region with shared interests, worked assiduously to maintain a stranglehold on state politics from the time Mississippi entered the union until the 1830s. "The nearest thing to a political machine in the state," in the words of Natchez historian D. Clayton James, the group achieved remarkable success in placing men it supported in office in the state's early years. Through the behind-the-scenes machinations of such power brokers as Robert H. Adams, James C. Wilkins, Stephen Duncan, and Robert J. Walker, the Junto successively built bridges of consensus, aimed at regional hegemony, between Democratic- and Whig-leaning groups. The group supported four of the first five Mississippi state senators, captured the lone seat the state held in the House of Representatives in five of the first seven elections, and proved instrumental in placing favored candidates in office for statewide positions, including the governor's office and attorney general. Acutely aware of the growth of the eastern section of the state and the looming expansion in its northern reaches as time progressed, they took steps to downplay the aristocratic reputation of the region's political leaders and instead emphasized the Democratic philosophies many of its allies tacitly espoused. Still, to many outside of the comparatively wealthy plantation district in the environs of Natchez, it seemed as if the town and the communities within its orbit literally thought they alone comprised the state.[7]

With each section of the state jealously looking after its own interests, internal improvements became a hot-button topic in early state politics. The legislature did attempt to study improvement needs objectively from time to time. In 1829 it established a Board of Internal Improvements consisting of the governor and three commissioners representing the state's western, eastern, and northern sections. Each section was to conduct an independent survey of needs and recommend projects based on priorities. Within a year, disagreement over how to rank those priorities on a statewide basis and how to fund them doomed the commission. Even the opening of land in areas of the state ceded by the Choctaw and Chickasaw proved contentious. The Mississippi River counties were lukewarm in their endorsement of the state's expansion, as they worried about the adverse economic impact it would have on their section. They fretted with good reason, for by 1840 approximately one-half of Mississippi's white population would reside in counties in the central and northern sections that had not even existed ten years earlier.[8]

Nowhere did the sectional rivalry appear more visible than in the several debates in the 1820s and 1830s over the location of the state capital. Originating as a conversation about how to most centrally locate government headquarters as the state experienced dramatic growth in terms of territory and population, the argument over where to place Mississippi's seat of government devolved into a free-for-all driven by shameless localism. The debate began in earnest once the political center of the state unmistakably moved away from Natchez. The "backwoods," as just about everything outside of Natchez became known during the territorial period, had steadily, if slowly, grown in both population and influence during the era, but it dated its arrival to the 1820 Treaty of Doak's Stand. The compact ceded more than five million acres of Choctaw land in the central portion of the state to the federal government, effectively doubling the area available for settlement. The cession virtually demanded the state's administrative center be moved from its extreme southwestern border. In 1821, the state legislature directed that its next session would be held in the town of Columbia, along the Pearl River in the south-central section of the state, but it almost simultaneously appointed a three-member commission to select a location for a permanent capital within the former Choctaw territory. State officials eventually settled on LeFleur's Bluff along the Pearl River, the site of modern Jackson, as meeting all their criteria. It lay situated on high ground along a navigable waterway, offered plentiful fresh water, had fertile soil, and lay near the geographic center of the state. In the spring of 1822 the commissioners laid out the town, and by December of that year, the first state capitol building actually owned by the state had been constructed and stood ready for the legislature's use.[9]

There was anything but general agreement about the capital staying in Jackson, however. In a confusing series of maneuvers reaching their height in the 1828, 1829, and 1830 legislative sessions, at least a dozen other communities in every corner of the state were considered to replace Jackson as the seat of government. Monticello, Madisonville, Centreville, Washington, Gallatin, Georgetown, Westville, Liberty, Covington, Port Gibson, Natchez, and Vicksburg all received some consideration as the site for the state capital, even if primarily by local representatives hoping to seize on the lack of consensus. The town of Clinton, a short distance from Jackson but much more established as a community at the time, came very near being designated the new capital on more than one occasion during all this debate. In 1829 the town came within one vote of being named the seat of government. In the end, indecision growing out of regional factionalism saved Jackson long enough for it to host the 1832 constitutional convention. A major topic of debate at the gathering, Jackson's fate as capital was ultimately secured by a provision contained in the new constitution stipulating the capital remain in the city until at least 1850.[10]

The year after declaring Jackson to be the capital for the immediate future, the legislature began planning for a new capitol building. Truly needing something larger and desiring something grander than the simple structure in which it had met in for the previous decade, they first authorized a Gothic Revival plan by Tennessee architect John Lawrence. Financial setbacks plagued the project, and what halting progress Lawrence made over two years clearly suited nobody and exhibited poor workmanship. In 1835 officials fired Lawrence and replaced him with William Nichols, a noted and accomplished architect who had built both the North Carolina and Alabama capitols. The edifice of Nichols's stunning Greek Revival design soon began climbing into view on the bluff overlooking the Pearl River. When completed in 1839 the structure towered over everything in the young town and in truth over virtually every other building in the state. Its imposing three stories and massive copper-plated rotunda, visible on the horizon for miles around, served as a physical expression of the strength and stability state leaders had hoped to convey. One contemporary, recording for posterity the thoughts of many at the time, observed that "it is doubtful if there is a more magnificent public hall in the United States, except in the capitol at Washington." The editor of a Jackson newspaper praised the building in similarly lavish terms, declaring that because "ours is a rich state," "she should have a house for her Legislature built upon a plan corresponding with that wealth."[11]

The same sectional partisan spirit that animated the debate over the selection of the capital also lay at the heart of the movement for the writing of a new constitution. Barely had Mississippi's first constitution been in use for a decade before calls for revising it began to be heard throughout the state. The eastern Mississippi "backwoods" settlements felt neglected by the original compact, specifically viewing the judicial districts it created in their region as inadequate. They also resented the appointed positions and lifetime tenure specified for many offices. More generally, the backwoods people became frustrated with the dominance of the river region in the state's affairs, which the document perpetuated. Dramatic changes in population were taking place in Mississippi by the 1820s; this began to render Natchez increasingly less central to the functioning of the state, and as previously discussed, the enormous territorial gains resulting from the Treaties of Doak's Stand and Dancing Rabbit Creek literally moved the geographic and population center of the state eastward and northward. By 1831, with the Chickasaw barely holding on to their lands in the northern portion of the state, both the river region and the eastern backwoods could read the proverbial writing on the wall. Finally, at the suggestion of Governor Gerard C. Brandon, the longtime antagonists agreed to submit the matter of a new constitution to referendum in August 1831. Many feared that the avalanche of new counties in northern Mississippi and those that would inevitably come into existence would syphon off the political power that then exclusively resided in the southern portion of the state. Before the signing of the Treaty of Doak's Stand in 1820 opened the central portion of Mississippi to American settlement, the state consisted of a mere sixteen counties, all in its southern reaches. It claimed only twenty-five as

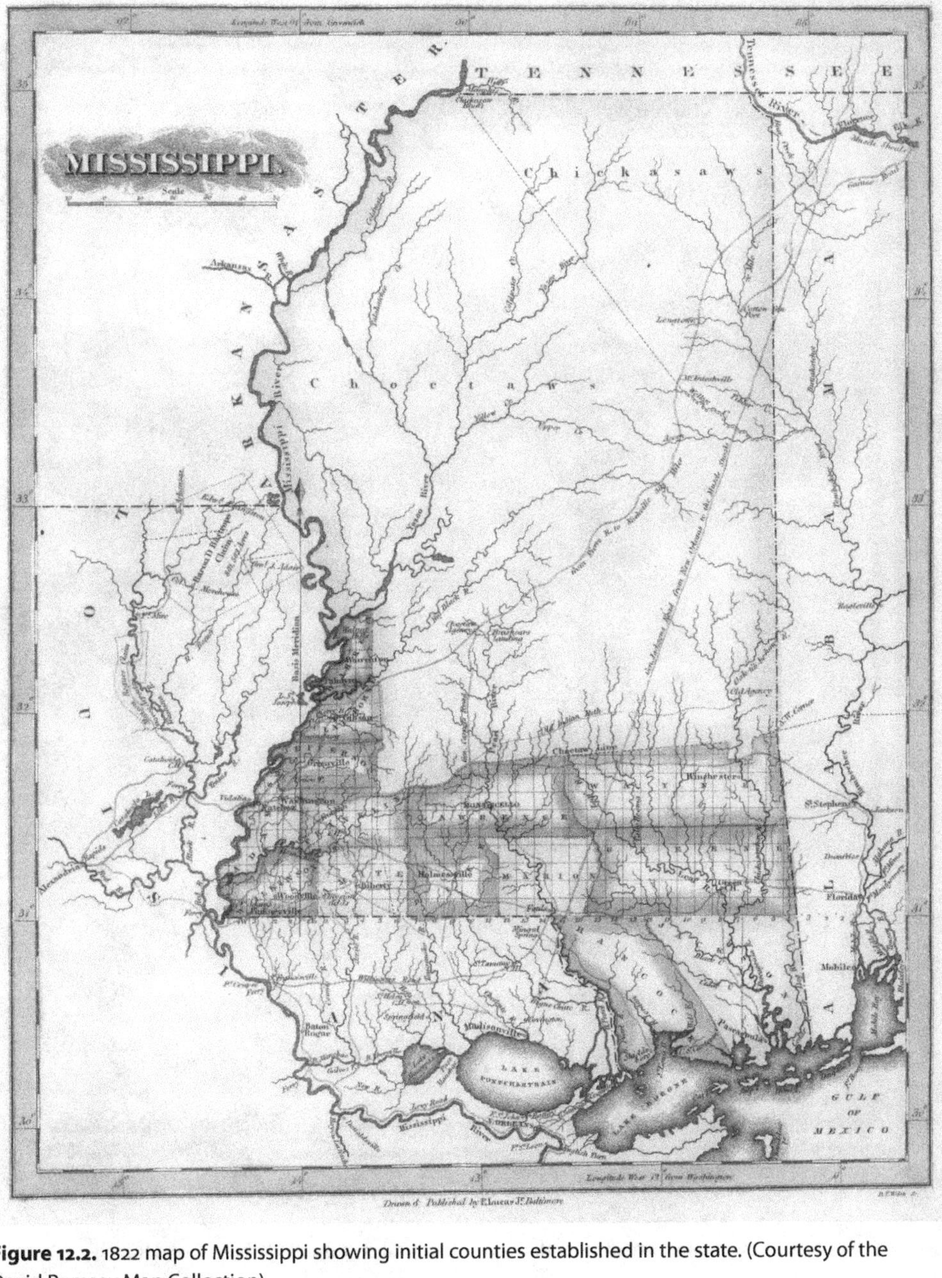

Figure 12.2. 1822 map of Mississippi showing initial counties established in the state. (Courtesy of the David Rumsey Map Collection)

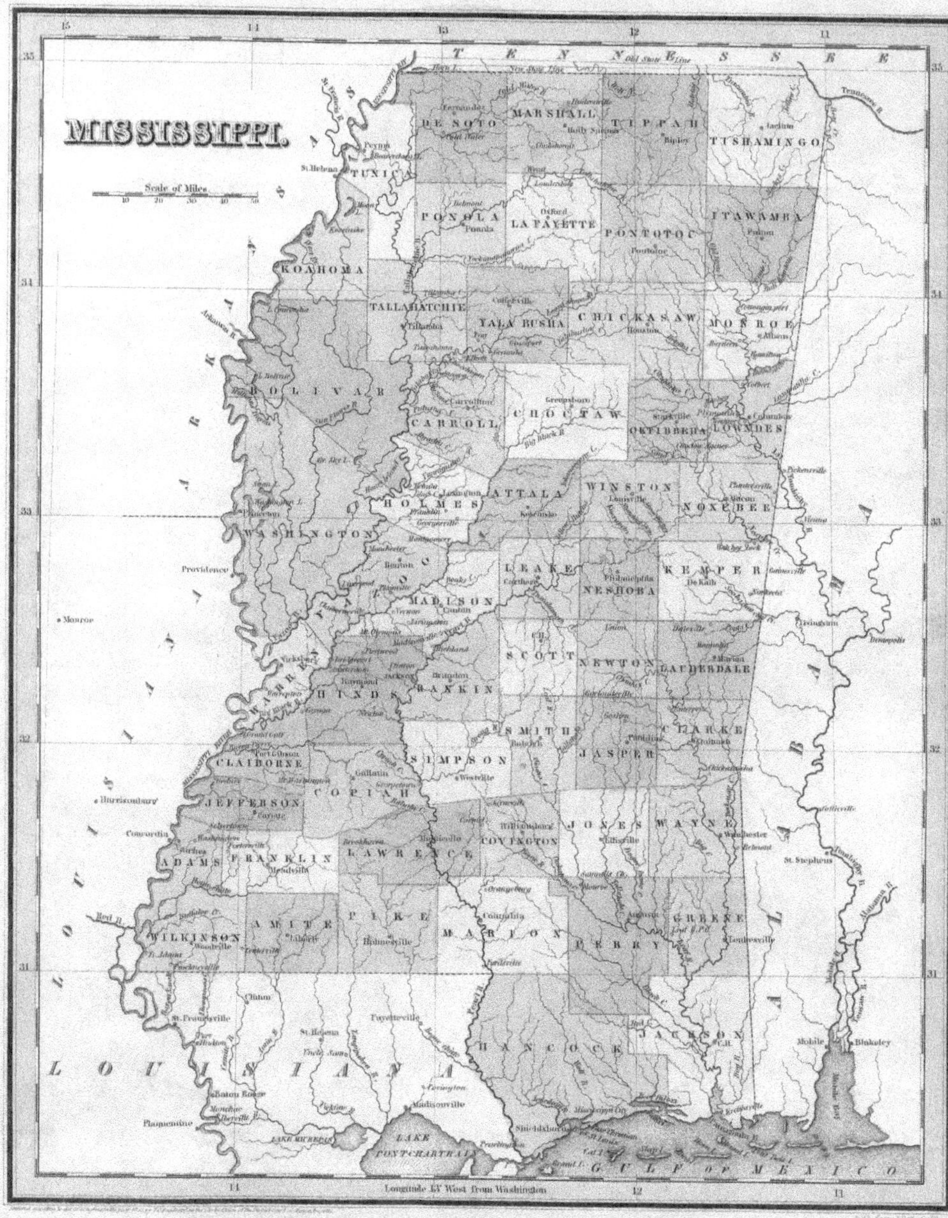

Figure 12.3. 1841 map showing entirety of state divided into counties. (Courtesy of the David Rumsey Map Collection)

late as 1829, just prior to the cession of the remaining Choctaw and Chickasaw territory within the state's borders. By 1836 the millions of acres of former Native American land brought under its administration in the central and northern sections of the state had been organized into more than double the number of counties. By 1840 Mississippi comprised some fifty-six counties.[12]

The forty-eight delegates to the convention, only five of whom had been involved in framing the state's first constitution, assembled in Jackson in the balmy late summer of 1832. It would be the defining event of the administration of Governor Abram M. Scott (1832–33), who had taken office in January. Opening their deliberations at 11:00 a.m. on September 10 in the simple state house at the corner of Capitol and President Streets, they worked for six weeks on the state's new governing document. By the time they adjourned on October 26, they had produced one of the most democratic constitutions in the nation. The document can be understood as in many ways a radical departure from the original state constitution, as it placed more power directly in the hands of free white males than most territorial officials would have ever contemplated. With the exception of US Senators, all state officers were to be elected and legislative or executive appointments virtually banned along with any lifetime tenures of office. This included every post from militia general to judges. The fight over the selection of judges actually came to be one of the most contentious of the convention, with "whole hogs" insisting on direct election of all judges and the "half hogs" asking for election of only the circuit courts while continuing to have the members of the Supreme Court appointed. In a stunning testimony to the unprecedented power given to the electorate, the "whole hogs" won out. Electors, as defined by the 1832 constitution, were to be resident white males over the age of twenty-one; all property ownership provisions were eliminated. To ensure the new counties being formed in the state had a fair chance at electing their own officials, residence requirements for voters within their districts were shortened to a mere four months. The constitution abolished the office of lieutenant governor and limited any governor from serving more than two terms in office in any six-year period. In an expression of fiscal conservatism and suspicion of unaccountable government spending, it included a provision that any loan on the state's credit must be approved by two successive legislatures. As a last, subtle, statement on the impending end of Mississippi's frontier era, the name of the House of Representatives and the Senate were changed officially from "General Assembly," the term originally assigned to the legislative body under the territorial government, to the more contemporary "Legislature."[13]

The practical implementation of the new constitution did lead to a bit of temporary confusion at the top levels of state government. When the first legislature to meet under the terms of the constitution convened in January 1833, it authorized a special election to be held in May to elect the officials called for by the compact. Although the wording of the constitution specified terms of office would begin in the November following their election, the legislature authorized the new officers to assume their duties immediately after the special election. Hiram G. Runnels defeated Abram M. Scott for governor in the special election, but in the confusion over legitimate terms of office, Runnels determined to assume his duties in November as spelled out in the constitution while Scott continued to serve until that time. When Scott suddenly died in June 1833, president of the state senate Charles Lynch stepped into the role of acting governor, as the constitution had eliminated the office of lieutenant governor. Runnels began his term (1833–35) in November 1833, as originally scheduled, for a tenure that would be remembered most for the addition of some sixteen new Mississippi counties. When defeated in his bid for reelection two years later, Runnels vacated office immediately in accordance with the wording of the constitution. However, the document called for inauguration of governors in January following election. Mississippi lay without a governor for nearly two weeks before a special session of the legislature elected a president of the senate who could finish out Runnels's term. Hence John A. Quitman served a monthlong term (1835–36) as Mississippi's chief executive until Lynch, who won office by the narrowest margin in state history, took office.[14]

Confusion over terms of office aside, conservatives such as former judge George Winchester decried the new constitution as "a full definition of mobocracy." Governor Alexander McNutt echoed this sentiment, voicing the concerns of many when he complained that the document may have given Mississippi a bit "too much Democracy." In an ironic statement on the nature of democratic reform ushered in by the new constitution, voters never got a chance to express their opinion on its merits. Its passage required only the approval of the legislature to go into effect. A few conservative political leaders sarcastically expressed concern over this glaring abandonment of democratic principle, but more because they saw a vote as the only means of defeating it than any civic philosophy. By modern standards the 1832 constitution was anything but liberal, as it continued to sanction slavery, left power exclusively in the hands of the free white male population, and left women, minorities, and natives virtually without a voice in government and little protection in the law. At the time, however, the democratic provisions it included placed Mississippi in the vanguard of an unprecedented shifting of power into the hands of the people.[15]

A landmark vote by the state legislature a few years later provided a glimmer of the types of reform possible as Mississippi began its maturation as a state. During the frontier era, women enjoyed essentially no independent property rights. Even property owned by a woman prior to marriage, or otherwise acquired independently, technically became her husband's upon marriage and might be subject to seizure if her husband became indebted. The issue first became a matter of note

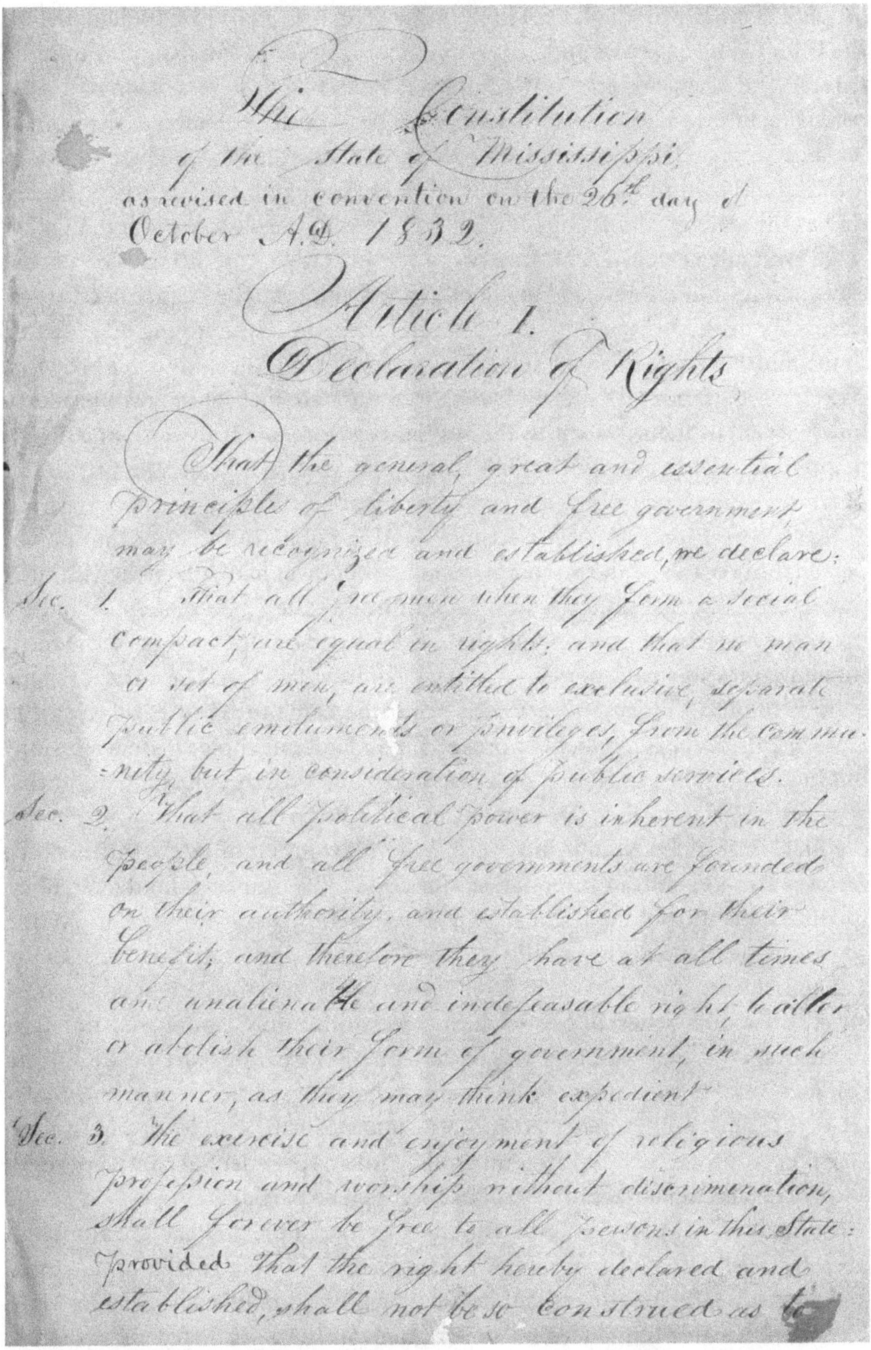

The Constitution
of the State of Mississippi,
as revised in convention on the 26th day of
October A.D. 1832.

Article 1.
Declaration of Rights

That the general, great and essential principles of liberty and free government may be recognized and established, we declare:

Sec. 1. That all freemen when they form a social compact, are equal in rights; and that no man or set of men, are entitled to exclusive, separate public emoluments or privileges, from the community, but in consideration of public services.

Sec. 2. That all political power is inherent in the people, and all free governments are founded on their authority, and established for their benefit; and therefore they have at all times an unalienable and indefeasable right to alter or abolish their form of government, in such manner, as they may think expedient.

Sec. 3. The exercise and enjoyment of religious profession and worship without discrimination, shall forever be free to all persons in this State: provided that the right hereby declared and established, shall not be so construed as to

Figure 12.4. Title page of Mississippi's 1832 state constitution, which granted voting rights to all white men in Mississippi. (Courtesy of Mississippi Department of Archives and History)

for public officials in Mississippi in the wake of an 1837 court case brought before the High Court of Errors and Appeals (the forerunner of Mississippi's Supreme Court). The case featured the attempt by a creditor to take possession of a slave belonging to a woman to satisfy a debt owed by her husband. However, the woman had been married in the Chickasaw Nation, and according to Chickasaw custom a wife could own property separately from her husband. The judges concluded that as the state of Mississippi officially recognized the customs of Indian marriage even after extension of state laws over all Native American residents, the slave in question did indeed belong to her and could not be confiscated for her husband's debt. In 1839 the state legislature, allegedly at the urging of a senator in the midst of some financial setbacks who sought to protect his wife's property, passed a bill granting all married women in the state the right to own property independent of their husbands. While a far cry from any true sense of equality before the law, the passage of the legislation did make the state the first in the nation to extend such rights to married women.[16]

To the great majority of Mississippi's voting public in the 1830s, notions of personal freedom and the proper distribution of power had little to do with such protections afforded minority groups within the state. Instead, they lay bound up in the concept of government that became personified by one of the most influential leaders in American history—Andrew Jackson. The very presence of Jackson and the redistribution of power he came to represent during the close of Mississippi's frontier era proved pivotal not only in individual elections but in knitting the very fabric of Mississippi's antebellum political party infrastructure. Dating to the appointment of aloof Federalist Winthrop Sargent as the first territorial governor in 1798 and the "Revolution of 1800," which swept Democratic-Republican Jeffersonian allies into power throughout the territory, the state's chaotic politics had always featured factionalism in some form. While some of this political rivalry aligned with national party organizations, to the extent that it did it was usually in favor or in opposition to the current presidential administration. Parties, in the modern sense of the word, simply did not exist in the Magnolia State until the rise of Jackson on the national scene. "Pluralistic and localistic" in the words of one leading scholar of politics in frontier Mississippi, the state's politics reflected an "intrastate localism" with weak and shifting allegiances before the Jackson–John Quincy Adams presidential contest brought about a coalescing of factions that operated as true parties.[17]

In many ways Mississippi stood at the epicenter of the political phenomenon known as Jacksonian Democracy. The movement empowered the "common man" and consequently broadened public participation in politics. Among its main tenets it advocated limited federal government and a full-throated endorsement of the concept of Manifest Destiny, construed in the South to mean in immediate terms the removal of any native groups who stood in the way of the expansion

Figure 12.5. Engraving of Andrew Jackson from 1829 when he served as the nation's seventh president and continued to affect Mississippi's future. (Courtesy of the Library of Congress)

of slavery and the Cotton Kingdom. While popular to some degree nationally, it had special appeal in the South during Mississippi's formative statehood years, and it swept all that came before it in the region. It gave shape and direction to a wide variety of political questions and helped the region find a collective sectional voice under which it could unite in arguing for its interests.

Andrew Jackson, the movement's namesake and in large part its inspiration, became its guiding force and paramount champion during two terms as the nation's chief executive. Mississippians viewed Jackson as practically one of their own, being at heart a frontiersman whom they believed understood their concerns. In the words of one historian, the military exploits that gave rise to his ascendancy as a political figure had occurred "almost in their own backyard." Indeed, Jackson had first come to fame through his exploits during the Creek War and the War of 1812, the former occurring almost exclusively within the borders of the Mississippi Territory and the latter just a short distance to the south in the commercial emporium every bit as important to the state's economy as Natchez or Vicksburg. It became common throughout the state in the 1820s for toasts to be given at political functions or community celebrations to "the glorious Eighth of January" or similar praise of Jackson's role of ridding the territory of both domestic and foreign menaces. Mississippians viewed it as a point of intense regional pride that he had taught Europe the "valor of the West" just a stone's throw from their borders. Jackson's association with Mississippi extended back much earlier than his campaigning during the War of 1812, for he had visited Natchez as early as 1790, married his wife near there, and made many friends throughout the state over the course of the decades as a planter and land speculator while residing in neighboring Tennessee. When Mississippi planned its capital city in territory ceded by the Choctaws through a treaty he helped negotiate in the 1820s, it was named in his honor.[18]

The 1828 presidential campaign between Jackson and John Quincy Adams pitted the archetypes of champion of the common man and his antagonist that were at the center of the Jacksonian movement—and Mississippi politics—for nearly a generation. The campaign in some ways became more about personality than policy, as supporters of both candidates in an unprecedented way emphasized personal attributes and backgrounds as proof of suitability or inability to govern the nation effectively. On the one hand stood the backwoods-born and self-made man whose sweat-of-the-brow heroics occurred largely in Mississippi and the surrounding region. On the other stood the privileged, aristocratic heir to a northeastern political dynasty who seemingly could not possibly understand southwesterners. "The symbolic contrast between Jackson and Adams," has asserted one historian of the topic, "could not have been much starker in the Magnolia State." Jackson garnered nearly two-thirds of the vote on his way to a resounding victory, gaining revenge for his loss to Adams four years prior. Jackson had polled a majority of votes in every county in the state in that controversial election, which many viewed as having been stolen from him via the famed "corrupt bargain" that swung an extremely tight race in Adams's favor. He won by even larger margins in his bid for reelection in 1832. His handpicked successor, Martin Van Buren, won the state in 1836.[19]

Rallying around Jackson and all he represented, the newly defined Democratic Party portrayed itself as "champions of egalitarian democracy." The party provided the proverbial big tent under which could gather all those who believed strongly in local self-determination and held in suspicion large bureaucratic institutions, such as banks and corporations. Fundamentally western in orientation and outlook, party supporters found common ground in questions of state sovereignty, Indian policy, and agricultural trade regulation. Aligned in opposition to the Democrats were the Whigs—so designated in reference to the English party that had sought to limit the power of the king—who seized on an undercurrent of revulsion to Jackson's autocratic nature and skepticism of progressive government. In stark contrast to Democratic principles stressing individualism, Whigs endorsed tenets of Henry Clay's "American System," which offered protective tariffs, banks, and internal improvements as the path to modernization. Both parties found room to thrive in Mississippi in the late 1830s despite an apparent overwhelming Democratic advantage. By 1840 Democrats controlled the state legislature, but the Whigs carried the state in the presidential election of that year and had actually managed to briefly seize the governor's mansion even during Jackson's second term as the nation's chief executive.[20]

The Natchez area—and its largely Whig leadership—did not relinquish control of the state's political power without a fight. Twice in the 1830s, Whig politicians from the region attempted to block the seating in the legislature of largely Democratic representatives from the new counties carved from lands ceded by the Choctaws (Treaty of Dancing Rabbit Creek) and the Chickasaws (Treaty of Pontotoc Creek). Hoping to forestall the inevitable for at least one more legislative session, the Whig-dominated Senate in 1835, during a special session of the legislature, refused to seat the sixteen delegates representing the counties formed from the Choctaw cession, on the basis that their method of selection had been unconstitutional. The discord became so severe that the legislature temporarily adjourned before reluctantly allowing the new delegates to take their seats. A reprisal of the same controversy occurred in the next regular legislative session. In January 1837 representatives of the ten counties formed from the recent Chickasaw cession attempted to take their seats, only to have Whigs, led by Seargent S. Prentiss, block them on the grounds that their selection had also been unconstitutional. It seems that the sitting Whig governor, Charles Lynch, purposefully had not ever authorized elections for representatives in the new counties, so local boards of police had undertaken the task themselves. Despite vocal protests, the delegates inevitably took their seats. While the sparring over seats in the legislature had nearly as much basis in party as sectional rivalry, the two were in fact inextricably linked. The corresponding shift in political power finally wrested control away from the Natchez region, where it had resided since the formation of the Mississippi Territory. The Piney Woods and "New Purchase" counties proved willing allies in working together to trump the political power of the river region.[21]

The one event of the era that threatened to fracture existing political alliances in Mississippi arose in South Carolina as a direct challenge to federal authority. In 1832 that state's legislature declared null and void within its boundaries a controversial tariff, or tax, on imported manufactured items. The tariff had been aimed at protecting Northern industry, which found itself frequently undercut by European manufacturers in pricing. It had the practical effect, however, of making those in states with little industrial presence, especially the Southern states, pay significantly higher prices for imported goods with little apparent benefit. Further, it complicated the South's vital cotton trade with Great Britain by creating an imbalance in that nation's import/export balance and, observers feared, would lead to less cotton exportation. Though the tariff was roundly denounced in the South, including Mississippi, where Jackson enjoyed substantial support, as hostile to sectional interests, the president refused to countenance South Carolina's belligerence. He threatened to send federal troops to enforce federal law within the state's borders if it proved unwilling to do so itself. These events caused consternation and equivocation in Mississippi, forcing its political leaders to choose between the two causes that underlay any concerted action in the state—state rights and support for Jackson. The nascent minority Whig party, which had virtually come into existence in opposition to Jackson and his "bottom-up" view of government, seized on the issue and suddenly put itself on the forefront of the state rights cause. The Democratic party, which coalesced in the state largely around Jackson, found itself ironically in the position of championing federal prerogative. In the end, Jackson's personal popularity triumphed in the state, but not without hesitation. The Mississippi legislature officially denounced South Carolina's stance and remained strongly unionist in the midst of the controversy, even though it had earlier passed resolutions condemnming the tarriff as "impolitic" and urging resistance by all constitutional means. The situation made for some strange allies, as defectors from both parties formed minority dissenting factions that blurred the lines between platforms for the remainder of the 1830s.[22]

One of the most significant aftershocks of this temporary realignment of political factions manifested itself in the formation of the short-lived Mississippi State Rights Association. Spearheaded by firebrand Southern partisan John Anthony Quitman, a self-styled "State Rights Convention" met in Jackson in May 1834 to discuss the proper course of coordinated action for all those who felt the federal response to the nullification issue represented an ominous precedent posing a serious threat to liberty. About fifty delegates from at least ten Mississippi counties assembled in the chancery court chambers of the capitol in Jackson on May 19 for the ad hoc convention. After Chief Justice William Lewis Sharkey called the gathering to order, Quitman motioned to adopt an impassioned resolution in which the collective body foamed with outrage at the nation's chief executive having threatened to send "mercenaries" to "butcher citizens before their own altars." The resolution assured readers that before that would be allowed to happen, a cry of "To the rescue!" would arise in the Magnolia State "from the Leaf to the Mississippi, from the Yazoo to the Homochitto." The convention chose officers, officially brought the State Rights Association of Mississippi into existence, and extended an invitation to all citizens of the state to join them in their crusade against perceived tyranny. Within months, local auxiliary chapters of the association sprang to life in several communities across the state including Adams, Amite, Hinds, and Wilkinson counties.[23]

Despite the intensity with which it briefly burned in 1834, enthusiasm for the state rights cause faded within a year in Mississippi as the nullification controversy found resolution and people turned their attention to other matters in the midst of one of the greatest economic booms the state has ever experienced. The consequences of the formal expression of state rights as an umbrella under which a political party might coalesce would be felt far into the future, however. A "state rights" faction took root in both the Mississippi Democratic and Whig parties in the wake of the nullification controversy, ultimately being transformed during the remainder of the antebellum era from a platform plank into a general rallying cry in political discourse. While Quitman and his associates had framed the movement's argument in a philosophical assertion that the sovereignty of the people had been infringed upon by executive action and drew inspiration from the celebrated Virginia and Kentucky Resolutions, one need not be clairvoyant to see a primary impetus for their defensive posture lay in perceived threats to slavery. Mississippians were acutely aware of the growing momentum of the antislavery movement in the North even in the early 1830s, and instinctively reacted to any alleged overreach of federal authority within their borders for fear of what the setting of the precedent might one day mean for their "peculiar institution." When the issue of the boundary between state and federal authority took center stage in state politics some two decades later, Mississippi would find itself in the forefront of the movement that led to secession. For the time being, however, local statesmen such as Seargent S. Prentiss attempted to calm the bitter sectional animus with a voice of objectivity that would soon be entirely drowned out in Mississippi politics. "Southern Democracy," he observed, "consists in general abuse of the rest of the Union, a denial of the existence of any common interest with the North, and a bitter denunciation of every man who has the independence to refuse assent to these strange dogmas."[24]

Mississippians found other outlets for state rights sentiment in the early statehood era, some far beyond the state's borders. They especially attached themselves to the cause of Texas independence because of the economic and political opportunities associated with the expansion of slavery it represented. Mississippi-based filibustering efforts aimed at capturing Texas from Spain began as early as 1819 with the failed expedition led by merchant and physician James Long. By the 1830s, many observers looked on Texas as a physical and cultural extension of the South, and took an interest in its political fortunes for both philosophical and pecuniary reasons. Not only was much of the region well-suited for cotton production, but many anticipated a financial bonanza falling to enterprising investors and planters if it could be wrested from Mexico and established as an independent nation or even annexed into the United States. When the long-simmering movement for independence got underway in earnest in 1835 and grew to involve armed conflict with Mexican authorities, Mississippians took notice.

A number of communities across the state raised money to support the cause. The citizens of Vicksburg gathered some $3,500 via a public appeal.[25]

Meanwhile prominent Mississippi political leaders such as United States Senator Robert J. Walker began advocating for the recognition of Texas independence by the United States in Congress. As early as the fall of 1835 and increasingly in the spring and summer of 1836, volunteer militia groups were organized to assist the Texas cause militarily. Six Mississippians arrived in time to participate in the ill-fated defense of the Alamo in March 1836. Most of the larger groups, however, were raised in response to the massacre at the Alamo and exhorted that "the proud dictator, Santa Anna, must fall like the Alamo, and the blood there shed for liberty and glory must be avenged." They would arrive too late to engage in actual combat before the fighting effectively concluded in the spring of 1836. Texas would remain in Mississippians' collective consciousness for another generation, as it became an asylum for those fleeing the financial collapse that struck the state shortly after Texas established its independence, and its annexation by the United States would become a hotly contested point in national politics within the decade. In the war eventually fought to secure Texas from Mexico once and for all, Mississippians would play an important role in both the political and military fighting.[26]

Mississippi's stunning transformation from backwoods frontier to heart of the Deep South is perhaps best illustrated in its political development. When the state entered the union in 1817, it lay along a fractious frontier, riven by sectionalism, whose internal politics virtually eschewed national party cooperation and in truth bordered on insularity. As it approached maturity as a state in the 1830s, Mississippi's political scene could arguably be understood as the very pulse of the national phenomenon known as Jacksonian Democracy. Increasingly assertive of its sovereignty, aggressively expansionistic in its outlook, and skeptical of federal prerogative, the state assumed a position in the vanguard of the movement that would in a few short decades lead to secession, war, and a reevaluation of the definition of the American republic.

Epilogue

In January 1840, former president Andrew Jackson undertook a journey to New Orleans to participate in the twenty-fifth anniversary celebration of his greatest triumph. In 1815, he had turned back what many believed to be the world's finest army on the very doorstep of the city, solidifying his place as America's foremost military hero and laying the foundation for a political career that would allow him to exert incredible influence on the development of the young nation. Though the journey to the Crescent City would be a long and taxing one for the seventy-three-year-old former president, he had agreed to pay a visit to the state of Mississippi on his way back home, accepting an invitation to be feted at the capitol in his namesake city of Jackson. Organizers of the event believed his appearance would be a landmark event in the history of the state, especially coming at a time in which many thought he might be making his last journey. It was widely known that the aging former president had suffered from ill health for some time. Little did they suspect him to be in such frail condition that exhaustion would prevent him from even seeing the battlefield at Chalmette where he had crushed the British during his stay in New Orleans, spending all his energies attending a dizzying series of formal receptions and ceremonies held in his honor throughout the city. With the steely determination characteristic of the man nicknamed "Old Hickory," he chose to keep his appointment in the Magnolia State nevertheless. Jackson took a steamer upriver from New Orleans to Natchez, where he stayed one night before proceeding to Vicksburg. There he spent an evening in the home of friend William Gwin, and the next morning boarded a train for the capital of Mississippi. At the terminus of the railroad, in Raymond, he boarded a stagecoach for the final leg of his journey.[1]

While we do not know Jackson's thoughts that day, it is not difficult to imagine him in a reflective mood during the roughly ten hours it took to traverse the state to his destination. Jackson had first visited what became Mississippi as a young man in the 1790s while the area still lay in Spanish hands. Romantic memories of his days courting the woman who became the love of his life probably sprang to mind, as his first sojourn in the region had come about as a result of his infatuation with the unhappily married Rachel Donelson Robards. Rachel had friends living outside of Natchez at the time, and had come from Tennessee for an extended visit to get away from her husband. Passionately in love with each other, Jackson and Robards visited and allegedly married in a house in Bayou Pierre after getting word that Mr. Robards had made official his divorce from her. Jackson could not have helped but think of that era of his life as a simpler time, for it predated his political career and he could at that moment have had no idea how his actions regarding the marriage of his wife would one day be a point of public discussion across the nation during presidential campaigns. He had famously traveled the Natchez Trace during the War of 1812, earning the nickname that would stick with him the rest of his life for his leadership of men in a moment of crisis. He had spent a considerable amount of time in Mississippi since then on various errands personal and professional: selling slaves, opening roads, and negotiating treaties with Native Americans for cessions of land. He could, in fact, on reflection be excused if he looked upon his time and various activities in the state as having played a part in its transition from a frontier wilderness to a dynamic part of the American union.[2]

His current whirlwind trip provided evidence of just how far that coming of age had progressed between his first visit and what he almost certainly knew would be his last. He had visited the state's two metropolises along the way, one of which had not existed in his youth and one which was but a shadow of what it would become when he first viewed it. Both featured urban refinements that compared favorably with what could be found anywhere along the developing inland trading corridor defined by the Mississippi. In practicality, the western "coast" of the nation at the time fronted the mighty river, and the state that bore its name occupied a prime spot along its course. Jackson's mode of travel, an elegant steamboat that must have even then seemed an engineering marvel, offered a luxuriant style of travel he could scarcely have imagined during his youth. He would have seen bustling harbors choked with vessels as he pulled into and out of Mississippi's two largest ports on his journey. Later, as he swayed and bounced with the rhythms of the train as it clicked and clattered over the iron rails that connected the river and the central area of the state, he may have been struck by the speed with which the machine allowed him to move through the countryside. What had taken days on foot—and he had traveled hundreds of miles on foot in the state—took mere hours. Gazing out his window throughout the journey he would have caught glimpses of the essential reason for Mississippi's economic ascendancy in the form of cotton fields. Jackson traversed the region in late January, so he would not have seen stands of the fiber waiting to be picked by the thousands of slaves that underlay so much of the region's economic activity, but he would have seen many openings settlers had cleared in the wilderness, and may have seen fields in the process of being prepared for the next crop as he jostled and rocked along the road.

The railroad along which he traveled cut through one of the fastest-developing agricultural districts in the state. Visible to him would have been the signs of rather recent settlement and repurposing of the former Choctaw lands, which Jackson himself had actually helped secure less than two decades ago: modest homes, ostentatious plantation houses, barns, schoolhouses, churches, and courthouses that stood as the centerpieces of the new types of communities being developed throughout this land. Within them and their environs these Mississippians, a great majority of them, white and black alike, of rather recent arrival here, were busily engaged in building on the foundations of the state laid during the territorial period in which Jackson had played so prominent a part. Yeoman farmers, many working alongside a slave or two and a large number possessing none at all, carved a living for themselves and their families through the tillage of soil that had for so long been part of Native domains. Nearby were the increasingly numerous ornate manses and expansive tracts owned by well-off planters and maintained and operated by dozens of enslaved laborers—an ever-present reminder of the potential wealth that was attainable for the few under the social and economic systems upon which the young state was being constructed. Jackson was certainly aware that his final destination, a growing city named in his honor, had been nothing more than a trading post in the heart of Indian country just a few decades before—yet today it stood as the political nerve center for a young but rapidly growing state with a distinctive culture, economy, and government reflecting to a great degree all he held dear and had advocated for over the course of his several decades of public service.

In the gathering dark of a winter's dusk on Friday, January 17, Jackson's coach rolled into the capital. Passing an assortment of homes and businesses as the wheels of the carriage steadily ground along over the dirt streets, he saw rising before him in the distance the grand capitol building that ranked among the largest and most ornate structures for hundreds of miles in any direction. As the carriage pulled to a halt in front of the building, a cannon shattered the stillness with booming salute. Jackson alighted to a grand welcome weeks in the making that had been arranged by a special committee of community leaders and the volunteer labor of several local women. The capitol, carefully decorated with their handiwork and magnificently "illuminated" with candles, served as the backdrop for the former president's official greeting to the city. Bands played and a crowd of onlookers, some scattered around the grounds and some crowding windows of the building itself, cheered and strained for a glimpse of Jackson as he strolled to the entrance of the facility. Stepping inside for a brief tour and a courtesy visit with Governor Alexander McNutt, he probably stopped briefly to gaze up at its centerpiece, a magnificent rotunda, as he made his way to the first-floor executive office at the end of the south hall. The former president's steps were probably a bit slow and a little unsteady, as the day had no doubt exhausted

Figure 13.1. Reputedly one of the oldest images of Mississippi's old state capitol in Jackson, the state's most historic building and lasting monument to the state's growth and development. (Courtesy of Mississippi Department of Archives and History)

him. He nevertheless summoned the strength to afterward make an appearance that night at a ball given in his honor in the city theater before retiring for the evening to a room in the Eagle Hotel.

The next day Jackson and his entourage were escorted the short distance from the hotel to the capitol by a procession of dignitaries for a formal reception by the state legislature. Either owing to the size of the large crowd that had gathered on the capitol green to witness the occasion or in recognition that Jackson's frail health might prevent him from making a dignified climb up the stairs to the second-floor legislative chambers where the event had been originally planned, organizers moved the entire ceremony to the portico. Speaker of the House Jesse Speight provided the state's address, greeting him as "the General," "fresh from the former theatre of your glory." With a flourish, Speight suggested he had won fame "as durable as the rock of ages" for his actions both military and political. He called attention to "the great improvements, both physical and moral," that had been made since his last visit to the region, and assigned Jackson a paramount role in their realization.

Too weak to address the crowd himself, Jackson had his nephew, Andrew Jackson Donelson, read his prepared remarks for him. Donelson related how Jackson felt unable to "express the emotions which are awakened by the cordial greeting you offer me . . ." and thanked them "from the bottom of my heart." He acknowledged having been "an actor in many of the events which had a bearing upon prosperity and welfare of the State," but modestly cautioned his hosts that they had "assigned too prominent a place to my character and services." In his estimation, "The great changes which have taken place and the still greater that await you in the prosecution of the improvements which are the result of virtue, enterprise, and wealth, are to be attributed to the irresistible influence of our happy institutions, when exerted upon a free population and upon a genial soil and climate."[3]

Jackson ate dinner that night in the home of former governor Hiram Runnels (during which time he negotiated an extension of terms for payment for the purchase of a Coahoma County plantation that his son Andrew Jr. had bought from Runnels) and afterward attended a levee at the home of Governor McNutt. Bidding adieu to Mississippi for a last time, Jackson left for Vicksburg on Sunday morning to take a steamboat on his journey home to Nashville. The former president likely looked as much to the future as much as the past on his way back across the state as the well-wishes and expressions of gratitude from leaders of the state perhaps most shaped by his vision of what America should be rang in his ears. At virtually every stop in his travels around the South since he had left office as the nation's chief executive, admiring dignitaries had publicly hailed him as the living embodiment of the age—a "second [Washington was the first] great benefactor of their country," in the words of Speaker Speight the previous day. Jackson, acutely aware of himself in the process of stepping off the national stage literally and figuratively, may have wondered how the next act in the nation's story would unfold and to what degree it would be influenced by his long and celebrated career.

In the span of his adult life, Jackson had witnessed a doubling of the number of states that originally created the American union. Mississippi stood in many ways as the epitome of the emergence from wilderness frontier to statehood so many, especially in the South, had experienced. Within the course of only four decades the state had made a remarkable transition from a remote colonial borderland to one of the most prosperous and vital states in the nation. That prosperity had come about largely at the expense of its native inhabitants and through the toil of its enslaved population, much as it had throughout the Deep South. But in the pursuit of the very same visions that had guided Jackson's ascendancy to become a spokesman for Southern interests, those who wielded power and influence in Mississippi had wrought tremendous change upon the land and given rise to a culture that fiercely clung to a sense of self-determination as its guiding force. The future promised nothing if not continued, and fast-paced, physical and cultural development animated by the ideals and attitudes of its formative era. Just like Jackson himself had participated in many of the increasingly bitter political contests and events that guided Mississippi's path, exactly how that continued trajectory might mesh with that of the nation as a whole would remain to be seen. The only thing certain was that Mississippi would be front and center.

Notes

PREFACE

1. John Ray Skates, *Mississippi's Old Capitol: Biography of a Building* (Jackson: Mississippi Department of Archives and History, 1990), 7–10.

2. Skates, *Mississippi's Old Capitol*, 7–10. The full report of the commissioners can be found in Dunbar Rowland, *History of Mississippi, The Heart of the South*, vol. 1 (Chicago: S. J. Clarke Publishing, 1925), 516–28.

3. Skates, *Mississippi's Old Capitol*, 9.

4. Thomas D. Clark and John D. W. Guice, *Frontiers in Conflict: The Old Southwest, 1798–1830* (Norman: University of Oklahoma Press, 1989); Robert V. Haynes, *The Mississippi Territory and the Old Southwest, 1798–1817* (Louisville: University Press of Kentucky, 2010); Richard A. McLemore, ed., *A History of Mississippi*, 2 vols. (Jackson: University Press of Mississippi, 1973).

5. Porter L. Fortune Jr., "The Formative Years," in McLemore, *A History of Mississippi*, I, 251–83.

6. James F. Barnett Jr., *Mississippi's American Indians* (Jackson: University Press of Mississippi, 2012); Randy J. Sparks, *Religion in Mississippi* (Jackson: University Press of Mississippi, 2001); Joseph Glover Baldwin, *The Flush Times of Alabama and Mississippi: A Series of Sketches* (New York: D. Appleton, 1854).

INTRODUCTION

1. Edouard de Montule, *Montule's Voyage to North America and the West Indies in 1817* (London: Sir Richard Phillips, 1821), 93 (first quote); Joseph Holt Ingraham, *The Southwest: By a Yankee* (New York: Harper and Brothers, 1835), 104–5 (second quote).

2. Christian Schultz, *Travels on an Inland Voyage through the States of New York, Pennsylvania, Virginia, Ohio, and Tennessee* (New York: Isaac Riley, 1810), 118 (quote); Noel Polk, ed., *Natchez before 1830* (Jackson: University Press of Mississippi, 1989), 115; Orrin Scofield, *Perambulations of Cosmopolite, Or the Travels and Labors of Lorenzo Dow* (Rochester: Scofield, 1842), 156–57.

3. Jacob Young, *Autobiography of a Pioneer* (Cincinnati: L. Swormstedt and A. Poe, 1857), 224; Bradley G. Bond, *Political Culture in the Nineteenth Century South: Mississippi 1830–1900* (Baton Rouge: Louisiana State University Press, 1995), 20; Jerry Bryan Lincecum and Edward Hake Phillips, *Adventures of a Frontier Naturalist: The Life and Times of Dr. Gideon Lincecum* (College Station: Texas A&M University Press, 1994), 60–62; Scofield, *Perambulations of Cosmopolite*, 156–57; Abiezer Clark Ramsey, *Memoirs of a Circuit Rider, Being Excerpts from the Life*

and Times of A. C. Ramsey and Others (Birmingham, AL: Birmingham Southern College, 1951), 11; George Rogers, *Memoranda of the Experience, Labor, and Travels of a Universalist Preacher* (Cincinnati: John A. Gurley, 1845), 271; Schultz, *Travels on an Inland Voyage*, 143.

4. Montule, *Montule's Voyage to North America*, 97 (first quote); James R. Creecy, *Scenes in the South, and Other Miscellaneous Pieces* (Washington, DC: Thomas McGill, 1860), 60 (second quote); Arthur H. DeRosier Jr., "Natchez and the Formative Years of William Dunbar," *Journal of Mississippi History* 34 (February 1972): 34 (third quote).

5. William Darby, *The Emigrants Guide to the Western and Southwestern States and Territories: Comprising a Geographical and Statistical Description of the States of Louisiana, Mississippi, Tennessee, Kentucky, and Ohio* (New York: Kirk and Mercein, 1818), 121 (first quote); Tyrone Power, *Impressions of America, During the Years 1833, 1834, and 1835* (London: Richard Bentley, 1836), 188 (second quote); John Hawkins Napier III, *Lower Pearl River's Piney Woods: Its Land and People* (Jackson: University of Mississippi Center for the Study of Southern Culture, 1985), 53.

6. Charles Lyell, *A Second Visit to the United States of America* (New York: Harper and Brothers, 1849), 207–8 (first quote); Horatio Eustis Letters, Mississippi Department of Archives and History; R. Bruce Davis, "The Tornado of 1840 Hits Mississippi," *Journal of Mississippi History* 36 (February 1974): 43 (second quote).

7. A. B. Meek, *Romantic Passages in Southwestern History* (Mobile, AL: S. H. Goetzel, 1857), 18–20.

8. Bernard Bailyn, *Voyagers to the West: A Passage in the Peopling of America on the Eve of the Revolution* (New York: Random House, 1986), 480 (first and second quotes); Charles D. Lowery, "The Great Migration to the Mississippi Territory, 1798–1819," *Journal of Mississippi History* 30 (August 1968): 178 (third and fourth quotes).

CHAPTER 1: BECOMING AMERICAN

1. Samuel F. Bemis, "The Settlement of the Yazoo Boundary Dispute: The First Step in Southern Expansion," *Magazine of History* 17 (1913): 131–34; Isaac J. Cox, *The West Florida Controversy, 1798–1813: A Study in American Diplomacy* (Baltimore: Johns Hopkins University Press, 1918), 2–26; John Ray Skates, *Mississippi: A History* (New York: W.W. Norton, 1979), 44–45.

2. Thomas D. Clark and John D. W. Guice, *The Old Southwest, 1795–1830* (Norman: University of Oklahoma Press, 1989), ix; D. Clayton James, *Antebellum Natchez* (Baton Rouge: Louisiana State University Press, 1968), 42.

3. Richard A. McLemore, "Factionalism: A Fruit of Spanish-American Rivalry on the Mississippi Frontier," *Journal of Mississippi History* 6 (1944): 237.

4. Consult J. Michael Bunn and Clay Williams, *Mississippi: The Bulwark of New Spain* (Jackson: Mississippi Department of Archives and History, 2003) for a concise overview of Spanish control of Mississippi.

5. Jack D. L. Holmes, "A Spanish Province, 1779–1798," in Richard A. McLemore, ed., *History of Mississippi*, 2 vols. (Jackson: University of Mississippi Press, 1973), 1: 171. For a detailed account of the treaty, consult Samuel Flagg Bemis, *Pinckney's Treaty: Advantage from Europe's Distress, 1783–1800* (New Haven, CT: Yale University Press, 1960).

6. Arthur Preston Whitaker, *The Mississippi Question, 1795–1803, A Study in Trade, Politics, and Diplomacy* (New York: D. Appleton-Century, 1934), 51; John C. Van Horne, "Andrew Ellicott's Mission to Natchez (1796–1798)," *Journal of Mississippi History* 45 (1983): 161;

Thomas P. Abernathy, *The South in the New Nation, 1789–1819* (Baton Rouge: Louisiana State University Press, 1961), 206–7.

7. Whitaker, *The Mississippi Question*, 53–54; Franklin L. Riley, "Spanish Policy in Mississippi After Treaty of San Lorenzo," *Publications of the Mississippi Historical Society* 1 (1898): 50–66.

8. James, *Antebellum Natchez*, 31–53; Robert V. Haynes, "The Formation of the Territory," in McLemore, *History of Mississippi*, 1: 174–75.

9. Arthur S. DeRosier Jr., *William Dunbar, Scientific Pioneer of the Old Southwest* (Lexington: University Press of Kentucky, 2007), 48; Jack D. L. Holmes, *Gayoso: The Life of a Spanish Governor in the Mississippi Valley, 1789–1799* (Baton Rouge: Louisiana State University Press, 1965), 91–95; Robert Haynes, *The Mississippi Territory and the Southwest Frontier, 1795–1817* (Lexington: University Press of Kentucky, 2010), 11–12 (first quote); James, *Antebellum Natchez*, 50 (second quote).

10. Clayton Rand, *Men of Spine in Mississippi* (Gulfport, MS: Dixie Press, 1940), 85–87; Van Horne, "Andrew Ellicott's Mission," 163–64 (quote); Catherine VanCortlandt Matthews, *Andrew Ellicott: His Life and Letters* (Alexander, NC: WorldComm, 1997), 107 (quote).

11. Van Horne, "Andrew Ellicott's Mission," 165; Matthews, *Andrew Ellicott*, 107.

12. Ellicott, *The Journal of Andrew Ellicott*, 32–38; Matthews, *Andrew Ellicott*, 121–22.

13. Ellicott, *The Journal of Andrew Ellicott*, 39; Riley, "Spanish Policy in Mississippi," 56.

14. Ellicott, *The Journal of Andrew Ellicott*, 43–44 (quote); Van Horne, "Andrew Ellicott's Mission," 169; Whitaker, *The Mississippi Question*, 59; Riley, "Spanish Policy in Mississippi," 57.

15. Riley, "Spanish Policy in Mississippi," 59 (quote).

16. James, *Antebellum Natchez*, 66; Van Horne, "Andrew Ellicott's Mission," 164–75; Ellicott, *The Journal of Andrew Ellicott*, 57–67.

17. Jack D. L. Holmes, "Barton Hannon in the Old Southwest," *Journal of Mississippi History* 44 (1982): 69–78; Ellicott, *The Journal of Andrew Ellicott*, 97–100 (first quote); Haynes, *The Mississippi Territory*, 16 (second quote).

18. James, *Antebellum Natchez*, 70–74; Haynes, *The Mississippi Territory*, 16; Holmes, "A Spanish Province," 172.

19. James, *Antebellum Natchez*, 71; John F. H. Claiborne, *Mississippi as a Province, Territory and State* (Jackson: Power and Barksdale, 1880), 170–71; Ellicott, *The Journal of Andrew Ellicott*, 112–17; Clarence Carter, ed., *The Territorial Papers of the United States, Vol. V* (Washington DC: Government Printing Office, 1937–1938), 11–12; Franklin L. Riley, "Transition From Spanish to American Rule," *Publications of the Mississippi Historical Society* 3 (1901): 281.

20. William S. Coker and Jack D. L. Holmes, eds., "Daniel Clark's Letter on the Mississippi Territory," *Journal of Mississippi History* 32 (1970): 161–62; Haynes, *The Mississippi Territory*, 18 (quote).

21. Van Horne, "Andrew Ellicott's Mission," 181–82; Haynes, "The Formation of the Territory," 175–77; James, *Antebellum Natchez*, 68–74 (quote); Robert V. Haynes, "Law Enforcement in Frontier Mississippi," *Journal of Mississippi History* 22 (1960): 29; Haynes, *The Mississippi Territory*, 21.

22. Claiborne, *Mississippi as a Province*, 178–84 (first quote); Isaac Guion, "Military Journal of Captain Isaac Guion, 1797–1799," Dunbar Rowland, ed., *Annual Report of the Mississippi Department of Archives and History* (Nashville: Brandon Printing, 1909), 68–69; Riley, "Transition From Spanish to American Rule," 305 (second quote); Haynes, *The Mississippi Territory*, 23–24 (third quote).

23. Holmes, "The Formation of the Territory," 172; Ellicott, *The Journal of Andrew Ellicott*, 176 (first quote); Guion, "Military Journal," 74 (second quote).

24. Peter J. Hamilton, "Running Mississippi's South Line," *Publications of the Mississippi Historical Society* 2 (1899): 167; Whitaker, *The Mississippi Question*, 66–67 (first quote); DeRosier, *William Dunbar*, 72 (second quote); Andro Linklater, *The Fabric of America, How Our Borders and Boundaries Shaped the Country and Forged Our National Identity* (New York: Walker & Company, 2007), 152–62: Rand, *Men of Spine*, 85–87.

25. Claiborne, *Mississippi as a Province*, 202 (quote); Carter, *The Territorial Papers, Volume V*, 18–22; Skates, *Mississippi: A History*, 67.

26. Westley F. Busbee Jr., *Mississippi: A History* (Wheeling, IL: Harland Davidson, 2005), 54; John Wunder, "American Law and Order Comes to the Mississippi Territory: The Making of Sargent's Code, 1798–1800," *Journal of Mississippi History* 38 (1976): 132–33.

27. Haynes, "The Formation of the Territory," 178; James, *Antebellum Natchez*, 74–75; Rand, *Men of Spine*, 93–95; Skates, *Mississippi: A History*, 53; Dunbar Rowland, ed., *The Mississippi Territorial Archives, 1798–1803. Vol. I* (Nashville: Press of Brandon, 1905), 9–10 (quote).

28. Haynes, "The Formation of the Territory," 180; Haynes, *The Mississippi Territory*, 28, DeRosier, *William Dunbar*, 180 (quote).

29. Robert V. Haynes, "The Disposal of Lands in the Mississippi Territory," *Journal of Mississippi History* 24 (1962): 227–38; William Rawlings, "The Great Yazoo Fraud," *Georgia Backroads* 8 (Spring 2009): 56–61; DeRosier, *William Dunbar*, 89 (quote).

30. Haynes, *The Mississippi Territory*, 34–35 (first quote); Rowland, *Mississippi Territorial Archives, I*, 32, 69 (second quote).

31. Haynes, "The Formation of the Territory," 179 (first quote); Rowland, *Mississippi Territorial Archives, I*, 104 (second quote).

32. Robert V. Haynes, "Law Enforcement in Frontier Mississippi," *Journal of Mississippi History* 22 (1960): 27–40; Rowland, *Mississippi Territorial Archives*, 1, 89–92; Jack D. L. Holmes, "Law and Order in Spanish Natchez," *Journal of Mississippi History* 25 (1963): 194–95 (quote).

CHAPTER 2: TUMULTUOUS TERRITORIAL GOVERNMENT

1. Harnett T. Kane, *Natchez on the Mississippi* (New York: Bonanza Books, 1947), 114; Haynes, "Formation of the Territory," 178; Dunbar Rowland, *History of Mississippi, The Heart of the South* (Jackson, MS: S. J. Clarke, 1925), vol. 1, 348; Haynes, *Mississippi Territory*, 27. Clark and Guice, *The Old Southwest*, 207–11, provide a summary of the political climate and personalities of this period. Haynes is by far the leading expert on the territorial period in Mississippi and has written on this topic for over fifty years. In this book, we have chosen to provide a quick overview of the political factionalism of the period and suggest readers consult Haynes's *The Mississippi Territory and the Southwest Frontier, 1795–1817* for a detailed analysis of the political landscape.

2. Rowland, *Mississippi Territorial Archives*, 25–29; Rowland, *Heart of the South*, vol. 1, 349.

3. Haynes, *Mississippi Territory*, 30; Claiborne, *Mississippi as a Province*, 206; William S. Coker and Jack D. L. Holmes, eds., "Daniel Clark's Letter on the Mississippi Territory," *Journal of Mississippi History* 23 (1970): 165.

4. Haynes, *Mississippi Territory*, 31; Haynes, "Formation of Territory," 180–81; Claiborne, *Mississippi as a Province*, 208.

5. Haynes, *Mississippi Territory*, 35–36; Haynes, "Formation of Territory," 181–82; Rowland, *Territorial Archives*, 110.

6. John Wunder, "American Law and Order Comes to Mississippi Territory: The Making of Sargent's Code, 1798–1800," *Journal of Mississippi History* 38 (1976): 131–55; William B.

Hamilton, "The Printing of the 1799 Laws of the Mississippi Territory," *Journal of Mississippi History* 2 (1940): 88–99.

7. Haynes, *Mississippi Territory*, 39–40; Claiborne, *Mississippi as a Province*, 205; Haynes, "Formation of Territory," 179.

8. Haynes, *Mississippi Territory*, 41; Haynes, *Formation of Territory*, 188; Carter, *Territorial Papers*, 5, 67.

9. Carter, *Territorial Papers*, 5, 78–82; Haynes, *Mississippi Territory*, 41–44; Haynes, "Formation of Territory," 188–90.

10. Haynes, "Formation of Territory," 193–94; Carter, *Territorial Papers*, vol. 5, 95–103.

11. Rowland, *Mississippi Territorial Archives*, 185; Haynes, *Mississippi Territory*, 45; Busbee, *Mississippi: A History*, 58.

12. Haynes, *Mississippi Territory*, 48; John Ray Skates, *Mississippi: A History* (New York: W. W. Norton, 1979), 59.

13. Haynes, "Formation of Territory," 196.

14. Rowland, *Mississippi Territorial Archives*, 351–55.

15. Haynes, "Formation of Territory," 197; Haynes, *Mississippi Territory*, 55.

16. Haynes, "Formation of Territory," 198; Haynes, *Mississippi Territory*, 62–63.

17. William B. Hamilton, "Jefferson College and Education in Mississippi, 1798–1817," *Journal of Mississippi History* 3 (1941): 259–76; Haynes, *Mississippi Territory*, 63–65; James, *Antebellum Natchez*, 105.

18. Carter, *Territorial Papers*, vol. 5, 192–205; Haynes, "Formation of Territory," 200–201; Haynes, *Mississippi Territory*, 57–61.

19. Haynes, "Formation of Territory," 201–2; Haynes, *Mississippi Territory*, 65–69.

20. Haynes, "Formation of Territory," 204; Haynes, *Mississippi Territory*, 56–60, 72; Carter, *Territorial Papers*, vol. 5, 290–92.

21. Haynes, *Mississippi Territory*, 89–90.

22. Haynes, *Mississippi Territory*, 80.

23. Skates, *Mississippi*, 62; Haynes, *Mississippi Territory*, 82; Haynes, "Formation of Territory," 207.

24. Haynes, *Mississippi Territory*, 85–86.

25. Haynes, *Mississippi Territory*, 91.

26. Dennis J. Mitchell, *Mississippi: A New History.* (Jackson: University Press of Mississippi, 2015), 67–70; James, *Antebellum Natchez*, 107–8; Robert Haynes devoted a complete chapter on Burr and his appearance and trial in Mississippi in Haynes, *Mississippi Territory*, 139–66. There are no shortages of biographies of Aaron Burr and books on the alleged conspiracy. One of the latest is James E. Lewis Jr., *The Burr Conspiracy: Uncovering the Story of an Early American Crisis* (Princeton, NJ: Princeton University Press, 2017).

27. Mitchell, *Mississippi: A New History*, 67–69.

28. Mitchell, *Mississippi: A New History*, 68–69; Haynes, *Mississippi Territory*, 158–61.

29. Busbee, *Mississippi: A History*, 61; Haynes, *Mississippi Territory*, 174.

30. Haynes, *Mississippi Territory*, 169; Carter, *Territorial Papers*, vol. 5, 654–57; James, *Antebellum Natchez*, 106.

31. Haynes, *Mississippi Territory*, 199–201.

32. Robert Haynes, "The Road to Statehood," in Richard McLemore , ed., *History of Mississippi*, 2 vols. (Jackson: University of Mississippi Press, 1973), 1: 217–18; Carter, *Territorial Papers*, vol. 6, 12–13.

33. James, *Antebellum Natchez*, 109–10; Haynes, "The Road to Statehood," 218–20.

34. Haynes, *Mississippi Territory*, 324–29.

35. Haynes, *Mississippi Territory*, 324–29.

36. William B. Hamilton. "Politics in the Mississippi Territory." *Huntington Library Quarterly* 11 (1948): 285.

CHAPTER 3: THE LAND OF PROMISE

1. William B. Hamilton, "Mississippi in 1817: A Sociological and Economic Analysis," *Journal of Mississippi History* 34 (November 1967): 282 (first quote); Bradley G. Bond, ed., *Mississippi: A Documentary History* (Jackson: University Press of Mississippi, 2003), 44 (second quote).

2. Haynes, "Disposal of Lands," 226–28; Clark and Guice, *The Old Southwest*, 80–82. Concise overviews of French, British, and Spanish claims to Mississippi are provided in several state histories. Among the best accounts is Busbee, *Mississippi: A History*. The complicated affair arising from the Georgia's claims to what became the Mississippi Territory is likewise chronicled in numerous histories of Georgia. For a unique assemblage of primary materials related to these claims, see Edmund C. Burnett, ed., "Papers Related to Bourbon County, Georgia, 1785–1786," *American Historical Review* 15 (October 1909–July 1910): 66–353.

3. Haynes, "Disposal of Lands," 233–37.

4. Haynes, *The Mississippi Territory*, 60; Clark and Guice, *The Old Southwest*, 78.

5. Carter, *The Territorial Papers*, vol. 5, 545–46, 599–600; Everett Dick, *The Dixie Frontier: A Social History* (New York: Knopf, 1948), 67.

6. Dick, *Dixie Frontier*, 67–68; Haynes, "Disposal of Lands," 242; Carter, *The Territorial Papers*, vol. 6, 491–98, 646–47 (quote); Thomas P. Abernathy, *The South in the New Nation* (Baton Rouge: Louisiana State University Press, 1961), 459.

7. Dick, *Dixie Frontier*, 11; Albert James Pickett, *History of Alabama, and Incidentally of Georgia and Mississippi, From the Earliest Period* (Charleston, SC: Walker and James, 1851), 470; Abernathy, *The South in the New Nation*, 458.

8. Surveyor's Record Book, Levin Wailes Collection, Mississippi Department of Archives and History.

9. Robert V. Haynes, "The Formation of the Territory," in McLemore, *A History of Mississippi*, 200; Haynes, "Disposal of Lands," 241; Abernathy, *South in the New Nation*, 451, 458, 460 (quote).

10. Dick, *Dixie Frontier*, 65; Joan E. Cashin, *A Family Venture: Men and Women on the Southern Frontier* (New York: Oxford University Press, 1991), 61; Adam Rothman, *American Expansion and the Origins of the Deep South* (Cambridge, MA: Harvard University Press, 2007), 45.

11. Carter, *Territorial Papers*, vol. 6, 226; Haynes, "Disposal of Lands," 239; Ray Allen Billington, *Westward Expansion: A History of the American Frontier* (New York: Macmillan, 1967), 350; Mike Bunn, *Early Alabama: An Illustrated Guide to the Formative Years, 1798–1826* (Tuscaloosa: University of Alabama Press, 2019), 75.

12. Dick, *Dixie Frontier*, 70–75; Haynes, "Disposal of Lands," 246; Edward M. Steel Jr., "A Pioneer Farmer in the Choctaw Purchase," *Journal of Mississippi History* 16 (October 1954): 229.

13. Abernathy, *The South in the New Nation*, 466 (first quote); Lowery, "The Great Migration to the Mississippi Territory," 177 (second quote); Frank L. Owsley, "The Pattern of Migration and Settlement on the Southern Frontier," *Journal of Southern History* 11 (May 1945): 147; Clark and Guice, *The Old Southwest*, 180–82.

14. Abernathy, *The South in the New Nation*, 444; Lowery, "The Great Migration," 173; Charles D. Lowery, "The Great Migration to the Mississippi Territory, 1798–1819," Mississippi

History Now, November 2000, http://mshistorynow.mdah.state.ms.us/articles/169/the-great-migration-to-the-mississippi-territory-1798–1819 (accessed June 2015).

15. Abernathy, *The South in the New Nation*, 465; Lowery, "The Great Migration."

16. Abernathy, *The South in the New Nation*, 465, 468, 471; George W. Featherstonhaugh, *Excursion through the Slave States, from Washington on the Potomac to the Frontier of Mexico; with sketches of Popular Manners and Geographical Notices* (New York: Harper and Brothers, 1844), 120; *Natchez Mississippi Republican*, March 12, 1818.

17. Abernathy, *The South in the New Nation*, 465; Hamilton, "Mississippi in 1817," 270.

18. Abernathy, *The South in the New Nation*, 472 (first quote); Lowery, "The Great Migration," 173–75, 183 (second quote).

19. Abernathy, *The South in the New Nation*, 468–71; C. W. Grafton, "A Sketch of the Old Scotch Settlement at Union Church," *Publications of the Mississippi Historical Society* 9 (1906): 263–71; Jesse M. Wilkins, "Early Times in Wayne County," *Publications of the Mississippi Historical Society* 6 (1902): 265–72.

20. For a detailed account of the history of the Vine and Olive Company, see Rafe Blaufarb, *Bonapartists in the Borderlands: French Exiles and Refugees on the Gulf Coast, 1815–1835* (Tuscaloosa: University of Alabama Press, 2005).

21. Charles S. Sydnor, *Slavery in Mississippi* (Baton Rouge: Louisiana State University Press, 1966), 161, 165, 171; Arthur H. DeRosier Jr., "Pioneers with Conflicting Ideals: Christianity and Slavery in the Choctaw Nation," *Journal of Mississippi History* 21 (July 1959): 174–89.

CHAPTER 4: NEW BEGINNINGS

1. Lowery, "The Great Migration," 182 (quote).

2. Cashin, *A Family Venture*, 45; Susan Dabney Smedes, *Memorials of a Southern Planter* (Baltimore: Cushing and Bailey, 1888), 49–65.

3. Abernathy, *South in the New Nation*, 466; Jesse M. Wilkins, "Early Times in Wayne County," *Publications of the Mississippi Historical Society* 6 (1902): 265–72.

4. J. F. H. Claiborne, *Life and Times of General Sam Dale* (New York: Harper and Brothers, 1860), 45, 168 (quote).

5. Cashin, *A Family Venture*, 37, 39, 46.

6. Cashin, *A Family Venture*, 41–78, 81.

7. Cashin, *A Family Venture*, 55; Walter Johnson, *River of Dark Dreams: Slavery and Empire in the Cotton Kingdom* (Cambridge, MA: Harvard University Press, 2013), 159; Ira Berlin, *Generations of Captivity: A History of African-American Slaves* (Cambridge, MA: Harvard University Press, 2004), 169, 171 (quote); Robert Gudmestad, *A Troublesome Commerce: The Transformation of the Interstate Slave Trade* (Baton Rouge: Louisiana State University Press, 2003), 191.

8. Frank L. Owsley, *Plain Folk of the Old South* (Baton Rouge: Louisiana State University Press, 1949), 57–65.

9. Owsley, *Plain Folk of the Old South*, 54, 56 (quote).

10. Owsley, *Plain Folk of the Old South*, 38.

11. Gideon Lincecum, "Autobiography of Gideon Lincecum," *Publications of the Mississippi Historical Society* 8 (1905): 468–69.

12. Dick, *Dixie Frontier*, 98; Robert Bowman, "Early History and Archaeology of Yazoo County," *Publications of the Mississippi Historical Society* 8 (1904): 429; Clark and Guice, *The Old Southwest*, 195–96.

13. Robert M. Coates, *The Outlaw Years: The History of the Land Pirates of the Natchez Trace* (New York: Macauley, 1930), 12–13; Lincecum, "Autobiography," 471 (quote).

14. Mary J. Welsh, "Recollections of Pioneer Life in Mississippi," *Publications of the Mississippi Historical Society* 4 (1901): 344–45; Jesse L. Boyd, *A Popular History of the Baptists in Mississippi* (Jackson: Baptist Press, 1930), 66; Hamilton, "Mississippi in 1817," 288–89 (quote).

15. Randy J. Sparks, *Religion in Mississippi* (Jackson: University Press of Mississippi, 2001), 34 (first quote); Marius M. Carriere Jr., "Mount Locust Plantation: The Development of Southwest Mississippi during the Frontier Period, 1810–1830," *Journal of Mississippi History* 48 (August 1986), 188 (second quote); Ingraham, *The Southwest*, 33 (third quote); John Hebron Moore, *Agriculture in Ante-Bellum Mississippi* (New York: Bookman, 1958), 39 (fourth, fifth, sixth, and seventh quotes); Cashin, *A Family Venture*, 66.

16. Francis Baily, *Journal of a Tour in Unsettled Parts of North America in 1796 and 1797* (London: Baily Brothers, 1856), 283 (first quote); Mack Swearingen, *The Early Life of George Poindexter: A Story of the Old Southwest* (New Orleans: Tulane University Press, 1934), 37–41; William C. Davis, *A Way Through the Wilderness: The Natchez Trace and the Civilization of the Southern Frontier* (New York: HarperCollins, 1995), 87–88; Boyd, *A Popular History of the Baptists in Mississippi*, 66; Dick, *Dixie Frontier*, 299–302, 304–5 (second quote), 324; Welsh, "Recollections," 346; Coates, *The Outlaw Years*, 14; Walter B. Posey, "The Public Manners of Ante-Bellum Southerners," *Journal of Mississippi History* 19 (October 1957): 220.

17. Coates, *The Outlaw Years*, 14; Sam Bowers Hilliard, *Hog Meat and Hoecake: Food Supply in the Old South, 1840–1869* (Carbondale: Southern Illinois University Press, 1972), 40, 47; Dick, *Dixie Frontier*, 287–92; Lincecum, "Autobiography," 471 (quote).

18. Coates, *The Outlaw Years*, 15–16; Dick, *Dixie Frontier*, 287–92; Hilliard, *Hog Meat and Hoecake*, 37, 49, 178; Creecy, *Scenes in the South*, 84; Swearingen, *Early Life of George Poindexter*, 37–41 (first quote); J. F. H. Claiborne, "A Trip Through the Piney Woods," *Publications of the Mississippi Historical Society* 9 (1906): 533 (second quote).

19. William B. Hamilton, *Thomas Rodney: Revolutionary and Builder of the West* (Durham, NC: Duke University Press, 1953), 89; Hilliard, *Hog Meat and Hoecake*, 39; Creecy, *Scenes in the South*, 105 (quote).

20. Coates, *The Outlaw Years*, 14; Percy L. Rainwater, "Indian Missions and Missionaries," *Journal of Mississippi History* 28 (February 1966): 38; Dick, *Dixie Frontier*, 287–92; Hilliard, *Hog Meat and Hoecake*, 39; Ingraham, *The Southwest*, 172 (quote).

21. Boyd, *A Popular History of the Baptists in Mississippi*, 66; Coates, *The Outlaw Years*, 13; Dick, *Dixie Frontier*, 293, 295–97; Ingraham, *The Southwest*, 171 (first quote); Robert E. May, *John A. Quitman: Old South Crusader* (Baton Rouge: Louisiana State University Press, 1985), 21; Swearingen, *Early Life of George Poindexter*, 161 (second quote).

22. Lincecum and Phillips, *Adventures of a Southern Naturalist*, 75–76; James Taylor Carson, *Searching for the Bright Path: The Mississippi Choctaws from Prehistory to Removal* (Lincoln: University of Nebraska Press, 1999), 73; Dick, *Dixie Frontier*, 287–92; Lincecum, "Autobiography," 476 (first and second quotes); Christopher Morris, *Becoming Southern: The Evolution of a Way of Life, Warren County and Vicksburg, Mississippi, 1770–1860* (New York: Oxford University Press, 1995), 35 (third quote).

23. Morris, *Becoming Southern*, 30, 85, 135; Alan Huffman, *Mississippi in Africa: The Saga of the Slaves of Prospect Hill Plantation and Their Legacy in Liberia Today* (New York: Penguin Group, 2004), 26; Dick, *Dixie Frontier*, 99; Cashin, *A Family Venture*, 40; Owsley, *Plain Folk*, 67–75; Theodora Britton Marshall and Gladys Crail Evans, *They Found It in Natchez* (New Orleans: Pelican, 1939), 76; Walter Sillers Jr., "Flood Control in Bolivar County, 1838–1924," *Journal of Mississippi History* 9 (January 1947): 3–5; Robert W. Harrison, "Early State Flood-Control

Legislation in the Mississippi Alluvial Valley," *Journal of Mississippi History* 23 (April 1961): 110–14.

24. Dick, *Dixie Frontier*, 334 (first quote); William H. Sparks, *The Memories of Fifty Years* (Macon, GA: J. W. Burke, 1872), 331–33 (second quote); Owsley, *Plain Folk*, 38 (third quote); Carl D. Arfwedson, *The United States and Canada in 1832, 1833, and 1834* (London: Richard Bentley, 1834), 99 (fourth quote).

25. Lowery, "The Great Migration," 191.

26. Rogers, *Memoranda*, 265 (first quote); Moore, *Agriculture in Ante-Bellum Mississippi*, 41 (second quote); Dick, *Dixie Frontier*, 25; Bond, *Mississippi: A Documentary History*, 45; Lowery, "The Great Migration," 188; Basil Hall, *Travels in North America, in the Years 1827 and 1828* (London: Simpkin and Marshall, 1830), 131–32 (third and fourth quotes).

27. Moore, *Agriculture in Ante-Bellum Mississippi*, 72; Miles, *Jacksonian Democracy*, 56–57 (first quote); Bond, *Political Culture*, 63 (second quote); Cashin, *A Family Venture*, 73–74.

28. Moore, *Agriculture in Ante-Bellum Mississippi*, 69; Hamilton, "Mississippi in 1817," 271–72, 276–77.

29. Miles, *Jacksonian Democracy in Mississippi*, 18–20; James C. Cobb, *The Most Southern Place on Earth: The Mississippi Delta and the Roots of Regional Identity* (New York: Oxford University Press, 1992), 7; Bowman, "Early History and Archaeology of Yazoo County," 427–41, 430.

CHAPTER 5: WAR ON THE FRONTIER

1. There is a tremendous and growing body of literature devoted to interpreting the complexities of international diplomacy, trade, and immigration that affected the development of the Old Southwest and its impact on Creek society. Among the principal sources consulted for this study included Robbie Ethridge, *Creek Country: The Creek Indians and Their World* (Chapel Hill: University of North Carolina Press, 2003); Andrew K. Frank, *Creeks and Southerners: Biculturalism on the Early American Frontier* (Lincoln: University of Nebraska Press, 2005); Angela Pulley Hudson, *Creek Paths and American Roads: Indians, Settlers, and Slaves and the Making of the American South* (Chapel Hill: University of North Carolina Press, 2010); Claudio Saunt, *A New Order of Things: Property, Power, and the Transformation of the Creek Indians, 1733–1816* (Cambridge: Cambridge University Press, 1999); Mark E. Fretwell, *This So Remote Frontier: The Chattahoochee Country of Alabama and Georgia* (Historic Chattahoochee Commission, 1980); Kathryn E. Holland Braund, *Deerskins and Duffels: The Creek Indian Trade with Anglo-America, 1685–1815* (Lincoln: University of Nebraska Press, 1996); Michael D. Green, *The Politics of Removal: Creek Government and Society in Crisis* (Lincoln: University of Nebraska Press, 1982); Vernor W. Crane, *The Southern Frontier, 1670–1732* (Tuscaloosa: University of Alabama Press, 2004); Thomas Foster, *The Collected Works of Benjamin Hawkins, 1796–1810* (Tuscaloosa: University of Alabama Press, 2003); C. L. Grant, *Letters, Journals, and Writings of Benjamin Hawkins* (Savannah: Beehive Press, 1980); H. Thomas Foster II, *Archaeology of the Lower Muskogee Creek Indians, 1715–1836* (Tuscaloosa: University of Alabama Press, 2007); William S. Coker, *Indian Traders of the Southeastern Spanish Borderlands: Panton, Leslie, and Company and John Forbes and Company, 1783–1847* (Gainesville: University Press of Florida, 1986); Florette Henri, *The Southern Indians and Benjamin Hawkins, 1796–1816* (Norman: University of Oklahoma Press, 1986); Henry DeLeon Southerland Jr. and Jerry Elijah Brown, *The Federal Road Through Georgia, the Creek Nation and Alabama, 1806–1836* (Tuscaloosa: University of Alabama Press, 1989); Thomas D. Clark and John D. W. Guice, *The Old Southwest, 1795–1830* (Albuquerque: University of New Mexico, 1989); Amos J. Wright Jr., *McGillivray and McIntosh:*

Traders on the Old Southwest Frontier 1716–1815 (Montgomery: NewSouth Books, 2001); Robert V. Haynes, *The Mississippi Territory and the Southwest Frontier, 1795–1817* (Lexington: University Press of Kentucky, 2010).

2. The term "Old Southwest" generally refers to the early nineteenth-century frontier region that includes the area that became the states of Tennessee, Georgia, Alabama, Mississippi, Louisiana, and Florida. The borders of the territory controlled by the Creeks underwent considerable change in the late 1700s and early 1800s as a result of a series of treaties, cessions, and population movements. Whereas boundaries with the United States and Spain were generally understood, even if disputed, not all of the boundaries between Creek lands and those of neighboring tribes were clearly marked or agreed upon. For purposes of this manuscript, "Creek territory" refers to the heartland of the Creek Confederacy along the lower reaches of the Chattahoochee River in modern-day Alabama and Georgia and the areas through which the Coosa, Tallapoosa, and Alabama Rivers flow in Alabama today. During the period under discussion, the western boundary of authorized American settlement in Georgia was the Ocmulgee River in the central area of the current state. Tennessee had achieved statehood in 1796. Spain had taken over administration of the province of West Florida, whose effective northern boundary generally conforms with today's boundary between Alabama and Florida, in 1783 from the British. The province stretched from the Mississippi River in the west to the Atlantic Coast in the east. The French presence in the region dates to the early 1700s, but effectively disappeared with France's defeat in the French and Indian War in 1763.

3. The most concise and inclusive scholarly account of the interplay of the War of 1812 and the Creek War in bringing underlying tensions in the region to the surface is Frank L. Owsley Jr., *Struggle for the Gulf Borderlands: The Creek War and the Battle of New Orleans 1812–1815* (Tuscaloosa: University of Alabama Press, 1981); see also his "British and Indian Activities in Spanish West Florida During the War of 1812," *Florida Historical Quarterly* 46 (October 1967): 111–23.

4. The long-running feud between the United States and the Spanish over the exact boundaries of the Louisiana Purchase has been chronicled in a number of excellent books on Gulf Coast history. Among the best recent work is William C. Davis, *The Rogue Republic: How Would-Be Patriots Waged the Shortest Revolution in American History* (Boston: Houghton Mifflin Harcourt, 2011); Frank L. Owsley Jr. and Gene A. Smith, *Filibusters and Expansionists: Jeffersonian Manifest Destiny, 1800–1821* (Tuscaloosa: University of Alabama Press, 2004); Andrew McMichael, *Atlantic Loyalties: Americans in Spanish West Florida, 1785–1810* (Athens: University of Georgia Press, 2008). For accounts of the capture of Mobile by Wilkinson, see Peter J. Hamilton, *Colonial Mobile: An Historical Study* (Cambridge, MA: Riverside Press, 1910), 357–65; Owsley, *Struggle for the Borderlands*, 21–23; Clark and Guice, *The Old Southwest*, 63–65.

5. A number of studies detail to various degrees the American policy of assimilation in bringing about the Creek War. Critical to understanding American-Creek relations are the writings of Creek Agent Benjamin Hawkins, made available in edited volumes in Foster, *The Collected Works of Benjamin Hawkins*; and Grant, *Letters, Journals, and Writings of Benjamin Hawkins*. Of the works already cited as used in this study, among the most informative in this regard are Ethridge, *The Creek Indians and Their World*; Braund, *Deerskins and Duffels*; Hudson, *Creek Paths and Federal Roads*; Henri, *The Southern Indians and Benjamin Hawkins*; and Merrit B. Pound, *Benjamin Hawkins, Indian Agent* (Athens: University of Georgia Press, 1951). See also Frank L. Owsley Jr., "Benjamin Hawkins, The First Modern Indian Agent," *Alabama Historical Quarterly* 30 (Summer 1968): 7–14.

6. The most in-depth account of the Federal Road and the role it played in the history of the region through which it cut before, during, and after the war is Southerland Jr. and Brown's

The Federal Road Through Georgia, the Creek Nation and Alabama, 1806–1836. See also Hudson, *Creek Paths and Federal Roads*; and Green, *Politics of Removal*.

7. Of the studies previously cited, the most useful in delineating the differences between Lower and Upper Creeks and the associated internal conflict that played a role in bringing about the war is Ethridge, *The Creek Indians and Their World*; and Saunt, *A New Order of Things*. See also Waselkov, *A Conquering Spirit: Fort Mims and the Redstick War of 1813–1814*; Benjamin W. Griffith Jr., *McIntosh and Weatherford: Creek Indian Leaders* (Tuscaloosa: University of Alabama Press, 1988); Douglas Barber, "Council Government and the Genesis of the Creek War," *Alabama Review* 38 (July 1985): 163–74; and Ross Hassig, "Internal Conflict in the Creek War of 1813–14," *Ethnohistory* 21 (Summer 1974): 251–71. For information on slaveholding among the Lower Creeks specifically, see Anthony Gene Carey, *Sold Down the River: Slavery in the Lower Chattahoochee Valley of Alabama and Georgia* (Tuscaloosa: University of Alabama Press, 2011).

8. The quality of scholarship on Tecumseh and Tenskatawa's efforts to form a pan-Indian confederacy is uneven and sometimes conflicting. Sources consulted for this book include John Sugden, *Tecumseh: A Life* (New York: Henry Holt, 1997); R. David Edmunds, *Tecumseh and the Quest for Indian Leadership* (New York: Little, Brown, 1984); Joel Martin, *Sacred Revolt: The Muskogees' Struggle for a New World* (Boston: Beacon Press, 1991); Benjamin Drake, *Life of Tecumseh, and His Brother the Prophet: With a Historical Sketch of the Shawnee Indians* (Cincinnati: E. Morgan, 1841); R. David Edmunds, *The Shawnee Prophet* (Lincoln: University of Nebraska Press, 1983); George Stiggins, *Creek Indian History* (Birmingham, AL: Birmingham Public Library Press, 1989), 83–96; John Sugden, "Early Pan-Indianism: Tecumseh's Tour of the Indian Country, 1811–12," *American Indian Quarterly* (Fall 1986): 273–304; H. B. Cushman, *History of the Choctaw, Chickasaw, and Natchez Indians* (Greeneville, TX: Headlight Printing House, 1899), 318 (quote).

9. Tecumseh's appearance at Tuckaubatchee is chronicled in dozens of volumes about the era. Among the most detailed accounts of the event and his trip south in general is found in Sugden, *Tecumseh*, 215–51. An account of Tecumseh's speech "as recorded from eyewitness accounts," which first appeared in J. F. H. Claiborne's *Mississippi as a Province, Territory and State*, has been quoted in several histories of the Creek War. While the accuracy of the alleged transcript is highly suspect and refuted by most modern historians who have researched the topic, there is general agreement among scholars of the era that his message contained an implied, if not overt, call for a rejection of American culture, return to ancestral ways, and military preparedness. Among the most comprehensive accounts of the remarkable natural phenomena that coincided with Tecumseh's appeal to the Creeks is Jay Feldman, *When the Mississippi Ran Backwards: Empire, Intrigue, Murder, and the New Madrid Earthquakes of 1811–12* (New York: Free Press, 2005).

10. Griffith, *McIntosh and Weatherford*, 79–89; Braund, *Deerksins and Duffels*, 186–87; "Creek Indian Letters, Talks, and Treaties 1705–1839 in Four Parts, Compiled, Copied and Bound with Authority of John B. Wilson, Secretary of State, Under Direction of Mrs. J. E. Hays, State Historian, 1939," Georgia Archives.

11. For an account of the murders on the Ohio, see Griffith, *McIntosh and Weatherford*, 85–86. An account of the murder of Little Warrior and his band, who had committed the atrocities, is contained in *American State Papers: Documents, Legislative and Executive, of the Congress of the United States, From the First Session of the First to the Third Session of the Thirteenth Congress* (Washington, DC: Gales and Seaton, 1832), 843–44. For the retaliatory attack on McIntosh's party, see Griffith, *McIntosh and Weatherford*, 88. Many histories document the Red Sticks' communication with Spanish authorities; among the most concise are Owsley, *Struggle for the Gulf Borderlands*, 24–26; and Haynes, "The Road to Statehood," 228–29.

12. The best modern summary of the situation in the Tensaw region in 1813 is found in Waselkov, *A Conquering Spirit*. H. S. Halbert and T. H. Ball's seminal history, *The Creek War of 1813 and 1814* (Chicago: Donohue and Henneberry, 1895), which was informed by interviews with those who lived through the panic of 1813, contains the most detailed study of the numerous settler stockades in the region, 105–19. Over a dozen settler or military forts eventually stood in the Tensaw region. An insightful firsthand perspective of the fear and reactions among Tensaw area settlers is found in Margaret Ervin Austill, "Memories of Journeying Through Creek Country and Childhood in Clarke County, 1811–14," *Alabama Historical Quarterly* 6 (Spring 1944): 92–98. The term "Tensaw" has specific reference to the Mobile-Tensaw delta region and has roots in the "Tensaw Settlement" of the mid-eighteenth century that was located just south of the junction of the Alabama and Tombigbee Rivers. For purposes of this narrative, "Tensaw region" refers broadly to the general area of modern-day southwestern Alabama, located immediately north of Mobile, through which the Alabama, Tombigbee, Tensaw, and Mobile Rivers flow.

13. For information on the Red Sticks' visit to Pensacola and the ensuing Battle of Burnt Corn Creek and its aftermath, see Owsley, *Struggle for the Gulf Borderlands*, 30–33; Waselkov, *A Conquering Spirit*, 98–102; Elizabeth Howard West, "A Prelude to the Creek War of 1813–14," *Florida Historical Quarterly* 18 (April 1940): 247–66; Stiggins, *Creek Indian History*, 98–103; Halbert and Ball, *The Creek War*, 125–42; Albert James Pickett, *History of Alabama and Incidentally of Georgia and Mississippi From the Earliest Period* (Montgomery, AL: River City Publishing, 2003), 521–27; Thomas S. Woodward, *Woodward's Reminiscences of the Creek, or Muscogee Indians, Contained in Letters to Friends in Georgia and Alabama* (Montgomery, AL: Barrett and Wimbush, 1859), 84–85; Benjamin Hawkins to General John Floyd, September 30, 1813, in Thomas Joseph Peddy, "Creek Letters from United States Government Publications Pertaining to the Creek Indian Nation," Peddy Collection, Columbus State University Archives. Moniac's account of Red Stick activity in the Tensaw region is found in the Deposition of Samuel Moniac, Alabama Department of Archives and History.

14. Owsley, *Struggle for the Gulf Borderlands*, 30–32; Waselkov, *A Conquering Spirit*, 98–102; interviews with Colonel G. W. Creagh, General Patrick May, and Doctor Thomas G. Holmes in Pickett Papers, Alabama Department of Archives and History.

15. Stiggins, *Creek Indian History*, 101.

16. Waselkov, *A Conquering Spirit*, is the most detailed study of the Battle of Fort Mims yet published. Incorporating the great majority of known primary and secondary sources, the book is also informed by the author's archaeological investigation of the site. Waselkov's analysis forms the basis for the summary of the battle presented here.

17. Waselkov, *A Conquering Spirit*; Daniel Beasley to General Ferdinand L. Claiborne, August 30, 1813, J. F. H. Claiborne Collection, Book F, "Letters and Papers Relating to the Fort Mims Massacre," Mississippi Department of Archives and History.

18. Waselkov, *A Conquering Spirit*, 116–38.

19. Waselkov, *A Conquering Spirit*, 116–38. The day after the affair at Fort Mims, Red Sticks massacred an entire family near a settler stockade in the vicinity known as Fort Sinquefield. A pitched battle took place there on September 2, 1813. See Halbert and Ball, *The Creek War*, 177–89; O'Brien, *In Bitterness and Tears*, 48–49.

20. Halbert and Ball, *The Creek War*, 116, 122, 296–300; Claiborne, *Mississippi as a Province, Territory, and State*, 326 (first quote), 336–37, 356; Letter of E. O. W. Andrews to "Uncle," September 19, 1813, Andrew Family Papers, Mississippi Department of Archives and History. The locations of the forts referenced near Port Gibson have not been documented. For information on Fort Smith, see Jack D. Elliott, "The Plymouth Fort and Creek War: A

Mystery Solved," *Journal of Mississippi History* 62 (Fall 2000): 328–70. Proclamation of Governor David Holmes, October 8, 1813, in Clarence Edwin Carter, ed., *The Territorial Papers of the United States, Volume VI: The Territory of Mississippi, 1809–1817* (Washington, DC: United States Government Printing Office, 1938), 399–400 (second quote).

21. Owsley, *Struggle for the Gulf Borderlands*, 43–46; Haynes, "The Formative Period," 230–31; Haynes, *The Mississippi Territory*, 307, 321. Pinckney commanded the Sixth Military District, which included Georgia and the Carolinas, at the start of the war but was eventually given overall command of the U.S. war effort. This was due in large part to more reliable communications between his district, headquartered in Charleston, and the nation's capital than those of the Seventh Military District, headquartered in New Orleans, in which most of the war was actually fought. For a fuller discussion of the progress of the fighting in the Creek War, see Mike Bunn and Clay Williams, *Battle for the Southern Frontier: The Creek War and War of 1812* (Charleston: History Press, 2008).

22. Owsley, *Struggle for the Gulf Borderlands*, 47–48; Waselkov, *A Conquering Spirit*, 164–66; Griffith, *McIntosh and Weatherford*, 126–32; Halbert and Ball, *The Creek War*, 241–65; Pickett, *History of Alabama*, 574–77; Stiggins, *Creek Indian History*, 116–21; Dunbar Rowland, "Military History of Mississippi 1803–1898," in *The Official and Statistical Register of the State of Mississippi, 1908* (Jackson: Mississippi Department of Archives and History, 1908), 399; General Ferdinand Claiborne to Secretary of War John Armstrong, January 1, 1814, in John Brannan, *Official Letters of the Military and Naval Officers of the United States, During the War with Great Britain in the Years 1812, 13, 14, and 15* (Washington, DC: Way and Gideon, 1823).

23. The campaigns of the Georgia militia are by far the least studied of those of the Creek War, and there is currently no in-depth study focusing on them solely. Among the sources consulted for this paper are Owsley, *Struggle for the Gulf Borderlands*; Sean Michael O'Brien, *In Bitterness and in Tears: Andrew Jackson's Destruction of the Creeks and Seminoles* (Guilford, CT: Lyons Press, 2003); Gordon Burns Smith, *History of the Georgia Militia, 1783–1861* (Milledgeville, GA: Boyd Publishing, 2000); Griffith, *McIntosh and Weatherford*; Stiggins, *Creek Indian History*; Pickett; *History of Alabama*; Eggleston, *Red Eagle*; Halbert and Ball, *The Creek War*; Robert S. Quimby, *The U.S. Army in the War of 1812: An Operational and Command Study* (East Lansing: Michigan State University Press, 1997); Brannan, *Official Letters*; Hugh M. Thomason, "Governor Peter Early and The Creek Indian Frontier, 1813–1815," *Georgia Historical Quarterly* 45 (Fall 1961): 223–37; "Notes and Documents: Letters of John Floyd, 1813–1838," *Georgia Historical Quarterly* 33 (September 1949): 228–41. For information on the allied Creek attacks and the siege of Coweta, see Owsley, *Struggle for the Gulf Borderlands*, 52; Griffith, *McIntosh and Weatherford*, 117–18; Peddy, "Creek Letters." Big Warrior, William McIntosh, Little Prince, and Alexander Cornells to General Floyd, November 18, 1813, and Big Warrior and Little Prince to Col. Hawkins, October 7, 1813, "Creek Indian Letters, Talks, and Treaties 1705–1839 in Four Parts, Compiled, Copied and Bound with Authority of John B. Wilson, Secretary of State, Under Direction of Mrs. J. E. Hays, State Historian, 1939," Georgia Archives (quotes).

24. The best work on the campaigns of the Tennessee militia and Andrew Jackson is Volume 1 of Robert Remini's three-volume masterpiece, *Andrew Jackson: The Course of American Empire, 1767–1821* (New York: Harper and Row, 1977). Other great sources that cover Jackson and the Creek War are Owsley, *Struggle for the Gulf Borderlands*, O'Brien, *In Bitterness and in Tears*; and Robert Remini, *Andrew Jackson and His Indian Wars* (New York: Viking, 2001). There are several great biographies of Andrew Jackson that also cover his involvement in these conflicts. They include James Parton, *Life of Andrew Jackson*, 3 vols. (New York: Mason Brothers, 1861); John Reid and John Henry Eaton, *The Life of Andrew Jackson, Major General in the Service of the United States, Comprising a History of the War in the South from the*

Commencement of the Creek Campaign to the Termination of Hostilities Before New Orleans (Philadelphia: M. Carey and Son, 1817); and more recently, H. W. Brands, *Andrew Jackson: His Life and Times* (New York: Doubleday, 2005).

25. Remini, *Andrew Jackson: Course of American Empire*, 170–80; Brands, *Andrew Jackson*, 179–87; Parton, *Life of Andrew Jackson*, I, 384 (quote).

26. Remini, *Andrew Jackson and His Indian Wars*, 62–64; Davy Crockett, *Life of Davy Crockett* (New York: 1854); Remini, *Andrew Jackson and His Indian Wars*, 65–66; Remini, *Andrew Jackson: Course of American Empire*, 194–97; O'Brien, *In Bitterness and in Tears*, 73–74, 76–79; Jackson to Willie Blount, November 15, 1813, in Bassett, *Correspondence*, I, 348–50.

27. Remini, *Andrew Jackson: Course of American Empire*, 197–205, 207–8; Reid and Eaton, *Life of Andrew Jackson*, 136.

28. Holland, *Victory at the Horseshoe*, 20; Jackson to Pinckney, March 31, 1814, in Bassett, *Correspondence*, I, 488–89 (quote); Remini, *Andrew Jackson: Course of American Empire*, 213–14. An excellent discussion of the Battle of Horseshoe Bend can be found in Tom Kanon, "'A Slow, Laborious Slaughter': The Battle of Horseshoe Bend," *Tennessee Historical Quarterly* 58 (Spring 1999): 2–15.

29. Holland, *Victory at the Horseshoe*, 23–24; Brands, *Andrew Jackson*, 216–17; Remini, *Andrew Jackson: Course of American Empire*, 214–15; O'Brien, *In Bitterness and in Tears*, 146–47.

30. Remini, *Andrew Jackson: Course of American Empire*, 215–16; Holland, *Victory at the Horseshoe*, 26–27; Jackson to Blount, March 31, 1814, in Bassett, *Correspondence*, I, 489–92.

31. Remini, *Andrew Jackson and His Indian Wars*, 80–81.

32. Remini, *Andrew Jackson: Course of American Empire*, 221–22.

33. The full text of the Treaty of Fort Jackson can be found in Charles J. Kappler, *Indian Treaties, 1778–1883* (New York: Interland Publishing, 1972), 107–10; Remini, *Andrew Jackson: Course of American Empire*, 224–32.

34. Reid and Eaton, *Life of Andrew Jackson*, 190–91 (quote); O'Brien, *In Bitterness and in Tears*, 163; Remini, *Andrew Jackson: Course of American Empire*, 231.

35. Remini, *Andrew Jackson: Course of American Empire*, 232–36.

36. Jackson to Monroe, September 17, 1814, in Bassett, *Correspondence*, II, 50–51; Owsley, *Struggle for the Gulf Borderlands*, 109–12.

37. Jackson to Monroe, October 26, 1814, in Bassett, *Correspondence*, II, 82–83 (quote); Remini, *Andrew Jackson: Course of American Empire*, 239–41; Jackson to Manrique, August 6, 1814 (notes 1 and 2), Jackson to Monroe, November 14, 1814, in Bassett, *Correspondence*, II, 92–93, 96–99; Owsley, *Struggle for the Gulf Borderlands*, 112–19.

38. Robert Remini, *The Battle of New Orleans: Andrew Jackson and America's First Military Victory* (New York: Penguin, 1999), 24, 42–49.

39. Remini, *Battle of New Orleans*, 60–67; Reilly, *British at the Gates*, 237–40, 256–58; Latour, *Historical Memoir*, 69–83; Remini, *Battle for New Orleans*, 74–81; Hickey, *The War of 1812*, 281–99.

40. Remini, *Andrew Jackson: Course of American Empire*, 265; Reilly, *British at the Gates*, 311–14, 307–20; Remini, *Battle of New Orleans*, 140–45, 167, 169–76, 181; letter to John Coffee, April 24, 1815, in Harold Moser, David Hoth, Sharon Macpherson, and John Reinhold, eds., *The Papers of Andrew Jackson, Volume III, 1814–1815* (Knoxville: University of Tennessee Press, 1991), 348–49; William S. Coker, *The Last Battle of the War of 1812: New Orleans, No, Fort Bowyer!* (Pensacola, FL: Perdido Bay Press, 1981).

CHAPTER 6: TWENTIETH STAR ON THE AMERICAN FLAG

1. Richard A. McLemore, "The Division of the Mississippi Territory," *Journal of Mississippi History* 5 (1943): 79–80.

2. Franklin L. Riley, "Location of the Boundaries of Mississippi," *Publications of the Mississippi Historical Society* 3 (1900): 170; Carter, *Territorial Papers*, vol. 5, 290 (second quote), 297–98 (first quote).

3. Riley, "Location of the Boundaries," 170; Clark and Guice, *The Old Southwest*, 210; Carter, *Territorial Papers*, vol. 6, 26 (quote).

4. Carter, *Territorial Papers*, vol. 6, 26–31.

5. Carter, *Territorial Papers*, vol. 6, 36–39.

6. McLemore, "Division of the Mississippi Territory," 79–80; Carter, *Territorial Papers*, vol. 6, 3 (quote); Claiborne, *Mississippi as a Province, Territory, and State*, 297; Laura D. S. Harrell, "Imprints Toward Statehood," *Journal of Mississippi History* 29 (November 1967): 429–42.

7. Thomas Hart Benton, ed., *Abridgement of the Debates of Congress, from 1789 to 1856, Vol. IV* (New York: D. Appleton, 1857), 411 (quote); Harrell, "Imprints Toward Statehood," 429–31; Riley, "Location of the Boundaries," 170, 173; Carter, *Territorial Papers*, vol. 6, 253–57; Richard A. McLemore and Nannie P. McLemore, "The Birth of Mississippi," *Journal of Mississippi History* 39 (November 1967): 258; McLemore, "Division of the Mississippi Territory," 80. For a detailed account of the West Florida Rebellion, see William C. Davis, *The Rogue Republic: How Would-Be Patriots Staged the Shortest Revolution in American History* (New York: Houghton Mifflin Harcourt, 2011).

8. Clark and Guice, *The Old Southwest*, 50, 63; Haynes, *The Mississippi Territory*, 115, 117.

9. "The Louisiana Purchase," National Archives and Records Administration, https://www.archives.gov/exhibits/american_originals/louistxt.html; Haynes, *The Mississippi Territory*, 107–8; Smith, *Louisiana and the Gulf South Frontier*, 225.

10. Haynes, *The Mississippi Territory*, 108, 263, 267; McLemore, *History of Mississippi*, 223; Clark and Guice, *The Old Southwest*, 51–52.

11. Haynes, *The Mississippi Territory*, 109, 116, 224, 261.

12. Clark and Guice, *The Old Southwest*, 46, 47; Haynes, *The Mississippi Territory*, 111.

13. Clark and Guice, *The Old Southwest*, 46–48; Haynes, *The Mississippi Territory*, 110–15; Davis, *The Rogue Republic*, 69–83.

14. For the most detailed account of the rebellion, see Davis, *The Rogue Republic*.

15. McLemore, *History of Mississippi*, 225.

16. Clark and Guice, *The Old Southwest*, 54, 58; Haynes, *The Mississippi Territory*, 270, 272, 276.

17. Haynes, *The Mississippi Territory*, 267–68, 273; Clark and Guice, *The Old Southwest*, 56–57; McLemore, *History of Mississippi*, 226.

18. Davis, *The Rogue Republic*, 225; Haynes, *The Mississippi Territory*, 274; Clark and Guice, *The Old Southwest*, 59.

19. Haynes, *The Mississippi Territory*, 276–78; Clark and Guice, *The Old Southwest*, 60; Davis, *The Rogue Republic*, 233–34.

20. Clark and Guice, *The Old Southwest*, 61; Haynes, *The Mississippi Territory*, 278; Davis, *The Rogue Republic*, 226–27, 238, 244–45.

21. Clark and Guice, *The Old Southwest*, 60; Haynes, *The Mississippi Territory*, 278–80.

22. Haynes, *The Mississippi Territory*, 281; McLemore, *History of Mississippi*, 226–27; Davis, *The Rogue Republic*, 253, 258, 264, 267, 271–73; Clark and Guice, *The Old Southwest*, 118.

23. Haynes, *The Mississippi Territory*, 281; McLemore, *History of Mississippi*, 226–27; Davis, *The Rogue Republic*, 253, 258, 264, 267, 271–73; Clark and Guice, *The Old Southwest*, 118.

24. McLemore, *History of Mississippi*, 227.

25. Haynes, *The Mississippi Territory*, 282; McLemore, *History of Mississippi*, 228; Clark and Guice, *The Old Southwest*, 64–65; Smith, *Louisiana and the Gulf South Frontier*, 225.

26. Carter, *Territorial Papers*, vol. 6, 331 (quote), 332–34, 337, 339, 347; Robert V. Haynes, *The Mississippi Territory and the Southwest Frontier, 1795–1817* (Lexington: University Press of Kentucky, 2010), 336; Clark and Guice, *The Old Southwest*, 211–14.

27. Claiborne, *Mississippi as a Province, Territory, and State*, 298; McLemore and McLemore, "The Birth of Mississippi," 258–59; Haynes, *The Mississippi Territory and the Southwest Frontier*, 338.

28. Carter, *Territorial Papers*, vol. 6, 358–59.

29. William Warren Rogers, Robert David Ward, Leah Rawls Atkins, and Wayne Flynt, *Alabama: The History of a Deep South State* (Tuscaloosa: University of Alabama Press, 1994), 62.

30. Haynes, "The Road to Statehood," 234; Riley, "Location of the Boundaries," 175.

31. Carter, *Territorial Papers*, vol. 6, 507–11 (quote), 601–5; Haynes, *The Mississippi Territory and the Southwest Frontier*, 333; Harrell, "Imprints Toward Statehood," 430, 432.

32. Carter, *Territorial Papers*, vol. 6, 593–94 (first and second quotes), 601–5 (third and fourth quotes); Clark and Guice, *The Old Southwest*, 215.

33. McLemore, "Division of the Mississippi Territory," 80; Haynes, "The Formation of the Territory," in McLemore, ed. *A History of Mississippi*, 244–45; Riley, "Location of the Boundaries," 170–73; Haynes, *The Mississippi Territory and the Southwest Frontier*, 341–42; Carter, *Territorial Papers*, vol. 6, 708–17 (quotes); Clark and Guice, *The Old Southwest*, 217–18.

34. McLemore and McLemore, "The Birth of Mississippi," 260; Claiborne, *Mississippi as a Province, Territory, and State*, 299. For biographical information on Toulmin, see Paul McWhorter Pruitt Jr., "Harry Toulmin," *Encyclopedia of Alabama*, July 13, 2011. http://www.encyclopediaofalabama.org/article/h-3108 (accessed June 2015).

35. Haynes, *The Mississippi Territory and the Southwest Frontier*, 341–42; Riley, "Location of the Boundaries," 178; Carter, *Territorial Papers*, vol. 6, 731–35 (quote), 744–46.

36. Carter, *Territorial Papers*, vol. 6, 748–49, 763–64.

37. *A Century of Lawmaking for a New Nation: U.S. Congressional Documents and Debates, 1774–1875: Statutes at Large*, 14th Congress, 2nd Session. http://memory.loc.gov/ammem/amlaw/lawhome.html (accessed June 2015), 348–49, 370–73.

38. Riley, "Location of the Boundaries," 180 (quote); Clark and Guice, *The Old Southwest*, 220.

39. Riley, "Location of the Boundaries," 180 (first quote); Haynes, "The Formation of the Territory," in McLemore, *A History of Mississippi*, 246; William Magruder Drake, "The Framing of Mississippi's First Constitution," *Journal of Mississippi History* 29 (November 1967): 301–27 (second quote); Clark and Guice, *The Old Southwest*, 226–27.

40. McLemore, "The Division of the Mississippi Territory," 80; Abernathy, *The Formative Period in Alabama: 1815–1828* (Tuscaloosa: University of Alabama Press, 1990), 49.

41. Drake, "The Framing of Mississippi's First Constitution," 304–7, 309–12, 321–22, 324; McLemore and McLemore, "The Birth of Mississippi," 265–66; David G. Sansing, "George Poindexter," Mississippi Encyclopedia. https://mississippiencyclopedia.org/entries/george-poindexter/.

42. McLemore and McLemore, "The Birth of Mississippi," 265–66; Drake, "The Framing of Mississippi's First Constitution," 312, 320, 324–27.

43. Drake, "The Framing of Mississippi's First Constitution," 313–16; George R. Stewart, *Names on the Land: A Historical Account of Place-Naming in the United States* (New York: New York Review of Books, 2008).

44. Drake, "The Framing of Mississippi's First Constitution," 308, 310, 312, 322–24.

CHAPTER 7: LAND AND LABOR

1. For those seeking a comprehensive examination of Choctaw and Chickasaw culture and the institution of slavery, both of which are beyond the purview of this book, please consult the two volumes in the Heritage of Mississippi Series that are devoted to those topics: James F. Barnett Jr., *Mississippi's American Indians* (Jackson: University Press of Mississippi, 2012); and Max L. Grivno, *From Bondage to Freedom: Slavery in Mississippi, 1719–1865* (forthcoming, University Press of Mississippi).

2. Clark and Guice, *The Old Southwest*, 20–22; Greg O'Brien, *Choctaws in a Revolutionary Age, 1750–1830* (Lincoln: University of Nebraska Press, 2002), 110–11.

3. Arrell Gibson, "The Indians of Mississippi," in McLemore, *History of Mississippi*, 1: 69–81; Westley F. Busbee Jr., *Mississippi: A History* (Wheeling, IL: Harland Davidson, 2005), 18–19; Greg O'Brien, "Mushulatubbee and Choctaw Removal: Chiefs Confront a Changing World," Mississippi History Now. http://www.mshistorynow.mdah.ms.gov/articles/12/mushulatubbee-and-choctaw-removal-chiefs-confront-a-changing-world; Arthur H. DeRosier Jr., *The Removal of the Choctaw Indians* (Knoxville: University of Tennessee Press, 1970), 7–11.

4. Busbee, *Mississippi: A History*, 20; Greg O'Brien, "Chickasaws: The Unconquerable People," Mississippi History Now. http://www.mshistorynow.mdah.ms.gov/articles/8/chickasaws-the-unconquerable-people. Also see James R. Atkinson, *Splendid Land, Splendid People: The Chickasaw to Removal* (Tuscaloosa: University of Alabama Press, 2004).

5. Gibson, "Indians of Mississippi," 79–81; Barnett, *Mississippi's American Indians*, 96–98, 166; Clark and Guice, *The Old Southwest*, 235–36.

6. Arrell Gibson, *The Chickasaws* (Norman: University of Oklahoma Press, 1972), 91–93; Barnett, *Mississippi's American Indians*, 166.

7. DeRosier, *The Removal of the Choctaw Indians*, 24–28; Gibson, *The Chickasaws*, 104; Barnett, *Mississippi's American Indians*, 148–49. For a unique perspective on alcohol's role, see Richard White, *The Roots of Dependency: Subsistence, Environment, and Social Change Among the Choctaws, Pawnees, and Navajos* (Lincoln: University of Nebraska Press, 1983)

8. Barnett, *Mississippi's American Indians*, 169–72.

9. Gibson, "Indians of Mississippi," 86–87; Gibson, *The Chickasaws*, 106.

10. DeRosier, *The Removal of the Choctaw Indians*, 38–41.

11. DeRosier, *The Removal of the Choctaw Indians*, 41–44.

12. Barnett, *Mississippi's American Indians*, 165–66; James Taylor Carson, "States Rights and Indian Removal in Mississippi," *Journal of Mississippi History* 57 (1995): 27–28.

13. Porter L. Fortune, "The Formative Period," in McLemore, *History of Mississippi*, 1: 260–61; Barnett, *Mississippi's American Indians*, 181; DeRosier, *The Removal of the Choctaw Indians*, 48–49, 54–55.

14. Fortune, "The Formative Period," 261; DeRosier, 54–56.

15. DeRosier, *The Removal of the Choctaw Indians*, 62–67; Barnett, *Mississippi's American Indians*, 183–87.

16. Fortune, "The Formative Period," 262; Barnett, *Mississippi's American Indians*, 185.

17. DeRoiser, *The Removal of the Choctaw Indians*, 67–68.

18. John Ray Skates, *Mississippi's Old Capitol: Biography of a Building* (Jackson: Mississippi Department of Archives and History, 1990), 7.

19. Fortune, "The Formative Period," 262–63; Barnett, *Mississippi's American Indians*, 187–88; DeRoiser, *The Removal of the Choctaw Indians*, 98.

20. DeRosier, *The Removal of the Choctaw Indians*, 91–93; Busbee, *Mississippi: A History*, 80.

21. DeRosier, *The Removal of the Choctaw Indians*, 91–93, 113–14.

22. Gibson, *The Chickasaws*, 142–50; Barnett, *Mississippi's American Indians*, 189.

23. Clark and Guice, *The Old Southwest*, 245; DeRosier, *The Removal of the Choctaw Indians*, 104; Barnett, *Mississippi's American Indians*, 193–94.

24. Barnett, *Mississippi's American Indians*, 192–93.

25. Clark and Guice, *The Old Southwest*, 246–47; Barnett, *Mississippi's American Indians*, 195–98; Fortune, "The Formative Period," 265; DeRosier, *The Removal of the Choctaw Indians*, 119–20.

26. Barnett, *Mississippi's American Indians*, 197; DeRosier, *The Removal of the Choctaw Indians*, 128.

27. Gibson, *The Chickasaws*, 170–80; Barnett, *Mississippi's American Indians*, 204; Fortune, "The Formative Period," 266.

28. Barnett, *Mississippi's American Indians*, 205.

29. Barnett, *Mississippi's American Indians*, 200; Gibson, *The Chickasaws*, 187.

30. Clark and Guice, *The Old Southwest*, 252; Gibson, *The Chickasaws*, 215.

31. Thomas D. Cockrell, "The Politics of Land in Jacksonian Mississippi," *Journal of Mississippi History* 47 (1985): 5–6; Clark and Guice, *The Old Southwest*, 252–53.

32. Barnett, *Mississippi's American Indians*, 208; Carson, "States Rights and Indian Removal," 27.

33. Clark and Guice, *The Old Southwest*, 253.

34. Berlin, *Generations of Captivity*, 163 (first quote); Rothman, *Slave Country*, 188, 198, 200; David J. Libby, *Slavery and Frontier Mississippi, 1720–1835* (Jackson: University Press of Mississippi, 2004), 64; Jim Barnett and Clark Burkett, "The Forks of the Road Slave Market at Natchez," *Journal of Mississippi History* 63 (Fall 2001): 169–88; Sydnor, *Slavery in Mississippi*, 149–51; Berlin and Morgan, *Cultivation and Culture*, 158–59; Baptist, *The Half Has Never Been Told*, 2; Joseph Holt Ingraham, *The Southwest: By a Yankee* (New York: Harper and Brothers, 1835), 185 (second quote), 235 (third quote).

35. Sydnor, *Slavery in Mississippi*, 149–51; Barnett and Burkett, "The Forks of the Road Slave Market," 169; Thom Rosenblum, "Driving Out the Slave Traders: The Natchez Uprising of 1833," *Journal of Mississippi History* 67 (Spring 2005): 45–67.

36. For information on the market at Forks of the Road, see Wendell H. Stephenson, *Isaac Franklin, Slave Trader and Planter of the Old South* (Baton Rouge: Louisiana State University Press, 1938); and Barnett and Burkett, "The Forks of the Road Slave Market."

37. Ingraham, *The Southwest*, 192–97.

38. Rosenblum, "Driving Out the Slave Traders," 45–67; William J. Anderson, *Life and Narrative of William J. Anderson: Twenty Four Years a Slave* (Chicago: *Daily Tribune* Book and Job Printing Office, 1857), 14 (quote). For a broad outline of the many ways slaves were bought and sold in the American South, see Walter Johnson, *Soul by Soul: Life Inside the Antebellum Slave Market* (Cambridge, MA: Harvard University Press, 1999).

39. Rosenblum, "Driving Out the Slave Traders," 45–67; Sydnor, *Slavery in Mississippi*, 157; Rothman, *Slave Country*, 202; Gudmestad, *A Troublesome Commerce*, 95–96.

40. Rosenblum, "Driving Out the Slave Traders," 45–67; Edwin A. Miles, *Jacksonian Democracy in Mississippi* (Chapel Hill: University of North Carolina Press, 1960), 24, 42; Stephenson, *Isaac Franklin, Slave Trader*, 61; Libby, *Slavery and Frontier Mississippi*, 66; Todd A. Herring, "Kidnapped and Sold in Natchez: The Ordeal of Aaron Cooper, a Free Black Man," *Journal of Mississippi History* 60 (December 1998): 341–53; Rothman, *Slave Country*, 201; Ira Berlin, *Generations of Captivity: A History of African-American Slaves* (Cambridge, MA: Harvard University Press, 2004), 169–70.

41. Berlin, *Generations of Captivity*, 168; Rosenblum, "Driving Out the Slave Traders," 45–67; Sydnor, *Slavery in Mississippi*, 171. Overviews of slave pricing can be found in Libby, *Slavery and Frontier Mississippi*; Johnson, *Soul by Soul*.

42. Sydnor, *Slavery in Mississippi*; Libby, *Slavery and Frontier Mississippi*; Anderson, *Life and Narrative of William J. Anderson*, 14–31. The broad outlines of slavery in the antebellum South are chronicled in a host of outstanding studies focusing on the South at large and individual states. Among the most useful for understanding the daily lives of slaves consulted for this study are Andrew Waters, ed., *Prayin' to Be Set Free: Personal Accounts of Slavery in Mississippi* (Winston-Salem, NC: John F. Blair, 2002); Eugene D. Genovese, *Roll Jordan Roll: The World the Slaves Made* (New York: Random House, 1976); Elizabeth Fox-Genovese, *Within the Plantation Household: Black and White Women of the Old South.* (Chapel Hill: University of North Carolina Press, 1988); John W. Blassingame, *The Slave Community: Plantation Life in the Antebellum South* (New York: Oxford University Press, 1979); Kenneth M. Stampp, *Peculiar Institution: Slavery in the Ante-Bellum South* (New York: Random House, 1989); Johnson, *River of Dark Dreams*, 190; Rothman, *Slave Country*, 51.

43. Swearingen, *Early Life of George Poindexter*, 152; Sydnor, *Slavery in Mississippi*, 68–71; Pearse, *A Narrative of the Life of James Pearse*, 34–37. For perhaps the best overview of the role of the overseer on Mississippi plantations, see William K. Scarborough, *The Overseer: Plantation Management in the Old South* (Athens: University of Georgia Press, 1984).

44. Rothman, *Slave Country*, 189 (quote); Waters, *Prayin' to Be Set Free*, 106, 167–69; Sydnor, *Slavery in Mississippi*, 65; Johnson, *River of Dark Dreams*, 161, 198.

45. Waters, *Prayin' to Be Set Free*, 18, 65, 103, 167–69; Sydnor, *Slavery in Mississippi*, 22–40, 48, 52–53; Moore, *Emergence of the Cotton Kingdom*, 88–91; Johnson, *River of Dark Dreams*, 187.

46. Sydnor, *Slavery in Mississippi*, 54; Bond, *Mississippi: A Documentary History*, 66–69; Governor's Correspondence, Appeals for Clemency, Mercy, Pardon, (Gov. Leake, 5/21/23, 1/29/1824), (Gov. Holmes, 5/19/181, 7/26/1819), Mississippi Department of Archives and History; Libby, *Slavery and Frontier Mississippi*, 66; Drake, "The Framing of Mississippi's First Constitution," 321; Rowland, *History of Mississippi*, 573; Johnson, *River of Dark Dreams*, 171; Rothman, *Slave Country*, 197.

47. Anderson, *Life and Narrative of William J. Anderson*, 14–31; Rothman, *Slave Country*, 53; Johnson, *River of Dark Dreams*, 194–96; Camp, *Closer to Freedom*, 40.

48. Sydnor, *Slavery in Mississippi*, 104; *Mississippi Herald and Natchez Gazette*, September 23, 1806, and July 15, 1807; *Natchez Ariel*, May 25, 1827, and October 24, 1825.

49. Berlin, *Generations of Captivity*, 173, 190–92; Berlin and Morgan, *Cultivation and Culture*, 166; Johnson, *River of Dark Dreams*, 9, 168; Kaye, *Joining Places*, 34, 37, 42, 44, 122; Sydnor, *Slavery in Mississippi*, 140; Waters, *Prayin' to Be Set Free*, 120; Claiborne, *Correspondence of John A. Quitman*, 84–86 (quotes); Libby, *Slavery and Frontier Mississippi*, 55, 88.

50. Smedes, *Memorials of a Southern Planter*, 70; Sydnor, *Slavery in Mississippi*, 96; Waters, *Prayin' to Be Set Free*, 21, 168–69; Johnson, *River of Dark Dreams*, 212; Berlin, *Generations of Captivity*, 185–86; Stephanie M. H. Camp, *Closer to Freedom: Enslaved Women and Everyday Resistance in the Plantation South* (Chapel Hill: University of North Carolina Press, 2004), 60, 65, 85–90; Anthony E. Kaye, *Joining Places: Slave Neighborhoods in the Old South* (Chapel Hill: University of North Carolina Press, 2007), 104; Berlin and Morgan, *Cultivation and Culture*, 168; Dylan C. Penningroth, *The Claims of Kinfolk: African-American Property and Community in the Nineteenth-Century South* (Chapel Hill: University of North Carolina Press, 2003), 47–52, 66.

51. Waters, *Prayin' to Be Set Free*, 21–22; Rogers, *Memoranda*, 267–68; Claiborne, *Correspondence of John A. Quitman*, 84–86 (quotes).

52. Libby, *Slavery and Frontier Mississippi*, 85; Ben E. Bailey, "Music in Slave Era Mississippi," *Journal of Mississippi History* 54 (February 1992): 3, 40; Boyd, *A Popular History of the Baptists in Mississippi*, 70; Sparks, *Religion in Mississippi*, 80–82, 91; Berlin, *Generations of Captivity*, 206.

53. *Vicksburg Register*, September 16, 1831 (first quote); Carter, *Territorial Papers*, vol. 6, 299 (second quote); J. Michael Crane, "Controlling the Night: Perceptions of the Slave Patrol System in Mississippi," *Journal of Mississippi History* 61 (Summer 1999): 120; Bond, *Mississippi: A Documentary History*, 66–69.

54. The revolts mentioned are chronicled in dozens of books focusing on each event. For a summary of them and others that were significant in shaping the institution of slavery in America, see Eugene D. Genovese, *From Rebellion to Revolution: Afro-American Slave Revolts in the Making of the Modern World* (Baton Rouge: Louisiana State University Press, 1979); Berlin, *Generations of Captivity*, 175.

55. Augustus Q. Walton, *A History of the Detection, Conviction, Life and Designs of John A. Murel, the Great Western Land Pirate . . .* (Athens, TN: The Journal, 1835); Bond, *Political Culture*, 93–94; Libby, *Slavery and Frontier Mississippi*, 103–14. For more information on the Murrell affair, see Joshua D. Rothman, *Flush Times and Fever Dreams: The Story of Capitalism and Slavery in the Age of Jackson* (Athens: University of Georgia Press, 2012); and James L. Penick, *The Great Western Land Pirate: John A. Murrell in Legend and History* (Columbia: University of Missouri Press, 1981).

56. Libby, *Slavery and Frontier Mississippi*, 114–18; Sparks, *Religion in Mississippi*, 89; Rothman, *Slave Country*, 209; Cameron B. Strang, *Frontiers of Science: Imperialism and Natural Knowledge in the Gulf South Borderlands, 1500–1800* (Chapel Hill: University of North Carolina Press, 2018), 278.

57. Jones, *Concise History of the Introduction of Protestantism*, 186–88.

58. Ray Holder, ed., "On Slavery: Selected Letters of Parson Winans, 1820–1844," *Journal of Mississippi History* 46 (November 1984): 326 (first quote); Dickey, *Seargent S. Prentiss*, 41 (second and third quotes); Dunbar, *History of Mississippi*, 547 (fourth through seventh quotes); Sydnor, *Slavery in Mississippi* (last quote).

59. Randy J. Sparks, "Mississippi's Apostle of Slavery: James Smylie and the Biblical Defense of Slavery," *Journal of Mississippi History* 49 (May 1989): 89–106; Sparks, *Religion in Mississippi*, 120–21; Frances Allen Cabaniss and James A. Cabaniss, "Religion in Ante-Bellum Mississippi," *Journal of Mississippi History* 6 (October 1944): 221–22. The biblical passage about Ham is found in Genesis 9:20–27.

60. Sparks, "Mississippi's Apostle of Slavery"; Sparks, *Religion in Mississippi*, 120–21; Cabaniss and Cabaniss, "Religion in Ante-Bellum Mississippi," 219, 221–22.

61. Norwood Allen Kerr, "The Mississippi Colonization Society (1831–1860)," *Journal of Mississippi History* 43 (February 1981): 1–30. Huffman, *Mississippi in Africa*, 45–47, 156; Sydnor, *Slavery in Mississippi*, 204. For more on the history of the American Colonization Society, see Eric Burin, *Slavery and the Peculiar Solution: A History of the American Colonization Society* (Gainesville: University Press of Florida, 2008).

62. Kerr, "The Mississippi Colonization Society"; Huffman, *Mississippi in Africa*, 49–52 (quote), 153–54; Sydnor, *Slavery in Mississippi*, 204–14; Sparks, *Religion in Mississippi*, 98–104.

63. McLemore, *A History of Mississippi*, 325.

CHAPTER 8: AN AGRICULTURAL ECONOMY

1. Frank L. Owsley, "The Pattern of Migration and Settlement on the Southern Frontier," *Journal of Southern History* 11 (May 1945): 147–76 (first quote, 149); John Solomon Otto, "The Migration of the Southern Plain Folk: An Interdisciplinary Synthesis," *Journal of Southern History* 51 (May 1985): 183–200; Lowery, "The Great Migration," 187; Swearingen, *The Early Life*

of George Poindexter, 37 (second quote); Napier, *Lower Pearl River's Piney Woods*, 44; Hamilton, "Mississippi in 1817," 281; Hilliard, *Hog Meat and Hoecake*, 112; Clark and Guice, *The Old Southwest*, 99–116.

2. Ellicott, *The Journal of Andrew Ellicott*, 135 (quote); John Hebron Moore, *The Emergence of the Cotton Kingdom in the Old Southwest* (Baton Rouge: Louisiana State University Press, 1998), 146; Hilliard, *Hog Meat and Hoecake*, 99, 113, 116; DeRosier, "Natchez and the Formative Years of William Dunbar," 31; Jack D. L. Holmes, "Livestock in Spanish Natchez," *Journal of Mississippi History* 23 (January 1961): 17; Carson, *Searching for the Bright Path*, 174; Richard S. Lackey, ed., *Frontier Claims in the Lower South* (Baton Rouge, LA: Provincial Press, 1977), 21–54; Jack Temple Kirby, *Mockingbird Song: Ecological Landscapes of the South* (Chapel Hill: University of North Carolina Press, 2006), 114; Nollie W. Hickman, "Logging and Rafting Timber in South Mississippi, 1840–1910," *Journal of Mississippi History* (July 1957): 154; Claiborne, "A Trip Through the Piney Woods," 515; Owsley, *Plain Folk*, 34.

3. Hilliard, *Hog Meat and Hoecake*, 98–99; Morris, *Becoming Southern*, 35; Claiborne, "A Trip Through the Piney Woods," 521–22; Traugott Broome, *Mississippi: Geographic, Statistic, Typographic Sketch for Immigrants and Friends of Geography and Ethnology* (Hattiesburg, MS: Book Farm, 1942), 102; Carson, *Searching for the Bright Path*, 74.

4. Owsley, *Plain Folk*, 67–75; Sparks, *Memories of Fifty Years*, 331 (first quote); Moore, *Emergence of the Cotton Kingdom*, 116; Young, *Autobiography of a Pioneer*, 222–23; James Pearse, *A Narrative of the Life of James Pearse* (Rutland, VT: William Fay, 1825), 51–52 (second and third quotes).

5. Hilliard, *Hog Meat and Hoecake*, 118–20; Claiborne, "A Trip Through the Piney Woods," 521–22; Moore, *Emergence of the Cotton Kingdom*, 147; Sparks, *Memories of Fifty Years*, 331–33; Moore, *Agriculture in Ante-Bellum Mississippi*, 64.

6. Claiborne, "A Trip Through the Piney Woods," 521–22.

7. Moore, *Agriculture in Ante-Bellum Mississippi*, 62–63; Hickman, "Logging and Rafting Timber," 154.

8. Moore, *Agriculture in Ante-Bellum Mississippi*, 10 (first quote); Dunbar Rowland, *History of Mississippi: The Heart of the South* (Jackson: S. J. Clarke, 1925), 621; Ingraham, *The Southwest*, 86 (second quote).

9. Holmes, "Cotton Gins," 159; Moore, *Agriculture in Ante-Bellum Mississippi*, 28, 34; James L. Watkins, *King Cotton: A Historical and Statistical Review, 1790–1808* (New York: James J. Watkins and Sons, 1908), 161–64; Carriere, "Mount Locust Plantation," 191; Moore, *Emergence of the Cotton Kingdom*, 12; Walter Johnson, *River of Dark Dreams: Slavery and Empire in the Cotton Kingdom* (Cambridge, MA: Harvard University Press, 2013), 152.

10. Moore, *Agriculture in Ante-Bellum Mississippi*, 32; Benjamin L. C. Wailes, *Report on the Agriculture and Geology of Mississippi* (Philadelphia: Lippincott, Grambo, 1854), 143; Jane Thompson-Stahr, *The Burling Books: Ancestors and Descendants of Edward and Grace Burling, Quakers* (Baltimore: Gateway Press, 2001), 321–22;Watkins, *King Cotton*, 165; Hamilton, "Mississippi in 1817," 284.

11. Haynes, "Disposal of Lands," 226; Claiborne, *Mississippi as a Province, Territory, and State*, 143 (first quote); Moore, *Agriculture in Ante-Bellum Mississippi*, 25, 69, 164; Watkins, *King Cotton*, 162, 166, 170–71; Hamilton, "Mississippi in 1817," 283; Ingraham, *The Southwest*, 86.

12. Moore, *Agriculture in Ante-Bellum Mississippi*, 30, 42–43; Libby, *Slavery and Frontier Mississippi*, 41–44; Wailes, *Report on the Agriculture and Geology*, 155; Johnson, *River of Dark Dreams*, 154–58, 162–63.

13. Moore, *Agriculture in Ante-Bellum Mississippi*, 42; Libby, *Slavery and Frontier Mississippi*, 41–44; Wailes, *Report on the Agriculture and Geology*, 154; Watkins, *King Cotton*, 163; Moore,

Emergence of the Cotton Kingdom, 12, 85; Ira Berlin and Phillip D. Morgan, eds., *Cultivation and Culture: Labor and the Shaping of Slave Life in the Americas* (Charlottesville: University of Virginia Press, 1993), 164; Johnson, *River of Dark Dreams*, 153, 246.

14. Moore, *Emergence of the Cotton Kingdom*, 37–44; Moore, *Agriculture in Ante-Bellum Mississippi*, 45–46.

15. Angela Lakwete, *Inventing the Cotton Gin: Machine and Myth in Antebellum America* (Baltimore: Johns Hopkins University Press, 2003), 38; Watkins, *King Cotton*, 161; John Hebron Moore, "Mississippi's Search for a Staple Crop," *Journal of Mississippi History* 29 (November 1967): 379; Libby, *Slavery and Frontier Mississippi*, 40; Holmes, "Cotton Gins," 161 (quote); Moore, *Agriculture in Ante-Bellum Mississippi*, 20–24.

16. Moore, "Mississippi's Search for a Staple Crop," 380–82; Watkins, *King Cotton*, 162, 166; Moore, *Agriculture in Ante-Bellum Mississippi*, 48; McLemore and McLemore, "The Birth of Mississippi," 255–69.

17. Moore, *Agriculture in Ante-Bellum Mississippi*, 47, 54–55, 161; Moore, *Emergence of the Cotton Kingdom*, 23–234; James Silk Buckingham, *The Slave States of America* (London: Fisher, Son, 1842), 447; Rothman, *Slave Country*, 46.

18. Moore, "Mississippi's Search for a Staple Crop," 379, 384; John G. Jones, *Concise History of the Introduction of Protestantism into Mississippi and The Southwest* (St. Louis: Pinckard, 1866), 113; Robert C. Weems, "Mississippi's First Banking System," *Journal of Mississippi History* 29 (November 1967): 389; Watkins, *King Cotton*, 166; Moore, *Agriculture in Ante-Bellum Mississippi*, 20–24.

19. Dick, *Dixie Frontier*, 114–17.

20. Charles Hillman Brough, "Historic Clinton," *Publications of the Mississippi Historical Society* 3 (1903), 318; Miles, *Jacksonian Democracy*, 23–24; Robert C. Weems, "The Makers of the Bank of Mississippi," *Journal of Mississippi History* 15 (July 1953): 138; Larry Schweikart, *Banking in the American South from the Age of Jackson to Reconstruction* (Baton Rouge: Louisiana State University Press, 1987), 203; Richard H. Kilbourne Jr., *Slave Agriculture and Financial Markets in Antebellum America: The Bank of the United States in Mississippi, 1831–1852* (London: Pickering and Chatto, 2006), 25–29, 57–105; Martha Jane Brazy, *An American Planter: Stephen Duncan of Antebellum Natchez and New York* (Baton Rouge: Louisiana State University Press, 2006), 69–70.

21. Reuben Davis, *Recollections of Mississippi and Mississippians* (Cambridge, MA: Riverside Press, 1890), 78 (first and second quotes); Moore, *Agriculture in Ante-Bellum Mississippi*, 68; Schweikart, *Banking in the American South*, 179 (third quote); Bond, *Political Culture in Antebellum Mississippi*, 83; Marvin Bentley, "Incorporated Banks and the Economic Development of Mississippi, 1829–1837," *Journal of Mississippi History* 35 (November 1973): 382–83; Charles Hillman Brough, "The History of Banking in Mississippi," *Publications of the Mississippi Historical Society* 3 (1900): 324.

22. Miles, *Jacksonian Democracy in Mississippi*, 118, 119 (quote); Moore, *Emergence of the Cotton Kingdom*, 18; Schweikart, *Banking in the American South*, 59; Dennis East, "The New York and Mississippi Land Company and the Panic of 1837," *Journal of Mississippi History* 33 (November 1971): 300.

23. Ingraham, *The Southwest*, 84–85 (quote); Hamilton, "Mississippi in 1817," 284; Watkins, *King Cotton*, 167–71; Bond, *Mississippi: A Documentary History*, 46; Abernathy, *The South in the New Nation*, 473; Moore, *Agriculture in Ante-Bellum Mississippi*, 69–71; Huffman, *Mississippi in Africa*, 18; Morris, *Becoming Southern*, 162.

24. Ingraham, *The Southwest*, 89–91.

25. J. F. H. Claiborne, *Life and Correspondence of John A. Quitman, Major-General, U.S.A., and Governor of the State of Mississippi* (New York: Harper and Brothers, 1860), 72 (first and second quotes), 83 (third quote).

26. Claiborne, *Life and Correspondence of John A. Quitman*, 72 (quotes); W. T. Scott, "Natchez Ante-bellum Theatricals" (unpublished manuscript), Mississippi Department of Archives and History.

27. Mack Swearingen, "Luxury at Natchez in 1801: A Ship's Manifest from the McDonogh Papers," *Journal of Southern History* 3 (May 1937): 188–90; Sparks, *Memories of Fifty Years*, 326.

28. Ingraham, *The Southwest*, 26 (first quote); James, *Antebellum Natchez*, 136; Tyrone Power, *Impressions of America, During the Years 1833, 1834, and 1835* (London: Richard Bentley, 1836), 190 (second quote).

29. Seargent S. Prentiss, *A Memoir of S. S. Prentiss* (New York: Scribner, 1856), 42 (first and second quotes); Ingraham, *The Southwest*, 102 (third and fourth quotes); Carriere, "Mount Locust Plantation," 189.

30. Haynes, "Disposal of Lands," 226 (first quote); Creecy, *Scenes in the South*, 106 (second quote); Henry Ker, *Travels Through the Western Interior of the United States* (Elizabethtown, NJ: Ker, 1816), 42 (third quote); Moore, *Agriculture in Ante-Bellum Mississippi*, 27, 57–61, 94, 128; Dick, *Dixie Frontier*, 84–85; Hamilton, "Mississippi in 1817," 287; Moore, *Emergence of the Cotton Kingdom*, 23.

31. Miles, *Jacksonian Democracy in Mississippi*, 75–76; Peter L. Rousseau, "Jacksonian Monetary Policy, Specie Flows, and the Panic of 1837," *Journal of Economic History* 62 (June 2002): 457–88; John Edmond Gonzales, "Flush Times, Depression, War, and Compromise," in McLemore, *Mississippi: A History*, 292. For a good overview of the depression and its effects, see Alasdair Roberts, *America's First Great Depression: Economic Crisis and Political Disorder After the Panic of 1837* (Ithaca, NY: Cornell University Press, 2012).

32. David G. Sansing, "Charles Lynch," Mississippi Encyclopedia. https://mississippiencyclopedia.org/entries/charles-lynch/; Rowland, *Encyclopedia of Mississippi History*, 153.

33. Moore, *Agriculture in Ante-Bellum Mississippi*, 70–74; Gonzales, "Flush Times," in McLemore, *Mississippi: A History*, 292; Bond, *Political Culture*, 85; Schweikart, *Banking in the American South*, 180; Dick, *Dixie Frontier*, 123; Davis, *Recollections of Mississippi and Mississippians*, 105 (first quote); Joseph G. Baldwin, *The Flush Times of Alabama and Mississippi* (New York: D. Appleton, 1853), 65 (second quote); Moore, *Emergence of the Cotton Kingdom*, 20.

34. Bond, *Political Culture*, 83; Gonzales, "Flush Times," in McLemore, *Mississippi: A History*, 292–93; Rowland, *History of Mississippi*, 604; Horatio Eustis Letters, March 5, 1840, Mississippi Department of Archives and History (quote).

35. Edwin A. Miles, "Joseph Seawell Jones," NCpedia.org January 1988, http://ncpedia.org/biography/jones-joseph-seawell (accessed June 2015); Edwin A. Miles, "Francis Leech's 'The Mammoth Humbug, or the Adventures of Shocco Jones in Mississippi, in the Summer of 1839,'" *Journal of Mississippi History* 21 (January 1959): 1–39; Schweikart, *Banking in the American South*, 83–91.

36. Miles, *Jacksonian Democracy in Mississippi*, 151, 155; Bond, *Political Culture*, 85; Rowland, *History of Mississippi*, 617; Schweikart, *Banking in the American* South, 180; David G. Sansing, "Alexander G. McNutt," Mississippi Encyclopedia, https://mississippiencyclopedia.org/entries/alexander-g-mcnutt/. An excellent and concise summary of the bond controversy and its effects is contained in Busbee, *Mississippi: A History*, 94–96.

37. Charles S. Sydnor, *A Gentleman of the Old Natchez Region: Benjamin L. C. Wailes* (Durham, NC: Duke University Press, 1938), 156 (first quote); Moore, *Emergence of the Cotton Kingdom*, 86–87; Hamilton, "Mississippi in 1817," 286–87; McLemore and McLemore, "The Birth of Mississippi," 255–69; Ingraham, *The Southwest*, 86–87 (second and third quotes); Moore, *Agriculture in Ante-Bellum Mississippi*, 38 (fourth quote), 41.

38. Hamilton, "Mississippi in 1817," 284; Moore, *Agriculture in Ante-Bellum Mississippi*, 70–74 (quote), 110–12.

39. Moore, *Agriculture in Ante-Bellum Mississippi*, 75, 81–82, 85, 95, 101, 165; James H. McLendon, "The Development of Mississippi Agriculture: A Survey," *Journal of Mississippi History* 13 (April 1951): 79.

40. Moore, *Emergence of the Cotton Kingdom*, 204–5; Claiborne, "A Trip Through the Piney Woods," 523 (quote); Richard W. Griffin, "Manufacturing Interests of Mississippi Planters, 1810–1832," *Journal of Mississippi History*, 22 (April 1960): 110–22; Les Crocker, "An Early Iron Foundry in Northern Mississippi," *Journal of Mississippi History* 35 (May 1973): 113–26; John Hebron Moore, "Mississippi's Ante-bellum Textile Industry," *Journal of Mississippi History* 16 (April 1954): 83–83; William Larry Ziglar, "Shipbuilding on the Pascagoula River," *Journal of Mississippi History* 36 (February 1974): 2.

CHAPTER 9: DYING (AND LIVING) IN EARLY MISSISSIPPI

1. Carter, *Territorial Papers*, vol. 6, 322–26.

2. Libby, *Slavery and Frontier Mississippi*, 79.

3. Owsley, *Plain Folk*, 95 (first quote); Cashin, *A Family Venture*, 11, 21–23; Dick, *Dixie Frontier*, 326 (second quote); Donna Elizabeth Sedevie, "The Prospect of Happiness: Women, Divorce and Property," *Journal of Mississippi History* 52 (February 1995): 189–206.

4. Cashin, *A Family Venture*, 13; Ingraham, *The Southwest*, 69 (first quote); Claiborne, "A Trip Through the Piney Woods," 488 (second and third quotes).

5. Lucie Robertson Bridgforth, "Medicine in Antebellum Mississippi," *Journal of Mississippi History* 46 (May 1984): 83.

6. Scofield, *Perambulations of Cosmopolite*, 640 (first quote); Bridgforth, "Medicine in Antebellum Mississippi," 89; George Rogers, *Memoranda of the Experience, Labor, and Travels of a Universalist Preacher* (Cincinnati: John A. Gurley, 1845), 276; Rebecca Ruth Hogg Young to sister, February 19, 1838, in Gage-Hogg-Young Family Papers, Mississippi Department of Archives and History (second quote); Pearse, *A Narrative of the Life of James Pearse*, 22 (third quote); Hamilton, "Mississippi in 1817," 275.

7. Lattimore-Lea Papers, January 13, 1823, Mississippi Department of Archives and History (first quote); Gage-Hogg-Young Family Papers, February 19, 1838 (second quote).

8. D. Clayton James, "Municipal Government in Territorial Natchez," *Journal of Mississippi History* 27 (May 1965): 164. There are several good studies of individual yellow fever epidemics in American history, most focusing on the deadly outbreaks in the second half of the nineteenth century, such as the 1878 epidemic, with staggering death tolls. For a good overview of the disease, its spread, methods of control, and influence in Southern history, see Margaret Humphreys, *Yellow Fever and the South* (Baltimore: Johns Hopkins University Press, 1999).

9. Edith W. Moore, *Natchez Under-the-Hill* (Natchez: Southern Historical Publications, 1958), 79–82; Claiborne, *Life and Correspondence of John A. Quitman*, 83 (second and third quotes), 86–87 (first and fourth quotes).

10. Rowland, *History of Mississippi*, 580; Bridgforth, "Medicine in Antebellum Mississippi," 89; Claiborne, *Life and Correspondence of John A. Quitman*, 132 (quotes).

11. Gordon-Calhoun-Ross Family Papers, May 5, 1840, Mississippi Department of Archives and History (first quote); Elijah Steele Letters, August 16, 1839, Mississippi Department of Archives and History (second quote); Nancy McDougall Robinson Collection, Diary, April 1833 (no date given), Mississippi Department of Archives and History (third quote); Gideon

Lincecum, *Autobiography of Gideon Lincecum* (Brenham, TX: New Creek Settlers Association, 1997), 476 (fourth quote).

12. *Natchez Mississippi Republican*, September 17, 1818 (first, second, and third quotes); Henry B. Fearon, *Sketches of America: A Narrative of a Journey of Five Thousand Miles Through the Eastern and Western States* (London: Longman, Hurst, Rees, Orme, and Brown, 1818), 270 (fourth quote).

13. Dick, *Dixie Frontier*, 200, 215; Bridgforth, "Medicine in Antebellum Mississippi," 90; Ingraham, *The Southwest*, 153 (first quote); Davis, *A Way Through the Wilderness*, 98; Pearse, *A Narrative of the Life of James Pearse*, 21 (second and third quotes).

14. Bridgforth, "Medicine in Antebellum Mississippi," 97; Eron Rowland, *Life, Letters and Papers of William Dunbar of Elgin, Morayshire, Scotland, and Natchez, Mississippi: Pioneer Scientist of the Southern United States* (Jackson: Press of the Mississippi Historical Society, 1930), 101; *Natchez Free Trader and Gazette*, January 2, 1838 (quote).

15. Lincecum, *Autobiography*, 477 (quote).

16. "Franklin L. Riley, "Life and Literary Services of Dr. John W. Monette," *Publications of the Mississippi Historical Society* 9 (1906): 199–237.

17. Bertram Wyatt-Brown, *Southern Honor: Ethics and Behavior in the Old South* (New York: Oxford University Press, 1982); Clark and Guice, *The Old Southwest*, 92–93, 203; Swearingen, *The Early Life of George Poindexter*, 348 (first quote); Timothy R. Buckner, "Vicksburg's War on Vice: Drinking, Gambling, and Race in the Antebellum South," *Journal of Mississippi History* 67 (Winter 2005): 323 (second quote); Rogers, *Memoranda*, 266 (third quote); Dick, *Dixie Frontier*, 322; Cashin, *A Family Venture*, 102 (fourth quote).

18. Buckingham, *The Slave States of America*, 446 (first quote); Ingraham, *The Southwest* (second quote); Creecy, *Scenes in the South*, 54–58 (third quote); James, "Municipal Government in Territorial Natchez," 153.

19. James, "Municipal Government in Territorial Natchez," 159; Michael Allen, *Western Rivermen, 1763–1861: Ohio and Mississippian Boatmen Myth of the Alligator Horse* (Baton Rouge: Louisiana State University Press, 1990), 199.

20. Wilmuth S. Rutledge, "Dueling in Antebellum Mississippi," *Journal of Mississippi History* 26 (1964): 181 (first quote), 182 (second quote); D. C. Dickey, *Seargent S. Prentiss* (Baton Rouge: Louisiana State University Press, 1945), 45–73; Haynes, "Law Enforcement in Frontier Mississippi," 36–37; David G. Sansing, "Hiram G. Runnels," Mississippi Encyclopedia, https://mississippiencyclopedia.org/entries/hiram-g-runnels/.

21. Rogers, *Memoranda*, 269 (quote); Rutledge, "Dueling in Antebellum Mississippi," 185; Cashin, *A Family Venture*, 104; Davis, *A Way Through the Wilderness*, 256; James, *Antebellum Natchez*, 264–65.

22. Rutledge, "Dueling in Antebellum Mississippi," 182 (first quote), 184–85 (second quote), 187; David G. Sansing, "Walter Leake," Mississippi Encyclopedia, https://mississippiencyclopedia.org/entries/walter-leake/.

23. Sparks, *Religion in Mississippi*, 32, 33 (first quote); Arthur Hornblow, *A History of the Theatre in America from Its Beginnings to the Present Time* (Philadelphia: J. B. Lippincott, 1919), 334; Joseph Miller Free, "The Ante-Bellum Theater of the Old Natchez Region," *Journal of Mississippi History* 5 (April 1941): 21; Dick, *Dixie Frontier*, 131–32; Davis, *A Way Through the Wilderness*, 193.

24. Rowland, *History of Mississippi*, 597; Claiborne, *Life and Correspondence of John A. Quitman*, 91; Davis, *Recollections of Mississippi*, 113 (quotes); Dick, *Dixie Frontier*, 158–67, 226; Howard S. Fulkerson, *Random Recollections of Early Days in Mississippi* (Vicksburg, MS: Vicksburg Printing and Publishing, 1885), 9; Ben E. Bailey, "The Minstrel Show in Mississippi,"

Journal of Mississippi History 57 (Summer 1995): 140–44; Harris Gaylord Warren, "Vignettes of Culture in Old Claiborne," *Journal of Mississippi History* 20 (1958): 141; Davis, *A Way Through the Wilderness*, 149.

25. Edwin A. Miles, "The Mississippi Press in the Jackson Era, 1824–1841," *Journal of Mississippi History* 19 (January 1957): 1–20; Warren, "Vignettes of Culture," 142; John Hebron Moore, ed., "Claiborne's Journal in 'Mississippi': A Fragment from the Unpublished Second Volume of History of Mississippi," *Journal of Mississippi History* 22 (April 1960): 95; Robert A. Gross and Mary Kelley, eds., *A History of the Book in America, Volume 2: An Extensive Republic: Print, Culture, and Society in the New Nation, 1790–1840* (Chapel Hill: University of North Carolina Press, 2014), 391.

26. Gross and Kelley, *History of the Book*, 396; Miles, "The Mississippi Press," 1–20; Swearingen, *Early Life of George Poindexter*, 58 (quote); Haynes, "The Formation of the Territory," in McLemore, *Mississippi: A History*, 193.

27. David N. Young, "The Mississippi Whigs" (PhD dissertation, University of Alabama, 1968), 93; Claiborne, *Life and Times of General Sam Dale*, 189–90 (quote).

28. Robert V. Haynes, "The Road to Statehood," in McLemore, *Mississippi: A History*, 238–41; William B. Hamilton, "The Printing of the 1799 Laws of the Mississippi Territory," *Journal of Mississippi History* 2 (April 1940): 88–90; Charles S. Sydnor, "The Beginning of Printing in Mississippi," *Journal of Southern History* 1 (February 1935): 51–54.

29. Mary J. Welsh, "Recollections of Pioneer Life in Mississippi," *Publications of the Mississippi Historical Society* 4 (1901): 349; Waldo W. Braden, *The Oral Tradition in the South* (Baton Rouge: Louisiana State University Press, 1983), 26–27; Owsley, *Plain Folk*, 97.

30. Fortescue Cuming, *Cuming's Sketches of a Tour of the Western Country, 1807–1809* (Pittsburgh: Cramer, Spear, and Richbaum, 1810), 319–21 (first quote); Warren, "Vignettes of Culture," 126; Jonathan H. Green, *An Exposure of the Arts and Miseries of Gambling* (Cincinnati: U.P. James, 1843); Horatio B. Cushman, *History of the Choctaw, Chickasaw, and Natchez Indians* (Norman: University of Oklahoma Press, 1999), 124–25 (second quote); Clark and Guice, *The Old Southwest*, 198.

31. Herbert Asbury, *Sucker's Progress; An Informal History of Gambling in America* (New York: Thunder's Mouth Press, 1938), 204–13; Green, *Miseries of Gambling*, 104–5.

32. Creecy, *Scenes in the South*, 110 (quotes).

33. Asbury, *Sucker's Progress*, 218 (quote), 220–24; Fulkerson, *Random Recollections*, 96–97; Morris, *Becoming Southern*, 121; John Morris, *Wanderings of a Vagabond: An Autobiography* (New York: John Morris, 1873), 341–43; Buckner, "Vicksburg's War on Vice."

34. Alethia Adam Gordon to sister, May 5, 1840, Gordon-Calhoun-Ross Family Papers, Mississippi Department of Archives and History (quote); Rowland, *History of Mississippi*, 607.

35. Laura D. S. Harrell, "Jockey Clubs and Race Tracks in Antebellum Mississippi," *Journal of Mississippi History* 28 (November 1966): 304–18.

36. Harrell, "Jockey Clubs and Race Tracks"; Sparks, *Religion in Mississippi*, 33 (quote).

37. Free, "The Ante-Bellum Theater," 14, 17, 26–27; William Bryan Gates, "The Theater in Natchez," *Journal of Mississippi History* 3 (April 1941): 71–129; Hornblow, *A History of the Theatre*, 339; *Mississippi Free Trader*, January 6, 1838 (first quote), January 8, 1838 (second quote); Scott, "Natchez Ante-bellum Theatricals."

38. Fulkerson, *Random Recollections*, 30 (first quote); *Mississippi Free Trader*, January 1, 1838 (second quote).

CHAPTER 10: NURTURING MIND AND SPIRIT

1. Gross and Kelley, *History of the Book*, 250; Alfred Benjamin Butts, "Public Education," *Publications of the Mississippi Historical Society, Centenary Series* 3 (1919): 20–23 (first quote); Julia Huston Nguyen, "The Value of Learning: Education and Class in Antebellum Natchez," *Journal of Mississippi History* 61 (Fall 1999): 262; Polk, *Natchez Before 1830*, 128; Abernathy, *The South in the New Nation*, 451 (quote).

2. Robert J. Bailey, "The Gubernatorial Administration of George Poindexter, 1820–1822," *Journal of Mississippi History* 35 (August 1973): 235 (first quote); Correspondence of Governor George Poindexter, 1820, Mississippi Department of Archives and History; Rowland, *History of Mississippi*, 530; Butts, "Public Education," 22–23; Laura D. S. Harrell, "The Development of the Lyceum Movement in Mississippi," *Journal of Mississippi History* 31 (August 1969): 191.

3. Rowland, *History of Mississippi*, vol. 1, 556–58.

4. Rowland, *History of Mississippi*, vol. 1, 608; Butts, "Public Education," 25; Nita Katharine Pyburn, "Public Schools in Mississippi Before 1860," *Journal of Mississippi History* 21 (1959): 115; Davis, *A Way Through the Wilderness*, 170.

5. Nguyen, "The Value of Learning," 239, 256; Polk, *Natchez Before 1830*; 126; Dickey, *Seargent S. Prentiss*, 38–39.

6. Harrell, "The Development of the Lyceum Movement," 190; Aubrey K. Lucas, "Education in Mississippi from Statehood to the Civil War," in McLemore, *A History of Mississippi*, 356; Margaret DesChamps Moore, "Early Schools and Churches in Natchez," *Journal of Mississippi History* 24 (October 1962): 253; Margaret DesChamps Moore, "Protestantism in the Mississippi Territory," *Journal of Mississippi History* 29 (November 1967): 367; Nguyen, "The Value of Learning," 240–55; William D. McCain, *The Story of Jackson: A History of the Capital of Mississippi, 1821–1951* (Jackson, MS: J.R. Hyer, 1953), 17.

7. Richard A McLemore, "The Roots of Higher Education in Mississippi," *Journal of Mississippi History* 26 (1964): 208; Butts, "Public Education," 21; Nguyen, "A History of Women's Higher Education," 291-305; Trey Berry, "A History of Women's Higher Education in Mississippi, 1819–1882," *Journal of Mississippi History* 53 (November 1991): 303–20.

8. Rowland, *History of Mississippi*, 499–500; Bishop Charles G. Galloway, "Elizabeth Female Academy—The Mother of Female Colleges," *Publications of the Mississippi Historical Society* 2 (1899): 169–73; Polk, *Natchez Before 1830*, 128; Berry, "A History of Women's Higher Education," 306 (quote); Forrest Lamar Cooper, *Looking Back: Mississippi Towns and Places* (Jackson: University Press of Mississippi, 2011), 23.

9. McLemore, "The Roots of Higher Education," 208, 210; W. T. Blain, *Education in the Old Southwest: A History of Jefferson College, Washington, Mississippi* (Washington, MS: Friends of Jefferson College, 1976), 1, 4, 10–12, 23, 32, 68–73; J. K. Morrison, "Early History of Jefferson College," *Publications of the Mississippi Historical Society* 2 (1899): 183; Polk, *Natchez Before 1830*, 130.

10. W. H. Weathersby, "A History of Mississippi College," *Publications of the Mississippi Historical Society* 5 (1901): 184–220; Tommy Wayne Rogers, "Oakland College, 1830–1871," *Journal of Mississippi History* 36 (May 1974): 143–60; Warren, "Vignettes of Culture," 136; Ray Holder, "Centenary: Roots of a Pioneer College (1838–1844)," *Journal of Mississippi History* 42 (May 1980): 77–98; Tommy Wayne Rogers, "The Schools of Higher Learning at Sharon, Mississippi," *Journal of Mississippi History* 28 (February 1966): 40–55.

11. Lucas, "Education in Mississippi," in McLemore, *A History of Mississippi*, 364; McLemore, "Roots of Higher Education," 213.

12. Haynes, "The Formation of the Territory," in McLemore, *A History of Mississippi*, 198; Blain, *Education in the Old Southwest*, 54.

13. Harrell, "The Development of the Lyceum Movement," 187–201; Warren, "Vignettes of Culture," 139–40; William B. Hamilton, "The Southwestern Frontier, 1795–1817: An Essay in Social History," *Journal of Southern History* 10 (1944): 396.

14. Angela G. Ray, *The Lyceum and Public Culture in the Nineteenth-Century United States* (East Lansing: Michigan State University Press, 2005); *South-Western Journal*, February 15, 1838, Mississippi Department of Archives and History.

15. Steel, "A Pioneer Farmer," 239.

16. Claiborne, *Mississippi as a Province, Territory, and State*, 201 (first quote); Cameron B. Strang, *Frontiers of Science: Imperialism and Natural Knowledge in the Gulf South Borderlands, 1500–1800* (Chapel Hill: University of North Carolina Press, 2018), 178 (second quote); Arthur H. DeRosier Jr., "William Dunbar, Explorer," *Journal of Mississippi History* 25 (July 1963): 166–68; Franklin L. Riley, "Sir William Dunbar—The Pioneer Scientist of Mississippi," *Publications of the Mississippi Historical Society* 2 (1899): 86–88; Arthur H. DeRosier Jr., "Natchez and the Formative Years of William Dunbar," *Journal of Mississippi History* 34 (February 1972): 30.

17. John D. W. Guice, "BLC Wailes, the Natchez District, and the Mississippi Historical Society," Mississippi History Now, December 2010, http://mshistorynow.mdah.state.ms.us/articles/357/b-l-c-wailes-the-natchez-district-and-the-mississippi-historical-society (accessed June 2015); Diary of Levin Covington, May 21, 1825, Mississippi Department of Archives and History. For more information on early Mississippi's intellectual community, see Strang, *Frontiers of Science*.

18. McLemore, *History of Mississippi*, 378; Moore, "Protestantism in the Mississippi Territory," 370; Lorenzo Dow, *History of Cosmopolite, Or the Four Volumes of Lorenzo Dow's Journal* (Washington, DC: Joshua Martin, 1849), 142; Bishop Charles G. Galloway, "Lorenzo Dow in Mississippi," *Publications of the Mississippi Historical Society* 4 (1901): 234, 236; Scofield, *Perambulations of Cosmopolite*, 156–57; Peattie, *Audubon's America*, 151 (first quote); Polk, *Natchez Before 1830*, 114 (second quote); Schultz, *Travels on an Inland Voyage*, 134 (third quote).

19. Nathon O. Hatch, *Democratization of American Christianity* (New Haven, CT: Yale University Press, 1989), 10 (quote); Cashin, *A Family Venture*, 96.

20. Charles A. Johnson, *The Frontier Camp Meeting: Religion's Harvest Time* (Dallas: Southern Methodist University Press, 1955), 25, 39, 87; James J. Pillar, "Religious and Cultural Life, 1817–1860," in McLemore, *A History of Mississippi*, 402; Boyd, *A Popular History of the Baptists in Mississippi*, 69; Clark and Guice, *The Old Southwest*, 190–93.

21. Bruce A. Rosenberg, *The Art of the American Folk Preacher* (New York: Oxford University Press, 1970), 10, 15; Sparks, *Religion in Mississippi*, 39, 42; Johnson, *The Frontier Camp Meeting*, 46–48; Sparks, *The Memories of Fifty Years*, 115; Dick, *Dixie Frontier*, 195–203.

22. Sparks, *Religion in Mississippi*, 34–43; Dow, *History of Cosmopolite*, 142 (first quote); Johnson, *The Frontier Camp Meeting*, 242 (second quote).

23. Jones, *Concise History of the Introduction of Protestantism*, 103; Percy L. Rainwater, "Conquistadors, Missionaries, and Missions," *Journal of Mississippi History* 26 (May 1965): 137 (first and second quotes); Boyd, *A Popular History of the Baptists in Mississippi*, 71.

24. Young, *Autobiography of a Pioneer*, 224 (first, second, and third quotes); McCain, *The Story of Jackson*, 150 (fourth quote); Cabaniss and Cabaniss, "Religion in Ante-Bellum Mississippi," 202 (fifth, sixth, and seventh quotes); Rush G. Miller, "John G. Jones: Pioneer Circuit Rider and Historian," *Journal of Mississippi History* 39 (February 1977): 24.

25. Henry Blackburn Eaton, *Descendants of the Jersey Settlers: Kingston, Adams County, Mississippi* (Woodriver, IL: self-published, 1950), 8; Cabaniss and Cabaniss, "Religion in

Ante-Bellum Mississippi," 193; James L. Pillar, *The Catholic Church in Mississippi, 1837–1865* (New Orleans: Hauser Press, 1964), xvii, 1.

26. Moore, "Protestantism in the Mississippi Territory," 361; Z. T. Leavell, "Early Beginnings of Baptists in Mississippi," *Publications of the Mississippi Historical Society* 4 (1901): 245–53; Boyd, *History of the Baptists in Mississippi*, 17–20, 24–25, 32–38, 43; Jones, *Concise History of the Introduction of Protestantism*, 48, 52–53; Cabaniss and Cabaniss, "Religion in Ante-Bellum Mississippi," 194; Walter B. Posey, "The Early Baptist Church in the Lower Southwest," *Journal of Southern History* 10 (May 1944): 162; Sparks, *Religion in Mississippi*, 50, 107.

27. Sparks, *Religion in Mississippi*, 107, 110; Allen Cabaniss, *The Life and Thought of a Country Preacher: C. W. Grafton, D.D., LL.D.* (Richmond: John Knox Press, 1942), 23, 140; Rainwater, "Conquistadors, Missionaries, and Missions," 139; Walter B. Posey, "The First Session Book of the Oldest Presbyterian Church in Mississippi," *Journal of Mississippi History* 10 (April 1948): 132–49; Cabaniss and Cabaniss, "Religion in Ante-Bellum Mississippi," 196–97; T. L. Haman, "Beginnings of Presbyterianism in Mississippi," *Publications of the Mississippi Historical Society* 10 (1909): 203–21.

28. Sparks, *Religion in Mississippi*, 107; Cabaniss and Cabaniss, "Religion in Ante-Bellum Mississippi," 195–96; Moore, "Protestantism in the Mississippi Territory," 362–64; Jones, *Concise History of the Introduction of Protestantism*, 99–100, 107; Ray Holder, *William Winans: Methodist Leader in Antebellum Mississippi* (Jackson: University Press of Mississippi, 1977).

29. Nash K. Burger, "Adam Cloud, Mississippi's First Episcopal Clergyman," *Journal of Mississippi History* 9 (April 1947): 88–97; Nash K. Burger and Charlotte Capers, "Episcopal Clergy of Mississippi, 1790–1940," *Journal of Mississippi History* 8 (April 1946): 59–66; Nash K. Burger, "The Rt. Rev. William Mercer Green, First Episcopal Bishop of Mississippi," *Journal of Mississippi History* 12 (January 1950): 3–27; Cabaniss and Cabaniss, "Religion in Ante-Bellum Mississippi," 195, 197; Sparks, *Religion in Mississippi*, 110, 114; Jones, *Concise History of the Introduction of Protestantism*, 60, 78; Turitz and Turitz, *Jews in Early Mississippi*, xiii–xvi, 12, 43.

CHAPTER 11: TRAVEL, TRADE, AND URBAN CENTERS

1. Seymour Dunbar, *A History of Travel in America* (New York: Tudor, 1937), 752, 755; Jeffrey C. Benton, *The Very Worst Road: Travellers' Accounts of Crossing Alabama's Old Creek Indian Territory, 1820–1847* (Eufaula, AL: Historic Chattahoochee Commission, 1998), 70 (first and second quotes); Dawson A. Phelps, "The Choctaw Mission: An Experiment in Civilization," *Journal of Mississippi History* 14 (January 1952): 41 (third and fourth quotes); Jack D. Elliott Jr., "Three Chopped Way and Representations of Yesteryear," *Journal of Mississippi History* 61 (Fall 1999): 215–16.

2. Richard B. Doss, "Andrew Jackson, Road Builder," *Journal of Mississippi History* 16 (January 1954): 3; Stephen Cresswell, *Rednecks, Redeemers, and Race: Mississippi After Reconstruction, 1877–1917* (Jackson: University Press of Mississippi, 2010), 169; David G. Sansing, "Gerard Chittocque Brandon," Mississippi Encyclopedia, https://mississippiencyclopedia.org/entries/gerard-chittocque-brandon/; David G. Sansing, "Walter Leake," Mississippi Encyclopedia, https://mississippiencyclopedia.org/entries/walter-leake/.

3. Dunbar, *History of Travel in America*, 741; Dick, *Dixie Frontier*, 206–9.

4. Lena Mitchell Jamison, "The Natchez Trace: A Federal Highway of the Old Southwest," *Journal of Mississippi History* 1 (April 1939): 83; Doss, "Andrew Jackson, Road Builder," 3; Carter, *The Territorial Papers*, vol. 6, 404–6; Abernathy, *The South in the New Nation*, 468; Bond, *Political Culture*, 30–32.

5. Doss, "Andrew Jackson, Road Builder," 1–21; William Love, "General Jackson's Military Road," *Publications of the Mississippi Historical Society* 11 (1910): 404; Clark and Guice, *The Old Southwest*, 176–78; George J. Leftwich, "Some Main Traveled Roads, Including Cross-Sections of Natchez Trace," *Publications of the Mississippi Historical Society* 11 (1916): 466; W. A. Evans, "Gaines Trace in Monroe County, Mississippi," *Journal of Mississippi History* 1 (April 1939): 100–109; Dawson A. Phelps, "The Robinson Road," *Journal of Mississippi History* 12 (July 1950): 153–61; Elliott, "Three Chopped Way and Representations of Yesteryear," 213–36.

6. Jamison, "The Natchez Trace," 82–83, 85–91; Dawson A. Phelps, "Travel on the Natchez Trace," *Journal of Mississippi History* 15 (July 1953): 155–64; Leftwich, "Some Main Traveled Roads," 465–66; Clarke and Guice, *The Old Southwest*, 86–89.

7. Moore, *Emergence of the Cotton Kingdom*, 156; Dick, *Dixie Frontier*, 113; Allen, *Western Rivermen*, 78; Clark Hunter, ed., *The Life and Letters of Alexander Wilson* (Philadelphia: American Philosophical Society, 1983), 360 (quote).

8. Jamison, "The Natchez Trace," 99; Phelps, "Travel on the Natchez Trace," 155–64; Jonathan Daniels, *The Devil's Backbone* (New York: McGraw-Hill, 1962), 237–38.

9. Daniels, *The Devil's Backbone*; Davis, *A Way Through the Wilderness*, 273; Coates, *The Outlaw Years*, 16, 102; *Mississippi Herald and Natchez Gazette*, September 15, 1807 (quote); Clark and Guice, *The Old Southwest*, 90–92.

10. Claiborne, *Mississippi as a Province, Territory, and State*, 225–26; Coates, *The Outlaw Years*, 105; Davis, *A Way Through the Wilderness*, 272–76.

11. Samuel B. Olden Jr., "Hotels, Inns, and Taverns in Mississippi, 1830–1860," *Journal of Mississippi History* 5 (October 1943): 171–84; Coates, *The Outlaw Years*, 84 (first and second quotes); Dick, *Dixie Frontier*, 211–13; Fulkerson, *Random Recollections of Early Days in Mississippi*, 9; Alfred W. Garner, "Folsom's Pigeon Roost, the Nineteenth Century Stage Traveler's Mecca, on the Natchez Trace," *Journal of Mississippi History* 4 (January 1942): 34–37; Young, *Autobiography of a Pioneer*, 213 (third quote); Charles L. Sullivan, *Mississippi Gulf Coast: Portrait of a People* (Sun Valley, CA: American Historical, 1999), 46; Darby, *The Emigrant's Guide*, 117; Ruth Irene Jones, "Ante-Bellum Watering Places of the Mississippi Gulf Coast," *Journal of Mississippi History* 18 (December 1956): 268–301.

12. Timothy Flint, *A Condensed Geography and History of the Western States . . .* (Cincinnati: E. H. Flint, 1828), vol. 1, 229 (quote); Davis, *A Way Through The Wilderness*, 37; Adam I. Kane, *The Western River Steamboat* (College Station: Texas A&M University Press, 2004) 8–9; Dunbar, *History of Travel in America*, 281; Moore, *Emergence of the Cotton Kingdom*, 157–58; Dick, *Dixie Frontier*, 119; John G. Clark, *New Orleans 1718–1812: An Economic History* (Baton Rouge: Louisiana State University Press, 1970), 313; John W. Monette, "The Progress of Navigation and Commerce on the Waters of the Mississippi River and the Great Lakes AD 1700–1846," *Publications of the Mississippi Historical Society* 7 (1903): 479–523.

13. Kane, *The Western River Steamboat*, 12; Dunbar, *History of Travel in America*, 393; Joseph D. Shields, *Natchez: Its Early History* (Louisville: Morton, 1930), 84 (quote). Among the best summaries of the invention of the steamboat and its rise as a primary transportation device in the first half of the nineteenth century can be found in S. L. Kotar and J. E. Gessler, *The Steamboat Era: A History of Fulton's Folly on American Rivers, 1807–1860* (Jefferson, NC: McFarland, 2009).

14. Moore, *Emergence of the Cotton Kingdom*, 156–58, 161; Monette, "The Progress of Navigation," 505; Kane, *The Western River Steamboat*, 10–20; Louis C. Hunter, *Steamboats on the Western Rivers: An Economic and Technological History* (Cambridge, MA: President and Fellows of Harvard College, 1949), 27–37; Johnson, *River of Dark Dreams*, 77.

15. Dick, *Dixie Frontier*, 112; Hunter, *Steamboats on the Western Rivers*, 256–89; Paul S. Paskoff, *Troubled Waters: Steamboat Disasters, River Improvements, and American Public Policy, 1821–1860* (Baton Rouge: Louisiana State University Press, 2007), 138–39; Dunbar, *History of Travel in America*, 296; Kane, *The Western River Steamboat*, 71–72; Arfwedson, *The United States and Canada*, 72–73 (quotes); James Neal Primm, *Lion of the Valley St. Louis, Missouri, 1764–1980* (St. Louis: Missouri Historical Society Press, 1981), 163.

16. Moore, *Emergence of the Cotton Kingdom*, 159–60.

17. Dick, *Dixie Frontier*, 60.

18. Allen, *Western Rivermen*, 50; James, "Municipal Government in Territorial Natchez," 162; Schultz, *Travels on an Inland Voyage*, 135 (quote); Dick, *Dixie Frontier*, 111; Moore, *Emergence of the Cotton Kingdom*, 159, 163–64; McCain, *The Story of Jackson*, 57; Napier, *Lower Pearl River's Piney Woods*, 47–48; W. A. Evans, "Steamboats on the Upper Tombigbee in the Early Days," *Journal of Mississippi History* 4 (October 1942): 216–24.

19. Una Pope Hennessey, ed., *The Aristocratic Journey, Being the Outspoken Letters of Mrs. Basil Hall Written During a Fourteen Months Sojourn in America* (New York: G. P. Putnam's Sons, 1931), 264; Reuben Gold Thwaites, *Early Western Travels, 1748–1846* (Cleveland: Arthur H. Clark, 1905), 128; James Stuart, *Three Years in North America* (Edinburgh: Robert Cadell, 1833), 299; Simon O. Ferrall, *A Ramble of Six Thousand Miles Through the United States of America* (London: Effingham Wilson, 1832), 216; Paul Wilhelm, Duke of Wurttemberg, *Travels in North America 1822–24* (Norman: University of Oklahoma Press, 1973), 136–37; Rogers, *Memoranda*, 262 (quote).

20. Wilhelm, *Travels in North America*, 136–37; Power, *Impressions of America*, 197 (quote).

21. Paul Schneider, *Old Man River: The Mississippi River in North American History* (New York: Henry Holt, 2013), 212; Allen, *Western Rivermen*, 126; Arthur Palmer Hudson, ed., *Humor of the Old Deep South* (New York: Macmillan, 1936), 57–61; Dunbar, *History of Travel in America*, 292–93 (first quote); Schultz, *Travels on an Inland Voyage*, 145 (second quote).

22. Coates, *The Outlaw Years*, 111. The Mike Fink legend is chronicled in dozens of histories of the region. Among the best studies of the legend, its origins, and its proliferation is Walter Blair and Franklin J. Meine, eds., *Half Horse, Half Alligator: The Growth of the Mike Fink Legend* (Chicago: University of Chicago Press, 1956).

23. Charles Ripley Johnson, "Railroad Legislation and Building in Mississippi, 1830–1840," *Journal of Mississippi History* 4 (October 1942): 196–97; John Hebron Moore, "Railroads of Antebellum Mississippi," *Journal of Mississippi History* 41 (February 1979): 53–82; Christian Wolmar, *The Great Railroad Revolution: The History of Trains in America* (New York: PublicAffairs, 2012).

24. Gonzales, "Flush Times," in McLemore, *A History of Mississippi*, 291; Moore, "Railroads of Antebellum Mississippi," 59; Johnson, "Railroad Legislation," 205; Moore, *Emergence of the Cotton Kingdom*, 167–68.

25. Moore, "Railroads of Antebellum Mississippi," 60–61; Johnson, "Railroad Legislation," 198.

26. Moore, *Emergence of the Cotton Kingdom*, 177, 180, Dick, *Dixie Frontier*, 151; Creecy, *Scenes in the South*, 106 (first and second quotes); Ingraham, *The Southwest*, 95 (third quote); Moore, *Agriculture in Ante-Bellum Mississippi*, 68.

27. Morris, *Becoming Southern*, 123. This summary of early Mississippi urban life is derived from a number of studies of individual communities across the antebellum South such as James, *Antebellum Natchez*; and Harriet E. Amos, *Cotton City: Urban Development in Antebellum Mobile* (Tuscaloosa: University of Alabama Press, 2001).

28. For information on the history of Mobile, see Michael V. R. Thomason, ed., *Mobile: The New History of Alabama's First City* (Tuscaloosa: University of Alabama Press, 2001); Amos, *Cotton City*; Hamilton, *Colonial Mobile*. For more information on the early history of St. Stephens, see Herbert James Lewis, *Lost Capitals of Alabama* (Charleston, History Press, 2014). For more information on the American settlement of the Tensaw region, see Waselkov, *A Conquering Spirit*.

29. Lewis, *Lost Capitals*, 42–44. For information on the history of Huntsville, see Edward Chambers Betts, *Early History of Huntsville, Alabama 1804–1870* (Montgomery: Brown Printing, 1916); and Daniel S. Dupre, *Transforming the Cotton Frontier: Madison County, Alabama 1800–1840* (Baton Rouge: Louisiana State University Press, 1997).

30. James, *Antebellum Natchez*, 160; James, "Municipal Government in Territorial Natchez," 148, 162; Hamilton, "The Southwestern Frontier," 394 (quote); Clark and Guice, *The Old Southwest*, 185.

31. Polk, *Natchez Before 1830*, 112, 321; Fortescue Cuming, *Sketches of a Tour to the Western Country* . . . (Pittsburgh: Cramer, Spear, and Richbaum, 1810), 321 (first quote); James, *Antebellum Natchez*, 184; Claiborne, *Life and Correspondence of John A. Quitman*, 71 (third quote), 72 (second quote); James, "Municipal Government in Territorial Natchez," 153.

32. Fearon, *Sketches of America*, 270 (quote); Moore, *Emergence of the Cotton Kingdom*, 190.

33. Hamilton, "The Southwestern Frontier," 395; Polk, *Natchez Before 1830*, 115; James, *Antebellum Natchez*, 97, 116; Cecil L. Summers, *The Governors of Mississippi* (Gretna, LA: Pelican Publishing, 1988), 46.

34. DeRosier, "Natchez and the Formative Years of William Dunbar," 32 (quote); Polk, *Natchez Before 1830*, 114, 143; James, *Antebellum Natchez*, 83; DeRosier, "Natchez and the Formative Years of William Dunbar," 32–33; James, "Municipal Government in Territorial Natchez," 161; Hamilton, "Mississippi in 1817," 278; Coates, *The Outlaw Years*, 137; Moore, *Emergence of the Cotton Kingdom*, 121.

35. Virginia Parks Matthias, "Natchez-Under-the-Hill: As It Developed Under the Influence of the Mississippi River and the Natchez Trace," *Journal of Mississippi History* 7 (1945): 201–21.

36. Matthias, "Natchez-Under-the-Hill," 201 (first, second, and third quotes); Fearon, *Sketches of America*, 267; Ingraham, *The Southwest*, 20 (fourth quote).

37. Ingraham, *The Southwest*, 59 (first quote); Hamilton, "The Southwestern Frontier," 395 (second quote); Ker, *Travels Through the Western Interior of the United States*, 41 (third and fourth quotes); Claiborne, *Life and Correspondence of John A. Quitman*, 71 (fifth quote).

38. Francis Baily, *Journal of a Tour in Unsettled Parts of North America in 1796 and 1797* (London: Baily Brothers, 1856), 276 (quote); Morris, *Becoming Southern*, 108–9, 123; Moore, *Emergence of the Cotton Kingdom*, 195, 243.

39. Rogers, *Memoranda*, 269 (quotes).

40. George H. Gibson, ed., "The Mississippi Market for Woolen Goods: An 1822 Analysis," *Journal of Southern History* 31 (February 1965): 80; Cuming, *Cuming's Sketches of a Tour of the Western Country*, 319–21 (second quote); Gaylord, "Vignettes of Culture," 126; H. G. Hawkins, "History of Port Gibson, Mississippi," *Publications of the Mississippi Historical Society* 10 (1909): 279–99.

41. Hamilton, "Mississippi in 1817," 278; Claiborne, *Mississippi as a Province, Territory, and State*, 258–60; McLemore and McLemore, "The Birth of Mississippi," 262–63; Susanna Smith, "Washington, Mississippi: Antebellum Elysium," *Journal of Mississippi History* 40 (May 1978): 143–65 (quote); Haynes, "The Formation of the Territory," in McLemore, *A History of Mississippi*, 197. Unfortunately, DeFrance's Tavern was lost to a fire a few decades ago. A historic marker near the site commemorates its role in Mississippi's territorial history.

42. W. L. Lipscomb, *A History of Columbus, Mississippi During the Nineteenth Century* (Birmingham, AL: Press of Dispatch Printing, 1909); Moore, *Emergence of the Cotton Kingdom*, 198–200; Jack D. Elliott Jr. and Mary Ann Wells, *Cotton Gin Port: A Frontier Settlement on the Upper Tombigbee* (Jackson, MS: Quail Ridge Press, 2003); Jay Higginbotham, *Pascagoula: Singing River City* (Mobile, AL: Gill Press, 1967), 17; Sullivan, *Mississippi Gulf Coast*, 34–41; Hubert H. McAlexander, "Flush Times in Holly Springs," *Journal of Mississippi History* 48 (February 1986): 1–13.

43. Eron Rowland, *History of Hinds County, Mississippi, 1821–1922* (Jackson: Jones Printing, 1922), 15; Fearon, *Sketches of America*, 270 (first and second quotes); Charles Hillman Brough, "Historic Clinton," *Publications of the Mississippi Historical Society* 3 (1903): 283–89; McCain, *The Story of Jackson*, 22–27, 31–32; Rowland, *History of Mississippi*, 565; Holder, *William Winans*, 103 (third quote); McCain, *The Story of Jackson*, 1, 4, 10–13, 21 (fourth quote), 22; Skates, *Biography of a Building*, 9–11, 16, 26 (fifth quote).

CHAPTER 12: THE RISE OF JACKSONIAN DEMOCRACY

1. Swearingen, *The Early Life of George Poindexter*, 32 (first quote); Lincecum and Phillips, *Adventures of a Southern Naturalist*, 72 (second quote); Haynes, "Law Enforcement," 33; Pickett, *History of Alabama*, 475 (third quote); Bond, *Political Culture*, 2–3; Lewis L. Gould, Katherine J. Adams, and Shearer D. Bowman, eds., *Inside Natchez Trace Collection: New Sources for Southern History* (Baton Rouge: Louisiana State University Press, 1999), 148–49.

2. Dick, *Dixie Frontier*, 239; Prentiss, *A Memoir*, 62; Charles S. Sydnor, ed., "A Description of Seargent S. Prentiss in 1838," *Journal of Southern History* 10 (November 1944): 479 (quote); Franklin L. Riley, "Life of Col. J. F. H. Claiborne," *Publications of the Mississippi Historical Society* 7 (1903): 218–20; Fulkerson, *Random Recollections of Early Days in Mississippi*, 14.

3. Claiborne, *Mississippi as a Province, Territory, and State*, 360 (first and second quotes), 372; Thomas D. Cockrell, "United States Senators and Representatives From Mississippi, 1828–1836: An Introduction," *Journal of Mississippi History* 49 (February 1987): 36–38; Miles, *Jacksonian Democracy in Mississippi*, 48, 53, 103, 113; Mack Swearingen, "George Poindexter," *Journal of Mississippi History* 29 (1967): 356 (second quote); Thomas D. Cockrell, "The Politics of Land in Jacksonian Mississippi," *Journal of Mississippi History* 47 (February 1985): 4–6; Cleo Hearon, "Nullification in Mississippi," *Publications of the Mississippi Historical Society* 12 (1912): 54; Robert J. Bailey, "The Gubernatorial Administration of George Poindexter, 1820–1822," *Journal of Mississippi History* 35 (August 1973): 227–46.

4. Edwin A. Miles, "Franklin E. Plummer: Piney Woods Spokesman of the Jackson Era," *Journal of Mississippi History* 14 (January 1952): 1–34; Miles, *Jacksonian Democracy in Mississippi*, 30, 80, 115; Cockrell, "United States Senators and Representatives," 45; Gould, Adams, and Bowman, *Inside the Natchez Trace Collection*, 45 (first quote); *Woodville Democrat*, February 5, 1831 (second quote).

5. William E. Dodd, *Robert J. Walker, Imperialist* (Chicago: Chicago Literary Club, 1914), 9–18; Cockrell, "United States Senators and Representatives," 41–42; May, *John A. Quitman*, 19–20, 49; Claiborne, *Life and Correspondence of John A. Quitman*, 165 (quote).

6. Sparks, *The Memories of Fifty Years*, 332 (quote).

7. Jeffrey Normand Bourdon, "Soldier Versus Statesman: The Primacy of Symbols during the Elections of 1824 and 1828 in Mississippi and Alabama," *Journal of Mississippi History* 73 (Winter 2011): 302–3, 314; Young, "The Mississippi Whigs," 48–50; James, *Antebellum Natchez*, 113–14 (second quote); Miles, *Jackson Democracy in Mississippi*, 28.

8. Miles, *Jacksonian Democracy in Mississippi*, 20–21, 24; Bond, *Political Culture*, 52.

9. Skates, *Mississippi's Old Capitol*, 7–17.

10. Eron Rowland, *History of Hinds County, Mississippi, 1821–1922* (Jackson: Jones Printing, 1922), 15; Fearon, *Sketches of America*, 270 (quotes); Charles Hillman Brough, "Historic Clinton," *Publications of the Mississippi Historical Society* 3 (1903): 283–89; McCain, *The Story of Jackson*, 22–27, 31–32; Rowland, *History of Mississippi*, 565; Skates, *Biography of a Building*, 16.

11. McCain, *The Story of Jackson*, 34–37; Skates, *Mississippi's Old Capitol*, 22–25; Rogers, *Memoranda*, 277–78 (first quote); *Jackson Southern Sun*, December 15, 1838 (second quote).

12. Wilbourne Magruder Drake, "The Mississippi Constitutional Convention of 1832," *Journal of Southern History* 23 (August 1957): 354–70; Miles, Jackson Democracy in Mississippi, 33–35.

13. *Journal of the Convention of the State of Mississippi Held in the Town of Jackson* (1832), printed by Peter Isler, Mississippi Department of Archives and History; Drake, "The Mississippi Constitutional Convention of 1832," 354–70; Miles, *Jacksonian Democracy in Mississippi*, 37–38.

14. David G. Sansing, "Abram M. Scott," Mississippi Encyclopedia, https://mississippiencyclopedia.org/entries/abram-m-scott/; "Hiram G. Runnels," Mississippi Encyclopedia, https://mississippiencyclopedia.org/entries/hiram-g-runnels/; "Charles Lynch," Mississippi Encyclopedia, https://mississippiencyclopedia.org/entries/charles-lynch/.

15. Drake, "The Mississippi Constitutional Convention of 1832," 362–70; Miles, *Jacksonian Democracy in Mississippi*, 42 (first quote), 43 (second quote).

16. Skates, *Biography of a Building*, 52–54; Anna F. Kaplan, "Married Women's Property Act," Mississippi Encyclopedia, https://mississippiencyclopedia.org/entries/married-womens-property-act/. A provision of the act excluded such protections to property acquired by the wife by virtue of the marriage, thus preventing married borrowers from shielding their assets through a manipulation of the law.

17. M. Philip Lucas, "Beyond McCormick and Miles: The Pre-Partisan Political Culture of Mississippi," *Journal of Mississippi History* 44 (November 1982): 329–50 (first quote); Gould and Bowman, *Inside the Natchez Trace Collection*, 164 (second quote); Bourdon, "Soldier Versus Statesman," 300, 333; Young, "The Mississippi Whigs," 8; Hamilton, "Mississippi in 1817," 278.

18. Miles, *Jacksonian Democracy in Mississippi*, 4–5 (second quote), 16–17 (first quote); Bourdon, "Soldier Versus Statesman," 309 (third quote).

19. Bourdon, "Soldier Versus Statesman," 305–33 (quote); Bette B. Tilly, "The Jackson-Dinsmoor Feud: A Paradox in a Minor Key," *Journal of Mississippi History* 39 (May 1977): 117; Miles, *Jacksonian Democracy in Mississippi*, 9, 16–17. Election results found at Dave Liep's Atlas of U.S. Elections, http://uselectionatlas.org/ (accessed August, 2015). In the 1824 presidential campaign, Jackson won a plurality of the vote in a tight race featuring four major candidates. The election was decided in the US House of Representatives, where Speaker and candidate Henry Clay threw his support to John Quincy Adams, who had placed second in the popular vote. Clay was subsequently selected to be Adams's Secretary of State. Jackson and his supporters decried what they viewed as this "corrupt bargain" between Adams and Clay.

20. Bond, *Political Culture*, 82 (first quote); Schweikart, *Banking in the American South*, 12; Rowland, *History of Mississippi*, 612–13; Robert V. Remini, "Henry Clay and the Natchez Connection," *Journal of Mississippi History* 54 (August 1992): 269; Young, "The Mississippi Whigs," 1–7, 98; Bourdon, "Soldier Versus Statesman," 333.

21. Young, "The Mississippi Whigs," 154; Rowland, *History of Mississippi*, 585–86; Dickey, *Seargent S. Prentiss*, 82; Miles, *Jacksonian Democracy in Mississippi*, 32; Dallas C. Dickey, "The Disputed Mississippi Election of 1837–1838," *Journal of Mississippi History* 1 (October 1939): 217–34.

22. Miles, *Jacksonian Democracy in Mississippi*, 61–68; Young, "The Mississippi Whigs," 140; Lucie Robertson Bridgforth, "Mississippi's Response to Nullification, 1833," *Journal of Mississippi History* 45 (February 1983): 2–7; Hearon, "Nullification in Mississippi," 38–41, 42 (quote). The Nullification Controversy is chronicled in a number of books. Among the best is William W. Freehling, *Prelude to Civil War: The Nullification Controversy in South Carolina, 1816–1836* (New York: Harper and Row, 1965).

23. Hearon, "Nullification"; *Vicksburg Register*, June 12, 1834 (quotes).

24. May, *John A. Quitman*, 60–61, 70; Miles, *Jacksonian Democracy in Mississippi*, 68–69; Michael F. Holt, *The Rise and Fall of the American Whig Party: Jacksonian Politics and the Onset of the Civil War* (New York: Oxford University Press, 1999), 35; Young, "The Mississippi Whigs," 156; Hearon, "Nullification," 64; Dickey, *Seargent S. Prentiss*, 146 (quote). In the 1840s Mississippi would host some of the first public debates in the South on the issue of secession. The long path toward secession in the state is chronicled uniquely in Christopher J. Olsen, *Political Culture and Secession in Mississippi, 1830–1860* (New York: Oxford University Press, 2000).

25. William C. Davis, *Lone Star Rising: The Revolutionary Birth of the Texas Republic* (New York: Free Press, 2004), 45–51; Carter Gallagher, *A Critical Study of the Mississippians that Fought in the Texas War for Independence, 1835–1836* (unpublished manuscript), Mississippi Department of Archives and History; James E. Winston, "Mississippi and the Independence of Texas," *Southwestern Historical Quarterly* 21 (July 1917): 36–60.

26. Winston, "Mississippi and the Independence of Texas"; May, *John A. Quitman*, 78–79; Rowland, *History of Mississippi*, 591; Gallagher, "A Critical Study"; Claiborne, *Life and Correspondence of John A. Quitman*, 140. The Mississippians present at the Alamo were William Charles Baker, James C. Gwyne, Isaac Millsaps, Willis Moore, George Pagan, and Christopher C. Parker.

EPILOGUE

1. Information on Jackson's visit to Jackson is taken in large part from Skates, *Mississippi's Old Capitol*, 55–57.

2. H. W. Brands, *Andrew Jackson: His Life and Times* (New York: Doubleday, 2005), 64–65; Jon Meachem, *American Lion: Andrew Jackson in the White House* (New York: Random House, 2009), 22–23. Among the best summaries of Jackson's influence on the development of the American Southwest are the writings of Robert V. Remini: *Andrew Jackson and His Indian Wars* (New York: Viking Penguin, 2001) and *The Battle of New Orleans: Andrew Jackson and America's First Military Victory* (New York: Penguin Books, 1999).

3. *The Globe*, February 15, 1840.

Bibliography

MANUSCRIPTS AND ARCHIVAL COLLECTIONS

Mississippi Department of Archives and History

B. L. C. Wailes Papers
Carter Gallagher, *A critical study of the Mississippians that fought in the Texas War for Independence, 1835–1836* (unpublished manuscript)
Correspondence of Governor Walter Leake
Correspondence of Governor David Holmes
Correspondence of Governor George Poindexter
Diary of Levin Covington
Elijah Steele Letters
Elizabeth Female Academy Subject File
Executive Journals of Governors Holmes, Poindexter, Leake, Brandon, 1817–1827, Governor's Records
Gage-Hogg-Young Family Papers
Gordon-Calhoun-Ross Family Papers
Horatio Eustis Letters
Hutchins Family Papers
Hughes, Henry, and Family Papers
J. F. H. Claiborne Papers
James Weir Journal
Journal of the Convention of the State of Mississippi Held in the Town of Jackson (1832)
Lattimore-Lea Papers
Levin Wailes Papers
Lyman Copeland Draper Papers
McDougall Robinson Collection
Natchez History Files
Philander Smith Papers
Secretary of State Archives
South-Western Journal
Territorial Governor's Records
Territorial Legislative Records
Thomas Rodney Papers
United States Land Grants Collection (Mississippi)
William Dunbar Papers
W. T. Scott, *Natchez Ante-bellum Theatricals* (unpublished manuscript)

Alabama Department of Archives and History

Albert J. Pickett Papers

NEWSPAPERS

The Globe
Jackson Mississippian
Mississippi Free Trader
Mississippi Herald and Natchez Gazette
Mississippi Messenger
Natchez Ariel
Natchez Mississippi Messenger
Natchez Mississippi Republican
Natchez Weekly Chronicle
Vicksburg Register
Vicksburg Whig
Washington Republican
Washington Republican and Natchez Intelligencer
Woodville Democrat

PRIMARY AND SECONDARY BOOKS

Abernathy, Thomas. *The Burr Conspiracy*. New York: Oxford University Press, 1954.
Abernathy, Thomas Perkins. *The Formative Period in Alabama: 1815–1828*. Tuscaloosa: University of Alabama Press, 1990.
Abernathy, Thomas Perkins. *The South in the New Nation*. Baton Rouge: Louisiana State University Press, 1961.
Adair, James, and Kathryn E. Holland Braund, eds. *The History of the American Indians*. Tuscaloosa: University of Alabama Press, 2005.
Akin, Edward N., and Charles C. Bolton. *Mississippi: An Illustrated History*. Sun Valley, CA: American Historical Press, 2002.
Alford, Terry. *Prince among Slaves: The True Story of an African Prince Sold into Slavery in the American South*. New York: Oxford University Press, 1977.
Allen, Michael. *Western Rivermen, 1763–1861: Ohio and Mississippian Boatmen Myth of the Alligator Horse*. Baton Rouge: Louisiana State University Press, 1990.
Ambrose, Stephen E. *Undaunted Courage: Meriwether Lewis, Thomas Jefferson, and the Opening of the American West*. New York: Simon & Schuster, 1996.
Amos, Harriet E. *Cotton City: Urban Development in Antebellum Mobile*. Tuscaloosa: University of Alabama Press, 2001.
Anderson, William J. *Life and Narrative of William J. Anderson: Twenty Four Years a Slave*. Chicago: *Daily Tribune* Book and Job Printing Office, 1857.
Arfwedson, Carl D. *The United States and Canada in 1832, 1833, and 1834*. London: Richard Bentley, 1834.
Arthur, Stanley C. *The Story of the West Florida Rebellion*. St. Francisville, LA: *St. Francisville Democrat*, 1935.

Asbury, Herbert. *Sucker's Progress: An Informal History of Gambling in America*. New York: Thunder's Mouth Press, 1938.

Atkinson, James R. *Splendid Land, Splendid People: The Chickasaw Indians to Removal*. Tuscaloosa: University of Alabama Press, 2004.

Badger, Reid, and Lawrence A. Clayton, eds. *Alabama and the Borderlands: From Prehistory to Statehood*. Tuscaloosa: University of Alabama Press, 1985.

Bailey, Robert J., and Priscilla M. Lowrey. *Historic Preservation in Mississippi: A Comprehensive Plan*. Jackson: Mississippi Department of Archives and History, 1975.

Baily, Francis. *Journal of a Tour in Unsettled Parts of North America in 1796 and 1797*. London: Baily Brothers, 1856.

Bailyn, Bernard. *Voyagers to the West: A Passage in the Peopling of America on the Eve of the Revolution*. New York: Random House, 1986.

Baldwin, Joseph G. *The Flush Times of Alabama and Mississippi*. New York: D. Appleton, 1853.

Ball, T. H. *A Glance into the Great South-East, Or, Clarke County, Alabama, and Its Surroundings from 1540–1877*. Tuscaloosa: Willo Publishing, 1962.

Baptist, Edward E. *The Half Has Never Been Told: Slavery and the Making of American Capitalism*. New York: Basic Books, 2014.

Barnett Jr., James F. *Mississippi's American Indians*. Jackson: University Press of Mississippi, 2012.

Bassett, John Spencer, ed. *Correspondence of Andrew Jackson. Vol. 1*, to April 30, 1814. *Vol. 2*, May 1, 1814, to December 31, 1819. Washington, DC: Carnegie Institution of Washington, 1926.

Bemis, Samuel Flagg. *Pinckney's Treaty: Advantage from Europe's Distress, 1783–1800*. New Haven, CT: Yale University Press, 1960.

Benn, Carl. *The War of 1812*. Oxford, UK: Osprey Publishing, 2002.

Benton, Jeffrey C. *The Very Worst Road: Travellers' Accounts of Crossing Alabama's Old Creek Indian Territory, 1820–1847*. Eufaula, AL: Historic Chattahoochee Commission, 1998.

Benton, Thomas Hart, ed. *Abridgement of the Debates of Congress, from 1789 to 1856, Vol. IV*. New York: D. Appleton, 1857.

Berlin, Ira. *Generations of Captivity: A History of African-American Slaves*. Cambridge, MA: Harvard University Press, 2004.

Berlin, Ira. *Many Thousands Gone: The First Two Centuries of Slavery in North America*. Cambridge, MA: Harvard University Press, 2000.

Berlin, Ira, and Philip D. Morgan, eds. *Cultivation and Culture: Labor and the Shaping of Slave Life in the Americas*. Charlottesville: University of Virginia Press, 1993.

Bettersworth, John K. *Mississippi: A History*. Austin: Steck, 1959.

Betts, Edward Chambers. *Early History of Huntsville, Alabama 1804–1870*. Montgomery: Brown Printing, 1916.

Billington, Ray Allen. *Westward Expansion: A History of the American Frontier*. New York: Macmillan, 1967.

Blackshear, David, and Stephen F. Miller, eds. *Memoir of General David Blackshear, Including Letters from Governors Irwin, Jackson, Mitchell, Early, and Rabun, and from Major General McIntosh, Brigadier-General Floyd, and Other Officers of the Army in the War of 1813–14, on the Frontier and Sea-Coast of Georgia; and Also Letters from Members of Congress, Dr. Moses Waddel, and Others: Together with a Muster Roll of Troops under his Command*. Philadelphia: J.B. Lippincott, 1858.

Blain, W. T. *Education in the Old Southwest: A History of Jefferson College, Washington, Mississippi*. Washington, MS: Friends of Jefferson College, 1976.

Blair, Walter, and Franklin J. Meine, eds. *Half Horse, Half Alligator: The Growth of the Mike Fink Legend*. Chicago: University of Chicago Press, 1956.

Blassingame, John W. *The Slave Community: Plantation Life in the Antebellum South*. New York: Oxford University Press, 1979.

Blaufarb, Rafe. *Bonapartists in the Borderlands: French Exiles and Refugees on the Gulf Coast, 1815–1835*. Tuscaloosa: University of Alabama Press, 2005.

Bond, Bradley G., ed. *Mississippi: A Documentary History*. Jackson: University Press of Mississippi, 2003.

Bond, Bradley G. *Political Culture in the Nineteenth Century South: Mississippi 1830–1900*. Baton Rouge: Louisiana State University Press, 1995.

Borneman, Walter R. *1812: The War That Forged a Nation*. New York: Harper-Collins, 2004.

Boyd, Jesse L. *A Popular History of the Baptists in Mississippi*. Jackson, MS: Baptist Press, 1930.

Braden, Waldo W. *The Oral Tradition in the South*. Baton Rouge: Louisiana State University Press, 1983.

Brands, H. W. *Andrew Jackson: His Life and Times*. New York: Doubleday, 2005.

Brannan, John. *Official Letters of the Military and Naval Officers of the United States, During the War with Great Britain in the years 1812, 13, 14, and 15*. Washington: Way and Gideon, 1823.

Braund, Kathryn E. Holland. *Deerskins and Duffels: The Creek Indian Trade with Anglo-America, 1685–1815*. Lincoln: University of Nebraska Press, 1996.

Brazy, Martha Jane. *An American Planter: Stephen Duncan of Antebellum Natchez and New York*. Baton Rouge: Louisiana State University Press, 2006.

Brewer, Willis. *Alabama: Her History, Resources, War Record, and Public Men*. Montgomery, AL: Barrett and Brown, 1872.

Broome, Traugott. *Mississippi: Geographic, Statistic, Typographic Sketch for Immigrants and Friends of Geography and Ethnology*. Hattiesburg, MS: Book Farm, 1942.

Brown, Wilburt S. *The Amphibious Campaign for West Florida and Louisiana, 1814–1815*. Tuscaloosa: University of Alabama Press, 1969.

Bryant, Charles E. *The Tensaw Country North of the Ellicott Line, 1800–1860*. Bay Minette, AL: Lavender Press, 1998.

Buchanan, John. *Jackson's Way: Andrew Jackson and the People of the Western Waters*. New York: John Wiley and Sons, 2001.

Buckingham, J. S. *The Slave States of America*. London: Fisher, Son & Company, 1842.

Bunn, Mike. *Early Alabama: An Illustrated Guide to the Formative Years, 1798–1826*. Tuscaloosa: University of Alabama Press, 2019.

Bunn, Mike, and Clay Williams. *Battle for the Southern Frontier: The Creek War and the War of 1812*. Charleston: History Press, 2008.

Bunn, Mike, and Clay Williams. *Mississippi: The Bulwark of New Spain*. Jackson: Mississippi Department of Archives and History, 2003.

Burin, Eric. *Slavery and the Peculiar Solution: A History of the American Colonization Society*. Gainesville: University Press of Florida, 2008.

Busbee Jr., Westley F. *Mississippi: A History*. Wheeling, IL: Harlan Davidson, 2005.

Cabaniss, Allen. *The Life and Thought of a Country Preacher: C. W. Grafton, D.D., LL.D.* Richmond: John Knox Press, 1942.

Camp, Stephanie M. H. *Closer to Freedom: Enslaved Women and Everyday Resistance in the Plantation South*. Chapel Hill: University of North Carolina Press, 2004.

Carson, James Taylor. *Searching for the Bright Path: The Mississippi Choctaws from Prehistory to Removal*. Lincoln: University of Nebraska Press, 1999.

Carter, Clarence, ed. *The Territorial Papers of the United States: The Territory of Mississippi, 1798–1817*. 2 vols. Washington, DC: Government Printing Office, 1937.

Carter, Samuel, III. *Blaze of Glory: The Fight for New Orleans, 1814–1815*. New York: St. Martin's Press, 1971.

Cashin, Joan E. *A Family Venture: Men and Women on the Southern Frontier*. New York: Oxford University Press, 1991.

A Century of Lawmaking for a New Nation: U.S. Congressional Documents and Debates, 1774–1875: Statutes at Large, 14th Congress, 2nd Session. http://memory.loc.gov/ammem/amlaw/lawhome.html (accessed June 2015).

Chaudhuri, Jean, and Joyotpaul Chaudhuri. *A Sacred Path: The Way of the Muscogee Creeks*. Los Angeles: UCLA American Indian Studies Center, 2001.

Claiborne, J. F. H. *Life and Correspondence of John A. Quitman, Major-General, U.S.A., and Governor of the State of Mississippi*. New York: Harper and Brothers, 1860.

Claiborne, J. F. H. *Life and Times of General Sam Dale*. New York: Harper and Brothers, 1860.

Claiborne, J. F. H. *Mississippi as a Province, Territory and State*. Jackson, MS: Power and Barksdale, 1880.

Clark, John G. *New Orleans 1718–1812: An Economic History*. Baton Rouge: Louisiana State University Press, 1970.

Clark, Thomas D., ed. *Travels in the Old South: A Bibliography, 1527–1860*. 3 vols. Norman: University of Oklahoma Press, 1956.

Clark, Thomas D., and John D. W. Guice. *The Old Southwest, 1795–1830: Frontiers in Conflict*. Norman: University of Oklahoma Press, 1996.

Coates, Robert M. *The Outlaw Years: The History of the Land Pirates of the Natchez Trace*. New York: Macauley, 1930.

Cobb, James C. *The Most Southern Place on Earth: The Mississippi Delta and the Roots of Regional Identity*. New York: Oxford University Press, 1992.

Coker, William S. *The Last Battle of the War of 1812: New Orleans. No, Fort Bowyer!* Pensacola, FL: Perdido Bay Press, 1981.

Cooper, Forrest Lamar. *Looking Back: Mississippi Towns and Places*. Jackson: University Press of Mississippi, 2011.

Corkran, David H. *The Creek Frontier, 1540–1783*. Norman: University of Oklahoma Press, 1967.

Cox, Isaac J. *The West Florida Controversy, 1798–1813*. Baltimore: Johns Hopkins Press, 1918.

Creecy, James R. *Scenes in the South, and Other Miscellaneous Pieces*. Washington, DC: Thomas McGill, 1860.

Cresswell, Stephen. *Rednecks, Redeemers, and Race: Mississippi after Reconstruction, 1877–1917*. Jackson: University Press of Mississippi, 2010.

Crutchfield, James A. *The Natchez Trace: A Pictorial History*. Nashville: Rutledge Hill Press, 1985.

Cuming, Fortescue. *Cuming's Sketches of a Tour of the Western Country, 1807–1809*. Pittsburgh: Cramer, Spear, and Richbaum, 1810.

Cushman, Horatio B. *History of the Choctaw, Chickasaw, and Natchez Indians*. Norman: University of Oklahoma Press, 1999.

Daniels, Jonathan. *The Devil's Backbone*. New York: McGraw-Hill, 1962.

Darby, William. *The Emigrants Guide to the Western and Southwestern States and Territories: Comprising a Geographical and Statistical Description of the States of Louisiana, Mississippi, Tennessee, Kentucky, and Ohio*. New York: Kirk and Mercein, 1818.

Davis, Edwin A., and William R. Hogan. *The Barber of Natchez*. Baton Rouge: Louisiana State University Press, 1954.

Davis, Reuben. *Recollections of Mississippi and Mississippians*. Cambridge, MA: Riverside Press, 1890.

Davis, William C. *A Way Through the Wilderness: The Natchez Trace and the Civilization of the Southern Frontier*. New York: HarperCollins, 1995.

Davis, William C. *Lone Star Rising: The Revolutionary Birth of the Texas Republic*. New York: Free Press, 2004.

Davis, William C. *The Pirates Laffite: The Treacherous World of the Corsairs of the Gulf.* Orlando: Harcourt, 2005.

Davis, William C. *The Rogue Republic: How Would-Be Patriots Staged the Shortest Revolution in American History.* New York: Houghton Mifflin Harcourt, 2011.

Debo, Angie. *The Road to Disappearance: A History of the Creek Indians.* Norman: University of Oklahoma Press, 1941.

DeRosier Jr., Arthur H. *The Removal of the Choctaw Indians.* Knoxville: University of Tennessee Press, 1970.

DeRosier Jr., Arthur H. *William Dunbar, Scientific Pioneer of the Old Southwest.* Lexington: University Press of Kentucky, 2007

Dick, Everett. *The Dixie Frontier: A Social History.* New York: Knopf, 1948.

Dickey, D. C. *Seargent S. Prentiss.* Baton Rouge: Louisiana State University Press, 1945.

Dixon, Richard R. *The Battle on the West Bank.* New Orleans: Louisiana Landmarks Society, 1965.

Dodd, Donald B. *Historical Atlas of Alabama.* Tuscaloosa: University of Alabama Press, 1974.

Dodd, William E. *Robert J. Walker, Imperialist.* Chicago: Chicago Literary Club, 1914.

Dow, Lorenzo. *History of Cosmopolite, Or the Four Volumes of Lorenzo Dow's Journal.* Washington, DC: Joshua Martin, 1849.

Dunbar, Seymour. *A History of Travel in America.* New York: Tudor Publishing, 1937.

Dupre, Daniel S. *Transforming the Cotton Frontier: Madison County, Alabama 1800–1840.* Baton Rouge: Louisiana State University Press, 1997.

Eaton, Henry Blackburn. *Descendants of the Jersey Settlers: Kingston, Adams County, Mississippi.* Woodriver, IL: self-published, 1950.

Edmunds, R. David. *The Shawnee Prophet.* Lincoln: University of Nebraska Press, 1983.

Edmunds, R. David. *Tecumseh and the Quest for Indian Leadership.* New York: Little, Brown, 1984.

Eggleston, George Cary. *Red Eagle and the Wars with the Creek Indians of Alabama.* New York: Dodd, Mead, 1878.

Ellicott, Andrew. *The Journal of Andrew Ellicott, Late Commissioner on Behalf of the United States during Part of the Year 1796, the Years 1797, 1798, 1799, and Part of the Year 1800; for Determining the Boundary Between the United States and the Possessions of His Catholic Majesty in America . . .* Philadelphia: Budd and Bartram, 1803.

Elliott Jr., Jack D., and Mary Ann Wells. *Cotton Gin Port: A Frontier Settlement on the Upper Tombigbee.* Jackson, MS: Quail Ridge Press, 2003.

Elting, John R. *Amateurs, To Arms! A Military History of the War of 1812.* Chapel Hill: Algonquin Books, 1991.

Etheridge, George H. *Mississippi, A History.* Hopkinsville, KY: Historical Record Association, 1938.

Ethridge, Robbie. *Creek Country: The Creek Indians and Their World.* Chapel Hill: University of North Carolina Press, 2003.

Fearon, Henry B. *Sketches of America: A Narrative of a Journey of Five Thousand Miles Through the Eastern and Western States.* London: Longman, Hurst, Rees, Orme, and Brown, 1818.

Featherstonhaugh, George W. *Excursion through the Slave States, from Washington On the Potomac to the Frontier of Mexico; with sketches of Popular Manners and Geographical Notices.* New York: Harper and Brothers, 1844.

Ferrall, Simon O. *A Ramble of Six Thousand Miles Through the United States of America.* London: Effingham Wilson, 1832.

Flint, Timothy. *A Condensed Geography and History of the Western States* . . . Cincinnati: E.H. Flint, 1828. 2 vols.

Flint, Timothy. *Recollections of the Last Ten Years Passed in Occasional Residences and Journeyings in the Valley of the Mississippi*. Boston: Cummings, Hilliard, 1826.

Foote, Henry S. *Casket of Reminiscences*. Washington, DC: Chronicle Publishing, 1874.

Foreman, Grant. *Indian Removal: The Emigration of the Five Civilized Tribes of Indians*. Norman: University of Oklahoma Press, 1974.

Foster, H. Thomas, II, ed. *The Collected Works of Benjamin Hawkins*. Tuscaloosa: University of Alabama Press, 2003.

Foster, John. *Southern Frontiersman: The Story of General Sam Dale*. New York: William Morrow, 1967.

Fox-Genovese, Elizabeth. *Within the Plantation Household: Black and White Women of the Old South*. Chapel Hill: University of North Carolina Press, 1988.

Fretwell, Mark E. *This So Remote Frontier: The Chattahoochee Country of Alabama and Georgia*. Historic Chattahoochee Commission, 1980.

Fulkerson, Howard S. *Random Recollections of Early Days in Mississippi*. Vicksburg, MS: Vicksburg Printing, 1885.

Gabriel, Ralph Henry, ed. *The Pageant of America: A Pictorial History of the United States*. New Haven, CT: Yale University Press, 1929.

Genovese, Eugene D. *From Rebellion to Revolution: Afro-American Slave Revolts in the Making of the Modern World*. Baton Rouge: Louisiana State University Press, 1979.

Genovese, Eugene D. *Roll Jordan Roll: The World the Slaves Made*. New York: Random House, 1976.

Gerow, Richard O. *Catholicity in Mississippi*. Natchez: self-published, 1939.

Gibson, Arrell. *The Chickasaws*. Norman: University of Oklahoma Press, 1972.

Gonzales, John Edmond, ed. *A Mississippi Reader: Selected Articles from* The Journal of Mississippi History. Jackson: Mississippi Historical Society, 1980.

Gould, Lewis L., Katherine J. Adams, and Shearer D. Bowman, eds. *Inside the Natchez Trace Collection: New Sources for Southern History*. Baton Rouge: Louisiana State University Press, 1999.

Grant, C. L., ed. *Letters, Journals and Writings of Benjamin Hawkins*. 2 vols. Savannah, GA: Beehive Press, 1980.

Gray, Lewis Cecil. *History of Agriculture in the Southern United States to 1860*. Washington, DC: Carnegie Institution, 1933.

Green, Jonathan H. *An Exposure of the Arts and Miseries of Gambling*. Cincinnati: U.P. James, 1843.

Green, Michael D. *The Politics of Removal: Creek Government and Society in Crisis*. Lincoln: University of Nebraska Press, 1982.

Green, Thomas Marshall. *The Spanish Conspiracy. A Review of Early Spanish Movements in the South-West*. Cincinnati: Robert Clarke, 1891.

Greenberg, Kenneth S. *Honor and Slavery: Lies, Duels, Noses, Masks, Dressing as a Woman, Gifts, Strangers, Humanitarianism, Death, Slave Rebellions, the Proslavery Argument, Baseball, Hunting, and Gambling in the Old South*. Princeton, NJ: Princeton University Press, 1997.

Griffith, Benjamin W., Jr. *McIntosh and Weatherford, Creek Indian Leaders*. Tuscaloosa: University of Alabama Press, 1988.

Griffith, Lucille. *Alabama: A Documentary History to 1900*, rev. ed. Tuscaloosa: University of Alabama Press, 1972.

Groom, Winston. *Patriotic Fire: Andrew Jackson and Jean Laffite at the Battle of New Orleans.* New York: Alfred A. Knopf, 2006.

Gross, Robert A., and Mary Kelley, eds. *A History of the Book in America: Volume 2: An Extensive Republic: Print, Culture, and Society in the New Nation, 1790–1840*. Chapel Hill: University of North Carolina Press, 2014.

Gudmestad, Robert. *A Troublesome Commerce: The Transformation of the Interstate Slave Trade.* Baton Rouge: Louisiana State University Press, 2003.

Halbert, Henry S., and Timothy H. Ball. *The Creek War of 1813 and 1814*. Chicago: Donohue and Henneberry, 1895.

Hall, Basil. *Travels in North America, in the Years 1827 and 1828.* London: Simpkin and Marshall, 1830.

Hamilton, Peter J. *Colonial Mobile: A Historical Study.* New York: Houghton, Mifflin, 1897.

Hamilton, Thomas. *Men and Manners in America.* New York: Johnson Reprint, 1968.

Hamilton, Virginia Van der Veer. *Alabama: A History.* New York: W.W. Norton, 1977.

Hamilton, William B. *Anglo-American Law on the Frontier: Thomas Rodney and His Territorial Cases.* Durham, NC: Duke University Press, 1953.

Hamilton, William B. *Thomas Rodney: Revolutionary and Builder of the West.* Durham, NC: Duke University Press, 1953.

Harmon, M. F. *A History of the Christian Churches (Disciples of Christ).* Louisville: Connors and Risdale, 1929.

Hatch, Nathon O. *Democratization of American Christianity.* New Haven, CT: Yale University Press, 1989.

Haynes, Robert V. *The Mississippi Territory and the Southwest Frontier, 1795–1817.* Lexington: University Press of Kentucky, 2010.

Heidler, Jeanne T., and David S. Heidler, eds. *Encyclopedia of the War of 1812.* Santa Barbara, CA: ABC-Clio, 1997.

Heidler, Jeanne T., and David S. Heidler, eds. *Old Hickory's War: Andrew Jackson and the Quest for Empire.* Mechanicsburg, PA: Stackpole, 1996.

Hennessey, Una Pope, ed. *The Aristocratic Journey, Being the Outspoken Letters of Mrs. Basil Hall Written During a Fourteen Months Sojourn in America.* New York: G.P. Putnam's Sons, 1931.

Hermann, Janet Sharp. *Joseph E. Davis: Pioneer Patriarch.* Jackson: University Press of Mississippi, 1990.

Higginbotham, Jay. *Pascagoula: Singing River City.* Mobile, AL: Gill Press, 1967.

Hilliard, Sam Bowers. *Hog Meat and Hoecake: Food Supply in the Old South, 1840–1869.* Carbondale: Southern Illinois University Press, 1972.

Hodgson, Adam. *Letters from North America, Written During a Tour in the United States and Canada.* London: Hurst, Robinson, 1824.

Holder, Ray. *William Winans: Methodist Leader in Antebellum Mississippi.* Jackson: University Press of Mississippi, 1977.

Holland, James W. *Andrew Jackson and the Creek War: Victory at the Horseshoe.* Tuscaloosa: University of Alabama Press, 1968.

Holmes, Jack D. L. *Gayoso: The Life of a Spanish Governor in the Mississippi Valley, 1789–1799.* Baton Rouge: Louisiana State University Press, 1965.

Holt, Michael F. *The Rise and Fall of the American Whig Party: Jacksonian Politics and the Onset of the Civil War.* New York: Oxford University Press, 1999.

Hood, Laura C., Sara M. Hood, Hugh M. Hood, and Jack B. Hood. *Alabama Historical Association Markers.* Bloomington, IN: AuthorHouse, 2006.

Hornblow, Arthur. *A History of the Theatre in America from Its Beginnings to the Present Time.* Philadelphia: J.B. Lippincott, 1919.

Hudson, Arthur Palmer, ed. *Humor of the Old Deep South.* New York: Macmillan, 1936.

Huffman, Alan. *Mississippi in Africa: The Saga of the Slaves of Prospect Hill Plantation and Their Legacy in Liberia Today.* New York: Penguin Group, 2004.

Hunter, Clark, ed. *The Life and Letters of Alexander Wilson.* Philadelphia: American Philosophical Society, 1983.

Hunter, Louis C. *Steamboats on the Western Rivers: An Economic and Technological History.* Cambridge, MA: President and Fellows of Harvard College, 1949.

Ingraham, Joseph Holt. *The Southwest: By a Yankee.* New York: Harper and Brothers, 1835.

Jacobs, James Ripley. *Tarnished Warrior: Major-General James Wilkinson.* New York: Macmillan, 1938.

James, D. Clayton. *Antebellum Natchez.* Baton Rouge: Louisiana State University Press, 1985.

Johnson, Charles A. *The Frontier Camp Meeting: Religion's Harvest Time.* Dallas: Southern Methodist University Press, 1955.

Johnson, Walter. *River of Dark Dreams: Slavery and Empire in the Cotton Kingdom.* Cambridge, MA: Harvard University Press, 2013.

Johnson, Walter. *Soul by Soul: Life Inside the Antebellum Slave Market.* Cambridge, MA: Harvard University Press, 1999.

Jones, John G. *Concise History of the Introduction of Protestantism into Mississippi and the Southwest.* St. Louis: Pinckard, 1866.

Kane, Adam I. *The Western River Steamboat.* College Station: Texas A&M University Press, 2004.

Kane, Harnett T. *Natchez on the Mississippi.* New York: Bonanza Books, 1947.

Kappler, Charles J. *Indian Treaties, 1778–1883.* New York: Interland Publishing, 1972.

Kaye, Anthony E. *Joining Places: Slave Neighborhoods in the Old South.* Chapel Hill: University of North Carolina Press, 2007.

Ker, Henry. *Travels Through the Western Interior of the United States.* Elizabethtown, NJ: Henry Ker, 1816.

Kidwell, Clara Sue. *Choctaws and Missionaries in Mississippi, 1818–1918.* Norman: University of Oklahoma Press, 1995.

Kilbourne, Richard H., Jr. *Slave Agriculture and Financial Markets in Antebellum America: The Bank of the United States in Mississippi, 1831–1852.* London: Pickering and Chatto, 2006.

Kirby, Jack Temple. *Mockingbird Song: Ecological Landscapes of the South.* Chapel Hill: University of North Carolina Press, 2006.

Kotar, S. L., and J. E. Gessler. *The Steamboat Era: A History of Fulton's Folly on American Rivers, 1807–1860.* Jefferson, NC: McFarland, 2009.

Lackey, Richard S., ed. *Frontier Claims in the Lower South.* Baton Rouge: Provincial Press, 1977.

Lakwete, Angela. *Inventing the Cotton Gin: Machine and Myth in Antebellum America.* Baltimore: Johns Hopkins University Press, 2003.

Langguth, A. J. *Union 1812: The Americans Who Fought the Second War of Independence.* New York: Simon and Schuster, 2006.

Latour, Arsene Lacarriere. *Historical Memoir of the War in West Florida and Louisiana in 1814–15.* Gainesville: Historic New Orleans Collection and University Press of Florida, 1999.

La Violette, Paul Estronza. *Sink or Be Sunk! The Naval Battle in the Mississippi Sound That Preceded the Battle of New Orleans.* Waveland, MS: Annabelle Publishing, 2002.

Leavell, Z. T., and T. J. Bailey. *A Complete History of Mississippi Baptists from the Earliest Times.* Jackson: Mississippi Baptist Publishing, 1903.

Lewis, Herbert James. *Lost Capitals of Alabama*. Charleston: History Press, 2014.

Lewis, James E., Jr. *The Burr Conspiracy: Uncovering the Story of an Early American Crisis*. Princeton, NJ: Princeton University Press, 2017.

Libby, David J. *Slavery and Frontier Mississippi, 1720–1835*. Jackson: University Press of Mississippi, 2004.

Lincecum, Gideon. *Autobiography of Gideon Lincecum*. Brenham, TX: New Creek Settlers Association, 1997.

Lincecum, Jerry Bryan, and Edward Hake Phillips. *Adventures of a Frontier Naturalist: The Life and Times of Dr. Gideon Lincecum*. College Station: Texas A&M University Press, 1994.

Linklater, Andro. *An Artist in Treason: The Extraordinary Life of General James Wilkinson*. New York: Walker, 2009.

Linklater, Andro. *The Fabric of America: How Our Borders and Boundaries Shaped the Country and Forged Our National Identity*. New York: Walker, 2007.

Lipscomb, W. L. *A History of Columbus, Mississippi During the Nineteenth Century*. Birmingham, AL: Press of Dispatch Printing, 1909.

Loewen, James W., and Charles Sallis, eds. *Mississippi: Conflict and Change*. New York: Pantheon Books, 1974.

Lowry, Robert, and William H. McCardle. *A History of Mississippi, from the Discovery of the Great River by Hernando DeSoto, including the Earliest Settlement made by the French, Under Iberville to the Death of Jefferson Davis*. Jackson: R.H. Henry, 1891.

Lyell, Charles. *A Second Visit to the United States of America*. New York: Harper and Brothers, 1849.

Lynch, James D. *The Bench and Bar of Mississippi*. New York: E.J. Hale and Son, 1881.

Marshall, Theodora Britton, and Gladys Crail Evans. *They Found It in Natchez*. New Orleans: Pelican, 1939.

Martin, Joel W. *Sacred Revolt: The Muskogees' Struggle for a New World*. Boston: Beacon Press, 1991.

Matthews, Catherine VanCortlandt. *Andrew Ellicott: His Life and Letters*. Alexander, NC: WorldComm, 1997.

May, Robert E. *John A. Quitman: Old South Crusader*. Baton Rouge: Louisiana State University Press, 1985.

Mayes, Edward. *History of Education in Mississippi*. Washington, DC: Government Printing Office, 1999.

McCain, William D. *The Story of Jackson: A History of the Capital of Mississippi, 1821–1951*. Jackson, MS: J.R. Hyer Publishing, 1953.

McCaleb, Walter F. *The Aaron Burr Conspiracy*. New York: Wilson-Ericksson, 1936.

McLemore, Richard A., ed. *A History of Mississippi*. Jackson: University and College Press of Mississippi, 1973.

Meacham, Jon. *American Lion: Andrew Jackson in the White House*. New York: Random House, 2009.

Meek, A. B. *Romantic Passages in Southwestern History*. Mobile, AL: S.H. Goetzel, 1857.

Miles, Edwin A. *Jacksonian Democracy in Mississippi*. Chapel Hill: University of North Carolina Press, 1960.

Mitchell, Dennis. *Mississippi: A New History*. Jackson: University Press of Mississippi, 2014.

Monette, John W. *History of the Discovery and Settlement of the Valley of the Mississippi*. New York: Harper and Brothers, 1848.

Montule, Edouard De. *Montule's Voyage to North America and the West Indies in 1817*. London: Sir Richard Phillips, 1821.

Moore, A. B. *History of Alabama*. Tuscaloosa: Alabama Book Store, 1951.

Moore, Edith W. *Natchez Under-the-Hill*. Natchez: Southern Historical Publications, 1958.

Moore, John Hebron. *Agriculture in Ante-Bellum Mississippi*. New York: Bookman, 1958.

Moore, John Hebron. *The Emergence of the Cotton Kingdom in the Old Southwest*. Baton Rouge: Louisiana State University Press, 1998.

Morris, Christopher. *Becoming Southern: The Evolution of a Way of Life, Warren County and Vicksburg, Mississippi, 1770–1860*. New York: Oxford University Press, 1995.

Morris, John. *Wanderings of a Vagabond: An Autobiography*. New York: John Morris, 1873.

Moser, Harold, David Hoth, Sharon Macpherson, and John Reinhold, eds. *The Papers of Andrew Jackson, Volume III, 1814–1815*. Knoxville: University of Tennessee Press, 1991.

Mosley, M. C. *The Negro in Mississippi History*. Jackson, MS: Hederman Brothers, 1950.

Murray, Charles. *Travels in North America During the Years 1834, 1835, and 1836*. London: Richard Bentley, 1839.

Napier, John Hawkins, III. *Lower Pearl River's Piney Woods: Its Land and People*. Jackson: University of Mississippi Center for the Study of Southern Culture, 1985.

Nichols, Thomas L. *Forty Years of American Life*. London: John Maxwell, 1864.

O'Brien, Greg. *Choctaws in a Revolutionary Age, 1750–1830*. Lincoln: University of Nebraska Press, 2002.

O'Brien, Michael. *In Bitterness and in Tears: Andrew Jackson's Destruction of the Creeks and Seminoles*. Westport, CT: Praeger, 2003.

O'Shea. Michael V. *Public Education in Mississippi*. Jackson, MS: Jackson Printing, 1927.

Oehler, Andrew. *The Life, Adventures, and Unparalleled Sufferings of Andre Oehler, Containing an Account of His Travels*. Trenton, NJ: D. Fenton, 1811.

Olsen, Christopher J. *Political Culture and Secession in Mississippi, 1830–1860*. New York: Oxford University Press, 2000.

Owsley, Frank. *Plain Folk of the Old South*. Baton Rouge: Louisiana State University Press, 1949.

Owsley, Frank L., Jr. *Struggle for the Gulf Borderlands*. Tuscaloosa: University of Alabama Press, 2000.

Paskoff, Paul S. *Troubled Waters: Steamboat Disasters, River Improvements, and American Public Policy, 1821–1860*. Baton Rouge: Louisiana State University Press, 2007.

Pate, James Paul, ed. *The Reminiscences of George Strother Gaines, Pioneer and Statesman of Early Alabama and Mississippi, 1805–1843*. Tuscaloosa: University of Alabama Press, 1998.

Peattie, Donald C., ed. *Audubon's America: The Narrative and Experiences of John James Audubon*. Boston: Houghton Mifflin, 1940.

Pearse, James. *A Narrative of the Life of James Pearse*. Rutland, VT: William Fay, 1825.

Penick, James L. *The Great Western Land Pirate: John A. Murrell in Legend and History*. Columbia: University of Missouri Press, 1981.

Penningroth, Dylan C. *The Claims of Kinfolk: African American Property and Community in the Nineteenth-Century South*. Chapel Hill: University of North Carolina Press, 2003.

Phares, Ross. *Reverend Devil*. New Orleans: Pelican Publishing, 1941.

Pickett, Albert James. *History of Alabama, and Incidentally of Georgia and Mississippi, From the Earliest Period*. Charleston: Walker and James, 1851.

Pillar, James L. *The Catholic Church in Mississippi, 1837–1865*. New Orleans: Hauser Press, 1964.

Polk, Noel, ed. *Natchez before 1830*. Jackson: University Press of Mississippi, 1989.

Posey, Walter Brownlow. *Frontier Mission: A History of Religion West of the Southern Appalachians to 1861*. Lexington: University Press of Kentucky, 1966.

Posey, Walter Brownlow. *The Presbyterian Church in the Old Southwest, 1778–1838*. Richmond: John Knox Press, 1952.

Power, Tyrone. *Impressions of America, During the Years 1833, 1834, and 1835*. London: Richard Bentley, 1836.

Prentiss, S. S. *A Memoir of S. S. Prentiss*. New York: Scribner, 1856.

Primm, James Neal. *Lion of the Valley: St. Louis, Missouri, 1764–1980*. St. Louis: Missouri Historical Society Press, 1981.

Quick, Edward. *Mississippi Steamboatin'*. New York: Holt, 1926.

Ramsey, Abiezer Clark. *Memoirs of a Circuit Rider, Being Excerpts from the Life and Times of A. C. Ramsey and Others*. Birmingham, AL: Birmingham-Southern College, 1951.

Rand, Clayton. *Men of Spine in Mississippi*. Gulfport, MS: Dixie Press, 1940.

Ray, Angela G. *The Lyceum and Public Culture in the Nineteenth-Century United States*. East Lansing: Michigan State University Press, 2005.

Ray, Florence Rebecca. *Chieftain Greenwood Leflore*. Memphis: C.A. Davis, 1936.

Reid, John, and John H. Eaton. *The Life of Andrew Jackson: The Original 1817 Edition*. Tuscaloosa: University of Alabama Press, 1974.

Register, James. *Views of Old Natchez*. Shreveport, LA: Mid-South Press, 1969.

Reilly, Robin. *The British at the Gates: The New Orleans Campaign in the War of 1812*. New York: G.P. Putnam's Sons, 1974.

Remini, Robert V. *Andrew Jackson and His Indian Wars*. New York: Viking Penguin, 2001.

Remini, Robert V. *Andrew Jackson: Volume One, The Course of American Empire, 1767–1821*. Baltimore: Johns Hopkins University Press, 1998.

Remini, Robert V. *The Battle of New Orleans: Andrew Jackson and America's First Military Victory*. New York: Penguin Books, 1999.

Richardson, William. *Journey from Boston to the Western Country and Mississippi River to New Orleans, 1815–1816*. New York: Valve Pilot Corporation, 1940.

Roberts, Alasdair. *America's First Great Depression: Economic Crisis and Political Disorder After the Panic of 1837*. Ithaca, NY: Cornell University Press, 2012.

Rogers, George. *Memoranda of the Experience, Labor, and Travels of a Universalist Preacher*. Cincinnati: John A. Gurley, 1845.

Rogers, William Warren, Robert David Ward, Leah Rawls Atkins, and Wayne Flynt. *Alabama: The History of a Deep South State*. Tuscaloosa: University of Alabama Press, 1994.

Rothman, Adam. *Slave Country: American Expansion and the Origins of the Deep South*. Cambridge, MA: Harvard University Press, 2007.

Rothman, Joshua D. *Flush Times and Fever Dreams: The Story of Capitalism and Slavery in the Age of Jackson*. Athens: University of Georgia Press, 2012.

Rosenberg, Bruce A. *The Art of the American Folk Preacher*. New York: Oxford University Press, 1970.

Rowland, Dunbar. *Biographical and Historical Memoirs of Mississippi*. Chicago: Goodspeed, 1891.

Rowland, Dunbar. *Courts, Judges, and Lawyers of Mississippi, 1798–1935*. Jackson, MS: Hederman Brothers, 1935.

Rowland, Dunbar. *Encyclopedia of Mississippi History*. Madison, WI: Selwyn A. Brant, 1907.

Rowland, Dunbar. *History of Mississippi: The Heart of the South*. Jackson, MS: S.J. Clarke, 1925.

Rowland, Dunbar, ed. *Mississippi Territorial Archives*. Nashville: Press of Brandon Printing, 1905.

Rowland, Eron. *Andrew Jackson's Campaign against the British, or the Mississippi Territory in the War of 1812*. New York: Macmillan, 1926.

Rowland, Eron. *History of Hinds County, Mississippi, 1821–1922*. Jackson, MS: Jones Printing, 1922.

Rowland, Eron. *Life, Letters and Papers of William Dunbar of Elgin, Morayshire, Scotland, and Natchez, Mississippi: Pioneer Scientist of the Southern United States*. Jackson: Press of the Mississippi Historical Society, 1930.

Rowland, Eron. *Mississippi Territory in the War of 1812*. Baltimore: Genealogical Publishing, 1968.
Sangster, Dess L., and Tom Sangster. *Fort Mims and the Tensaw Settlement*. Bay Minette, AL: Lavender Publishing, 1993.
Sansing, David G., Sim C. Callon, and Carolyn Vance Smith. *Natchez: An Illustrated History*. Natchez, MS: Plantation Publishing, 1992.
Scarborough, William K. *The Overseer: Plantation Management in the Old South*. Athens: University of Georgia Press, 1984.
Schneider, Paul. *Old Man River: The Mississippi River in North American History*. New York: Henry Holt, 2013.
Schultz, Christian. *Travels on an Inland Voyage through the States of New York, Pennsylvania, Virginia, Ohio, and Tennessee*. New York: Isaac Riley, 1810.
Schweikart, Larry. *Banking in the American South from the Age of Jackson to Reconstruction*. Baton Rouge: Louisiana State University Press, 1987.
Scofield, Orrin. *Perambulations of Cosmopolite, Or the Travels and Labors of Lorenzo Dow*. Rochester: Scofield, 1842.
Shields, Joseph D. *The Life and Times of Seargent Smith Prentiss*. Philadelphia: Lippincott, 1883.
Shields, Joseph D. *Natchez: Its Early History*. Louisville: Morton, 1930.
Silver, James W. *Edmund Pendleton Gaines, Frontier General*. Baton Rouge: Louisiana State University Press, 1949.
Simms, William Gilmore. *Border Beagles, a Tale of Mississippi*. Chicago: Donohue, Henneberry, 1890.
Skates, John Ray. *Mississippi: A History*. New York: W.W. Norton, 1979.
Skates, John Ray. *Mississippi's Old Capitol: Biography of a Building*. Jackson: Mississippi Department of Archives and History, 1990.
Smedes, Susan Dabney. *Memorials of a Southern Planter*. Baltimore: Cushing and Bailey, 1888.
Smith, Allene de Shazo. *Greenwood Leflore and the Choctaw Indians of the Mississippi Valley*. Memphis: C.A. Davis, 1951.
Smith, Dale Edwyna. *The Slaves of Liberty: Freedom in Amite County, Mississippi, 1820–1868*. New York: Routledge, 2012.
Smith, Dwight L., and Ray Swick, eds. *A Journey Through the West: Thomas Rodney's Journal from Delaware to the Mississippi Territory*. Athens: Ohio University Press, 1997.
Smith, Gene A. *Thomas ap Catesby Jones: Commodore of Manifest Destiny*. Annapolis: US Naval Institute Press, 2000.
Smith, Gene A., ed. *A British Eyewitness and the Battle of New Orleans: The Memoir of Royal Navy Admiral Robert Aitchison, 1808–1827*. New Orleans: Historic New Orleans Collection, 2004.
Summers, Cecil L. *The Governors of Mississippi*. Gretna, LA: Pelican Publishing, 1988.
Southerland, Henry deLeon, and Jerry E. Brown. *The Federal Road Through Georgia, the Creek Nation, and Alabama, 1806–1836*. Tuscaloosa: University of Alabama Press, 1990.
Sparks, Randy J. *Religion in Mississippi*. Jackson: University Press of Mississippi, 2001.
Sparks, William. H. *The Memories of Fifty Years*. Macon, GA: J. W. Burke, 1872.
Stampp, Kenneth M. *Peculiar Institution: Slavery in the Ante-Bellum South*. New York: Random House, 1989.
Starr, John W. *One Hundred Years of American Railroading*. New York: Dodd, Mead, 1928.
Stephenson, Wendell H. *Isaac Franklin, Slave Trader and Planter of the Old South*. Baton Rouge: Louisiana State University Press, 1938.
Stewart, George R. *Names on the Land: A Historical Account of Place-Naming in the United States*. New York: New York Review of Books, 2008.

Stiggins, George. *Creek Indian History: A Historical Narrative of the Geneaology, Traditions, and Downfall of the Ispacoga of Creek Tribe of Indians*. Birmingham, AL: Birmingham Public Library Press, 1989.

Strang, Cameron B. *Frontiers of Science: Imperialism and Natural Knowledge in the Gulf South Borderlands, 1500–1800*. Chapel Hill: University of North Carolina Press, 2018.

Stuart, James. *Three Years in North America*. Edinburgh: Robert Cadell, 1833.

Sugden, John. *Tecumseh: A Life*. New York: Henry Holt, 1998.

Sullivan, Charles L. *Mississippi Gulf Coast: Portrait of a People*. Sun Valley, CA: American Historical Press, 1999.

Sullivan, James. *Mississippi: The Land and the People*. Brandon, MS: Ollray Publishing, 1994.

Swearingen, Mack. *The Early Life of George Poindexter: A Story of the Old Southwest*. New Orleans: Tulane University Press, 1934.

Sydnor, Charles S. *A Gentleman of the Old Natchez Region: Benjamin L. C. Wailes*. Durham, NC: Duke University Press, 1938.

Sydnor, Charles S. *Slavery in Mississippi*. Baton Rouge: Louisiana State University Press, 1966.

Thomason, Michael V. R., ed. *Mobile: The New History of Alabama's First City*. Tuscaloosa: University of Alabama Press, 2001.

Thompson, Ernest Trice. *Presbyterian Missions in the Southern United States*. Richmond: Presbyterian Committee of Publication, 1934.

Thompson, Slason. *A Short History of American Railways, Covering Ten Decades*. New York: D. Appleton, 1925.

Thompson-Stahr, Jane. *The Burling Books: Ancestors and Descendants of Edward and Grace Burling, Quakers*. Baltimore: Gateway Press, 2001.

Tudor, Henry. *Narrative of a Tour in North America*. London: James Duncan, 1834.

Thwaites, Reuben Gold. *Early Western Travels, 1748–1846*. Cleveland: Arthur H. Clark, 1905.

Turitz, Rabbi Leo, and Evelyn Turitz. *Jews in Early Mississippi*. Jackson: University Press of Mississippi, 1995.

Wailes, Benjamin L. C. *Report on the Agriculture and Geology of Mississippi*. Philadelphia: Lippincott, Grambo, 1854.

Walton, Augustus Q. *A History of the Detection, Conviction, Life and Designs of John A. Murel, the Great Western Land Pirate* . . . Athens, TN: The Journal, 1835.

Waselkov, Gregory A. *A Conquering Spirit: Fort Mims and the Redstick War of 1813–1814*. Tuscaloosa: University of Alabama Press: 2006.

Waters, Andrew, ed. *Prayin' to Be Set Free: Personal Accounts of Slavery in Mississippi*. Winston-Salem, NC: John F. Blair, 2002.

Watkins, James L. *King Cotton: A Historical and Statistical Review, 1790–1808*. New York: James J. Watkins and Sons, 1908.

Whitaker, Arthur. *The Mississippi Question, 1795–1803*. New York: D. Appleton-Century, 1934.

Wilhelm, Paul, Duke of Wurttemberg. *Travels in North America 1822–24*. Norman: University of Oklahoma Press, 1973.

Wolmar, Christian. *The Great Railroad Revolution: The History of Trains in America*. New York: PublicAffairs, 2012.

Wood, Gordon S. *Empire of Liberty: A History of the Early Republic, 1789–1815*. Oxford: Oxford University Press, 2009.

Woodward, Thomas S. *Woodward's Reminiscences of the Creek, or Muscogee Indians, Contained in Letters to Friends in Georgia and Alabama*. Montgomery, AL: Berrett and Wimbush, 1859.

Wyatt-Brown, Bertram. *Southern Honor: Ethics and Behavior in the Old South*. New York: Oxford University Press, 1982.

Young, Jacob. *Autobiography of a Pioneer*. Cincinnati: L. Swormstedt and A. Poe, 1857.

THESES AND DISSERTATIONS

Drake, Wilbourne Magruder. "Constitutional Development in Mississippi, 1817–1865." PhD dissertation, University of North Carolina, 1954.

Elliott, Mary Joan. "Winthrop Sargent and the Administration of the Mississippi Territory, 1798–1801." PhD dissertation, University of Southern California, 1971.

Hamilton, William B. "American Beginnings in the Old Southwest: The Mississippi Phase." PhD dissertation, Duke University, 1938.

Moss, Henry Herbert. "Sectionalism in Mississippi 1817–1832." M.A. thesis, University of Mississippi, 1934.

Stampley, Herbert Glenn. "The Academy Movement in Mississippi During the Nineteenth Century." M.A. thesis, University of Mississippi, 1950.

Young, David N. "The Mississippi Whigs." PhD dissertation, University of Alabama, 1968.

ARTICLES

Abernathy, Thomas P. "Aaron Burr in Mississippi." *Journal of Southern History* 15 (1949): 9–21.

Abbott, Martin. "Indian Policy and Management in the Mississippi Territory." *Journal of Mississippi History* 14 (1952): 153–69.

Alford, Terry. "Some Manumissions Recorded in the Adams County Deed Books in Chancery Clerk's Office, Natchez, Mississippi, 1795–1835." *Journal of Mississippi History* 33 (February 1971): 39–50.

Austill, Jeremiah. (Autobiography). *Alabama Historical Quarterly* 6 (Spring 1944): 84–86.

Bailey, Ben E. "The Minstrel Show in Mississippi." *Journal of Mississippi History* 57 (Summer 1995): 139–52.

Bailey, Ben E. "Music in Slave Era Mississippi." *Journal of Mississippi History* 54 (February 1992): 29–58.

Bailey, Robert J. "The Gubernatorial Administration of George Poindexter, 1820–1822." *Journal of Mississippi History* 35 (August 1973): 227–46.

Barber, Douglas. "Council Government and the Genesis of the Creek War." *Alabama Review* 38 (July 1985): 163–74.

Barnett, Jim, and Clark Burkett. "The Forks of the Road Slave Market at Natchez." *Journal of Mississippi History* 63 (Fall 2001): 169–88.

Bemis, Samuel F. "The Settlement of the Yazoo Boundary Dispute: The First Step in Southern Expansion." *Magazine of History* 17 (1913): 129–40.

Bentley, Marvin. "Incorporated Banks and the Economic Development of Mississippi, 1829–1837." *Journal of Mississippi History* 35 (November 1973): 381–401.

Bentley, Marvin. "The State Bank of Mississippi: Monopoly Bank on the Frontier (1809–1830)." *Journal of Mississippi History* 40 (November 1978): 297–318.

Berry, Trey. "A History of Women's Higher Education in Mississippi, 1819–1882." *Journal of Mississippi History* 53 (November 1991): 303–20.

Blaufarb, Rafe. "Vine and Olive Company." *Encyclopedia of Alabama*, May 19, 2008. http://www.encyclopediaofalabama.org/article/h-1539 (accessed June 2015).

Bloom, Jo Tice. "Mississippi's Territorial Delegates." *Journal of Mississippi History* 37 (November 1975): 327–57.

Bourdon, Jeffrey Normand. "Soldier Versus Statesman: The Primacy of Symbols during the Elections of 1824 and 1828 in Mississippi and Alabama." *Journal of Mississippi History* 73 (Winter 2011): 299–333.

Bowman, Robert. "Early History and Archaeology of Yazoo County." *Publications of the Mississippi Historical Society* 8 (1904): 427–41.

Braden, Guy B. "A Jeffersonian Village: Washington, Mississippi." *Journal of Mississippi History* 30 (1968): 135–42.

Brannon, Peter A. "Fort Mitchell References." *Alabama Historical Quarterly* 21 (1959): 1–13.

Brannon, Peter A. "Journal of James Tait for the Year 1813." *Alabama Historical Quarterly* 2 (Winter 1940): 431–40.

Bretz, Julian P. "Early Land Communication with the Lower Mississippi Valley." *Mississippi Valley Historical Review* 13 (June 1926): 3–29.

Bridgforth, Lucie Robertson. "Medicine in Antebellum Mississippi." *Journal of Mississippi History* 46 (May 1984): 82–107.

Bridgforth, Lucie Robertson. "Mississippi's Response to Nullification, 1833." *Journal of Mississippi History* 45 (February 1983): 1–22.

Brough, Charles Hillman. "Historic Clinton." *Publications of the Mississippi Historical Society* 3 (1903): 281–311.

Brough, Charles Hillman. "The History of Banking in Mississippi." *Publications of the Mississippi Historical Society* 3 (1900): 317–40.

Brough, Charles Hillman. "The History of Taxation in Mississippi." *Publications of the Mississippi Historical Society* 2 (1899): 112–24.

Buckner, Timothy R. "Vicksburg's War on Vice: Drinking, Gambling, and Race in the Antebellum South." *Journal of Mississippi History* 67 (Winter 2005): 311–30.

Burger, Nash K. "Adam Cloud, Mississippi's First Episcopal Clergyman." *Journal of Mississippi History* 9 (April 1947): 88–97.

Burger, Nash K. "The Rt. Rev. William Mercer Green, First Episcopal Bishop of Mississippi." *Journal of Mississippi History* 12 (January 1950): 3–27.

Burger, Nash K., and Charlotte Capers. "Episcopal Clergy of Mississippi, 1790–1940." *Journal of Mississippi History* 8 (April 1946): 59–66.

Cabaniss, Frances Allen, and James A. Cabaniss. "Religion in Ante-Bellum Mississippi." *Journal of Mississippi History* 6 (October 1944): 191–224.

Cabaniss, James Allen. "The Mississippi Jus Circa Sacra: A Note." *Journal of Mississippi History* 12 (July 1950): 169–73.

Carriere, Marius M., Jr. "Mount Locust Plantation: The Development of Southwest Mississippi during the Frontier Period, 1810–1830." *Journal of Mississippi History* 48 (August 1986): 187–98.

Carson, James Taylor. "States Rights and Indian Removal in Mississippi: 1817–1835." *Journal of Mississippi History* 57 (1995): 25–41.

Claiborne, J. F. H. "A Trip Through the Piney Woods." *Publications of the Mississippi Historical Society* 9 (1906): 487–538.

Cobb, Edwin L. "Powhatan Ellis of Mississippi: A Reappraisal." *Journal of Mississippi History* (May 1968): 91–110.

Cockrell, Thomas D. "The Politics of Land in Jacksonian Mississippi." *Journal of Mississippi History* 47 (February 1985): 1–14.

Cockrell, Thomas D. "United States Senators and Representatives From Mississippi, 1828–1836: An Introduction." *Journal of Mississippi History* 49 (February 1987): 35–48.

Coleman, James P. "Two Irascible Antebellum Senators: George Poindexter and Henry S. Foote." *Journal of Mississippi History* 46 (February 1984): 17–27.

Coker, William S., and Jack D. L. Holmes, eds. "Daniel Clark's Letter on the Mississippi Territory." *Journal of Mississippi History* 32 (May 1970): 154–55.

Coley, C. J. "The Battle of Horseshoe Bend." *Alabama Historical Quarterly* 14 (January 1952): 129–35.

Coley, C. J. "Creek Treaties, 1790–1832." *Alabama Review* 11 (July 1958): 163–76.

Crane, J. Michael. "Controlling the Night: Perceptions of the Slave Patrol System in Mississippi." *Journal of Mississippi History* 61 (Summer 1999): 119–36.

Crocker, Les. "An Early Iron Foundry in Northern Mississippi." *Journal of Mississippi History* 35 (May 1973): 113–26.

Crowther, Edward R. "Mississippi Baptists, Slavery, and Secession, 1806–1861." *Journal of Mississippi History* 56 (May 1994): 129–48.

Davis, Edwin Adams. "A Northern Sojourners' Remembrances of the Mississippi." *Journal of Mississippi History* 12 (July 1950): 127–52.

Davis, Edwin Adams. "William Johnson: Free Negro Citizen of Ante-bellum Mississippi." *Journal of Mississippi History* 15 (April 1953): 57–72.

Davis, R. Bruce. "The Tornado of 1840 Hits Mississippi." *Journal of Mississippi History* 36 (February 1974): 43–51.

Dean, Lewis S. "Tecumseh's Prophecy: The Great New Madrid Earthquakes of 1811–1812 and 1843 in Alabama." *Alabama Review* 47 (July 1994): 163–71.

DeRosier, Arthur H., Jr. "Natchez and the Formative Years of William Dunbar." *Journal of Mississippi History* 34 (February 1972): 29–47.

DeRosier, Arthur H., Jr. "Pioneers with Conflicting Ideals: Christianity and Slavery in the Choctaw Nation." *Journal of Mississippi History* 21 (July 1959): 174–89.

DeRosier, Arthur H., Jr. "William Dunbar: A Product of the Eighteenth Century Scottish Renaissance." *Journal of Mississippi History* 28 (1966): 185–222.

DeRosier, Arthur H., Jr. "William Dunbar, Explorer." *Journal of Mississippi History* 25 (July 1963): 165–85.

Dickey, Dallas C. "The Disputed Mississippi Election of 1837–1838." *Journal of Mississippi History* 1 (October 1939): 217–34.

Doss, Richard B. "Andrew Jackson, Road Builder." *Journal of Mississippi History* 16 (January 1954): 1–21.

Doster, James F. "Early Settlements on the Tombigbee and Tensaw Rivers." *Alabama Review* 12 (April 1959): 83–94.

Doster, James F., ed. "Letters Relating to the Tragedy at Fort Mims: August-September, 1813." *Alabama Review* 14 (1961): 269–85.

Drake, Wilbourne Magruder. "The Framing of Mississippi's First Constitution." *Journal of Mississippi History* 29 (November 1967): 301–27.

Drake, Wilbourne Magruder. "The Mississippi Constitutional Convention of 1832." *Journal of Southern History* 23 (August 1957): 354–70.

Drake, Wilbourne Magruder. "Mississippi's First Constitutional Convention." *Journal of Mississippi History* 18 (April 1956): 79–110.

Dunbar, William. "Report of Sir William Dunbar to the Spanish Government, at the Conclusion of his Services in Locating and Surveying the Thirty-First Degree of Latitude." *Publications of the Mississippi Historical Society* 3 (1900): 185–206.

Dungan, James R. "Sir William Dunbar of Natchez Planter, Explorer, and Scientist." *Journal of Mississippi History* 23 (1961): 211–28.

East, Dennis. "The New York and Mississippi Land Company and the Panic of 1837." *Journal of Mississippi History* 33 (November 1971): 299–331.

Eichert, Magdalen. "Some Implications Arising from Robert J. Walker's Participation in Land Ventures." *Journal of Mississippi History* 13 (January 1951): 41–46.

Elliott, Jack D., Jr. "The Plymouth Fort and Creek War: A Mystery Solved." *Journal of Mississippi History* 62 (Fall 2000): 328–70.

Elliott, Jack D., Jr. "Three Chopped Way and Representations of Yesteryear." *Journal of Mississippi History* 61 (Fall 1999): 213–36.

Evans, W. A. "Gaines Trace in Monroe County, Mississippi." *Journal of Mississippi History* 1 (April 1939): 100–109.

Evans, W. A. "Steamboats on the Upper Tombigbee in the Early Days." *Journal of Mississippi History* 4 (October 1942): 216–24.

Faucette, Shirley. "Clinton-Yesterday." *Journal of Mississippi History* 40 (August 1978): 215–30.

Faust, Richard H. "Another Look at General Jackson and the Indians of the Mississippi Territory." *Alabama Review* 28 (July 1975): 202–17.

Fike, Claude E. "The Administration of Walter Leake (1822–1825)." *Journal of Mississippi History* 32 (May 1970): 103–15.

Fike, Claude E. "The Gubernatorial Administrations of Governor Gerard Chittocque Brandon, 1825–1832." *Journal of Mississippi History* 35 (August 1973): 247–65.

Floyd, John. "Letters of John Floyd, 1813–1838." *Georgia Historical Quarterly* 33 (September 1949): 228–69.

Frantz, Joe B. "Gail Borden: Amite County's First Inventor." *Journal of Mississippi History* 11 (October 1949): 223–30.

Free, Joseph Miller. "The Ante-Bellum Theater of the Old Natchez Region." *Journal of Mississippi History* 5 (April 1941): 14–27.

French, Warren Graham. "A Sketch of the Life of Joseph Holt Ingraham." *Journal of Mississippi History* 11 (July 1949): 155–71.

Galloway, Charles G. "Elizabeth Female Academy—The Mother of Female Colleges." *Publications of the Mississippi Historical Society* 2 (1899): 169–78.

Galloway, Charles G. "Lorenzo Dow in Mississippi." *Publications of the Mississippi Historical Society* 4 (1901): 233–44.

Garner, Alfred W. "Folsom's Pigeon Roost, the Nineteenth Century Stage Traveler's Mecca, on the Natchez Trace." *Journal of Mississippi History* 4 (January 1942): 34–37.

Gates, William Bryan. "Performances of Shakespeare in Ante-Bellum Mississippi." *Journal of Mississippi History* 5 (January 1943): 28–37.

Gates, William Bryan. "The Theater in Natchez." *Journal of Mississippi History* 3 (April 1941): 71–129.

Gibson, George H., ed. "The Mississippi Market for Woolen Goods: An 1822 Analysis." *Journal of Southern History* 31 (February 1965): 80–90.

Grafton, C. W. "A Sketch of the Old Scotch Settlement at Union Church." *Publications of the Mississippi Historical Society* 9 (1906): 263–71.

Griffin, Richard W. "Manufacturing Interests of Mississippi Planters, 1810–1832." *Journal of Mississippi History* 22 (April 1960): 110–22.

Guice, John D. W. "Cattle Raisers of the Old Southwest: A Reinterpretation." *Western Historical Quarterly* 8 (April 1977): 166–77.

Hall, James. "A Brief History of the Mississippi Territory." *Publications of the Mississippi Historical Society* 9 (1906): 539–75.

Halsell, Willie D. "A Vicksburg Speculator and Planter in the Yazoo Delta." *Journal of Mississippi History* 11 (October 1949): 231–42.

Haman, T. L. "Beginnings of Presbyterianism in Mississippi." *Publications of the Mississippi Historical Society* 10 (1909): 203–21.

Hamilton, Peter J. "Running Mississippi's South Line." *Publications of the Mississippi Historical Society* 2 (1899): 157–68.

Hamilton, William B. "Jefferson College and Education in Mississippi, 1798–1817." *Journal of Mississippi History* 3 (1941): 259–76.

Hamilton, William B. "Mississippi in 1817: A Sociological and Economic Analysis." *Journal of Mississippi History* 34 (November 1967): 270–92.

Hamilton, William B. "The Planters Society in Claiborne County: The First Incorporated Cooperative and the First Farmers' Purchasing Cooperative." *Journal of Mississippi History* 11 (January 1949): 67–70.

Hamilton, William. B. "Politics in the Mississippi Territory." *Huntington Library Quarterly* 11 (1948): 277–91.

Hamilton, William B. "The Printing of the 1799 Laws of the Mississippi Territory." *Journal of Mississippi History* 2 (April 1940): 88–99.

Hamilton, William B. "The Sources of History of the Mississippi Territory." *Journal of Mississippi History* 1 (1939): 29–36.

Hamilton, William B. "The Southwestern Frontier, 1795–1817: An Essay in Social History." *Journal of Southern History* 10 (1944): 389–403.

Harrell, Laura D. S. "The Development of the Lyceum Movement in Mississippi." *Journal of Mississippi History* 31 (August 1969): 187–201.

Harrell, Laura D. S. "Horse Racing in the Old Natchez District." *Journal of Mississippi History* 13 (1951): 123–37.

Harrell, Laura D. S. "Imprints Toward Statehood." *Journal of Mississippi History* 29 (November 1967): 429–42.

Harrell, Laura D. S. "Index to Minutes of the Orphans' (Probate) Court of Jefferson County, Mississippi, January 23, 1830–November 24, 1834." *Journal of Mississippi History* 33 (August 1971): 231–40.

Harrell, Laura D. S. "Jockey Clubs and Race Tracks in Antebellum Mississippi." *Journal of Mississippi History* 28 (November 1966): 304–18.

Harrison, Robert W. "Early State Flood-Control Legislation in the Mississippi Alluvial Valley." *Journal of Mississippi History* 23 (April 1961): 104–26.

Hassig, Ross. "Internal Conflict in the Creek War of 1813–1814." *Ethnohistory* 21 (Summer 1974): 251–71.

Hatfield, Joseph T. "Governor William Claiborne, Indians, and Outlaws in Frontier Mississippi, 1801–1803." *Journal of Mississippi History* 27 (May 1965): 323–26.

Hatfield, Joseph T. "William C. C. Claiborne, Congress, and Republicanism, 1797–1804." *Tennessee Historical Quarterly* 24 (Summer 1965): 156–80.

Hawkins, H. G. "History of Port Gibson, Mississippi." *Publications of the Mississippi Historical Society* 10 (1909): 279–99.

Haynes, Robert V. "The Disposal of Lands in the Mississippi Territory." *Journal of Mississippi History* 24 (October 1962): 226–52.

Haynes, Robert V. "Early Washington County, Alabama." *Alabama Review* 18 (July 1965): 183–200.

Haynes, Robert V. "Law Enforcement in Frontier Mississippi." *Journal of Mississippi History* 22 (January 1960): 27–42.

Haynes, Robert V. "The Southwest and the War of 1812." *Louisiana History* 5 (Winter 1964): 41–51.

Haynes, Robert V. "Territorial Mississippi, 1798–1817." *Journal of Mississippi History* 64 (2002): 283–305.

Hearon, Cleo. "Nullification in Mississippi." *Publications of the Mississippi Historical Society* 12 (1912): 37–71.

Heimstra, William L. "Early Presbyterian Missions Among the Choctaw and Chickasaw Indians in Mississippi." *Journal of Mississippi History* 10 (January 1948): 8–17.

Herring, Todd A. "Kidnapped and Sold in Natchez: The Ordeal of Aaron Cooper, a Free Black Man." *Journal of Mississippi History* 60 (December 1998): 341–53.

Hickman, Nollie W. "Logging and Rafting Timber in South Mississippi, 1840–1910." *Journal of Mississippi History* (July 1957): 154–72.

Hoagland, H. E. "Early Transportation on the Mississippi." *Journal of Political Economy* 19 (1911): 111–23.

Holder, Ray. "Centenary: Roots of a Pioneer College (1838–1844)." *Journal of Mississippi History* 42 (May 1980): 77–98.

Holder, Ray, ed. "On Slavery: Selected Letters of Parson Winans, 1820–1844." *Journal of Mississippi History* 46 (November 1984): 323–54.

Holder, Ray. "Parson Winans' Pilgrimage to 'The Natchez' Winter of 1810." *Journal of Mississippi History* 44 (February 1982): 47–67.

Holmes, Jack D. L. "Barton Hannon in the Old Southwest." *Journal of Mississippi History* 44 (1982): 69–78.

Holmes, Jack D. L. "Cotton Gins in the Spanish Natchez District, 1795–1800." *Journal of Mississippi History* 31 (August 1969): 159–71.

Holmes, Jack D. L. "Law and Order in Spanish Natchez." *Journal of Mississippi History* 25 (1963): 186–201.

Holmes, Jack D. L. "Livestock in Spanish Natchez." *Journal of Mississippi History* 23 (January 1961): 15–37.

Holmes, Jack D. L. "Stephen Minor: Natchez Pioneer." *Journal of Mississippi History* 42 (1980): 17–26.

Holmes, Jack D. L. "William Dunbar's Correspondence of the Southern Boundary of Mississippi, 1798." *Journal of Mississippi History* 27 (1965): 187–90.

James, D. Clayton. "Municipal Government in Territorial Natchez." *Journal of Mississippi History* 27 (May 1965): 148–67.

Jamison, Lena Mitchell. "The Natchez Trace: A Federal Highway of the Old Southwest." *Journal of Mississippi History* 1 (April 1939): 82–99.

Jenkins, William H. "Alabama Forts, 1700–1838." *Alabama Review* 12 (July 1959): 163–80.

Johnson, Charles Ripley. "Railroad Legislation and Building in Mississippi, 1830–1840." *Journal of Mississippi History* 4 (October 1942): 195–206.

Johnson, Christopher S. "Poor Relief in Antebellum Mississippi." *Journal of Mississippi History* 49 (February 1987): 1–21.

Jones, Ruth Irene. "Ante-Bellum Watering Places of the Mississippi Gulf Coast." *Journal of Mississippi History* 18 (December 1956): 268–301.

Jordan, Daniel P. "Mississippi's Antebellum Congressmen: A Collective Biography." *Journal of Mississippi History* 38 (May 1976): 157–82.

Kanon, Thomas. "Andrew Jackson Pays the Spanish a Visit: The Capture of Pensacola, November 7, 1814." *Journal of the War of 1812 and the Era 1800 to 1840* (Spring 1999): 5–8.

Kanon, Thomas. "The Other Battle of New Orleans: Andrew Jackson and the Louisianans." *Gulf South Historical Review* 17 (Spring 2002): 40–61.

Kanon, Thomas. "'A Slow Laborious Slaughter': The Battle of Horseshoe Bend." *Tennessee Historical Quarterly* 58 (Spring 1999): 2–15.

Keller, Mark A. "Horse Racing Madness in the Old South—The Sporting Epistles of William J. Minor of Natchez (1837–1860)." *Journal of Mississippi History* 47 (August 1985): 165–85.

Kerr, Norwood Allen. "The Mississippi Colonization Society (1831–1860)." *Journal of Mississippi History* 43 (February 1981): 1–30.

Lake, L. "Grenada and Neighboring Towns in the 30's." *Publications of the Mississippi Historical Society* 3 (1898): 313–16.

Leavell, Z. T. "Early Beginnings of Baptists in Mississippi." *Publications of the Mississippi Historical Society* 4 (1901): 245–53.

Leftwich, George J. "Robert J. Walker." *Publications of the Mississippi Historical Society* 6 (1902): 359–71.

Leftwich, George J. "Some Main Traveled Roads, Including Cross-Sections of Natchez Trace." *Publications of the Mississippi Historical Society* 11 (1916): 463–76.

Lengel, Leland L. "The Road to Fort Mims: Judge Harry Toulmin's Observations on the Creek War, 1811–1813." *Alabama Review* 29 (January 1976): 16–36.

Lincecum, Gideon. "Autobiography of Gideon Lincecum." *Publications of the Mississippi Historical Society* 8 (1905): 443–519.

Love, William A. "General Jackson's Military Road." *Publications of the Mississippi Historical Society* 11 (1910): 402–17.

Lowery, Charles D. "The Great Migration to the Mississippi Territory, 1798–1819." *Journal of Mississippi History* 30 (August 1968): 173–92.

Lowery, Charles D. "The Great Migration to the Mississippi Territory, 1798–1819." November 2000. http://mshistorynow.mdah.state.ms.us/articles/169/the-great-migration-to-the-mississippi-territory-1798–1819 (accessed June 2015).

Lucas, M. Philip. "Beyond McCormick and Miles: The Pre-Partisan Political Culture of Mississippi." *Journal of Mississippi History* 44 (November 1982): 329–50.

Matthias, Virginia Parks. "Natchez-Under-the-Hill: As It Developed Under the Influence of the Mississippi River and the Natchez Trace." *Journal of Mississippi History* 7 (1945): 201–21.

McAlexander, Hubert H. "Flush Times in Holly Springs." *Journal of Mississippi History* 48 (February 1986): 1–13.

McCain, William D. "The Administration of David Holmes, Governor of the Mississippi Territory." *Journal of Mississippi History* 29 (November 1967): 328–47.

McCain, William D. "The Charter of Mississippi's First Bank." *Journal of Mississippi History* 1 (October 1939): 251–63.

McDonald, Forrest, and Grady McWhiney. "The Antebellum Southern Herdsman: A Reinterpretation." *Journal of Southern History* 41 (May 1975): 147–66.

McLemore, Richard A. "The Division of the Mississippi Territory." *Journal of Mississippi History* 5 (1943): 79–82.

McLemore, Richard A. "Factionalism: A Fruit of Spanish-American Rivalry on the Mississippi Frontier." *Journal of Mississippi History* 6 (1944): 237.

McLemore, Richard A. "The Roots of Higher Education in Mississippi." *Journal of Mississippi History* 26 (1964): 207–18.

McLemore, Richard A., and Nannie P. McLemore. "The Birth of Mississippi." *Journal of Mississippi History* 39 (November 1967): 255–69.

McLendon, James H. "The Development of Mississippi Agriculture: A Survey." *Journal of Mississippi History* 13 (April 1951): 75–87.

Miles, Edwin A. "Andrew Jackson and Senator George Poindexter." *Journal of Southern History* 24 (February 1958): 51–66.

Miles, Edwin A. "Francis Leech's 'The Mammoth Humbug, or the Adventures of Shocco Jones in Mississippi, in the Summer of 1839.'" *Journal of Mississippi History* 21 (January 1959): 1–39.

Miles, Edwin A. "Franklin E. Plummer: Piney Woods Spokesman of the Jackson Era." *Journal of Mississippi History* 14 (January 1952): 1–34.

Miles, Edwin A. "Joseph Seawell Jones." NCpedia.org, January 1988. http://ncpedia.org/biography/jones-joseph-seawell (accessed June 2015).

Miles, Edwin A. "The Mississippi Press in the Jackson Era, 1824–1841." *Journal of Mississippi History* 19 (January 1957): 1–20.

Miles, Edwin A. "The Mississippi Slave Insurrection Scare of 1835." *Journal of Negro History* (January 1957): 48–60.

Miller, Rush G. "John G. Jones: Pioneer Circuit Rider and Historian." *Journal of Mississippi History* 39 (February 1977): 17–39.

Mitcham, Howard. "Old Rodney: A Mississippi Ghost Town." *Journal of Mississippi History* 15 (October 1943): 242–51.

Monette, John W. "The Progress of Navigation and Commerce on the Waters of the Mississippi River and the Great Lakes AD 1700–1846." *Publications of the Mississippi Historical Society* 7 (1903): 479–523.

Moore, A. B. "Rummaging in Alabama's Background." *Alabama Review* 4 (July 1951): 163–82.

Moore, E. W. "Audubon and Natchez." *Nature* 33 (1940): 147–48.

Moore, John Hebron, ed. "Claiborne's Journal in 'Mississippi': A Fragment from the Unpublished Second Volume of History of Mississippi." *Journal of Mississippi History* 22 (April 1960): 87–100.

Moore, John Hebron. "Local and State Governments of Antebellum Mississippi." *Journal of Mississippi History* 44 (May 1982): 104–35.

Moore, John Hebron. "Mississippi's Ante-bellum Textile Industry." *Journal of Mississippi History* 16 (April 1954): 81–90.

Moore, John Hebron. "Mississippi's Search for a Staple Crop." *Journal of Mississippi History* 29 (November 1967): 371–85.

Moore, John Hebron. "Railroads of Antebellum Mississippi." *Journal of Mississippi History* 41 (February 1979): 53–82.

Moore, Margaret DesChamps, ed. "Early Aerial Views of Mississippi." *Journal of Mississippi History* 20 (October 1958): 251–58.

Moore, Margaret DesChamps. "Early Schools and Churches in Natchez." *Journal of Mississippi History* 24 (October 1962): 253–55.

Moore, Margaret DesChamps. "Protestantism in the Mississippi Territory." *Journal of Mississippi History* 29 (November 1967): 358–70.

Moore, Margaret DesChamps. "Religion in Mississippi in 1860." *Journal of Mississippi History* 22 (October 1960): 223–38.

Morgan, Madel J. "Andrew Marschalk's Account of Mississippi's First Press." *Journal of Mississippi History* 8 (July 1946): 146–48.

Morrison, J. K. "Early History of Jefferson College." *Publications of the Mississippi Historical Society* 2 (1899): 179–88.

Nguyen, Julia Huston. "A History of Women's Higher Education in Mississippi, 1819–1882." *Journal of Mississippi History* 53 (1991): 303–19.

Nguyen, Julia Huston. "The Value of Learning: Education and Class in Antebellum Natchez." *Journal of Mississippi History* 61 (Fall 1999): 237–63.

Olden, Samuel B., Jr. "Hotels, Inns, and Taverns in Mississippi, 1830–1860." *Journal of Mississippi History* 5 (October 1943): 171–84.

Otto, John Solomon. "The Migration of the Southern Plain Folk: An Interdisciplinary Synthesis." *Journal of Southern History* 51 (May 1985): 183–200.

Owsley, Frank L. "The Pattern of Migration and Settlement on the Southern Frontier." *Journal of Southern History* 11 (May 1945): 147–76.

Owsley, Frank L., Jr. "Benjamin Hawkins, The First Modern Indian Agent." *Alabama Historical Quarterly* 30 (Summer 1968): 7–14.

Owsley, Frank L., Jr. "British and Indian Activities in Spanish West Florida during the War of 1812." *Florida Historical Quarterly* 46 (October 1967): 111–23.

Owsley, Frank L., Jr. "The Fort Mims Massacre." *Alabama Review* 24 (July 1971): 192–204.

Owsley, Frank L., Jr. "Jackson's Capture of Pensacola." *Alabama Review* 19 (July 1966): 175–85.

Owsley, Frank L., Jr. "Prophet of War: Josiah Francis and the Creek War." *American Indian Quarterly* 9, no. 3 (1985): 273–93.

Owsley, Frank L., Jr. "The Role of the South in the British Grand Strategy in the War of 1812." *Tennessee Historical Quarterly* 31 (Spring 1972): 22–38.

Phelps, Dawson A. "The Chickasaw Mission." *Journal of Mississippi History* 13 (October 1951): 226–35.

Phelps, Dawson A. "The Choctaw Mission: An Experiment in Civilization." *Journal of Mississippi History* 14 (January 1952): 35–62.

Phelps, Dawson A. "Excerpts from the Journal of the Reverend Joseph Bullen, 1799 and 1800." *Journal of Mississippi History* 17 (December 1955): 254–81.

Phelps, Dawson A. "The Robinson Road." *Journal of Mississippi History* 12 (July 1950): 153–61.

Phelps, Dawson A. "Stands and Travel Accommodations on the Natchez Trace." *Journal of Mississippi History* 11 (January 1949): 1–54.

Phelps, Dawson A. "Travel On the Natchez Trace." *Journal of Mississippi History* 15 (July 1953): 155–64.

Pineda, Marika. "Preserving Good Order: John Girault of Natchez, Mississippi, 1783–1813." *Journal of Mississippi History* 68 (2006): 307–45.

Posey, Walter B. "Advance of Methodism into the Lower Southwest." *Journal of Southern History* 2 (November 1936): 439–52.

Posey, Walter B. "The Early Baptist Church in the Lower Southwest." *Journal of Southern History* 10 (May 1944): 161–73.

Posey, Walter B. "The First Session Book of the Oldest Presbyterian Church in Mississippi." *Journal of Mississippi History* 10 (April 1948): 132–49.

Posey, Walter B. "The Public Manners of Ante-Bellum Southerners." *Journal of Mississippi History* 19 (October 1957): 219–33.

Pruitt, Paul McWhorter, Jr. "Harry Toulmin." *Encyclopedia of Alabama*. July 13, 2011. http://www.encyclopediaofalabama.org/article/h-3108 (accessed June 2015).

Pyburn, Nita Katharine. "Public Schools in Mississippi Before 1860." *Journal of Mississippi History* 21 (1959): 113–30.

Quinn, Yancey M., Jr. "Jackson's Military Road." *Journal of Mississippi History* 41 (November 1979): 335–50.

Rainwater, Percy L. "Conquistadors, Missionaries, and Missions." *Journal of Mississippi History* 26 (May 1965): 123–47.

Rainwater, Percy L. "Indian Missions and Missionaries." *Journal of Mississippi History* 28 (February 1966): 15–39.

Rawlings, William. "The Great Yazoo Fraud." *Georgia Backroads* 8 (Spring 2009): 56–61.

Remini, Robert V. "Henry Clay and the Natchez Connection." *Journal of Mississippi History* 54 (August 1992): 269–81.

Riley, Franklin L. "A Contribution to the History of the Colonization Movement in Mississippi." *Publications of the Mississippi Historical Society* 9 (1906): 331–414.

Riley, Franklin L. "Life and Literary Services of Dr. John W. Monette." *Publications of the Mississippi Historical Society* 9 (1906): 199–237.

Riley, Franklin L. "Life of Col. J. F. H. Claiborne." *Publications of the Mississippi Historical Society* 7 (1903): 217–44.

Riley, Franklin L. "Location of the Boundaries of Mississippi." *Publications of the Mississippi Historical Society* 3 (1900): 167–84.

Riley, Franklin L. "Sir William Dunbar—The Pioneer Scientist of Mississippi." *Publications of the Mississippi Historical Society* 2 (1899): 85–111.

Riley, Franklin L. "Spanish Policy in Mississippi After the Treaty of San Lorenzo." *Publications of the Mississippi Historical Society* 1 (1898): 50–66.

Riley, Franklin L. "Transition from Spanish to American Rule." *Publications of the Mississippi Historical Society* 3 (1901): 261–311.

Rousseau, Peter L. "Jacksonian Monetary Policy, Specie Flows, and the Panic of 1837." *Journal of Economic History* 62 (June 2002): 457–88.

Rogers, Tommy Wayne. "Oakland College, 1830–1871." *Journal of Mississippi History* 36 (May 1974): 143–60.

Rogers, Tommy Wayne. "The Schools of Higher Learning at Sharon, Mississippi." *Journal of Mississippi History* 28 (February 1966): 40–55.

Rosenblum, Thom. "Driving Out the Slave Traders: The Natchez Uprising of 1833." *Journal of Mississippi History* 67 (Spring 2005): 45–67.

Rowland, Dunbar, ed. "Military Journal of Captain Isaac Guion, 1797–1799." *Seventh Annual Report, Mississippi Department of Archives and History*. Nashville: Press of Brandon Printing, 1909.

Rutledge, Wilmuth S. "Dueling in Antebellum Mississippi." *Journal of Mississippi History* 26 (1964): 181–91.

Scarborough, William K. "Lords or Capitalists? The Natchez Nabobs in Comparative Perspective." *Journal of Mississippi History* 54 (August 1992): 239–67.

Seal, Albert Garrel. "John Carmichael Jenkins: Scientific Planter of the Natchez District." *Journal of Mississippi History* 1 (January 1939): 14–28.

Sedevie, Donna Elizabeth. "The Prospect of Happiness: Women, Divorce and Property." *Journal of Mississippi History* 52 (February 1995): 189–206.

Sillers, Walter, Jr. "Flood Control in Bolivar County, 1838–1924." *Journal of Mississippi History* 9 (January 1947): 3–20.

Smith, Susanna. "Washington, Mississippi: Antebellum Elysium." *Journal of Mississippi History* 40 (May 1978): 143–65.

Southerland, Henry. "The Federal Road: Gateway to Alabama, 1806–1836." *Alabama Review* 39 (April 1986): 96–109.

Sparks, Randy J. "Mississippi's Apostle of Slavery: James Smylie and the Biblical Defense of Slavery." *Journal of Mississippi History* 49 (May 1989): 89–106.

Steel, Edward M., Jr. "A Pioneer Farmer in the Choctaw Purchase." *Journal of Mississippi History* 16 (October 1954): 229–41.

Stephen, Walter B. "Andrew Jackson's 'Forgotten Army.'" *Alabama Review* 12 (April 1959): 126–31.

Swearingen, Mack. "George Poindexter." *Journal of Mississippi History* 29 (1967): 348–57.

Swearingen, Mack. "Luxury at Natchez in 1801: A Ship's Manifest from the McDonogh Papers." *Journal of Southern History* 3 (May 1937): 188–90.

Sydnor, Charles S. "The Beginning of Printing in Mississippi." *Journal of Southern History* 1 (February 1935): 49–55.

Sydnor, Charles S., ed. "A Description of Seargent S. Prentiss in 1838." *Journal of Southern History* 10 (November 1944): 475–79.

Taylor, George R. "Agrarian Discontent in the Mississippi Valley Preceding the War of 1812." *Journal of Political Economy* 39 (1913): 471.

Thomanson, Hugh M. "Governor Peter Early and the Creek Indian Frontier, 1813–1815." *Georgia Historical Quarterly* 45 (September 1961): 223–37.

Tilly, Bette B. "The Jackson-Dinsmoor Feud: A Paradox in a Minor Key." *Journal of Mississippi History* 39 (May 1977): 117–31.

Toulmin, George B. "The Political Ideas of Winthrop Sargent, A New England Federalist of the Frontier." *Journal of Mississippi History* 15 (1953): 207–29.

Van Horne, John C. "Andrew Ellicott's Mission to Natchez (1796–1798)." *Journal of Mississippi History* 45 (August 1983): 160–85.
Vogt, Daniel C. "Poor Relief in Frontier Mississippi, 1798–1832." *Journal of Mississippi History* 51 (August 1989): 181–98.
Warren, Harris Gaylord. "Vignettes of Culture in Old Claiborne." *Journal of Mississippi History* 20 (1958): 125–46.
Watkins, Col. John A. "The Mississippi Panic of 1813." *Publications of the Mississippi Historical Society* 4 (1901): 483–91.
Weathersby, W. H. "A History of Mississippi College." *Publications of the Mississippi Historical Society* 5 (1901): 184–220.
Weems, Robert C. "The Makers of the Bank of Mississippi." *Journal of Mississippi History* 15 (July 1953): 137–54.
Weems, Robert C. "Mississippi's First Banking System." *Journal of Mississippi History* 29 (November 1967): 286–408.
Welsh, Mary J. "Recollections of Pioneer Life in Mississippi." *Publications of the Mississippi Historical Society* 4 (1901): 343–56.
White, J. M. "Territorial Growth of Mississippi." *Publications of the Mississippi Historical Society* 2 (1899): 125–34.
Wilkins, Jesse M. "Early Times in Wayne County." *Publications of the Mississippi Historical Society* 6 (1902): 265–72.
Williams, Frederick D. "The Congressional Career of J. F. H. Claiborne." *Journal of Mississippi History* 17 (January 1955): 24–42.
Winston, James E. "Mississippi and the Independence of Texas." *Southwestern Historical Quarterly* 21 (July 1917): 36–60.
Winter, William F., ed. "The Journal of the Constitutional Convention of 1817." *Journal of Mississippi History* 29 (November 1967): 443–504.
Wunder, John. "American Law and Order Comes to the Mississippi Territory: The Making of Sargent's Code, 1798–1800." *Journal of Mississippi History* 38 (1976): 131–55.
Ziglar, William Larry. "Shipbuilding on the Pascagoula River." *Journal of Mississippi History* 36 (February 1974): 1–15.

ONLINE RESOURCES

Guice, John D. W. "B. L. C. Wailes, the Natchez District, and the Mississippi Historical Society." Mississippi History Now, December 2010. http://mshistorynow.mdah.state.ms.us/articles/357/b-l-c-wailes-the-natchez-district-and-the-mississippi-historical-society (accessed June 2015).
Kaplan, Anna F. "Married Women's Property Act." Mississippi Encyclopedia. https://mississippiencyclopedia.org/entries/married-womens-property-act/.
O'Brien, Greg. "Chickasaws: The Unconquerable People." Mississippi History Now. http://www.mshistorynow.mdah.ms.gov/articles/8/chickasaws-the-unconquerable-people.
O'Brien, Greg. "Mushulatubbee and Choctaw Removal: Chiefs Confront a Changing World." Mississippi History Now. http://www.mshistorynow.mdah.ms.gov/articles/12/mushulatubbee-and-choctaw-removal-chiefs-confront-a-changing-world.
Sansing, David, "Abram M. Scott." Mississippi Encyclopedia. https://mississippiencyclopedia.org/entries/abram-m-scott/.
Sansing, David. "Alexander G. McNutt." Mississippi Encyclopedia. https://mississippiencyclopedia.org/entries/alexander-g-mcnutt/.

Sansing, David. "Charles Lynch." Mississippi Encyclopedia. https://mississippiencyclopedia.org/entries/charles-lynch/.

Sansing, David. "George Poindexter." Mississippi Encyclopedia. https://mississippiencyclopedia.org/entries/george-poindexter/.

Sansing, David. "Gerard Chittocque Brandon." Mississippi Encyclopedia. https://mississippiencyclopedia.org/entries/gerard-chittocque-brandon/.

Sansing, David. "Hiram G. Runnels." Mississippi Encyclopedia. https://mississippiencyclopedia.org/entries/hiram-g-runnels/.

Sansing, David. "Walter Leake." Mississippi Encyclopedia. https://mississippiencyclopedia.org/entries/walter-leake/.

Index

About the Authors

Photo courtesy of the author

Mike Bunn is a historian and author who has worked with several cultural heritage institutions in the Southeast. He currently serves as director of Historic Blakeley State Park in Spanish Fort, Alabama, and is active with numerous local and regional history organizations. Mike and his wife Tonya live in Daphne, Alabama, with their daughter Zoey.

Photo courtesy of Mississippi Department of Archives and History

Clay Williams worked for the Mississippi Department of Archives and History for over twenty years before retiring from the state in 2022. A strong advocate for public history and the power of place, he has given numerous presentations and has been published in several venues. He and his wife Kym have one child, Sarah, who was born on Halloween 2002.